John Paul II

The Man, the Disciple, the Leader

The Complete Illustrated Biography

Reader's Digest

The Reader's Digest Association, Inc.
Pleasantville, New York/Montreal/London/Hong Kong/Sydney

Have no fear! Open the doors to Christ. Open them ever wider. Open the borders of your countries, your economic systems, your current customs and civilizations to his saving power. Do not be afraid! Christ knows all about humanity and who each of you is. Christ is the only one who really knows.

—John Paul II
October 22, 1978

❧ IN MEMORIAM ❧

He made pilgrimages. He preached of life as an incessant path to love and to the heart of humanity. He visited the most remote corners of the world and crossed hundreds of borders. He had a simple yet powerful message for mankind: "Do not be afraid."

Certainly John Paul II taught by example. There was little in life more terrifying than his early days in Poland when the Nazis ruled his country. With implacable serenity and inner strength, he coped with the loss of his mother, brother, and father at a young age; overcame the fears of a man forced to follow his faith in an underground seminary; and confronted physical suffering with grace and courage.

Throughout his life John Paul II eschewed hate, and whenever he met it, he countered that force with love. He embraced the modern world with all of its innovations and problems, and he stood ready to listen to new ideas but remained firm in his dedication to the traditional beliefs that were the bedrock of his faith. This was his way of effectively preserving Catholicism as he understood it, opposing those elements in society that he found threatening to the inner core of the church he loved.

John Paul II was, therefore, the first modern pope, the first to nurture a relationship with all aspects of the media and to use that relationship to strengthen his papacy. Many have likened his charisma to that of a rock star—and perhaps that's true. But he used that image to attract those he most wanted to reach: young people across all countries and all cultures. And the young flocked to him as he took his contemporary pilgrimage to more than 120 countries.

Yet the source of this attraction was not only the star power he exuded in person and across television screens. He had an inner core that provided the fire. His early training as an actor and his love of theater and poetry gave him dramatic persuasive powers.

This was a man of many personas: He was a trained theologian who was deeply attached to the basic tenets of his faith, convictions he embraced and that were the root of what so many saw as his conservatism. He was a philosopher and an original thinker who brought an open mind to discussions with those who championed other views. He was a man interested in science who believed that its findings could be made an integral part of his faith. For his resolute faith was the key to who he was.

John Paul II was a universal figure with a universal message that he carried through his long pilgrimage now ended. He truly believed all men are equal in the eyes of God and that his was the voice of those unheard—the poor, the sick, the defenseless. This book is a tribute to the life of an extraordinary man, a true pilgrim of hope. *Requiescat in pace.*

Previously published by Reader's Digest Mexico as
   Juan Pablo II, Peregrino de la Esperanza ©2004
Previously published by Reader's Digest Poland as
   Pielgrzym Nadziei, Jestem z wami ©2001

Address any comments about *John Paul II* to:
   The Reader's Digest Association, Inc.
   Adult Trade Publishing
   Reader's Digest Road
   Pleasantville, NY 10570-7000

For more Reader's Digest products and information, visit
   our website:
   www.readersdigest.co.uk
   www.readersdigest.co.au
   www.readersdigest.co.hk

Library of Congress Cataloging in Publication Data
John Paul II : the man, the disciple, the leader :
the complete illustrated biography.
   p.cm.
   Includes index.
   ISBN 0-7621-0657-3
   1. John Paul II, Pope, 1920-2. Popes—Biography.
   I. Reader's Digest Association.

BX1378.5.J43 2005
282'.092—dc22
(B)   2005046520

Spanish Language Translator: Mary T. Connell
Polish Language Consultant: The Reverend
   Miroslaw Pawlaczyk

Editors: Nancy Shuker and Tom Weyr

Project Editor: Marilyn J. Knowlton
Copy Editor: Barbara Booth
Indexer: Nan Badgett
Senior Designer: George McKeon
Interior Design Consultant: Nick Anderson
Prepress Manager: Douglas A. Croll
Manufacturing Manager: John L. Cassidy
Production Designer: Jennifer R. Tokarski
Executive Editor, Trade Publishing: Dolores York
Director of Production: Michael Braunschweiger
President & Publisher, Books & Music: Harold Clarke

Special thanks to:
   Kim Casey
   Pamela DelSonno
   Rich Kershner
   Mabel Zorzano

Original Polish Edition Editors:
   Wieslawa Lewandowska
   Zbignew Zbikowski
   The Reverend Professor Waldemar Chrostowski

Mexican Edition Editors:
   Arturo Ramos Pluma
   Beatriz E. Avalos Chávez

Printed in China

1 3 5 7 9 10 8 6 4 2

CONTENTS

Introduction

Unlike popes who preceded him, John Paul II distinguished himself by his tireless efforts to spread the Word of God throughout the world. This illustrated biography presents an in-depth portrait of the pope—as a man, a disciple, a leader. This personalized account will take you to the young Karol Wojtyla's hometown of Wadowice, Poland, where you will follow him through his university days at the Jagiellonian University in Kraków, accompany him throughout his career as a priest, a bishop, and a cardinal, and finally witness his extraordinary journey as pope.

As a native of Poland, Karol Wojtyla lived through both the dehumanizing Nazi occupation of his country in World War II and the Soviet takeover of his country immediately afterward. In his besieged Poland he learned to use his prodigious intellect and energy to effect compromise and change in the government while keeping the Catholic Church strong and effective.

As a prelate, he played a key role in bringing down Communism in Poland. As pope, he dared to apologize before the world for the Catholic Church's past treatment of the Jews and to the victims of religious wars.

Always fascinated by theater and science, John Paul II mastered the twentieth-century communications revolution with his brilliant use of television, radio, and print. As the first jet-setting pope, he traveled more than 600,000 miles. In his voice, language was a tool of faith that he was able to project around the globe. And because he spoke so many languages, he gave his message a personal touch that resonated in listeners' hearts as well as their minds.

John Paul II preached freedom as a characteristic of humanity. He supported the poor, the hungry, and the helpless in the undeveloped nations of the world and warned the capitalistic democracies of the dangers of liberty without an ethical framework. His staunch conservatism in matters of faith and morals often seemed at odds with his modern persona. Deploring the world's growing secularism, he saw a return to the one true faith as mankind's only salvation.

The first edition of this biography was researched, written, and produced by Reader's Digest Poland, where it had enormous success. That book is rich in revelations about John Paul II's early years not readily available outside his homeland. Reader's Digest Mexico then translated that edition into Spanish, producing the exquisite volume that Reader's Digest U.S. editors have now updated to include John Paul II's last days and the Vatican's final tribute to the pontiff. Through the book's photographs, friends' anecdotes, historical notes, and powerful text, this edition presents a fascinating chronicle of the latter half of the twentieth century on into the twenty-first, with a very personal look at one of the world's most beloved leaders.

On May 18, 1920, Karol Józef Wojtyla was born in Wadowice, a town in the newly established independent Republic of Poland. When his mother heard his first cries, she asked the midwife to open the windows so the baby could hear the music from the nearby Church of the Presentation of the Blessed Virgin Mary.

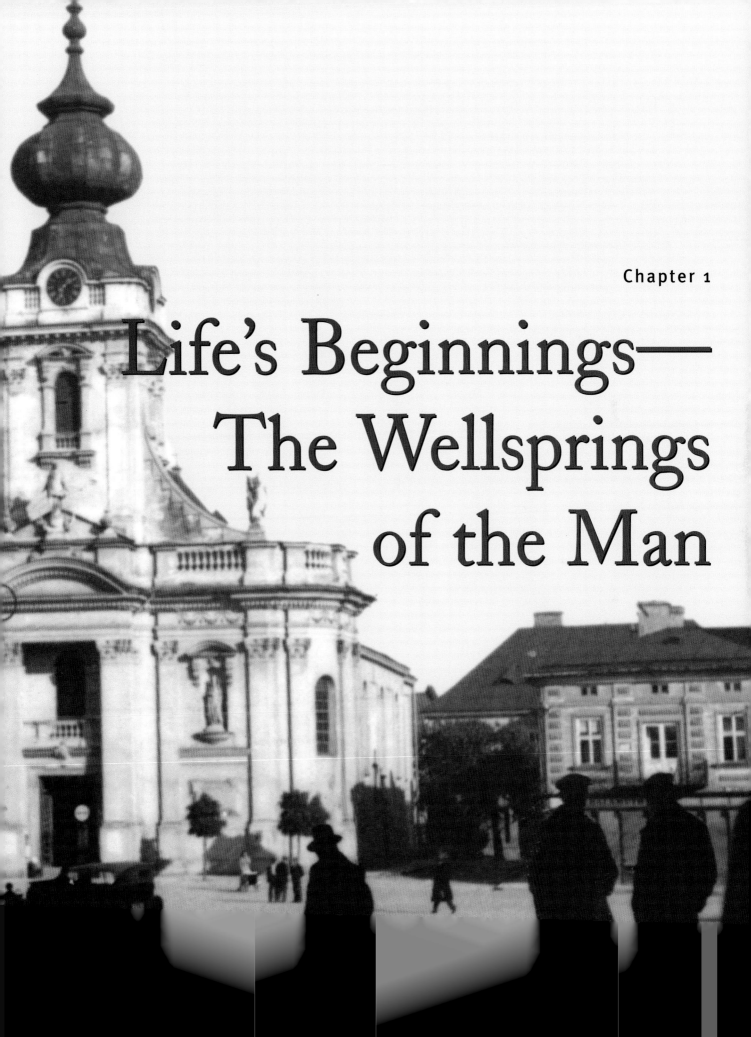

Chapter 1

Life's Beginnings— The Wellsprings of the Man

To understand the story of John Paul II, the first Polish pope, you must know something about the history of his country. Poland and the Roman Catholic Church have more than 1,000 years of shared trials and triumphs. The Slavic peoples who lived in the area of present-day Poland were first united in the tenth century under the Piast dynasty; at the same time, they were converted to Christianity. The Roman Catholic Piast dynasty managed in its 400-year history to establish a cosmopolitan empire that included Poles, Germans, Rutherians, Flemings, Walachians, Jews, Armenians, and even Tartars. The University of Kraków, founded in 1364, reflected this religious and political tolerance.

POLAND'S GOLDEN AGE

When the last Piet king died, the great Lithuanian prince, Jagiello, married the young queen of Poland, Jadwiga, and founded his own dynasty. In 1385 he initiated a long process of consolidation between Lithuania and Poland, which culminated in the signing of the Treaty of Lublin in 1569, providing for a joint *Sejm* (parliament), king, and foreign policy. During the fifteenth and sixteenth centuries the Republic of Two Nations, under the Jagiellonians, was one of the greatest European powers, controlling lands from the Baltic Sea in the North to the Black Sea in the South. When the Jagiellonians died out in 1572, an aristocratic republic was created in which the landed nobility elected a Polish king.

In the western territories of the Republic of Two Nations, people enjoyed peace, some prosperity, and religious tolerance—a rarity at that time in Europe. It was the most diverse state in Europe in regard to languages, nationalities, and religions. This was Poland's golden age. Extraordinary examples of Romanesque, Gothic, and Renaissance architecture from this period are still seen in Poland. Nicolaus Copernicus, the renowned astronomer and humanist, was born in Poland in 1473. He studied at the University of Kraków and was the first to theorize that Earth and other planets revolve around the sun. Until that time Earth was considered to be the center of the universe. Mikolaj Rej, the first significant writer in the Polish language, lived from 1504 to 1569. Poet Jan Kochanowski (1530–1584) wrote the first Polish tragedy, *The Dismissal of the Greek Envoys,* as well as humorous poems and cycles of sorrowful poems that are still read and performed to this day.

Karol Wojtyla's parents were married in 1904. They were both devout Catholics who observed religious rituals faithfully in their home.

LOSS OF AUTONOMY AND PARTITION

In the seventeenth century, however, the Polish-Lithuanian Republic fell prey to its Russian and Swedish neighbors, who annexed great tracts of territory without facing serious opposition. In this period, known as "the Deluge," a joint Cossack and Russian invasion put the entire eastern half of the country under the tsar.

A Swedish assault on Warsaw in 1655 seemed to signal yet another humiliating Polish defeat until, during 44 days of the Christmas season, a small band of monks and knights fought off the Swedes at the Battle of Czestochowa and sent them into retreat. This great victory was credited to the Virgin Mary and is still one of Poland's most sacred military miracles.

Czestochowa is an ancient town between Warsaw and Kraków, famous for its Pauline monastery that sits on a hill called Jasna Góra (Luminous Mountain). The monastery houses the shrine of the Virgin of Jasna Góra, or the Black Madonna. The Madonna is a Byzantine icon, said to have been painted by Saint Luke the Evangelist on a wooden plank that served as the Holy Family's table at Nazareth. She is called the "Black Madonna" because her face and hands and those of the child she holds in her arms have darkened with age. Her defense of Catholic Poland against the Protestant Swedes made the Polish king proclaim her the Queen of the Crown of Poland. The Black Madonna is still the most venerated Marian icon in Poland; her shrine draws thousands of pilgrims throughout the year.

CHALLENGE FROM THE TURKS

A brilliant victory against the Turks in 1673 brought the Polish crown to Jan Sobieski in 1674. Notwithstanding his seminal victory over the Turks outside Vienna in 1683, which prevented an Ottoman invasion of Europe, he was never able to regain all the southeastern lands that Poland had lost to the Ottomans. The Republic of Two Nations continued to lose ground. Finally, in 1697, the electors of Saxony took over the Polish throne, and the country lost its name and its independence.

By the end of the eighteenth century, Poland had been partitioned three separate times among three powerful neighbors: Prussia, Russia, and Austria. For the most part, all through the nineteenth century, what once was Polish territory formed the borders of these monarchies: Protestant Hohenzollerns in Prussia to the west, Orthodox Romanovs in Russia to the east, and Roman Catholic Hapsburgs in the Austro-Hungarian Empire to the south.

HELP FROM NAPOLÉON

The one exception was a brief period starting in 1807 when Napoléon, moving east, created the Duchy of Warsaw from land around the city and introduced the Napoleonic Code, which freed the peasants. (Without land, this freedom gave the peasants no advantage.) The Duchy of Warsaw acquired Galicia, a historic region south of Warsaw, in the War of 1809. Napoléon's disastrous failure in Russia, however, doomed the Duchy to Russian control by 1813.

Several failed insurrections in the nineteenth century brought reprisals from Poland's tsarist rulers: Lands were confiscated, cultural and educational institutions were closed, and more than 20,000 Poles left their homeland. Prince Adam Czartoryski headed a group of exiles in Paris. Poets Adam Mickiewizt, Zygmunt Krasinski, Juliusz Slowacki, and Cyprian Norwid also sought more freedom in France. Composer and pianist Frédéric Chopin, born and trained in Warsaw, made his career in Paris. Throughout these difficult times, however, Polish nationalism persisted.

POLAND IN WORLD WAR I
Poland became a pawn of the Germans and the Austrians during World War I, when each promised Poland autonomy in order to recruit more Poles into the fight against Russia. Some 800,000 Poles lost their lives in World War I. The Treaty of Versailles in 1919 settled the peace and mandated that the Republic of Poland be revitalized as an independent nation under Józef Pilsudski. This heroic military leader also became head of state. The German emperor and king of Prussia, William II, surrendered to the Allies; Austria also surrendered to the Allies. The Austro-Hungarian Empire collapsed, and many of its states became independent countries. United States president Woodrow Wilson presented a peace program at Versailles known as the Fourteen Points. The thirteenth point demanded that "an independent Polish state should be erected" with free and secure access to the sea.

The Russia that began World War I on the side of France and Great Britain was not the same Russia that now disputed Poland's eastern border. The tsarist regime had been toppled in February 1917. The following October a new political party, led by Vladimir Lenin, instigated a coup d'état that overthrew the new Russian parliamentary government, led by Aleksandr Kerensky. Lenin and his Bolsheviks quickly established a dictatorship. Their

objective was to create—with force if necessary—a Communist state, where the government would own everything, and the people would work on collective farms or in state-run factories and would theoretically share the bounty equally. In this new Marxist utopia there was no place for religion. Russia's Orthodox churches were expropriated by the state and used for other purposes.

FIGHTING FOR POLAND'S NEW BORDERS
The new Polish republic had to fight Russia's Red Army for its eastern border in 1920 and 1921. Pilsudski led a young Polish army first into the Ukraine far enough to seize Kiev. He couldn't hold the territory for long and later had to repulse a Russian counterattack at the gates of Warsaw. This extraordinary victory, known as the "miracle on the Vistula," effectively kept the Soviets at bay in Central Europe until after World War II. Poland's territorial claims were then settled in the Treaty of Riga.

A POLISH COURTSHIP
At the turn of the twentieth century, Karol Wojtyla (father of Pope John Paul II) was a lieutenant in the Austrian army stationed in Kraków. This area of southern Poland, Galicia, was then part of the Austro-Hungarian Empire. He came from strong peasant stock that could be traced back more than 100 years. Karol Wojtyla's father, Maciej Wojtyla, was a farmer from Lipniki, a small village near Wadowice, and his mother, Anna Przeczek, was the daughter of a local baker. She died when her only child was an infant. His father, Maciej, soon remarried. Since the Wojtyla farm was very small, Maciej Wojtyla also worked as a tailor to supplement the family income. Karol Wojtyla was apprenticed to his father to learn this trade. He did tailoring jobs up until 1900, when he turned twenty and was inducted into the Austro-Hungarian army.

No one knows where or when Karol met his future bride, Emilia Kaczorowska. Her family had been living for some years in Kraków, but they had originally come from Biala, a small town on the banks of the Biala River. Her father, Feliks Kaczorowski, owned a saddle and harness shop. Her mother, Maria Scholz

Karol Józef Wojtyla was baptized at this ornately gilded stone baptismal font in the military chapel of Wadowice's Church of the Presentation of the Blessed Virgin Mary. More than 50 years later a plaque was placed over it to commemorate the event.

Karol Wojtyla was a beloved youngest child. His mother affectionately called him "Lolek."

Kaczorowski, was a shoemaker's daughter, who died in 1897 when Emilia, the youngest of five children, was eight years old and a student at an elementary school run by the Sisters of the Love of God.

THE NEW FAMILY

Lieutenant Karol Wojtyla courted Emilia Kaczorowski for about a year. They were married in 1904 in the military chapel of the beautiful baroque Church of Saints Peter and Paul in Kraków. John Paul II used to keep his parents' wedding photograph on his desk in the Vatican. The groom is dressed in his Austrian army uniform and displays his military badges. His mustache is neatly trimmed, and his carefully combed hair looks healthy and thick because the photographer used a little ink to fill it out. A flower from the bride's bouquet is pinned to his uniform. The bride's eyes are large and dark. Her dress is high collared and trimmed with lace, and she is wearing a long white veil.

In 1906 Emilia Wojtyla gave birth to their first child, Edmund. Little is known about the family's early life except that in 1911 the Wojtylas attended the investiture of Lithuanian prince Adam Stefan Sapieha as bishop in the Wawel Cathedral, little knowing how he would affect their family's life in the future. Pope Pius X had decided to elevate Sapieha, his Polish chamberlain, to the rank of bishop.

In 1914 the Wojtylas had a second child, Olga, in

Benedict XV

Giacomo della Chiesa was born November 21, 1854, into an ancient noble family from Genoa. Ordained a priest when he was only twenty-four, he was soon assigned to the papal diplomatic corps, where he served from 1882 to 1907. He then became the archbishop of Bologna. In July 1914 he was made cardinal. Two months later, after the death of Pius X, della Chiesa was elected pope and took the name Benedict XV.

His papacy began on the brink of World War I. With Catholics involved on both sides of the conflict, the pope felt obliged to keep to a strictly neutral position that would be respected by all parties. He drew up several unsuccessful peace proposals. To alleviate the horrors he followed all over Europe, he founded the Vatican service for prisoners of war and gave generously to programs for war victims.

In 1917 he put forward a revised Code of Canon Law that remained in effect until 1983. Pope Benedict XV died on January 22, 1922.

Kraków, but she died in infancy. Emilia Wojtyla's parents also died in Kraków before the start of World War I. Karol Wojtyla fought bravely against the Russians in World War I and was awarded the Iron Cross of Merit with Cluster by the Austrians.

A Historical Note

In Portugal on May 13, 1917, near the tiny hamlet of Fatima, three young shepherds told their neighbors that they were having extraordinary visions on the thirteenth day of each month. Before they started having these visions, they said, an angel had appeared to them to prepare them for their future encounters with heaven. They saw the Mother of God—Our Lady, they called her—for the first time in a vision. The Blessed Virgin, Mother of God, returned and spoke again with them in five later apparitions. She asked them to say the Rosary and foretold the future. Her predictions dealt with how to combat atheistic forces that were attacking the church. She also foretold future events that would concern the papacy, including an assassination attempt against some Holy Father in the future. Lucia, the oldest of the three children, related one of their visions to a bishop: "We saw a brilliant light there, and it was God.... The Holy Father...was kneeling at the foot of a large cross. A group of soldiers were shooting at him, and he was riddled with bullets. The blasts swallowed him up in bursts of fire."

On October 13, 1917, a crowd of some 100,000 people accompanied the three children as they went to meet Our Lady at the appointed time and place. The crowd witnessed an extraordinary sight—a whirling multicolored orb in the sky, which they called the "Miracle of the Sun." This verified to many the supernatural nature of the apparitions and the truth of what the young shepherds were saying.

Lucia entered the Carmelite Order in 1925, where she lived and worked until her death in 2005. The other two children died soon after the apparitions, Francisco in April 1919 and Jacinta in February 1920.

MOVE TO WADOWICE

When Poland was granted independence in 1918, Karol Wojtyla joined the new Polish army as a full-fledged officer. He was assigned the rank of first lieutenant in the 12th Infantry Regiment in Wadowice, where he was to be quartermaster. The Wojtylas moved to Wadowice and settled into an apartment near the center of town.

In 1920, when the new Polish army took on the Soviets, Karol Wojtyla was forty-one years old and considered unfit for active combat. He followed Pilsudski's progress by scouring day-old Kraków newspapers every morning. He learned that Pilsudski was forcing the Red Army back over the Dnieper River.

When the Polish army column entered Kiev, he was not surprised to read that Pilsudski led the charge. Rumors spread that Pilsudski was triumphantly returning to Warsaw in a special train after his heroic victory in Kiev.

With the exception of the war news, most events that happened in Warsaw went unreported in Wadowice. At that time, there were no radio broadcasts.

A HAPPY BIRTH

On May 18, the day that Pilsudski arrived back in Warsaw, Emilia Wojtyla, in the ninth month of her third pregnancy, felt her first labor pains. Her fourteen-year-old son, Edmund, was at school, and her husband was at his military quarters, so she sent a neighbor to find the midwife.

After what had been a cold snap, the sun came out that day and warmed the air. The apartment building in which the Wojtylas lived was just down a narrow street from the main Roman Catholic church in Wadowice, the Church of Presentation of the Blessed Virgin Mary. Since it was May, the month of Our Lady, parishioners were celebrating the Marian liturgy. Emilia Wojtyla was not physically strong and had rarely felt well in the six years since baby Olga's death. She had been depressed much of that time, and now, at thirty-six, after an uncomfortable pregnancy, she awaited the impending birth with trepidation. Despite her fears, however, she clung to the hope that this new child would bring happiness and joy to her life.

While Mrs. Wojtyla was in labor, she could hear the mumbled voices of parishioners in the nearby church. When she heard the first cries of her newborn, she asked the midwife to open the windows. She could hear the Marian chant at the end of the service, and she wanted the first strains of music that her son would hear to be hymns of glory to the Holy Mother of God.

WHAT'S IN A NAME?

One month later the child was baptized in the Church of the Presentation of the Blessed Virgin Mary, whose Marian litanies and hymns had accompanied his birth. His mother's sister, Maria Wiadrowska, and brother-in-law, Józef Luczmierczyk, were the child's godparents. "I baptize you Karol Józef," pronounced the military chaplain as he bathed the tiny head with holy water.

Why the parents chose this name is not clear. They might have chosen Karol for his father and Józef in honor of the victorious Józef Pilsudski. If they had followed the usual custom, however, they would have named the first-born son Karol. Instead, they called him Edmund. It is also possible that Karol Wojtyla, a longtime and loyal military officer in the Austro-Hungarian Empire, picked out two names for his son in honor of the last reigning Hapsburgs: Francis Joseph I (Franz Józef in Polish), who died in 1916, and Charles I (Karol in Polish), his grand-nephew and successor to the throne, who abdicated in 1918 as the empire collapsed.

THE POLISH MIRACLE AT WARSAW

This picture of Emilia Wojtyla with her son Karol is now on display in the church dedicated to the Virgin Mary in Wadowice, where the family regularly attended Mass.

By the middle of August 1920, the Red Army was encamped on the banks of the Vistula River across from Warsaw. During the preceding year the Soviets had planned a march west that would meet up with German Communist groups to spread the Communist revolution across Central Europe, but they were forced to stop at the Vistula when the Polish army blockaded the roads. Now, however, two fresh Red Army divisions had arrived and set up a second camp beside the Vistula River. Berlin seemed to be within their reach. In fact, Monsignor Achille Ratti, apostolic delegate to Warsaw, informed Pope Benedict XV in horror that the church had not been in such a threatened state since Napoléon's time. The dread of Communism that took hold of Monsignor Ratti at that moment never left him. Three years later he became Pope Pius XI.

On August 15, while civilian Catholics in Poland celebrated the Feast of the Assumption of the Blessed Virgin Mary, Pilsudski launched the heavily outnumbered—three to one—Polish army in a daring counteroffensive. Polish soldiers penetrated the breach between the two Bolshevik forces and routed both in a ferociously

grace before each meal and before doing homework; and every night, Lieutenant Wojtyla read from the sacred scriptures. This practice was rare, even in Galicia, where people were thought to be very religious. One of the earliest memories John Paul II had of his father is the older man's kneeling at his prie-dieu, head bent forward and face enfolded in hands, praying before going to sleep.

When young Wojtyla was four years old, his brother, Edmund, finished high school with high honors and left for Kraków to study medicine at the Jagiellonian University (once the University of Kraków). For many years after that, the brothers saw each other only during holidays and vacations.

A SMALL GALESIAN TOWN IN THE 1920S

The building in which the Wojtylas lived was owned by a Jewish merchant, Chaim Balamuth. He operated a glass, crystal, and ceramic shop on the ground floor of the building. The Balamuth family lived in an apartment next to the shop. The Wojtylas' other neighbors were the Szczepanskis, who had no children, and the Beers, whose daughter, Regina, was one of young Wojtyla's friends.

Typical of Wadowice at the time, the building had electricity but no running water. Families got their water from a well in town. Neighbors remember Emilia Wojtyla chatting with them at the well. Holding her small son in her arms, she often said, "Someday you'll see. My little Lolek will be a great man."

The population of Wadowice was made up of merchants, skilled craftspeople, military personnel, clergy, municipal bureaucrats, and a small number of laborers who worked in local manufacturing plants. The largest of these were a producer of cable wire, a factory that made Holy Communion wafers for Roman Catholic liturgies, a plant that generated electricity, and a paper mill.

The town supported many small shops and at least two restaurants. Among the small businesses were a newspaper store, a tobacco shop, a pharmacy, a grocery store, a shoemaker's shop, and Hagenhuber's cafeteria, whose special buns stuffed with pastry cream became famous when John Paul II spoke of them in later years. There was a movie theater that showed the latest black-and-white film releases, though high school students were not allowed to see them. Iser Lauber, a businessman, owned a building near Chaim Balamuth's and rented out office space in it to the photographer Franciszek Lopatecki and the framer Adolf Zadora.

bloody battle. The Poles regained many of their eastern territories in the Battle of Warsaw, as it was then called. The outcome of this battle not only changed the course of the Polish-Soviet border but also saved Europe from the Communist advance for another 24 years. The victory at the Battle of Warsaw became known as the "Miracle on the Vistula."

The second-floor apartment where the Wojtylas lived in Wadowice is now a museum.

A DEVOUT HOUSEHOLD

The youngest Wojtyla was born during a war that established the borders of a newly independent Poland. The family was finally safe enough to live the kind of life they wanted. Their apartment on the second floor of a building near the Market Square in Wadowice had four rooms and a kitchen. The older brother, Edmund, was fourteen and already pursuing his high school degree. Emilia Wojtyla took care of the home and did sewing to earn extra income.

The atmosphere of the home in which the children grew up was extremely religious. A holy-water fountain hung near the front door so that family and guests could dip their fingers in the holy water and make the sign of the cross as they entered or left. Religious pictures and other holy objects that would remind them of their faith hung on the walls along with family portraits. The Wojtylas observed all the religious feast days, went to confession every first Friday of the month, and fasted on days specified by the church. They attended morning Mass at the Church of the Presentation of the Blessed Virgin Mary before going to work or school each day; they said

Young Karol Wojtyla (holding the ball) loved to play soccer with his friends. He was energetic and good at sports.

CATHOLICS AND JEWS LIVE SIDE BY SIDE

The Jewish community comprised one-fifth of Wadowice's total population, which at that time was about 7,000 people. Jews began arriving in Wadowice in the latter half of the nineteenth century when the Austro-Hungarian emperor, Francis Joseph I, granted equal rights to all his subjects. Before that, Jews were not allowed in many cities, including Wadowice.

Polish Catholics and Jews got along peacefully in Wadowice in the 1930s. It was commonplace to see the local parish priest, Father Leonard Prochownik, strolling along the main square with Anna Hubertow, an influential woman in the Jewish community. The mother-in-law of the Jewish community leader, she herself owned 11 buildings in Wadowice. They always conversed in loud voices because both of them were hard of hearing. Their leisurely strolls assured everyone in town, Christians and Jews alike, that relations between the two communities were harmonious.

The Jews had a synagogue; the Christians had the Church of the Presentation of the Blessed Virgin Mary, a monastery of Discalced (Shoeless) Carmelites at Gorka and another of Pallotine Fathers at Kopiec, as well as chapels of the Sisters of Nazareth and the Albertine Brothers.

The boundaries between congregations were not well defined. As a young boy, Karol Wojtyla went to the synagogue with his father to hear the cantor, an outstanding tenor, who was also in military service in Wadowice.

Likewise, the son of the Jewish community leader used to walk right into the church to recruit his friend for soccer games.

A BIPARTISAN GOALKEEPER?

Wadowice boys played soccer in the street every day but Thursday, which was market day. Traffic was not a problem: There were few automobiles in Wadowice, and their owners didn't take them out very often. The boys also played in the main square and nearby fields. No one could match young Wojtyla's skills except possibly Poldek Goldberg, a well-built Jewish boy. When the youngsters picked sides, a natural division arose between Catholics and Jews, and they formed separate Christian and Jewish teams. Whenever Goldberg was absent, everybody forgot about the separation and Wojtyla played on the Jewish team, defending the Jewish goal against Christian shots. Actually, as one of his school friends remembered, between studying and praying, Karol Wojtyla didn't have much time for soccer.

Wadowice had two excellent high schools: the Marcin Wadowita School, which was a national preparatory high school for young men, and its equivalent for young women, the Michalina Moscicka School. Students who lived outside Wadowice took the train to school. (A railroad linked Wadowice with the nearby cities of Kraków, Bielsk, and Andrychow.) The policy of the school administrators was to hire outstanding teachers. They wanted to be sure their students would receive a high level of instruction. Wadowice was also an important cultural center in the region, especially in the field of amateur theater. People who lived in surrounding towns benefited from the theatrical talent developed in Wadowice.

When young Wojtyla was six years old, his parents enrolled him in the primary school on Market Square. Even in first grade, he was a good student. Although the classroom was small and overcrowded, teachers never had any disciplinary

The elder Karol Wojtyla took his son (center) on a pilgrimage to Kalwaria Zebrzydowska after the boy's mother died. The oldest calvary in Poland, made up of 40 chapels, it was built in the early seventeenth century.

problems with him. Quite the contrary, they remarked on how well he got along with his classmates and respected his teachers.

A SAD INTERLUDE

As much as Emilia Wojtyla enjoyed caring for her second son, her health did not improve. In 1927 her husband took early retirement so that he could care for her and their young son full-time. The lieutenant had to forfeit a retirement rank and accept a meager pension. To help family finances, he took up tailoring again. Two years later, shortly before Karol's First Communion and Edmund's graduation from the university, Emilia died.

After the death of the boys' mother, the disconsolate father took his sons on a pilgrimage to Kalwaria Zebrzydowska, a calvary commissioned in 1600 by Mikolaj Zebrzydowski, the ruler of Kraków, who hoped to replicate the layout of Jerusalem. The calvary is made up of 40 chapels, each embellished with Dutch ornamentation, built between 1605 and 1632 on a series of

A Historical Note

Scarcely two months after the death of Emilia Wojtyla, on June 13, 1929, in the Spanish Carmelite Convent of Tuy, Sister Lucia experienced another apparition of the Blessed Virgin Mary. This second "Miracle of Fatima" would one day lead directly to young Karol Wojtyla. This time the Virgin asked Lucia to deliver a message to the pope. The Virgin Mary wanted the pope to dedicate Russia to God. She also gave Lucia instructions as to how she wanted this done. This request was never adequately fulfilled, however, until the pontificate of John Paul II.

hills not far from Wadowice. An outdoor path laid on the hillsides forms open-air stations of the cross, a meditative *Via Dolorosa*. Soon after the original complex was completed, a second well-planned labyrinth of paths, dedicated to Our Lady, was built. The paths of the labyrinth

Where It All Began

The world has come to know Wadowice, a small town in southern Poland, as the birthplace of Pope John Paul II. Located about 25 miles (40 km) southwest of Kraków on the banks of the Skawa River, it has a current population of 20,000. Ever since Karol Wojtyla's elevation to pope in 1978, people have made pilgrimages to Wadowice.

His family's apartment on 7 Koslielna Street became a museum—the Birthplace of the Holy Father John Paul II—in 1984, thanks to the efforts of Cardinal Franciszek Macharski and Father Edward Zacher. They resolved several legal difficulties, found alternative housing for the tenant at that time, and restored the apartment to the way it was when the Wojtylas lived there. The caretakers of this museum are the Nazarene Sisters, who have been in Wadowice for more than 100 years. They also operate a home for handicapped children.

Close to the town at Gorka is the monastery of the Discalced Carmelites. They built their home in 1892 as a reformed branch of the Carmelites of Czerna. In 1991 John Paul II canonized Rafael Kalikowski, prior of the order when Gorka was founded.

Pallotine Fathers live in the Collegium Marianum, which is also near Wadowice. After World War II they published religious books and magazines at this center. It currently houses the order's novitiate.

The Church of the Presentation of the Blessed Virgin Mary is the oldest one in Wadowice (completed in 1798). On its south side is a sundial with the Latin inscription *Tempus fugit; aeternitas manet.* (Time goes by; eternity is always there.) Recently Roman Catholics in Wadowice built a second parish church and dedicated it to Saint Peter.

Wadowice is proud of its high school. Marcin Wadowita was the patron of this school. He was born in Wadowice in the seventeenth century, was rector of the Kraków Academy of Polish Language and Culture, and founded a high school and a hospital in his native city.

No one knows when Wadowice was established as a town. It was first mentioned in a document dated February 24, 1327, during the reign of Ladislao I Lokietek.

intersect the route of the stations of the cross in several places.

It is evident that this holy place was built for children, especially for those in need of maternal help. Wojtyla had a reason for bringing his sons here. "Now that you no longer have an earthly mother, your Heavenly Mother will be the one who will protect you with her loving care. She will defend you from the evil in this world," he told them. Although young Karol Wojtyla was only nine years old and could not fully understand all his father wanted him to know, he has written that he felt, from that time on, the Blessed Virgin Mary would always take care of him.

Karol Wojtyla finished first grade in 1927. As this report card shows, he received high marks in all of his subjects.

The close bond between Wojtyla and the Virgin Mary grew deeper after that pilgrimage. The following year the Carmelite Sisters of Wadowice gave young Wojtyla a scapula—a long piece of cloth worn over the shoulders, front and back, as part of a monastic habit—with the image of the Mother of God on it. He took good care of this scapula and wore it on various occasions.

EDMUND WOJTYLA'S STORY

After receiving his medical degree, Edmund Wojtyla began practicing medicine in the hospital in Bielsk, a city not far from Wadowice, and he visited his father and brother often. After the death of their mother, he became more attentive to his little brother despite the difference in their ages. People who knew the brothers noticed that they seemed to have very similar personality traits. Edmund taught Karol how to climb mountains and how to ski. He also taught him how to skillfully dodge other soccer players.

The year Edmund received his medical degree, Lieutenant Wojtyla took his family to Czestochowa to worship at the shrine of the Black Madonna. Throughout his life Karol Wojtyla returned there quite often.

At the end of 1932, Edmund Wojtyla contracted scarlet fever from a patient. There were no cures for this disease in this era before antibiotics; the young doctor, who was only twenty-six, died on December 5 after four days of suffering.

The hospital director recalled that Wojtyla could not understand the meaning of his suffering and the mysterious ways of God. While he was dying, he kept asking, "Why me? And why now?"

For Karol Wojtyla, a boy of twelve in his third year of high school, this was a much harder blow than the death of his mother, possibly because he was more conscious of the reality of death than he had been three and a half years earlier. One of the most cherished mementos John Paul II used to keep in his desk at the Vatican was his brother's stethoscope.

A FRIEND IN THE CHURCH

In 1930 Father Kazimierz Figlewicz arrived in Wadowice to help out in the high school catechetical, or religious program. He was overwhelmed with work. That was the same year that Karol, who was eight years old, finished elementary school and began his high school studies. Father Figlewicz taught him religion and thus became the first catechist of the future pope.

The religion teacher liked his student very much. He described Wojtyla as "very alert, astute, intelligent, and a very good student." The two of them formed a close friendship not only in class but also on the altar and in the confessional. One of Father Figlewicz's duties was to train the altar boys in the parish, and he recruited Wojtyla to become one. The new catechetical teacher also became the student's first regular confessor. After three years Father Figlewicz was transferred to the cathedral at Wawel Castle in Kraków. The warm friendship between teacher and student continued for many years. The priest often invited

Karol Wojtyla (sitting on the priest's right) was an altar boy under the tutelage of Father Kazimierz Figlewicz, a curate of the church and religion teacher in the Wadowice young men's high school.

A Prince of Firm Convictions

Prince Adam Stefan Sapieha was born in 1867 into an aristocratic Lithuanian family. He was ordained a priest at the age of twenty-six. He served at the Vatican from 1906 to 1911, and then Pope Pius X made him a bishop. In March 1912 he came to Kraków for his installation. The first thing he did in Kraków was to visit a shelter for homeless people.

When Poland gained her independence, Bishop Sapieha refused to let Achille Ratti, the apostolic delegate, take part in the deliberations of the Polish Bishops' Conference. He argued that the Polish bishops should discuss issues just among themselves. Sapieha was also against signing a treaty with the Vatican.

In 1922 Achille Ratti was elected pope and took the name Pius XI. During the 17 years of his pontificate, he withheld the title of cardinal from Sapieha, even though Kraków became an archdiocese in 1926. It was Pope Pius XII who named Sapieha cardinal archbishop of Kraków on February 18, 1946.

Sapieha also confronted President Ignacy Moscicki and public opinion in 1937 when he ordered, without consulting anybody, the glass casket containing the remains of Marshal Józef Pilsudski to be moved from the royal crypt of Saint Leonard in Wawel Cathedral to the belfry—the Tower of the Silver Bells—arguing that the crowds who came to view the body in the church violated the sacred character of this holy sanctuary.

When World War II broke out, Sapieha was the head of the Polish Bishops' Conference, since Cardinal Hlond, primate of Poland, had fled to France. With the help of Lucina Frassati de Gawronski, wife of a Polish diplomat, Sapieha intervened with Mussolini on behalf of professors at the Jagiellonian University in Kraków who had been deported to the concentration camp in Dachau. During the war Sapieha set up a Public Service Board, the only organization apart from the Polish Red Cross that was recognized by the General Government designated by Germany in the occupied area around Kraków.

After the war, he protested the detention of soldiers in the Home Army, unfair trial procedures, and the deportation of Poles to forced labor and prison camps in the Soviet Union. In March 1945 Sapieha founded a weekly Catholic magazine, *Tygodnik Powszechny*. It was the only popular (and opposition) publication in Poland, and the Communist government censored it regularly.

Sapieha died on July 23, 1951, and was buried in the Wawel Castle Cathedral in Kraków.

Wojtyla to Kraków to take part in the liturgy, especially during Holy Week ceremonies. These visits were a great adventure for the young man, who was accustomed to a quiet life in his small town.

DEVELOPING AN INTELLECT

Father Edward Zacher took the place of Father Figlewicz in Wadowice. Ordained a priest in 1927, educated in Rome, and with a doctorate in theology, Father Zacher sparked Wojtyla's interest in natural science. The course of studies in the young men's high school concentrated on the classics and the humanities. The curriculum included Polish language and literature, history, Latin, and Greek. Scientific disciplines were not given equal status in this program, but first-year students were taught calculus, geometry, and natural science. In later years courses in physics and chemistry were added. These science courses were the only subjects in which Wojtyla did not receive high marks. It wasn't for lack of aptitude or study. According to the science teacher, no student was competent enough to receive high marks in these subjects.

Although he was a theologian, Father Zacher had a sound knowledge of physics and astrophysics. When he taught religion in class and directed his students' thoughts to God, he turned their attention to the cosmos, other galaxies, and unknown stars at the same time. Zbigniew Silkowski, a schoolmate of Karol Wojtyla's, remembered how attentively Wojtyla listened to Father Zacher's thoughts. He told his pupils that an open-minded and sincere quest for truth never obscures God's truth. On the contrary, it fosters humility before God, the Creator.

Other teachers in the Wadowice high school also influenced Wojtyla's intellectual development. Kazimierz Foryl, the Polish language professor, piqued Wojtyla's interest in romantic literature and the theater. Zygmunt Damasiewicz cultivated Wojtyla's love of Latin, a language that he mastered extraordinarily well.

A FIRST TASTE OF LEADERSHIP

Wojtyla was eleven when he was elected leader of the class and assumed responsibility for the first time. Father Figlewicz noticed that "he was always very loyal to his classmates, without getting into conflict with his teachers." He was also leader of the altar boys for a while, and later, in his last high school year, he became president of the Marian Sodality, moderated by Father Zacher. The purpose of this group was to strengthen each student's relationship with the Blessed Virgin Mary through prayer.

Zbigniew Silkowski was one of Karol Wojtyla's good school friends. He had to repeat a year because he was having problems with his studies. Wojtyla offered to tutor his friend and did such a good job that Silkowski became one of the best students in the class. From then on, Wojtyla was always ready to help other students who were having trouble with their schoolwork.

CHILDHOOD FRIENDS

One of Wojtyla's other close friends was Jerzy Kluger, son of a local lawyer who was the leader of the Jewish community, called a *kahal* in Hebrew. Kluger was a year younger than Wojtyla and had a totally different personality. He did not apply himself as a student. On the contrary, he was attracted to things that were permissible for young people, as well as those that were forbidden. He practiced his religion superficially. Despite this, their friendship lasted many years. Kluger, his British wife, and his daughter were among the first people from Poland that Pope John Paul II received in a special private audience.

In Wojtyla's fifth year in high school, he had a close call. After his mother died, his father used to take his son out to eat in a restaurant owned by Maria Banas. One day Mrs. Banas's son, one of young Wojtyla's friends, took a gun out of the cash-register drawer. The weapon belonged to a policeman in town, who, with the permission of the restaurant's owner, used to put it in the drawer whenever he stopped in to grab a bite before going on duty. Wojtyla's friend knew the gun was in the drawer, so he took it out and started fooling around with it. He pointed the gun at his friend Karol and shouted, "Hands up!" Then he pulled the trigger, and a shot rang out. It missed the head of the future pope by inches. Aghast and relieved, young Banas found his own behavior totally unbelievable.

THE LURE OF THE THEATER

Throughout his young life Wojtyla enjoyed the art of elocution. During his high school years he was always the one picked to give welcoming and farewell speeches, or speeches thanking someone for something. In 1933 he gave the altar-boy group's farewell address to Father Figlewicz, and in 1935 his teachers asked him to deliver the funeral oration for Marshal Józef Pilsudski on the day the head of state and army leader was buried.

Professor Kazimierz Foryl had revealed to Wojtyla the beauty and evocative force of language hidden in Polish romantic literature. However, the person who instilled in him a real love for the theater was Mieczyslaw Kotlarczyk, the history teacher in the women's high school. Theater was the very core of Kotlarczyk's being.

Wojtyla acted for the first time in November 1935, when

Aspiring actor Wojtyla plays a role in Zygmunt August, a play about the last Jagiellonian king by Stanislaw Wyspialski. He plays a soldier of the Light Brigade, near right.

the students staged *Antigone* by Sophocles. He played the part of Haemon, opposite his friend Halina Królikiewiczówna. She attended the young women's high school and was the daughter of the principal of the young men's high school.

Three months later Wojtyla interpreted the role of Gucio in *Sluby panienskie (Maiden Vows),* a comedy written by Aleksander Fredro. Here he played opposite his neighbor Regina Beer. He would appear with her in other plays later on. These three young people, under the direction of Kotlarczyk, were to become the backbone of the amateur theater in Wadowice in the 1930s. This theatrical circle of friends from a small town soon became a company of actors that won the applause of the entire region.

A DIRECTOR'S INFLUENCE

Wojtyla identified with the ideas of Mieczyslaw Kotlarczyk. The director affirmed that the role of the actor and of the priest were the same in some ways, since the job of both was to elaborate on the spoken word for the listener. The actor who recites a literary text is doing the same thing the priest does when he proclaims the Word of God. Each should perform his role in such a way that the truth hidden in the word reaches and touches the one who hears it, while the persona of the actor and that of the priest remain hidden behind the role. They operate only as intermediaries.

Following this philosophy, little by little Mieczyslaw Kotlarczyk got rid of all theatrical elements—sets, costumes, and actor's gestures—that would distract attention from the power of the Word. That way, the inner souls of both the epic text and the actor speaking the words were revealed. His two star adherents and performers were Karol Wojtyla and Halina Królikiewiczówna.

A THESPIAN RIVALRY

A not-too-serious rivalry sprang up between the two. On one occasion a famous actress from Kraków, Kazimiera

In July 1937 young Wojtyla finished his summer military training in Hermanowice and was promoted to the next rank. From left to right: Karol Wojtyla and his fellow trainees Zbigniew Silkowski, Stanislaw Zmuda, Tadeusz Zieba, Eugeniusz Filek, and Szczepan Mogielnicki.

Rychterówna, came to Wadowice and organized an oratorical competition. Królikiewiczówna recited a lighthearted piece, while Wojtyla chose a complicated poem. Despite the difficulty of the poem Wojtyla recited, the actress awarded the first prize to Królikiewiczówna and the second prize to Wojtyla. He was a gallant loser and gave his rival a bouquet of flowers.

His ability to act showed that Wojtyla had an excellent memory. When he played a long role, it was enough for him to read the text a few times to memorize it. Once, when an actor was let go, Wojtyla took on the part, since the character he played died before the other character came onstage. He learned the new lines in a day, telling everybody that it wasn't difficult, since he had begun picking up the lines during rehearsals.

AN AUSPICIOUS MEETING

Wojtyla's love of the spoken word consumed him during his last high school years. Though theater took up most of his free time, he still attended Mass each morning, did his school-work carefully, fulfilled his duties as leader of the Marian Sodality, and took a walk every afternoon with his father. In the spring of 1938, Prince Adam Stefan Sapieha, now arch-bishop of Kraków, arrived at the high school in Wadowice to confer the sacrament of confirmation. That was a big event for the school and for all of Wadowice.

Tadeusz Szeliski, who taught Greek, and Karol Wojtyla, his student, welcomed the archbishop on behalf of the school

Karol Wojtyla (left) and his father (on his right) made a pilgrimage with two friends to the sanctuary of Our Lady of Czestochowa.

community. Since the school curriculum emphasized the classics, Wojtyla gave his speech in fluent Latin. His performance impressed Archbishop Sapieha so much that he asked the school principal if that student, by any chance, had any intention of entering the seminary and becoming a priest. He was told that Wojtyla was going to study Polish language and literature at the university.

A FAREWELL TO HIGH SCHOOL

Wojtyla was not thinking of becoming a priest at that time. He loved literature and the theater and wanted to pursue these disciplines. On May 14, 1938, one week after his meeting with Archbishop Sapieha, Wojtyla passed his final high school exams. He got the highest marks in all his subjects, and the school board approved him to go on to study at the university.

At the end of May, the classmates had to say farewell to one another and to the school. Karol Wojtyla gave the farewell speech to the professors on behalf of his fellow students. It was a formal thank-you for their hard work. Wojtyla assured them that their students, with all the knowledge the professors had passed down to them, would start out upon, and stick to, the paths they had been taught.

Before entering the university, Wojtyla had to fulfill military duty required of all students. At the end of June, he and other recent Wadowice graduates reported to the military camp at Zubrzyca Gorna, where they were assigned to build roads. Wojtyla and his friends were sent out to do this construction work, but sometimes he found himself peeling potatoes in the camp's mess hall.

FOREBODINGS OF A BLEAK FUTURE

Karol Wojtyla arrived back in Wadowice in the last half of July 1938. His father had already been making preparations

for the family's move to Kraków. Wojtyla was scheduled to enter the Jagiellonian University, and now nothing would hold him back. The period of his life spent in the little town of Wadowice was over.

The atmosphere of Wadowice had changed. Forebodings of anti-Semitism filled the air, and Polish-Jewish relationships were no longer comfortable. Regina Beer's story is a case in point. She finished her final high school exams in 1936 and wanted to study medicine at the Jagiellonian University in Kraków. While Marshall Józef Pilsudski was still in power, radical anti-Semitic groups were not powerful. After his death, however, hate groups became more active. Education officials limited the number of Jewish students admitted to the university without specifying an exact number that would be allowed to enter. These rules allowed university officials to deny matriculation at any time to any Jewish candidate without further explanation. Regina Beer, despite excellent marks in all her high school exams, was not allowed to stay at the university.

ANTI-SEMITISM IS ANTI-CHRISTIAN

In the spring of 1937, Regina Beer returned home to Wadowice so that she and her parents could move to Palestine. Her sudden exit was due not only to anti-Semitic incidents at the university but also to an accusation that she had been in contact with the illegal Polish Communist Party. She lived with a roommate in a student residence. Her roommate's friend was a Communist, and the police arrested Beer because she knew him.

Many years later she wrote, "Only one family did not show racial hatred toward us. That was Karol and his father…. Mr. Wojtyla…told me many times, 'Not all Polish people are anti-Semitic. I want you to know that I am not anti-Semitic.' He was very sad that I had to go away, and I believe Karol was even sadder." Regina Beer Risenfeld met up with her old friend half a century later, during one of his audiences in St. Peter's Square, in Rome.

Anti-Semitism was not limited to certain social classes; workers, farmers, teachers, buisnessmen, housewives, and priests all participated in anti-Jewish activities. Karol Wojtyla was brought up in an environment in which Jewish people were thought of as "elder brothers in the faith" and anti-Semitism was antithetical to Gospel values. Father Leonard Prochownik, a priest at the Wadowice Catholic church, often repeated, "Anti-Semitism is anti-Christian," and his altar boy always remembered that.

On May 14, 1938, Karol passed his high school exams with the highest marks. On May 27 he gave the farewell address to the teachers on behalf of the students.

SURROUNDED BY HATE

By the end of the 1930s, Poland, caught between anti-Semitic and an anti-Christian dictatorship, was in mortal danger. Across Poland's western border, Germany's Third Reich had made anti-Semitism official policy. In 1933 Germans voted for Adolph Hitler in democratic elections. His party platform ostensibly was aimed against Communism. Communism was against religion, and the Nazi Party needed Christian votes, so they railed against the godless Communists, but their real target was the Jews. Across Poland's eastern border, the Communists of Stalin's Union of Soviet Socialist Republics (USSR) were a constant threat.

While Karol Wojtyla was taking his high school exams in 1938, Germany managed to annex Austria. Six months later, while the Wojtylas were moving to Kraków, the Germans marched into Czechoslovakia. Young Karol Wojtyla, captivated by dreams of the future, most likely had not yet recognized the peril of his country's situation.

In the autumn of 1938, Karol Wojtyla arrived in Kraków to begin his studies at the Jagiellonian University. A year later Poland was occupied by the German Reich, swastikas hung from Wawel Castle, and the university was shut down. Jews and monks were sent to concentration camps. Young Wojtyla worked as a manual laborer and acted in the underground theater directed by Mieczyslaw Kotlarczyk. It was during these difficult times that Wojtyla realized his vocation.

Chapter 2

The Nazis Take Over Poland

A photograph of Karol Wojtyla taken in Kraków in 1938 shows a thoughtful eighteen-year-old student with long hair. He was quiet, somewhat reserved, but well liked—and respected—by many.

When Lieutenant Wojtyla and his son left Wadowice for Kraków in the autumn of 1938, they moved into the basement apartment of a house at 10 Tyniecka Street that Emilia Wojtyla's younger brother, Robert Kaczorowski, had built. Upon his return to Kraków, after being interned in a Russian prison camp throughout most of World War I, Kaczorowski bought a plot of land with family money and chose a site on the river in Debnicki, a primarily working-class district. The house, which had a ground floor, a second story, and a basement apartment, was solid, although Kaczorowski had used recycled bricks, beams, and windows from demolition sites to construct it.

The basement apartment had a separate entrance. The senior Wojtyla's brother-in-law lived on the ground floor, and his unmarried sisters-in-law, Rudolfina and Anna, lived on the second floor. The Wojtylas' area was small—two rooms on one side of a hallway and a kitchen and bath on the other side. It was also quite a chilly and damp place.

The house sat on the right bank of the Vistula River and had a beautiful view of the historic section of Kraków. At one end of the old town, atop Wawel Hill, stood the Royal Castle and the imposing fourteenth-century Cathedral of Saints Stanislaw and Waclaw; on the other end was the Church of Saint Mary, another extraordinary fourteenth-century building, which faced Market Square. It took young Wojtyla about half an hour to walk to the university. First he had to cross the Debnicki Bridge, and then he walked along side streets that went around Market Square. On his daily route he passed the palatial residence of Archbishop Adam Stefan Sapieha, whose investiture as bishop had been witnessed by his parents many years before and whom he had welcomed to his high school with a speech given in fluent Latin.

UNIVERSITY LIFE BEGINS

Wojtyla began his courses at the university in October. He signed up for a language curriculum in the Polish philology department, which was run by the philosophy faculty at the university. In high school, Polish-language classes included grammar and literature. At the university the curriculum included linguistics, etymology, and phonetics as well. To his course list Karol Wojtyla added classes in Russian and Old Church Slavonic (the language Saints Cyril and Methodius spoke when they introduced Byzantine-rite Christianity to Eastern Europe). It was a heavy first-year schedule, but young Wojtyla had an extraordinary memory and a strong sense of self-discipline, so he assimilated the new course material as easily as he

had mastered high school Latin and Greek. For a time he even thought of majoring in linguistics.

Wojtyla was in excellent health that autumn. He was fit and tanned from his mandatory army training the summer before. His clothes were rough and rustic, but they were neat and clean. Fashion did not interest him. Actually, the senior Wojtyla tailored all his son's clothes from his own old military uniforms.

In the beginning of his university life, Wojtyla sat in the first row of every class and paid close attention to the lectures. In time, however, he made friends with Tadeusz Kwiatkowski, Wojciech Zukrowski, and Tadeusz Holuj and moved to the back of the room to sit with them. No matter where he sat, Karol Wojtyla was an outstanding student. His keen intellect and determination to learn were a winning combination. At times, he chose almost impossible assignments. Stanislaw Pigon, a well-known literary critic, conducted a seminar course. Not many first-year students other than Wojtyla were enrolled in it. When it was his turn to present a paper, Wojtyla was not intimidated by the upperclassmen—he chose a topic that required full command of French: "Madame de Staël as Theoretician of Romanticism," a study of the influence of this famous hostess who held "Literary Evenings" in her home in Paris. By the next meeting of the group, he had already finished a long and difficult analysis of her style, which he read aloud to the group. It took several sessions for him to present the entire paper, and to do the research in French, he had to work for some time with a private tutor.

STUDENT SOCIAL LIFE

Wojtyla didn't spend all his time studying. Although he was reserved when he met someone for the first time, he was genuinely interested in people and enjoyed the give-and-take of student discussions.

When he got to the university, he joined various student groups. Right from the start, he let it be known that he considered himself a poet and orator. Two weeks into the school year, he recited several of his poems at a Literary Evening organized by a group of budding poets in philology. The group charged a small admission fee. When they tallied up their earnings at the end of the evening, they were surprised to find that they had made a profit of 18 zlotys. The group decided to spend the windfall in a popular bar in Kraków. Karol Wojtyla declined. He

Above: The Wojtylas moved into a basement apartment at 10 Tyniecka Street. Located in a working-class district of Kraków, the house belonged, in part, to young Wojtyla's mother.

Right: Karol Wojtyla's student identification cards show his status at the university and his membership in one of the religious societies.

wasn't interested in going to bars, so his poet friends paid him his share 2 zlotys—and went without him.

A FIRST BRUSH WITH POLITICS

Next Wojtyla joined a literary society of students from the Polish philology department. Members of this group discussed and debated literature and other subjects that were of interest to them. They talked about restructuring the Polish philology department at the university into a separate department rather than a subdivision of the philosophy faculty.

They also protested the *Numerus Nullis* regulation at the university, a "zero number" provision that reflected the growing anti-Semitism in Poland. The purpose of the rule was to keep Jewish students from entering the university—in effect, actually preventing them from being accepted. Since boyhood, Wojtyla had always held the Jews in high regard. His university friends remembered his sticking close to Anka Weber in class. She was Jewish, and he wanted to protect her from members of the rightist-nationalist organization *Mlodziez Wszechpolska*. Wojtyla disapproved of this group because they openly attacked Jews simply for being Jews.

WEAVING A NETWORK OF FRIENDS

Karol Wojtyla made many friends during his university days. Sharing a common interest in the theater, he became close to Juliusz Kydrynski, whose father had been a

Right: Karol Wojtyla plays Taurus (right). Studio 39 staged *The Moon Cavalier* in a courtyard of the university at the Kraków Festival in June 1939.

Below: Photographs of the actors in Studio 39 that summer.

language professor at the Jagiellonian University. Kydryniski's father had died in 1937, and the fact that each young man had lost a parent likely made the two friends closer. Wojtyla was quickly accepted as a member of the Kydrynski family. He even called Mrs. Kydrynski "Mom." Wojtyla had a penchant for thinking of close friends as family. He looked upon his drama coach, Mieczyslaw Kotlarczyk, as an older brother, just as he looked upon Juliusz Kydrynski as a younger brother.

The Kydrynskis introduced Wojtyla to the Szkocki family. Leon Szkocki and his wife, Irena, had a large circle of friends in the arts. Their house, the Pod Lipkami (Under the Birches) Villa, was one of many homes in Kraków where poets, writers, and musicians used to gather. The Szkocki's daughter, Zofia Pozniak, was a pianist, and her husband was a musicologist. Karol called Irena Szkocki "Grandma," although he was not the only guest in her house who affectionately called her that. Wojtyla's French tutor, Jadwiga Lewaj, also lived with the Szkockis.

KEEPING UP WITH RELIGIOUS LIFE

Wojtyla's religious devotion did not change in his new environment. He began each day with morning Mass in the parish church. He went to confession regularly each month. On occasion he served as altar boy for Father Figlewicz, his former religion teacher, who now served at Wawel Castle Cathedral. But the idea of his becoming a priest was not in his thoughts at all.

On February 6, 1939, four days after the Blessed Virgin's Candlemas Day, Wojtyla was accepted into the Marian Sodality at Jagiellonian University, a branch of the Marian group he had belonged to in high school in Wadowice. He told the group that he intended to get involved in work that promoted social justice.

Four days later, on February 10, Pope Pius XI died. The Vatican secretary of state, Cardinal Eugenio Pacelli, was elected pope on the third vote. He took the name of his predecessor and became known as Pius XII.

A Historical Note

While Karol Wojtyla was embarking on his new life in Kraków, the famous visionary Sister Faustina was dying of tuberculosis in a convent there. In 1931 she had received revelations about God's Divine Mercy and dedicated herself to spreading this devotion. People in her familiar surroundings caused her much grief because of her visions, but the devotion she started spread rapidly among Catholics in Kraków and slowly but surely farther afield. Many years later Wojtyla, as Pope John Paul II, elevated her to sainthood.

The new pope's election took place during Lent in 1939, a time when Karol Wojtyla attended the washing-of-the-feet ceremony of the Holy Thursday liturgy at Wawel Cathedral. This ceremony commemorates the institution of the sacrament of holy orders. The celebrant was Archbishop Sapieha. Right after the service Wojtyla knelt in front of the tomb of King Jagiello, the Lithuanian prince who founded a great Polish and Lithuanian dynasty. Wojtyla seemed to be deep in thought. Then he stayed a while longer, praying in front of the Chapel of Our Lady.

That May he went on a student pilgrimage to one of the shrines where his father had taken him after his mother's death, Jasna Góra (Luminous Mountain), the Shrine of the Black Madonna, Our Lady of Czestochowa, Queen of Poland. He arrived at the shrine the day he turned nineteen years old.

FINISHING HIS FIRST YEAR

Final exams began in June. His first was in creative writing, given by Professor Kazimierz Nitsche, who was known for his challenging exams. Nitsche was also known to fail students who came to class unprepared. He even threw chalk, erasers, and chairs at them. Wojtyla passed that exam with a high mark and later the same day took one in Old Church Slavonic. Easily passing that exam, too, he had no trouble fulfilling his requirements and moving on to the second year.

To celebrate, a party was organized by several of Wojtyla's friends at the home of one of the women students in the Polish philology class. There was wine and dancing to the music of a record player. He may not have had any wine, but Wojtyla is reported to have joined in all the dancing. It may well have been the first and last time his friends ever saw him dance with anyone. He usually preferred to spend his time in lively conversation. "He didn't avoid the company of women, but he also didn't seek it out," Irena Orlewicz, a student friend, wrote in later years. She added that Wojtyla always came alone to classes and left alone.

AN ACTOR PREPARES

About this time the Theater Guild organized a drama workshop called Studio 39, and Wojtyla took up acting once again. Wojtyla, Halina Królikiewiczówna, Juliusz Kydrynski, and some other friends auditioned for a play. They got parts in a comedy, *The Moon Cavalier,* written by a young playwright named Marian Nizynski. In it, the actors played the signs of the zodiac. The protagonist was Lord Twardowski, a well-known character in Polish folklore. The play cast sarcastic allusions on social conditions of the time. Wojtyla played Taurus (his astrological sign) and wore a bull's mask. Taurus was a minor character in the play, but Wojtyla's energetic interpretation of the part—performed several times to the delight of audiences—was well received. The director recognized Wojtyla's acting talent and picked him to lead the parade of zodiac signs with his monologue, an important scene in the play.

Thus ended a full and busy school year. These joyful moments were most likely the last happy and carefree times in Wojtyla's young life. As a warm autumn rolled in, nothing would ever be the same again.

IN UNIFORM, CARRYING A RIFLE

Karol Wojtyla spent the better part of August at the military camp of the Academic Legion in Sadowa Wisznia, near Przemysl, a region inhabited mostly by Ukranians. This facility specialized in providing university students

Above: Karol Wojtyla spent the last month before the German occupation in a military camp for university students. Along with performing military exercises, he also swam and played soccer.

Left: His identity card shows that he fulfilled his Polish military requirements.

with military training that complemented their regular academic studies. Here Wojtyla learned to present arms, shoot, and drill.

He never took part in the boxing exercises that were offered, however, because he was not inclined to fight. Other legionnaires involved in these military exercises with him

Karol Wojtyla began working in this rock quarry at Zakrzówek in September 1940.

noticed that he seemed uncomfortable wearing a uniform and carrying a rifle. The last day of August, when Wojtyla handed in his uniform and other military equipment, the soldier on duty supposedly remarked, "You won't need these anymore." How wrong he was!

THE WAR IN POLAND BEGINS
On August 23, 1939, Germany's dictator, Adolph Hitler, and Russia's dictator, Joseph Stalin, concluded a cynical nonaggression pact that contained a secret protocol dividing Poland into German and Soviet spheres of interest. (Hitler actually wanted to use Poland as a staging area for a later planned attack on the Soviet Union.)

The first Friday of the month fell on September 1. Karol Wojtyla, just home from the Academic Legion, started out for confession, as usual. He found, however, that it was not a usual morning. German planes started bombing Kraków at dawn. Panic spread over the city, and people fled in all directions. Wojtyla crossed over the Debnicki Bridge and went straight to the cathedral, where he met Father Figlewicz. The priest was happy to see his former student—no one else was around to assist him at Mass. So after Father Figlewicz heard Wojtyla's confession, the young man served as altar boy while air-raid sirens howled and bombs exploded outside Wawel Cathedral.

THE SOVIETS BEGIN THEIR OWN AGGRESSION
The next day the Wojtylas packed two suitcases with bare necessities and started walking away from the Nazi bombs. They headed for the eastern border of Poland amid a flood of other refugees making their way by any means they could—car, train, wagon, on foot—and hiding from planes at every attack. The Wojtylas arrived at the San River a week later. The son was concerned that his sexagenarian father's health was not good enough to endure more travel, so the Wojtylas decided to turn around and head back home.

This decision may have saved their lives. An even greater danger lay farther ahead, toward the East. While the Wojtylas were fleeing from the Nazis, the Red Army was gearing up. The USSR invaded Poland on September 17 and began annexing territories it had disputed with Poland after World War I. Warsaw capitulated to the Germans on September 27, but the Wojtylas knew nothing of this. Nor did they know that the Soviets would press farther into Poland. Lithuania, which had previously been handed over to Germany, was now back under Moscow's control. The region between the Vistula and Bug rivers, so recently occupied by the Germans, now came under the Soviets. When the Wojtylas arrived at their basement apartment in the Debnicki neighborhood, Nazi police were already scouring Kraków for Polish officials, whom they were arresting, along with their entire families.

KRAKÓW UNDER THE NAZIS
Huge banners with swastikas waved over Wawel Castle. The historic royal fortress of ancient Polish kings became the residence of Hans Frank, the German-appointed

The Juliusz Slowacki Theater in Kraków flew swastikas when the Germans turned it into their own Staatstheater, or official state theater.

He Arrived with Empty Hands

—Lucjan Kydrynski, family friend

During the occupation we lived in a three-room apartment on the fourth floor of a building in Felicjanek Street in Kraków. A German officer's staff took over our biggest room. My mother, older brother, sister, and I lived in the remaining rooms.

Karol and his father spent Christmas 1940 with us. In February 1941, after his father died, Karol moved in with us and stayed for six months. My mother, my sister, and I slept in one bedroom, while Karol and my brother occupied the other. The apartment was very crowded; we all had to open and close our beds each day. Karol and my brother took turns bringing coal up from the cellar to the fourth floor.

Neither of them spent much time in the apartment. They left for work at six o'clock in the morning and didn't get back until after six in the evening. They usually arrived home exhausted. Karol put his few belongings in order in his little corner of our apartment. He didn't need any more space, since he didn't own many things. It was difficult to hold on to anything during the occupation, and he arrived at our house with practically nothing. Although he might have wanted to bring his furniture with him, there wasn't enough space in the apartment. Anyway, he really wasn't attached to material things. What Karol did bring with him was his friendship, his kindness, and his pleasant disposition, and that was enough.

The meals my mother prepared were never fancy, but Karol obviously enjoyed our family atmosphere. No one could prepare sumptuous meals during the occupation. We could buy only what was allotted to us with food-rationing coupons. While his father was still alive, Karol ate dinner with us and then took dinner to his father at their house in Debnicki. My sister went with Karol to help him care for his father.

Although I was almost 10 years younger than my brother and Karol, they shared their concerns with me. At any rate, in an apartment so small, with so many people packed in, we all had to stick together.

My brother and Karol liked the theater very much. A year before the war began, when they started their university studies, they joined the Theater Guild. During the Kraków Festival, they staged *The Moon Cavalier* by Marian Nizynski, out in the courtyard of the university, near Barbakan. The characters in this play were the signs of the zodiac. Karol played Taurus, and my brother played Aquarius.

During the occupation they acted in a kind of underground theater. The guild actors, dressed in black, recited plays in our largest room—until the Germans took it over—because there was no room to actually stage the production. These get-togethers were social as well as theatrical. The well-known actor Juliusz Osterwa attended performances that took place in our apartment. Usually 20 to 30 people came to watch them. Naturally, I saw them all. Once, I watched Karol portray the part of Smugon and my brother play Przelecki in *Przepióreczka* by Stefan Zeromski. Later on, when the Germans occupied the big room, we didn't have enough space to put on any plays.

Soon after that, Mieczyslaw Kotlarczyk from Wadowice came to Krakow and inaugurated the Rhapsodic Theater. Those plays took place in other people's houses. I loved all the plays very much, even though I didn't always understand what they were about. These were my first encounters with art. I also enjoyed the clandestine ambiance of those times—the fear the Germans caused and our constant dread of being reported.

I remember the time the police arrived when we were getting ready for a performance. As luck would have it, none of the guests had arrived yet, but the chairs and other furniture were already set up. The Germans asked why all the furniture was arranged in such a strange way all around the room. My mother explained she was right in the middle of giving the apartment a good overall housecleaning. Thank God this happened in the middle of the day, when Karol and my brother were away at work. The police actually believed the story.

During those difficult times Karol seemed very ordinary. He was no different from anyone else. He related to our family as a good son would; he was friendly and hardworking. We all prayed together—in those war times we had a lot to pray for—and that didn't seem strange to any of us. We've kept a close relationship ever since. When my mother was dying, we went to find Karol at the seminary. He arrived while she was in her last moments. He presided at her funeral, and later he officiated at my sister's wedding.

When he became Pope John Paul II, my old friend received me in a private audience at the Vatican. We reminisced about the old days. He also mentioned my family, the Kydrynskis, with much affection in his autobiography, *Dar i tajemnica (Gift and Mystery)*.

governor-general. Adolph Hitler gave him the power to govern that region of Poland just conquered by the Germans—up to a line where the Soviet armies had halted their invasion. The Germans designated their part of subjugated Poland as a protectorate, and it became known as the Designated General-Governorship. Kraków was proclaimed its capital, and according to German plans for it, Warsaw, which also lay within the

The Apostle of the Living Rosary
—Father Michal Szafarski

Jan Tyranowski was the leader of the Living Rosary youth group in St. Stanislas Kostka parish. He invited Karol Wojtyla to join the group. Tyranowski was an interesting man and also a demanding one. He was very disciplined and followed a strict schedule that began at five o'clock in the morning. Anyone who did not have a strong character quickly left his group. We used to pray at the meetings, and he taught us about the liturgy. Each month, we got out our little cards. In them were illustrations—a flower, for instance—and next to them a word like "Obedience." All during that month we had to put into practice what the word in the card said and then tell whether or not we had succeeded and why.

When Tyranowski eventually became ill with tuberculosis, that didn't stop him in his apostolate, not even while he was in the hospital. In the evening hours, other sick people sought him out, and he spoke with them all night long.

The nurses remembered that when someone was in pain and complaining, Tyranowski would say, "Pray that this suffering passes over to me," and then the sick person would stop moaning. Tyranowski endured his own pain and suffering and remained serenely calm in the face of them. He thanked God for suffering and asked God to forgive sin. Members of the Living Rosary group came to help take care of him.

During the war, 11 of the Salesian Fathers who were working in the parish died in concentration camps. Eleven of the Living Rosary group were eventually ordained as priests. Karol Wojtyla was the first among them to be ordained in 1946. Tyranowski did not attend his ordination and first Mass, because he was in the hospital. Instead, Father Wojtyla visited him to say good-bye, as the young priest was leaving soon after his ordination to continue his studies in Rome.

Jan Tyranowski died in 1947. A letter arrived for him from Rome, but unfortunately, it was too late. Karol Wojtyla wrote:

I know all that you went through, I know what type of Cross the most merciful God has nailed you to, and I know that God has accepted the sacrifice you offered him. I realize that in that hospital room, which you have come to know so well, you spread the Good News of the living God to many people. God afflicts his most devoted children. This is God the Father Who also did not deliver his own Son from suffering. I sense your suffering is not of the same measure as others. It is suffering in plenitude, and the type by which God is adored in small human undertakings. I know that God has accomplished His redemptive work in you as a brave collaborator. I see all this with the eyes of faith.

Two years later Karol Wojtyla wrote in the Catholic weekly *Tygodnik Powszechny*:

Jan was an apostle of the greatness of God, of the beauty of God, of the transcendence of God. God is not in us for us to limit him to the dimensions of our human spirituality. God is in us to pull us toward divine transcendence, above and beyond our nature. This was the underlying principle of Jan's strength. And in that, he was most strong, most tenacious, most persuasive, and most apostolic. God is within us. Jan knew that.

---

borders of the General-Governorship, would become a future "provincial way station on the German drive toward the East."

Living conditions were changing drastically. Everything from beets to coal became scarce. People lined up at daybreak to buy bread, and many prohibitions were imposed. Despite these bans, students from the Polish philology department continued to meet at the Kydrynskis' apartment for Literary Evenings. They read great literary works and assigned one another dramatic parts to read aloud since they didn't have enough room to actually stage any plays.

Mieczyslaw Kotlarczyk was unable to join them just then. Wadowice, where he was living at the time, was located west of the Skawa River from Kraków, so it was technically in another country. The German Reich had simply incorporated the whole region west of this border—a large part of western and northern Poland—into the German Reich, declaring this region "ancestral Germany" because a large part of the population had German roots.

CRACKDOWNS ON EDUCATION AND RELIGIOUS LIFE

Notice went out that despite the occupation, the university would open once again in November, and Karol Wojtyla registered for second-year Polish philology courses. But the Germans were only setting a trap. When 186 professors showed up on November 6 to start the school year, they were arrested and deported to the Sachsenhausen-Oranienburg concentration camp. Many of them lost their lives in the camp because of deplorable conditions, and the university remained closed until the end of the war.

Religious celebrations were forbidden. Archbishop Sapieha celebrated the last public Mass in Wawel Cathedral on October 29. Unlike Cardinal August Hlond, the primate of Poland who fled to France when World War II broke out, Archbishop Sapieha chose to remain in Poland. Governor Frank made a slight concession a short time later and allowed Mass to be celebrated. Two priests were authorized to celebrate two Masses per week in Wawel Cathedral. Father Figlewicz was one of those priests, but the Masses were only for Hitler's troops. No Poles were allowed to enter the Wawel Castle complex.

ROLE REVERSALS FOR THE WOJTYLAS

With the outbreak of World War II, roles in the Wojtyla family were reversed. With Poland under German control, the father lost his meager military pension—their only livelihood—and the son had to find a way to support them both.

By autumn of 1940, young Wojtyla was desperately looking for a paying job. He sought work in a theater, but the Germans had shut most of them down. The famous Juliusz Slowacki Theater became the German Staatstheater, or official state theater. Young Wojtyla then found a job as a delivery boy for a grocery store run by his godfather and a distant relative, Józef Kuczmierczyk. He registered with the Work Office, but German regulations were very stringent. This job, apart from being unstable, was not sufficiently important to the war effort to qualify for food-rationing tickets.

By this time the older Karol Wojtyla was becoming weaker. Not being able to support his son in his studies, which gave the father a reason to live, made the old lieutenant profoundly depressed. Their difficult circumstances aggravated his poor health. In addition to food, young Karol Wojtyla had another worry. During the occupation men between the ages of 18 and 60 were required to fulfill a "Public Labor Obligation." Karol had to find a type of work in Kraków that would support the war effort, not simply qualify him for food-ration coupons. This war-effort work could

Above: Karol Wojtyla in his work clothes. He preferred the night shift because he could find time to pray and read.

Right: St. Stanislas Kostka Church in the Debnicki district near the Wojtylas' apartment. Salesian Fathers, who specialized in working with young people, ran the parish.

protect him from being deported to a forced labor camp in Germany.

NEW WORKERS IN THE QUARRY

Jadwiga Lewaj, Wojtyla's French tutor who lived with the Szkocki family, helped him find a more secure job. In the autumn of 1940, thanks to her contacts, Wojtyla started working at Solvay Enterprises, a German chemical company with a subsidiary in Kraków. This manufacturing enterprise had, before the war, belonged to Belgian entrepreneurs, and the management team operated it out of Brussels. In 1940, when the Nazis occupied Belgium, Germans took control of the company, but their new directors didn't change the local administrative personnel in Kraków. Luckily for Wojtyla and his friends, the newly appointed German plant manager, a man named Foehl, maintained good relations with his Polish employees. The enterprise was also on good terms with the Gestapo, so the German secret police didn't pay too much attention to its payroll.

Many intellectuals in Kraków each day found work at the Solvay limestone quarry. Up until that time, Karol Wojtyla had lived in an intellectual milieu. This new job involved heavy manual labor, sometimes in freezing-cold weather. Although it was physically exhausting, Wojtyla later recognized it as an important social learning experience for him.

At first Wojtyla worked in the Zakrzówek quarry, which was almost an hour away from his home. His job

Below: The Solvay chemical plant where Wojtyla was transferred in October, 1941.

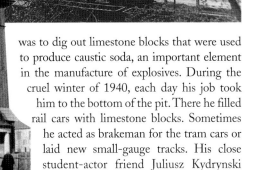

was to dig out limestone blocks that were used to produce caustic soda, an important element in the manufacture of explosives. During the cruel winter of 1940, each day his job took him to the bottom of the pit. There he filled rail cars with limestone blocks. Sometimes he acted as brakeman for the tram cars or laid new small-gauge tracks. His close student-actor friend Juliusz Kydrynski also worked in the quarry. Luckily, the manual laborers at the plant were Poles, so the students, who had no expertise in performing hard physical labor, could count on a certain amount of sympathy from the stronger and more experienced workers. Employees used their short lunch break to eat bread and drink ersatz coffee in a shack warmed by a small iron stove.

WOJTYLA'S FATHER'S FINAL DAYS

Despite the fact that the senior Wojtyla was eating better food, he was still sick and growing weaker by the day. On Christmas Day 1940 he accompanied his son to the Kydrynskis for dinner, but that was his last outing. He never left their apartment again. By February he wasn't

The palatial archbishop's residence still stands on Franciszkanska Street in Kraków.

able to cook for himself. His son used to go home from work with Juliusz Kydrynski and eat a dinner prepared by Mrs. Kydrynski. Then young Wojtyla took meals to his father.

On February 18, arriving with dinner as usual, Wojtyla found his father dead, most likely from a heart attack. Wojtyla burst into tears, sobbing, "I wasn't there at my mother's death. I wasn't there when my brother died. Now the same thing has happened with my father." He prayed by his father's bedside all night. Four days later, in bitter cold and accompanied by Father Figlewicz, Wojtyla buried his father in the military cemetery in Kraków.

Shortly after the burial, suffering from loss and loneliness, young Wojtyla moved in with the Kydrynskis for a while. (People who knew the

In Kraków, Wojtyla often visited his aunt Stefania, his father's half-sister.

Wojtylas at that time noticed that although the house on Tyniecka Street belonged to Wojtyla's maternal family, he and his father did not have a close relationship with the relatives who lived upstairs.)

BETTER DAYS AT THE QUARRY

With the end of the cold weather, Wojtyla's most difficult days at the quarry were over. That spring he became an assistant to Franciszek Labus, whose job was to set explosives in the rock and then detonate them. He and Wojtyla had to take cover when the explosions went off.

Wojtyla was helpful, friendly, hardworking, and very religious. He prayed silently whenever he got the slightest chance. At noon, when he heard the church bells ring out the *Angelus,* he used to stand still for a few moments beside the trays of explosives and collect himself. His coworkers called him "the student," and everyone who worked with him enjoyed being around him. Once Labus got to know Wojtyla, he, too, took a great liking to him and said to the younger man one day, "Wojtyla, you should be a priest."

STICKING TO CULTURE

But Wojtyla wasn't thinking along those lines yet. He spent his free time reading literary books, writing poetry, and acting in underground plays. In the autumn of 1941, he became a member of Unia, a Christian-Socialist organization. While Polish Resistance fighters wanted to resort to armed warfare to free Poland, Unia's basic objective was to transform community life in Poland (and in the whole world) by following and living Christian principles.

Unia was divided into various autonomous groups. Karol Wojtyla decided to join the Cultural Union, whose goal was to keep Polish cultural and Christian ideas alive; during the occupation the Germans had tried to suppress both religion and culture. Tadeusz Kudlinski was one of Unia's leaders in Kraków. In 1942 leaders of the Polish Resistance fighters decided to incorporate the entire Unia organization into the Home Army of the Resistance movement.

WORKING IN CHEMICALS, THINKING NEW THOUGHTS

After a year at the quarry, Wojtyla was transferred to the company's Borek Falecki plant that manufactured caustic soda. A narrow railroad linked it with the quarry. Work was lighter there, and the workers were allowed to take more time to eat their modest midday meal. Although this job paid a little more money than the quarry job, it still wasn't just compensation for the amount of work involved. Wojtyla had to carry buckets filled with milky limewater or bags of powdered reagents up to the men who needed them on the production line. He then had to stir new chemicals into the water buckets to start the process again.

It was at this time that the idea of dedicating himself to a religious life began to fill Wojtyla's mind. As he started to entertain thoughts of becoming a priest, people who could direct him along this spiritual path turned up in his life.

MEETING THE MYSTICAL TAILOR

While he was living in Debnicki, Wojtyla often attended Mass in St. Stanislas Kostka parish church, where the Salesian Fathers were in charge. He also went to services in the Dominican–parish and attended their theological and spiritual conferences. There he met Jan Tyranowski, the man who helped Wojtyla finally realize his priestly vocation. Although Tyranowski had taken business courses and was trained as an accountant, commerce didn't suit his personality. He took over his father's tailor shop instead. Short and mousy in appearance, he lived in the one-room shop, where he also did tailoring work for local Debnicki clients.

The shop was so sparsely furnished it looked like a monk's cell. Although Tyranowski had never taken vows to become a monk, he decided to remain celibate because he sensed that serving God was his true vocation. John Paul II would one day call Tyranowski "a hidden saint" because he had "opened the universe" for the pope when he was young.

A SAINTLY LIFE IN THE SECULAR WORLD

For Tyranowski it was possible to live a saintly life in the secular world—that was the ideal. He believed that anyone could be called to holiness. In 1935 Tyranowski had heard a Salesian priest confirm the concept that saintly holiness of life was indeed open to everyone, not just to priests or monks. Tyranowski strived to live this ideal

Saint John of the Cross

Juan (John) de Ypres y Álvarez lived from 1542 to 1591. He entered the Carmelite Order in 1563, taking the name of John of Saint Mathias. The Carmelite religious order was founded in the eleventh century by a group of hermits who lived on Mount Carmel in the Holy Land. Over time the strict rules established in the beginning became too difficult for some monasteries to follow, so, as requested by the general

chapter of the Carmelites, Pope Eugene IV approved a relaxation of their rules. This decision caused discord among the monks. Many believed that severe asceticism was an important means of spiritual development and helped souls draw closer to God.

In the second half of the sixteenth century, fearing practices were too lax in monasteries, Saint Teresa of Avila made the most effective attempt to revert to the original Carmelite rules. In 1562, with the approval of Pope Pius IV, she founded the first convent of reformed Carmelite Sisters. Saint John met her in 1567. Under her influence he founded the first reformed monastery for Carmelite monks in 1568 and took a new name in religion: John of the Cross.

During the pontificate of Pope Gregory XIII in 1582, the reformed Carmelites created their first province. To distinguish themselves from the traditional order, they were called "discalced" (shoeless) Carmelites. John of the Cross was elected provincial, but while he refused the nomination, he did accept the priory of the monastery in Granada.

In 1591 he was relieved of his responsibilities by a group of monks who wanted to follow a more relaxed rule. John of the Cross died in Ubeda the same year, a simple and unappreciated monk. Pope Benedict XIII canonized him in 1726, and in 1926 John of the Cross was proclaimed a Doctor of the Church.

He left behind many written works, but some were burned after his death. He is considered to be one of the greatest poets of the Spanish baroque era. Of the 22 volumes that were saved, the most important are *Dark Night of the Soul, The Spiritual Canticle, The Ascent of Mount Carmel,* and *The Living Flame of Love.*

The mysticism of Saint John of the Cross is based on the principle that the goal of human perfection is to be united with God, and the summit of this union is the fusion of one's will with the divine will. Before this can happen, the soul has to strive to purify itself of all sinful desires, to renounce the selfish "me."

and assiduously studied spiritual readings. His biggest premise was "Don't waste a minute" and with that, he arrived at a high level of spiritual awareness.

Tyranowski wanted to share his spiritual knowledge with young people. The Salesians of Debnicki encouraged such laypeople (those who were not ordained clergy) to help them in their apostolic work. The Salesians were the object of fierce Nazi persecution and lived under constant fear of being arrested by the Gestapo. If German troops

(CONTINUED ON PAGE 28)

Curtain Going Up!

—Danuta Michalowska, fellow actor

I got to know Karol much better during the occupation. Several of us young actors in the Theater Guild went to see Juliusz Osterwa, the fabulous actor, stage director, and ex-director of the Juliusz Slowacki Theater. All the guild members could not attend, because some were not in Kraków at the time. We decided to stage the play, *Ucieckla mi przepióreczka,* which everyone knew Zeromski had written especially for Osterwa, so he could play the famous role of Przelecki. So the members of our guild began to get to work on our version of this play. We had Juliusz Kydrynski, who was going to play the role of Przelecki; Karol Wojtyla, who would take the part of Smugon, and a few other actors. Kydrynski suggested that I take the role of Dorota, Smugon's wife. People in Kraków had heard about me because I won first prize in an oratorical competition when I was thirteen and I used to take part in Literary Evenings.

Staging this play turned out to be very difficult because there were a lot of parts to be played. We tried to get a larger group of actors together, but we failed. It wasn't easy to find actors during the occupation. Finally we decided to limit our production to the second act, which lasted an hour and a half but only called for three actors. Juliusz Kydrynski, Karol Wojtyla, and I were the ones who were interested in performing the roles. Karol also became the director; he was always the most enthusiastic person and would take on anything. We rehearsed every evening, since the men worked at the quarry and I was a typist at the "Spolem" Food Cooperative Association. At that time, nobody dared walk in the street without a work permit.

ARRIVAL OF KOTLARCZYK

Mieczyslaw Kotlarczyk arrived in Kraków in 1941 from Wadowice. He was a good friend of Karol's and was able to show us another method of acting. Kotlarczyk had a doctorate in philology from the Jagiellonian University and used to teach at the high school. Mieczyslaw had to leave Wadowice because the Nazis were looking for him. He crossed the border illegally. Once he managed to get to Kraków, he immediately sought out Karol because Kotlarczyk knew him very well. Everybody in Wadowice probably knows everybody else, since it is a small town.

The occupation forced theater director Mieczyslaw Kotlarczyk into a new role: ticket collector on the trolley cars in Kraków.

Our first meeting with Kotlarczyk took place in the home of Mrs. Debowska on Komorowskiego Street. She lived there with her daughters, Christine and Irene. Her husband, who was a high-ranking military officer, was killed by the Russians at Katyn. Their apartment was in a new modern building and had three rooms. Sometime after that, the Nazis evicted them.

In those days anything that had to do with the theater, above all the classic texts of Polish literature, impressed me. Kotlarczyk had a captivating personality and an exquisite speaking voice. He was a fanatic about the theater and saw the story of his life as if it were one big stage play. Everything he did, whether it was directing a play in Wadowice or living his everyday life, was all part of one big repertoire. Sometimes he played Wyspianski, other times Slowacki, and still others Mickiewicz. He was also interested in minor playwrights.

During the occupation he was unemployed and began to read all kinds of works, such as the lectures Mieckiewicz gave in Paris. Kotlarczyk discovered the idea for the Rhapsodic Theater in those Parisian lectures. The famous thesis Mickiewicz proposed in 1843 was the basic concept for his theater. Mickiewicz said that the Slavic theater is based, fundamentally and above all, on the spoken word. This affirmation of his own ideas kept Kotlarczyk's idea of theater alive, and in it he brought to life the great literary texts of the Polish culture.

Our first play was *Krol-Duch (King-Spirit)* by Slowacki. It was a poem, and it wasn't easy. Kotlarczyk was very intuitive in assigning parts. Krystyna Ostaszewska had a lovely deep voice, and she was almost always picked to play the most aggressive women's roles, while I got to play the lyrical ones because I was younger. Sometimes Halina Kwiatkowska—her name was Królikiewiczówna before she married Tadeusz Kwiatkowski after the war—took Krystyna's place.

INTERPRETING

Karol's acting in *King-Spirit* was very striking. His part included several monologues, but the main one was an excerpt from the fifth poem. It dealt with the story of the Polish king Boleslaw I the Brave and his conflict with Bishop Stanislaw. It was a very dramatic text, and Karol interpreted it with unusual intensity. Two weeks later, though, he totally changed his interpretation and spoke his part in a low, monotone voice. He had plenty of talent and could change his acting methods and modify his tone of voice whenever he needed to. In the play King Boleslaw, who kills the bishop, says, "I wasn't afraid the Lord would strike me down. I ran as a king would run to vanquish the bishop." That is the climactic moment of the play; the king says it in the dark of the night, cups overflowing with wine, as the embattled mob starts to go off and judge the bishop. And Karol unexpectedly toned down his acting and spoke in lifeless tones. This was Karol's last excerpt to recite, his final scene in the play, because *King-Spirit* ends with that poem about Boleslaw.

After the play we demanded an explanation from Karol as to why he made that change; the women especially wanted to know why. I don't know if Kotlarczyk said anything to Karol. At best, he might have known Karol was going to change his interpretation. The rest of us questioned Karol. "What have you done? How could you do that?" and I was the most assertive. He calmly listened to our accusations and then very calmly and clearly explained, "I thought about the story line. Boleslaw is making a confession." Slowacki, through the character of Boleslaw, was confessing all his sins, everything he did, all the evil he did.

Naturally, for us this wasn't a satisfactory explanation. Much later I arrived at the conclusion that Karol was right. As I reread the first octaves of *King-Spirit*, I noticed this text: "Woe to the one who, searching for vainglory and not revealing his soul, writes human books!"

That's what Slowacki was writing about his own works, a confession that applies to the king's confession as well, as it is repeated in different plays, time and again over the centuries. I preferred Karol's first interpretation at that time, the one we heard during rehearsals and in the premier performance. *King-Spirit* still had a few performances to go, and the Rhapsodic Theater always repeated that scene.

CHANGING THE WORLD

Sometime after the *King-Spirit* production, I lost contact with Wojtyla. After he was ordained a priest, he went abroad to study in Rome for a while. He visited some other countries and was sent to Niegowic as vicar when he returned. We met each other once again when he returned to Kraków and was assigned to St. Florian's parish.

We literally ran into each other on the staircase of the Polish philology building on Golebia Street. I was studying there and acting in the theater at the same time. I was going down the stairs, looking for the theology department. I knew there were some libraries and reading rooms on the third floor. All of a sudden I saw several priests on the stairs, and one of them was Karol. It was a shock to see him in a cassock. We hadn't seen each other for a long time. The world had changed, and classes had begun again after the liberation. I said hello to him, but we spoke only for a minute or two.

The theater that was on Warzawska Street where I worked was always full of people. Soviet artists, especially Sergiusz Obrazcov, helped us out. He put in a

Above: Actresses in the Rhapsodic Theater in 1942 included (from left) Halina Królikiewiczówna, Danuta Michalowska, and Krystyna Ostaszewska.

Left: Home of the Rhapsodic Theater was 2 Skarbowa Street in Kraków.

good word for us, and Wlodzimierz Sokorski, who was the minister of culture and very famous, said, "You find a place [for a theater], and I'll get the money for it." After a long search we found a building in Kraków and turned it into a theater. (Today it is the Kameralmy Theater.) The day we were finally ready, we put together a small informal ceremony to mark the opening of the theater. We held it on the revolving stage, where we had laid out old posters and documents from the Rhapsodic Theater.

Everybody came to the ceremony. Karol was dressed in his cassock, but nobody said anything. The workers seemed happy to see a quiet, meditative priest in our midst. They thought something was going to happen, but we were all just standing around. Hanging the commemorative plaque was an official event, but the priest's presence wasn't. Everybody was silent, thinking. Karol remained where he was, head bent and enfolded in his hands. He must have been praying. And that's all that happened.

found the Salesians teaching underground catechism classes to young people, for example, they would consider the crime worthy of arrest. The Salesians quite rightly worried that their parish would wind up without priests. On May 23, 1941, the Germans arrested all the Salesian priests and sent them to a concentration camp, where most of them died.

A TRUE SPIRITUAL LEADER

Jan Tyranowski was the out-standing lay catechist in the parish. He was certainly one of young Wojtyla's most influential spiritual guides. Even before they knew each other very well, the mystic tailor noticed how fervently the young man prayed.

In the autumn of 1942, Karol Wojtyla entered the under-ground seminary of the archdiocese of Kraków to begin theological studies.

Finally he decided to invite Wojtyla to become a mem-ber of the "Living Rosary" youth group.

One Saturday at a retreat conference, Tyranowski approached Wojtyla and asked to speak with him for a few minutes. After the conversation Wojtyla decided to join the Living Rosary (only later did he find out that it was an underground organization). Fifteen young men, who represented the Fifteen Mysteries of the Rosary, promised to live Jesus's commandment to love God and neighbor in all aspects of daily life. Given the political sit-uation, it was too risky for the members to meet as a large group, so Tyranowski met and conversed with each one individually.

A FATHER'S LEGACY

When Wojtyla was still a child and he and his father were living in Wadowice, the senior Wojtyla was the first

person to direct the boy's attention to the way the Holy Spirit acts. He listened while his son was praying to the Holy Spirit and noticed that his son was not addressing the Third Person of the Holy Trinity as his father thought he should. That's when the father taught his son a special prayer that emblazoned itself in the boy's heart, soul, and memory. Many years later Pope John Paul II included his father's ideas in his encyclical *Dominum et Vivificantem (On the Holy Spirit in the Life of the Church and the World)*.

For his part Tyranowski led the twenty-year-old Wojtyla into the depths of the spiritual life. He showed him a path of meditative prayer that leads directly to the experience of the presence of God, without and beyond resorting to thoughts, symbols, or words.

A TOUCH OF PASTORAL LIFE

After only a few meetings Tyranowski real-ized that his student needed pastoral experi-ence. Tyranowski asked Wojtyla to lead a new Living Rosary group. As his mystical teacher had done, Wojtyla confidently shouldered the responsibility of carefully guiding 15 young people in their spiritual life. This initial pastoral experience most likely influenced him in choosing the road to follow in his religious life.

RESTRICTIONS ON SEMINARIANS

In the autumn of 1939, the Nazis evicted the students from the seminary building on Podzameze Street. It became the offices of the SS (Nazi secret police) detachment in charge of protecting Hans Frank. No new seminarians were allowed to enter, and no theology or other university subjects were allowed. The only courses that could be taught to seminarians who were already there were purely spiritual and liturgical subjects. This lack of theological training kept the seminarians from being ordained.

Archbishop Sapieha ignored the restrictions for a while and gave orders to continue with the seminary edu-cation program, as usual. Classes were held in the arch-bishop's residence, and the seminarians lived incognito as parish clerks around Kraków.

When the Gestapo arrested some of these undercover seminarians, however, the bishop had to change his strategy. He decided that he would have to form an underground seminary. New seminarians wouldn't go into hiding. They would stay in their jobs and look and work just like everybody else in the city, but they would study secretly and take religious exams in the homes of individ-ual professors.

APPROACHING THE CARMELITES

When Wojtyla discovered his vocation to serve God, he first wanted to become a Carmelite. The Carmelite way of life was very near to his heart and akin to his natural disposition. On a few occasions he had crossed spiritual paths with Carmelite monks, first in Wadowice and later in Kraków. Jan Tyranowski further aroused Wojtyla's interest in the Carmelites with the writings of Saint John of the Cross, which Wojtyla tried to read in the original Spanish. He tackled the saint's lofty poetry enthusiastically but with great difficulty. The only dictionary he could find to help him learn Spanish—a new language for him—was a German-Spanish dictionary, and German was not one of his best foreign languages.

November 1942 was the 400th anniversary of the birth of Saint John of the Cross. Wojtyla took part in the commemoration observances at the Carmelite monastery in Kraków. He became friends with Father Józef Prus, the provincial, and told him he wanted to enter the monastery. But the Germans forbade any religious institution from accepting novices, because all Poles had to work. The monk advised him that if he really wanted to become a Carmelite, he should come back after the war.

A NEW UNDERGROUND SEMINARIAN

Wojtyla sought another way to follow his vocation. He went to speak with Father Jan Piworczyk, the father rector of the underground seminary organized by the archbishop, who agreed to accept him as a seminarian. Wojtyla had not formally met Archbishop Sapieha, but the archbishop must have known something about Wojtyla's wishes. Aspiring candidates to the priesthood had to be approved by the archbishop before the father rector could agree to accept them. Since in Wojtyla's case his acceptance was immediate, most likely the archbishop had been informed of the young man's petition and remembered the student from Wadowice who spoke fluent Latin.

The first face-to-face meeting between the archbishop and the new seminarian took place soon after Wojtyla arrived and became an acolyte, a beginning step to the priesthood.

In October two candidates for the priesthood took part in a weeklong retreat separately, because Nazi eyes were vigilant. They were supplied with books and other student materials. During his work shifts at the chemical plant,

Pope Pius XI

Achille Ratti was born on May 13, 1857, near Milan. After his ordination as a priest, he taught in a seminary in Padua for many years. In 1914 he became prefect at the Vatican Library. At the end of World War I, Pope Benedict XV sent him to Warsaw as apostolic visitor. A year later, in 1919, the pope appointed him apostolic delegate. He completed his assignment in Poland in 1921 and was named Cardinal Archbishop of Milan. Ratti was elected pope on February 2, 1922, and took the name Pius XI.

During his pontificate, reconciliation between the Holy See and the Italian government took place. In 1929 Pius XI signed the Lateran Accords with the Fascist government of Benito Mussolini, which recognized the Vatican as an independent state, but in 1931 he expressed strong disapproval of Fascist practices in a letter, *Non abbiamo bisogno.* He signed a concordat with the supposedly anti-Communist Hitler in 1933 to assure that the rights of the church would be respected, but Hitler disregarded this agreement. Pius XI condemned the Nazi government in Germany in 1937 in another encyclical, *Mit brennender Sorge.* The same year, he also condemned atheistic Communism.

Pius XI criticized laissez-faire capitalism and renewed a plea for social reform first put forth by Leo XIII 40 years before. In 1937 he established the Pontifical Academy of Science. In the Catholic Action program he called for greater lay participation in the religious life of the church. Pius XI died on February 14, 1939.

Pope Pius XII

Eugenio Pacelli was born on March 2, 1876, in Rome. After his ordination in 1899, he worked in the Vatican diplomatic offices. In 1917 Pope Benedict XV ordained him as bishop and appointed him apostolic delegate to Bavaria and then delegate to Berlin. Named a cardinal in 1929, a year later he became Vatican secretary of state. In that capacity he negotiated the ill-fated 1933 concordat with the Nazis. On March 12, 1939, on the eve of World War II, he was elected pope and took the name Pius XII.

With his diplomatic background, Pius XII believed that the church could best work for peace by keeping formal relationships with all the belligerents. He worked vigorously to help prisoners of war and displaced persons, but he was much criticized during the war and afterward for not speaking out against the Nazi persecution of the Jews.

After the war he opposed Communism and excommunicated Italian Catholics who joined the Communist Party. In the papal bull *Munificentissimus Deus,* issued in 1950, he defined the dogma of the Assumption of the Virgin Mary. In 1956 Pius XII reformed the Holy Week liturgy, relaxing the fasting rules and allowing evening Masses. He also encouraged the appointment of native hierarchies in overseas dioceses. Pius XII died on October 9, 1958.

coworkers became used to seeing the young seminarian read huge texts and write notes in the margins. (Fellow chemical workers in the plant in Borek Falecki even let him take reading breaks.) When Karol Wojtyla became one of the first 10 students in the underground seminary in Kraków, he told no one. This secret had to be strictly kept. Only Mieczyslaw Kotlarczyk was informed right away about Wojtyla's plans.

The tomb of the Wojtyla and Kaczorowski families in the Rakowiec cemetery in Kraków. Young Wojtyla visited his father's tomb nightly after work during World War II.

A NEW UNDERGROUND THEATER
In July 1941 Mieczyslaw Kotlarczyk and his wife moved to Kraków. They had to get out of Wadowice, which was part of the territory annexed to the German Reich. Hitler's reign of terror was bent on destroying all Polish intellectuals. To help him support his family, friends found a job for him in Kraków as a ticket collector on the streetcars. Wojtyla offered him lodging, since his apartment was vacant at that time. A month after his arrival in Kraków, on August 22, Kotlarczyk inaugurated the underground Rhapsodic Theater, linked it with the Cultural Union, and made Wojtyla the principal actor.

While Kotlarczyk was still living in Wadowice, he and Wojtyla had maintained contact through letters delivered by Halina Królikiewiczówna, who periodically visited her family in Wadowice. Wojtyla was writing dramas at the time, and he always asked Kotlarczyk for his opinion. He was also acting in underground plays directed by Tadeusz Kudlinski at the Kydrynskis. He and his friends, dressed

in black, used to recite their roles without costumes or scenery.

Juliusz Osterwa, who met Wojtyla through Kydrynski, joined them. He was a famous actor and theater director, who before the war had founded the Redoubt Theater for staging a repertory of the great Polish romantic playwrights. Although acting was Osterwa's profession, he collaborated with the group only until 1941. He left after producing *Uciekla mi przepióreczka (My Pen Got Away from Me)* by Stefan Zeromski.

A NEW APPROACH TO THEATER
Mieczyslaw Kotlarczyk, on the other hand, became wholeheartedly involved with the group at the Kydrynskis'. The Rhapsodic Theater became his personal project, a means of propagating his views of what theater should be. Juliusz Kydrynski left the group because of these ideas; his view of drama was completely different.

The Rhapsodic Theater presented its first play, *King-Spirit*, by Juliusz Slowacki, at the home of the Debowski family. Wojtyla played the part of Boleslaw the Brave, the Polish king who murdered Bishop Stanislaw, making him a martyr. He represented Boleslaw as being repentant after his foul deed. In February of the following year, the group presented another play *Beniowski*, also by Slowacki. After that, they staged a montage by Jan Kasprowicz *(Hymns)*, three dramas by Stanislaw Wyspialski, and *The Portrait of an Artist*, which was a montage of several poems by Cyprian Norwid, Wojtyla's favorite poet. They also performed *Pan Tadeusz (Professor Thaddeus)*.

One evening Karol Wojtyla, at that point a seminarian, was playing his part in that play—reciting the confession of Jacek Soplica. Suddenly everyone in the room could hear German loudspeakers blaring an announcement outside in the street. The orator did not stop speaking. His recitation of the playwright Mickiewicz's words drowned out the roar about the Nazi army's victories on the eastern front in North Africa. The audience was listening intently to both speakers. Osterwa, who was there at the time, criticized Wojtyla. He thought the actor should have stopped until everything was quiet again.

The last part Wojtyla played was the lead in *Samuel Zborowski* by Juliusz Slowacki in March 1943. This play was presented a total of six times, and at one of these underground performances, several members of the Polish government in exile in London were in the audience.

A THEATER LEGACY
Wojtyla never broke off his friendship with Kotlarczyk and his wife. He owed a great deal to Mieczyslaw Kotlarczyk, who honed Wojtyla's acting skills and taught him how to project his speech, deepening his sensitivity to the magic of poetic words. He also taught Wojtyla how to think about the Word in its spiritual and biblical sense. Through the power of the Word, Kotlarczyk suggested, anything can happen if it is spoken at the right moment

and with the right spirit. Nevertheless, once Wojtyla got closer to the core of spiritual living under the guidance of Jan Tyranowski, he arrived at the conclusion that "the priesthood of the Word," which he exercised by acting, wasn't the road in life he wanted to travel.

When Wojtyla realized what his true vocation was, he could no longer work at the chemical plant, study for the priesthood, and act in the Rhapsodic Theater all at the same time. On New Year's Day 1942 he told Kotlarczyk that he would no longer be accepting roles in his plays, because he was thinking about starting a religious life.

Though Kotlarczyk was a fervent Catholic, he didn't want to accept his friend's decision. He was sure that Wojtyla's future was linked to the theater. If Wojtyla had any vocation at all, it would be to proclaim the Word of God in religiously oriented mystery plays.

Kotlarczyk tried to get his promising actor-poet to change his mind and forget about the priesthood. He even urged Wojtyla's other close friends, such as Tadeusz Kudlinski, to try to dissuade him. However, nothing changed Wojtyla's decision. His mind was made up, and friends could not alter it.

Kotlarczyk finally gave in despite the fact that he had lost the best actor in his theater, and his personal artistic dreams were starting to fall apart. Wojtyla's oldest and closest friends consoled themselves with the thought that at least they had convinced him to become a priest rather than a monk.

THE SERIOUS SEMINARIAN

When the German occupation began, Wojtyla had taken an oath to become a member of the underground Unia organization. Before he entered the seminary, he wanted to take proper leave of this group. Stanislaw Bukowski freed him from his oath in the same congenial way he had accepted him into the group. Wojtyla also left Polish philology behind, since he was already secretly studying theology in the underground Jagiellonian University seminary.

Once he was admitted to the seminary, Wojtyla concentrated on his studies and on reading the Carmelite mystical writings that would deepen his spiritual life. The fervent devotion to Mary that had begun in his childhood came back to him in a deeper way. He was influenced by the writings of Saint Louis-Marie Grignon de Montfort, who was at that time being considered for sainthood by the church. Wojtyla's spiritual director at the seminary suggested he read de Montfort's treatise on *True Devotion to the Blessed Virgin*. Wojtyla studied the treatise over several months

and finally came to realize that "true devotion to the Mother of God stems from a profound understanding of the mystery of the Incarnation." Afterward, when he became Pope John Paul II, he borrowed the motto *Totus Tuus* (All Yours) from de Montfort's treatise on Mary.

A TERRIBLE HIT AND MISS

Very late one night in February 1944, Karol Wojtyla was returning home after working a double shift at the Borek Falecki plant. He was humming while he walked, glad he would be off from work the whole next day. He was thinking about how hungry he was when suddenly a truck flashed by, hit him from behind, and then sped away. Wojtyla was thrown to the ground unconscious. A woman, Józefa Florek, who was riding in a bus, spotted him at a distance and wondered if a huge package had fallen off the back of the truck. When she got off the bus to investigate, she saw that the object was a person. The accident victim was covered in blood, and she assumed he was dead. She was considering covering the body when a car stopped. A German officer got out and ordered the woman to get some water from a nearby stream to wash the man's face. Realizing that the wounded man was still alive, the officer stopped a passing delivery truck and ordered the driver to take the victim to the hospital.

The doctors diagnosed Wojtyla with a concussion and other head wounds, and they kept him in the hospital for two weeks. After a short convalescence with the Szkockis, Wojtyla went back to work, his studies, and his duties as an acolyte of the archbishop.

After the war in 1946, Wojtyla (center) and his fellow underground seminarians openly began fourth-year theology.

A list of students in the philosophy department of the Jagiellonian University before the Germans forced the university to close. The institution reopened in February 1946.

After the war Karol Wojtyla met with Józefa Florek and wrote her a formal letter thanking her for having saved his life. The German army official who had sent him to the hospital remains anonymous.

NO ONE IS SAFE

Two months after he left the hospital, Wojtyla had another reminder that life under the Nazis was perilous. Archbishop Sapieha had two acolytes who served him at morning Mass in his private chapel. One of them was Wojtyla; the other was Szczesny Zachuta, whom Wojtyla had known in the Living Rosary group. On April 30 Zachuta didn't show up at the archbishop's residence. They found out later that the Gestapo had picked him up during a raid because they had found his theology books and notes. He was executed one month later. After the war a parish priest learned that Zachuta was not only a student in the seminary; he also belonged to an underground organization that helped save Jews by preparing them for baptism. He was the only seminarian in Kraków to lose his life during the war.

PALATIAL INCARCERATION

In August 1944 the Red Army started moving toward Warsaw. It was headed for Berlin but this time not to help the German army. The former Allies, who had divided Poland between them such a short while before, were now mortal enemies. The Red Army tried courting the Poles in order to get them to join up, but only a small number responded. (The Polish people who went on the offensive against the Germans on August 1 in the Warsaw Uprising were not Communist partisans. The decision to start the uprising was made by the exiled Polish government, not from any alliance with the Bolsheviks.)

The German forces in Kraków, fearing a repeat of the Warsaw events, did a massive sweep of the city on August 6 to find and detain young Poles. Archbishop Sapieha, realizing what was going on, brought his seminarians to live in his official residence. He figured that the war in Poland would not last much longer and that they could be

These documents, including a class schedule from the Mutual Aid Society, relate to Karol Wojtyla's Jagiellonian University activities.

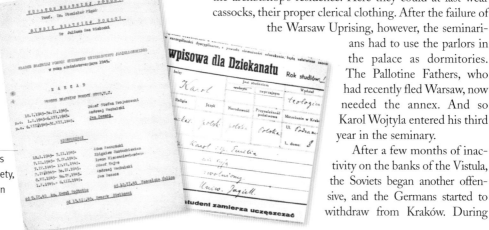

A Historical Note

In January 1941, at the request of the bishop of Leira-Fatima in Portugal, Sister Lucia, who had been living in a Carmelite convent for 25 years, wrote out the details of her last vision—the so-called third mystery of Fatima. The Mother of God had revealed the mystery's contents when she appeared to the children in 1917. Now, for the first time, Sister Lucia put in writing what she had long ago told a Dominican bishop: She was walking through a half-destroyed city, tormented by pain and suffering, while she prayed for the souls of the dead, whose bodies she passed on her way to the top of a mountain. A cross stood on the mountaintop.

Lucia had written down the first two mysteries in August 1941; they showed a vision of hell, revealed prophesies about the two world wars and Russia, and directed the church to establish a devotion to the Immaculate Heart of Mary.

safely hidden until the Germans finally left Kraków. The seminarians' "palatial incarceration" lasted almost six months.

THE MISSING CHEMICAL WORKER

Permanent residence in the archbishop's palace meant that Karol Wojtyla had to stop working at the Solvay chemical plant. When he didn't show up at Borek Falecki after a few days, the Work Office sent notices to his apartment on Tyniecka Street. When they weren't answered, the Germans started to investigate. Realizing the danger, Archbishop Sapieha asked Father Figlewicz to use his contacts to take care of the problem.

Father Figlewicz went to see the ex-director of Solvay, Henryk Kulakowski, whom the Germans had kept on to direct the factory operations, and asked if it were possible for Karol Wojtyla's name to be dropped from the list of missing employees that was sent to the German Work Office. "I'd throw myself into the fire for the archbishop," Kulakowski answered, "but this won't be easy." The problem was that the Germans at the Work Office suspected that Wojtyla had joined the Resistance. A short time later, however, the threatening notices stopped.

IMPROVISING LIVING QUARTERS

The seminarians started out living together in an annex of the archbishop's residence. Here they could at last wear cassocks, their proper clerical clothing. After the failure of the Warsaw Uprising, however, the seminarians had to use the parlors in the palace as dormitories. The Pallotine Fathers, who had recently fled Warsaw, now needed the annex. And so Karol Wojtyla entered his third year in the seminary.

After a few months of inactivity on the banks of the Vistula, the Soviets began another offensive, and the Germans started to withdraw from Kraków. During the night of January 17, 1945, the Germans blew up the Debnicki Bridge on their way out. The explosions smashed all the windows in the area, including those in the archbishop's residence, and the Red Army entered the city.

The seminarians kept on living in the archbishop's palace on Franciszkalska Street for a while. When they finally got their seminary on Podzameze Street back, it was a wreck. Only after they repaired the roof, installed new windows, and got rid of all traces of the SS who had been occupying the building could they move back into their rightful home.

TOUCHING THE SOUL OF A SOVIET SOLDIER

The frontal attack passed over Kraków, and the Red Army turned west and south. In May a Soviet soldier rang the seminary doorbell. He was curious about something and asked if he could please come in. Wojtyla, who spoke a little Russian, had a long conversation with him. The soldier wanted to find out about God. He said that schoolteachers had always told him God didn't exist, but he was certain that God did exist. When speaking at retreats in Rome many years later, Cardinal Wojtyla talked about this experience. He told how he had "learned a lot about how God enters into human thoughts and intelligence even in circumstances of complete, systematic negation."

Eventually Kraków started to get back to normal. Classes in the theology department of the Jagiellonian University started once again. When April came around, seminarian Wojtyla taught theology at the university as an adjunct professor. In the same month he was elected president of the students' Mutual Aid Society.

SECOND THOUGHTS ABOUT MONASTIC LIFE

Wojtyla, however, never stopped thinking about Mount Carmel and the Carmelites. The war was over, and since he had spoken with the provincial, he could now ask to be admitted into the Carmelite novitiate. After all, Father Leonard Kowalówka, Novice Master of the Carmelites in Czerna, was his friend. To change paths and become a Carmelite, Wojtyla would have to get the permission of his titular bishop, Archbishop Sapieha. The archbishop of Kraków put off the application of the seminarian, saying, "Let him finish what he started." Not for a moment would he deprive the diocesan clergy or the Catholics of the diocese of such a talented priest. Day by day, it seemed more and more likely that Wojtyla would fill an important role in the future of the church. The archbishop's reply settled the dilemma forever.

RECOGNIZING THE CARDINAL

The Kraków archbishop was a man of strong convictions that got him into trouble at times. That's why he was denied the title of cardinal for an extended period. He certainly merited being made a cardinal, based both on the

Wojtyla considered entering this Carmelite monastery at Czerna. He was attracted by the idea of a contemplative life.

tradition of elevating archbishops and on his own merits. But soon after Poland gained independence in 1918, when the apostolic delegate, Achille Ratti, asked to attend a meeting of the Conference of Polish Bishops, Sapieha refused him, saying the Polish bishops wanted to meet in private.

Ratti was elected Pope Pius XI soon after and clearly never forgot this incident. When new cardinals were nominated, Sapieha's name was never among them. But Pope Pius XII did justice for the "unshakable Prince," as Karol Wojtyla called him. On February 18, 1946, Pius XII made Sapieha a cardinal. In March the new cardinal returned to Kraków. Just as years earlier the inhabitants of Warsaw carried Józef Pilsudski's carriage on their shoulders, this time the people of Kraków picked up Sapieha's car and carried him to St. Mary's Church.

Karol Wojtyla must have recognized that life takes strange turns. He organized a celebration in honor of Sapieha's elevation to cardinal and welcomed him with a long speech on behalf of the students. Here was the same student who had welcomed Sapieha to the Wadowice high school. This time the cardinal didn't have to wonder if it would be a good idea to have the speaker become a priest.

Karol Wojtyla was an outstanding priest: He wrote poems and plays, he climbed mountains, he studied philosophy, he directed an amateur theater group, he prayed as he rowed a boat on Lake Mazuria. . .and he immersed himself in the mystery of salvation.

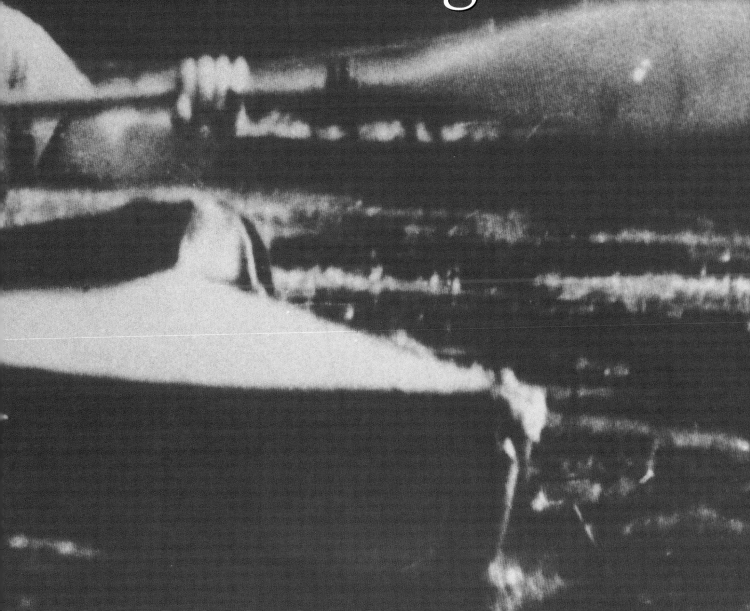

Chapter 3

The Almighty Has Done Great Things in Me

In October 1946 Karol Wojtyla took the first of several quick steps to the priesthood. On the twelfth he submitted a formal application for ordination as a subdeacon, the lowest order of the Latin clergy, and the next day Cardinal Stefan Adam Sapieha, the archbishop of Kraków and Wojtyla's mentor, performed the required service in his private chapel. A week later the archbishop granted Wojtyla's request for ordination as a deacon. Next Wojtyla spent a week in a private retreat under the archbishop's personal direction. On November 1, 1946, All Saints' Day, Sapieha consecrated the seminarian as a priest.

A MOVING CEREMONY

Again Wojtyla went to the archbishop's private chapel. He knelt down before Sapieha with a lit candle in his hand. Then he prostrated himself on the floor, putting his body in the form of a cross, and listened to the words of the sacrament pronounced over him: "Be perfect in faith and what you do, be steadfast in your love of God and of all others."

As the congregation recited the Litany of the Saints, the young man knelt again and the archbishop placed his hands on Wojtyla's head to invoke the power of the Holy Spirit. He then anointed his hands with holy oils while those in attendance sang *Veni Creator* ("Come, Holy Spirit"). After he gave Wojtyla the chalice and the other holy vessels needed to celebrate Mass, Wojtyla received Holy Communion. Once again the archbishop placed his hands on the other's head, saying, "Receive the Holy Spirit. Whose sins you shall forgive, they will be forgiven." The newly ordained priest swore an oath of obedience to the bishop and his successors, and then he and Sapieha exchanged the Kiss of Peace.

FIRST CELEBRATIONS OF MASS

Three days later Father Wojtyla celebrated his first Mass and attended a small reception given for him afterward. Guests were handed little commemorative cards upon which he had written *Fecit mihi magna....*" (The Almighty has done great things in me), the opening words of the Virgin Mary's prayer, the *Magnificat* (My Soul Magnifies the Lord).

On November 10 Wojtyla celebrated Mass in his hometown church in Wadowice. Since he could not attend the anniversary of the founding of the Rhapsodic Theater, he wrote the following letter of apology to Mieczyslaw Kotlarczyk.

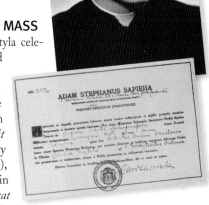

Perhaps it's God's will that prevented me from being with you at your joyous celebration. I think I have come to understand His will for us. As an actor, you have to live your life with an interior inspiration. As a priest, I have to draw upon that same type of interior motive as I live my life. I realize that interior inspiration, not outward appearances, is the strongest energizing force for the priest.

THE ARCHBISHOP'S PLANS

Under normal circumstances Wojtyla would have remained in the seminary until Palm Sunday 1947 and been consecrated with the other seminarians in their last year of study. But the archbishop—he was made a cardinal on February 18, 1946—had other plans for his brightest student. He wanted him to go to Rome and attend the Angelicum, the Pontifical University of Saint Thomas, where classes began in November.

Two weeks after his ordination Wojtyla and Father Stanislaw Starowieyski left for Rome via Paris, arriving in the Holy City toward the end of November. They were to stay at the Belgian College rather than the Polish College because the Poles attended the more liberal, Jesuit-run Gregorianum, or Gregorian University, and Sapieha wanted his protégés to study at the more conservative and traditional Dominican school.

At first they could not get into the Belgian residence, so they stayed with the Pallotine Fathers. Luckily, however, the Polish primate, Cardinal August Hlond, happened to be in Rome for an audience with Pope Pius XII, and he arranged for the two young priests to move into the Belgian College just before Christmas.

Left: Intense preparations for the ordination of Karol Józef Wojtyla took place in 1946. He was ordained subdeacon on October 13 and deacon one week later. Archbishop Sapieha ordained him a priest on November 1.

Below: The record of his ordination.

A BROADER EDUCATION

Cardinal Sapieha's reasons for choice of schools and residences were twofold: In the Belgian College the two priests would learn Italian and French and meet and build relationships with clergy from other countries. The Angelicum would provide a solid academic base for Father Wojtyla's natural inclination toward theological speculation. Its curriculum focused on the theology and philosophy of Saint Thomas Aquinas and that of other great Catholic mystics.

The Belgian College was located near the university. A 100-year-old building with three floors, it was surrounded by a garden, and at the time, more than 20 people lived there. For all its charm, living conditions were primitive: no showers, no heat in the cold winters, and no air-conditioning in the hot Roman summers. The rooms were tiny.

At Saint Leonard's crypt in Wawel Cathedral, Father Wojtyla celebrated his first Mass among the tombs of the ancient kings of Poland.

Padre Pío: First Beatified, Then Proclaimed a Saint

FRANCESCO FORGIONE, an Italian Capuchin Friar, was the first ordained priest in the history of the church to bear the stigmata. (Saint Francis of Assisi, who also bore the stigmata, was an ordained deacon.) Forgione was born in 1887 and entered the Capuchin order at age fifteen, taking his final vows as a priest in 1910. Five years later he felt the pain of Christ's wounds on the cross for the first time, and on September 20, 1918, blood flowed from them and would continue to do so until he died in 1968, a man with a global reputation for miraculous good works and a long history of suffering.

He was stricken with diseases doctors could not diagnose or explain. His body temperature rose at times to 108 degrees Fahrenheit (42 degrees Celsius) and perhaps even higher—when doctors took his temperature, the glass thermometer actually broke. Blood seeped from his hands. His chest bled. He had wounds on his feet that never healed, yet never became infected. The blood flowed most strongly from Friday evening to Sunday morning. He ate once a day—and very little—and he never slept much.

Examples of his clairvoyance abound. He once asked someone to fetch his handkerchief, and when the man returned, Padre Pío told him, "Now go back to my room and put back what you stuffed in your purse." On another occasion, during Mass, Pío told a man to visit his family before he died—in eight days' time. The man did, and he died on the eighth day. Pío could also read other people's minds. He would often tell his penitents that they had forgotten the circumstances around the sins they had confessed, or he would ask them why they had forgotten to confess certain sins.

Most dramatic, perhaps, he is said to have predicted Wojtyla's election as pope and his attempted assassination. The two met when the young priest was a theology student in Rome and had traveled to San Giovanni Rotondo, where Pío had his church and his hospital. Wojtyla attended Mass and went to confession, where Padre Pío told him he would be pope, adding, "I see blood during your pontificate."

Padre Pío also had a global reputation as a miraculous healer of the sick. In 1962 Bishop Wojtyla wrote and asked him to pray for Dr. Wanda Poltawaka, a mother of four children who suffered from cancer. A short time later he wrote the padre to say that the woman had made a miraculous recovery, one clearly beyond the bounds of medicine.

When Padre Pío was buried in 1968, some 300,000 people came to the funeral, and today his church and hospital receive close to 7 million visitors a year. Four years after Pío died, Cardinal Wojtyla, as Metropolitan archbishop of Kraków, signed a petition in the name of the Polish episcopate to beatify Padre Pío. The beatification process began in 1983, and as Pope John Paul II, Wojtyla pushed very hard to speed up the process. One day he told those in charge of the proceedings, "Hurry up. I want to canonize this saint."

On December 18, 1997, with the pope present, the decree on heroic virtue was promulgated. And at a solemn Mass in St. Peter's Square on May 2, 1999, the pope beatified Padre Pío. On June 16, 2002, he was canonized as a saint.

For the American students these less-than-perfect accommodations seemed more like jail cells than student dormitory rooms. But Father Wojtyla, who was used to extreme hardship, didn't mind them at all. On the contrary, he seemed very happy. He enjoyed the friendly atmosphere. He practiced his French with two Belgian priests and his English with the Americans. He played volleyball on the patio. Roaming the streets and byways of Rome, he discovered new places, taking in all the local color, "always enriching my mind," as he wrote back to friends in Kraków.

PADRE PÍO KNEELS TO KAROL WOJTYLA

A few days after Easter 1947, Fathers Karol Wojtyla and Stanislaw Starowieyski drove to San Giovanni Rotondo, the town where the Capuchin Franciscan Friar, Padre (Father) Pío, lived and worked. He was marked with the Stigmata of Christ (as was Saint Francis of Assisi). The people in Padre Pío's parish adored him, but the hierarchy of the church treated him with reserve. The two Polish priests visited the House of Relief of Suffering, the hospital

Padre Pío had built with donations, and the Church of Mary, Mother of the Loving God. Here in this church, Father Wojtyla waited in a long line to go to confession with Padre Pío, who spent many hours every day in the confessional.

For Wojtyla it would prove a terrifying experience (even though the Vatican has never taken an official position on what happened and the pope has never confirmed it). After hearing the young priest's confession, Padre Pío stepped out of the confessional, knelt down at his feet, and told him that he would one day become pope. He also predicted the attempted assassination and Wojtyla's survival.

Forty years later, in May 1987, six years after the attempt on his life and 19 years after Padre Pío's death, Karol Wojtyla went back to San Giovanni Rotondo, this time as Pope John Paul II.

TRAVELS THROUGH EUROPE

While studying at the Angelicum in 1947 Father Wojtyla traveled extensively through Italy, France, and the Low

Countries, mostly with Father Starowieyski and sometimes with other priests from the Belgian College. They went to Assisi, Siena, and other major Italian attractions, even visiting Monte Cassino and Subiaco, the monasteries Saint Benedict founded in the fifth century. Built in a huge cave inside a rocky slope, Subiaco was the site where, according to legend, Saint Benedict started the first monastery of the Benedictine Order. Starowieyski heard his friend murmur, "I must live my life to please God and praise him at all times."

In February they went to Marseille to begin a European trip Cardinal Sapieha had financed. There they met members of the "Mission de France," a worker-priest movement founded after the war to combat the de-Christianization of the working class. Wojtyla, who had done manual labor in the Solvay plant during the Nazi occupation of Poland, found their ideas attractive, especially those expounded by one of the founders, Father Loew, a Protestant convert who had entered the Dominican Order. Priests ministering to workers, Loew held, had to speak their language and understand where they were coming from.

They again made contact with the working-class ministry in Paris, where they arrived after a short trip to Lourdes. Father Michonneau, who ran a parish along the banks of the Seine, had written a book, *Paroisse communauté missionaire (The Parish, a Missionary Community)*, about the parish as an evangelizing community.

Belgium and Holland were the next stops on their tour. Wojtyla spent several weeks in the Belgian coal-mining region of Charleroi because many emigrant Poles worked there, and he had a chance to talk and minister to them. The experience was instructive and influential. Years later Michonneau's and Loew's ideas, as well as his own experience staying with Polish miners, would show up in the pope's writings about working with believers and non-believers alike, and about social welfare for labor.

A DIFFERENT POINT OF VIEW
When Wojtyla returned to the Angelicum, he found a new spiritual director, Father Reginald Garrigou-Lagrange, a Dominican theologian out of sympathy with the worker-priest movement. He had even written an article condemning their approach to Thomistic philosophy, which the worker priests dismissed as "theological imperialism." Nor did the Dominican priest share their open attitude toward other Christian denominations.

Wojtyla must have faced a dilemma when he returned to the university: On the one hand, he admired "the priests who forcibly confronted movements that were out to de-Christianize society, working amid the people as worker-priests," while on the other, he felt profound respect and admiration for his teacher's wisdom. Garrigou-Lagrange knew mystical theology in depth, and his personality was close to Wojtyla's own spiritual bent.

THE DOCTORAL DISSERTATION
The future pope wrote his doctoral dissertation on *Issues of Faith According to Saint John of the Cross*, with Garrigou-Lagrange as his mentor. The two did not always agree. Wojtyla's thought was shaped by what he had learned in Kraków from Jan Tyranowski, the accountant and tailor who had been his spiritual adviser and had introduced him to Saint John and Carmelite mysticism, which, in turn, had triggered his interest in the relationship between faith and reason. His mentor in Rome, however, thought the Spanish Carmelite too speculative—and too far from the strict canons of Thomistic philosophy.

Right: Father Wojtyla's diploma in theology, from the Pontifical University in Rome.

Below: Father Wojtyla with fellow priests on the terrace of the Marian Fathers' residence in Rome.

Wojtyla had discussed the writings of Saint John of the Cross in the first theological essay he wrote after the war. He focused on the idea of faith as the bridge linking the soul with God, which was central to Saint John's thinking. He was criticized at the time for failing to substantiate his basic hypothesis. At the Angelicum he would tackle the subject again, this time after exposure to the college's teaching.

The Dominican College in Rome was founded in the middle of the nineteenth century as a center of neo-Thomist thought—a modern reinterpretation of Saint Thomas Aquinas's medieval teaching. Man, Aquinas held, could find the truth about God through reason alone, provided he adhered to a rigid, logical progression. His argument followed the one laid out by Aristotle: Human reason is a path to understanding God, the Creator was "an object of factual knowledge," and man is "the subject who possesses this knowledge." Knowledge about God can be acquired "from outside the person" in the same way that objective scientific knowledge is obtained. However, Saint Thomas posits one caveat—divine revelation, mysteries the human mind cannot fathom, is the most important source of our knowledge about God, and faith is necessary to acquire it.

MENTOR VERSUS STUDENT

On this point the great Christian mystics, including Saint John of the Cross, differed with Saint Thomas. They wrote that only an act of faith is needed to achieve the union of the human soul with God the Creator. And it was here that Wojtyla and Garrigou-Lagrange did not agree. While both were interested in Spanish mysticism, the mentor felt that the great Carmelite had strayed too far from the teachings of strict Thomism, that his approach was too much conjecture. Wojtyla held that the mystical path to knowledge was more important than the rational one.

Located on a mountain slope, the Pontifical University of Saint Thomas (also known as the Angelicum) hasn't changed much since Karol Wojtyla studied there. Mediterranean plants adorn the courtyard, and the cloister provides a shaded area for walking.

His dissertation, written in Latin, makes no mention of the central Thomistic concept of the "divine object"—an absence his mentor criticized. Instead, Wojtyla argued that reason was not enough to achieve a true knowledge of God, because it does not give individuals the full experience of a personal God. Man's intellect can understand that God exists, but faith and a mystical experience are required for a *real encounter* with God.

AN UNPRINTED THESIS

Despite their differences, Garrigou-Lagrange gave his student high marks—17 out of a possible 20 points—and Wojtyla's oral defense of his thesis was widely applauded. Still, he returned to Poland without his degree. The Angelicum's regulations required publication before awarding the title, and the young priest lacked the funds to do so.

He was back in Kraków in mid-June 1948 and spent some time at his old apartment on Tyniecka Street, seeing old friends while he waited for the next job the archbishop would give him. In mid-July he was assigned to a small, out-of-the way rural parish in Niegowic, a village between Kraków and Tarnow, where he would arrive on July 28.

THE RURAL PASTOR

The "doctor in theology without a formal degree" packed his few personal belongings and some books into an old suitcase, went to the railroad station, and boarded a train to the country, specifically to the town of Gdow, the rail station closest to his new parish. He would have to walk the rest of the way. Luckily, he met a farmer who gave him a ride in his horse-drawn cart. The farmer was clearly surprised that the archbishop would send such a shabbily dressed priest to become assistant pastor. The farmer dropped Wojtyla off at a crossroad in Maszowic, giving him directions for a shortcut to Niegowic through ripening wheat fields. After saying good-bye, the young priest walked on alone, like a pilgrim, toward the church steeple he could see in the distance.

When he arrived at the border of the Assumption of the Blessed Virgin Mary parish church, Wojtyla knelt down in silence and kissed the ground. He had read about the gesture in the works of a nineteenth-century French priest, Father John Vianney, the Curé of Ars in France, during a visit to that town the year before. Vianney had gained a nationwide reputation in France as a confessor. He spent hours in the confessional ministering to thousands who came from across the country to see him, just as Padre Pio had done in Italy. Vianney became a role model for the future pope, and his kissing of the earth in each country he visited became a signature for Pope John Paul II's papacy.

Niegowic seemed to be the end of the earth. Karol's friends in Kraków thought the archbishop had sent him there as punishment, but it was anything but that. Father

Kazimierz Buzala had a reputation for training promising young priests, many of whom had gone on to become famous.

MAKING A FULL SCHEDULE

Wojtyla spent about eight months in Niegowic—time enough to unwind from the arduous course of study in Rome and to learn the ins and outs of becoming a good parish priest. He began his new mission with great enthusiasm. He taught religion together with the other young vicar, Father Kazimierz Ciuba. He started a Living Rosary group, and he organized an amateur theater in the

Father Wojtyla poses with his class of boys that will receive their first Holy Communion at the church in Niegowic.

Catholic House, where he staged a play called *Gose Oczekiwany* by Zofia Kossak-Szezucka. Wojtyla played a beggar whose opponents did not believe in Jesus Christ.

He quickly established close ties to his parishioners who often came to seek his advice and were regularly surprised by his insight and vision. Thus, when they asked him for ideas on an appropriate present for Father Buzala's twenty-fifth anniversary as a priest, he suggested raising funds for a new brick church rather than a new cassock or stole. The old church dated back to the eighteenth century but, like all houses in the village, was built of wood. The parishioners were poor and feared that so ambitious a project was beyond their means. But the new vicar so inspired them that they raised the money for a new church and moved the old one to another village.

Niegowic: First Assignment for the Young Priest

Father Karol Wojtyla began his first pastoral assignment in the parish of Niegowic, 25 kilometers south of Kraków. In July 1948 he boarded a train in Kraków and finished his trip in a farmer's wagon. Dropped off in the nearby town of Marszowice, Wojtyla continued his journey on foot, walking across the fields toward the church of the Assumption of the Mother of God.

Later, after Wojtyla became pope, he described this experience in his book *Gift and Mystery:* "I went through the wheat fields. Some were already cut; others were waiting to be harvested. I remember that when I crossed the boundary line of the Niegowic parish, I knelt down and kissed the ground." A bronze plaque commemorates the event he would repeat so often as pope.

The young priest assumed all the traditional duties of his office. "I taught religion classes in five primary schools in villages that were part of the Niegowic parish. I got around in a farmer's wagon or a buggy, and I remember how friendly the teachers and the parishioners were."

Some of his parishioners are still alive and well remember when the Holy Father, then a young priest, taught them religion or prepared them for their First Holy Communion; he loved working with young people and spent a great deal of time with them. He organized them for religious activities and even for theater productions.

He was very fond of children, very patient when they played tricks in class. Rather than shout at them, he would walk over to the windows and begin to pray.

People still remember him as a priest who was extremely sensitive to their poor living conditions and to their needs. Later, their village would become world famous because it was the place where Father Wojtyla began his priestly ministration. And for many of them, this is far more than ancient history. They remember, as an integral part of their lives, that this future pope had baptized their children or married them.

BACK TO SCHOOL

While taking care of his parish work, Father Wojtyla tried to enroll as a doctoral candidate in the faculty of theology at the Jagiellonian University. He planned to submit the same thesis he had written at the Angelicum because Kraków did not demand that candidates publish their dissertation. However, he lacked a key requirement—a teaching certificate, the equivalent of a master's degree, something he had not completed before going to Rome.

Undeterred, he took the necessary exam for the license and passed it with flying colors. His master's thesis, *The Concept of How the Soul Is United with God According to Saint John of the Cross,* was accepted, again with high

Winning the Hearts of the People

—Stanislaw Wyporek, a young parishioner

I was twelve years old when Father Karol Wojtyla arrived in Niegowic. He used to go to the university during the week and come back on weekends. My mother was a seamstress, my sister was in secondary school, and I had two younger brothers. We lived on a small farm that we couldn't work, because we didn't have any farm machinery. Before I entered the military, I was secretary of the Catholic Youth Organization, which was reactivated after the war. It was a very powerful organization, with several hundred young men from neighboring villages as members.

Around Niegowic, all the houses were run-down, poor, and dirty. There were no roads. We didn't have any radios, and there was no electricity. Karol Wojtyla was here as vicar for less than a year. Right from the start, he established contact with young people in the Catholic Organization and began an amateur theater, quickly making friends with everyone.

From his first days here, he won the hearts of the people. Everyone noticed that there was something special about him, something that other priests didn't seem to have. He had a manner that made us think he was "one of us." To put it simply, he was a very good priest.

His arrival coincided with the beginning of government persecution of Catholics. We had to get permission for everything we wanted to do. The Office of Security began to make a lot of trouble for us. Karol Wojtyla formed the Caritas (Love of God) group anyway, which organized plays, among other activities. This allowed us to hold benefit events.

The police kept their distance from Karol Wojtyla. They did not want to have to deal with him, because they knew he was so much smarter than they were. But they did try to get information about him from us—what he did, with whom, what he was saying, what he was thinking. They told us we shouldn't let ourselves be influenced by the clergy. But they had their ways of getting information and knew just about everything. Somebody always told them about what was happening and what we were doing.

There were underground anti-Communist groups in the area called "bands," and the Office of Security thought we were potential collaborators with the underground. They used to beat us up. One day they drove me to the municipal office in Niegowic and gave me a beating because I wouldn't confess that I collaborated with the bands. I didn't belong to any organization, not even the Home Army, because I was still too young. (The Home Army—the underground resistance to German occupation—was outlawed by the Communists, and many of its members were deported.)

The police accused me of carrying cards from the director of the school in Niepolomice with votes for underground trials that passed sentences on them and of being a member of the Home Army, but I insisted I was not and that I did not know what was in those letters. When I wouldn't sign the confession, they beat me up again and threw me into a dark closet under the staircase. I spent the whole night there.

They came to get me the next morning and beat me again, but I still didn't sign a confession. They handed me another confession form to sign. I read it, filled in all the blank white spaces so they could not add anything to it later, and signed it. To get back home, I had to walk 15 kilometers from Bochnia, and I was hungry, filthy, and hurting all over from the beatings.

When I arrived home, my father smacked me because I had stayed out all night. That's when I began to cry and couldn't stop. I didn't know what else to do, so I went to look for Father Wojtyla, and he comforted me. He said, "Don't cry. You'll see. The time will come when they'll end up destroying themselves."

After that, a person tried to convince me to collaborate with the security police and promised to get me a better job if I did. Wojtyla advised me, "Don't accept that offer. Tell them you wouldn't be any good at informing on people."

Karol Wojtyla didn't have any enemies in Niegowic. He always shook hands with every one of us, always had a few nice words to say, and everybody received his blessing. He was different from the priests before the war. He wanted to bring a new spirit to the church. He was a man who was always thinking about the church and wanted other people to do the same.

Father Wojtyla was poor and lived humbly. One day I went to ask him if he could help a mother with a new baby whose house had burned down. She was using a leather jacket for a pillow. One of the women had made an embroidered cushion for the priest, and he gave it to the woman. He always gave away whatever he had. When he was consecrated as bishop, his friends had to take up a collection for him because he owned practically nothing. People in the parish noticed that he had nothing when he came and nothing when he left.

Karol Wojtyla's experience in Niegowic shouldn't be considered insignificant. On the contrary, it was very important because that's where he had his first pastoral experiences. He came to know the poverty of the countryside in the postwar era of totalitarian Communism.

I knew a lot of priests, but he stood out from the rest. And I think that's why he ended up in Rome. Always into books, always busy. When he wasn't working, he was reading. Sometimes, when he wanted to be alone, he would walk along the little alleyways around the church or in the garden, reading from his breviary.

I was jealous of his intellectual ability and his philosophical knowledge. He was jealous of my ability to do manual work. Electricity frightened him, and he didn't know how to make a door key. He lost his key once, and I made him another one. "I don't know how to do that. I am not gifted that way," he told me. "I wouldn't even know how to begin."

honors. He then expanded and submitted the dissertation he had written for the Angelicum: *Issues of Faith According to Saint John of the Cross*. Before the end of 1949, he was awarded a doctorate in sacred theology, with high honors.

THE LIVING ROSARY ONCE AGAIN

Father Wojtyla remained in Niegowic until the spring when, on March 17, 1949, Archbishop Sapieha transferred him back to Kraków. He was to be one of three vicars assigned to St. Florian, a church affiliated with the university parish of St. Catherine and a favorite meeting place for young Catholics. Father Tadeusz Kurowski had been its pastor since 1945 and had proved to be very popular with his Catholic students.

Wojtyla moved into a two-room apartment in the rectory—luxurious compared to his accommodations in Rome and Niegowic. But he soon acquired a roommate, an exiled priest from Lvov in the Ukraine who did not want to return home and didn't have enough money to pay for lodgings in Kraków.

The new environment posed a much greater challenge for Father Wojtyla, as he would later admit, than the "simple but beautiful" rural parish community in Niegowic. But it was a challenge he met quickly. Parishioners, students, and university professors were attracted to his straightforward style, his willingness to engage in discussion, and his sensibilities.

He was active across the spectrum of parish activities, organizing a Living Rosary, then a Gregorian Choir and a study group that tackled the *Summa Theologiae* of Saint Thomas, which the group read in Latin. He also prepared religious education classes and established a pastoral outreach program for the sick.

A NEW WAY TO SERVE THE SICK

Back in Niegowic, Wojtyla had visited sick parishioners in their own homes. Now, in Kraków, he reversed his approach and brought the old and the sick to church, smiling and blessing the invalids as he walked among them, something no one had ever done before and which made parishioners very happy. No matter how busy he was, Father Wojtyla always had time to minister to the needy.

During this time he also paid close attention to the theater and his writing, working with his old colleague in drama, Mieczyslaw Kotlarczyk, and publishing in the opposition Catholic weekly *Tygodnik Powszechny*, which Archbishop Sapieha had launched after the war in 1945. In 1949, while still in Niegowic, he had submitted an

Below: The brick church in Niegowic was built under the direction of Father Wojtyla.

article about the *Mission de France*, the worker-priest movement in France. Jerzy Turowicz, the editor, had liked it so much that he put it on page one. In May 1950 Wojtyla published a second essay in the periodical, but this time he used the pseudonym Andrej Jawien. Thus began a very close relationship between Wojtyla and the whole circle involved with *Tygodnik Powszechny*, the center of Catholic intellectual life in Kraków at the time.

Above: Father Wojtyla (circled) seated in the first row among his parishioners in Niegowic.

THE DEATH OF CARDINAL SAPIEHA

Cardinal Adam Sapieha died in Kraków on July 23, 1951, at the age of ninety-three. The cardinal's body lay ad state at the foot of the tomb of Saint Stanislaw in Wawel Cathedral. Four days later Father Karol Wojtyla was among the priests assisting at his patron's funeral services at which Archbishop Stefan Wyszynski, the primate of Poland, officiated.

Pope Pius XII chose Eugeniusz Baziak, archbishop of Lvov, as the new archbishop of Kraków. Unable to exercise his duties in Lvov because of Communist pressure in the Ukraine, Baziak had accepted Sapieha's invitation to come to Kraków, where he became the de facto auxiliary bishop and the cardinal's natural successor.

ARCHBISHOP BAZIAK'S MANDATE

In September 1951 Archbishop Baziak told Wojtyla to take a leave of absence from his parish duties and concentrate on his theological studies in preparation for earning yet another doctorate and becoming a theology professor. Wojtyla moved into the Kanoniczna Street apartment of

No More Fooling Around!
—Boguslaw Sonik, a student activist

Everybody met at the student chapel very early on Sunday mornings. The student ministry at the university consisted of Mass at seven o'clock in the morning, and after that, there were lectures on the liturgy, the Bible, philosophy, as well as reflections on history and politics. I belonged to this group between 1973 and 1977, while I was a student. Karol Wojtyla was bishop of Kraków at the time, and he kept in close contact with young people through pastoral visits, meetings, and lectures.

Everybody knew that whenever Karol Wojtyla was in Kraków, on any given day between ten in the morning and noon, you could talk to him at least for a few minutes. Sometime later, especially during the second half of the 1970s, when the opposition started, we discussed how to organize an alternative student movement in response to the official Communist student organization.

Wojtyla frequently organized meetings in Franciskánska Street. These meetings were usually for priests, but sometimes chaplains, like Father Kloczkowski, would bring us along. I remember those meetings very well, especially ones we had with Father Stefan Kisielewski and Father Józef Tischner.

When the problems with the workers started after the repressions at Radom, we went to help them. We collected money and distributed bulletins and flyers from the Committee to Defend the Workers. Karol Wojtyla was interested in this aspect of our work, and Father Dziwisz, our chaplain, kept him up-to-date. When the secret police murdered Stanislaw Pyjas, a student activist, in May 1977, we began to demonstrate and still tried to keep in touch with Bishop Wojtyla.

Father Dziwisz advised us to give the bishop all the information we shared with the underground press, and we did that. Whenever he met us, Karol Wojtyla asked how we were doing. We told him about the arrests, the reprisals, and the raids that followed the formation of the "Solidarity" student committee in the wake of Pyjas's murder.

WOJTYLA SUPPORTS THE WORKERS
The famous sermon Karol Wojtyla gave on Corpus Christi was published in *Tygodnik Powszechny (Universal Weekly)*, the Catholic opposition newspaper. He delivered it before one of the altars set up for the procession in which we marched and where he supported us. We didn't know if we were going to be put in prison or not, and a wave of arrests followed the demonstrations in Kraków in 1977. Members of the Committee to Defend the Workers were also arrested in Warsaw. That's when we boycotted the *Juvenalia*, the traditional student festival at the university.

In his Corpus Christi sermon Bishop Wojtyla was very clear about what we should do. He said that instead of going to have a good time at the *Juvenalia*, we youths should choose to respect the dead. Naturally, mass-media coverage disseminated false information about the procession and our reaction, and that's when Karol Wojtyla set the record straight about what we had done. It was a marvelous moment, though the reprisals came along soon enough.

YOUNG PEOPLE PROTEST
The years 1975 to 1979 were marked by a popular rebellion against the Communist government. It started with young people proclaiming their opposition to the regime, an opposition sparked by a sociopolitical awakening in student ministry groups between 1974 and 1976.

We wanted to form a Catholic student organization. We felt that the church had not done all it could to help and we decided to take things a little further. We wanted to understand the church's reaction to our plans, and that's why we met with Karol Wojtyla and other church leaders.

Between 1974 and 1975 the goal of these meetings was to strengthen our sense of freedom by attending lectures held inside the churches. Father Tischner spoke about morality and ethics, for example. Wojtyla talked about personal responsibility. We were interested in the social aspect of Catholicism—what our religion could do to change the reality we were forced to live in. To us, Catholicism seemed the perfect way to revolt against lies and deception. We were sure Wojtyla thought about Catholicism the same way; he was a true people's priest.

The student ministry was not just prayer, reflections, and Masses; sometimes we played jokes and did tricks. I remember in 1976, when people had already started saying that Wojtyla could become pope, we still joked around with him. He was tolerant, but one day, after putting up with us for a half hour, he leaned over to me and said, "Wouldn't it be a good time to stop this foolishness now?"

In 1977 Father Kloczkowski took charge of letting him know our activities, so we did keep in touch. Soon after, Bishop Wojtyla left for Rome and was elected pope the following year.

Father Ignacy Rózycki, a leading theologian whom he knew from the Kraków seminary, where Rózycki had been his teacher and had inspired Wojtyla to study the works of Saint John of the Cross.

At the Church of St. Florian, named for the patron saint of Poland, Father Karol Wojtyla organized an adult religious education program and a residence for sick people.

Since the two men lived together, they had plenty of time to discuss philosophy and theology and to prepare the thesis Father Wojtyla would submit in order to teach theology at the university level. Father Rózycki introduced his roommate to the works of the German phenemonologist Max Scheler, who became the subject of Wojtyla's work. Specifically, the future pope examined the possibility of basing a system of Christian ethics on Scheler's system of thought. It took him two years to complete the thesis, but in the fall of 1953, Wojtyla had completed the text—175 typewritten pages—and it won unanimous approval from the theological faculty at the Jagiellonian University on December 12. By that time Communist control of church activities had progressed to the point where the ministry of education refused to allow the university to grant Wojtyla the degree.

BETWEEN MOSCOW AND THE VATICAN

When Father Wojtyla returned to Kraków from Rome in the summer of 1948, the Communists had already begun to consolidate their hold on power. Party leader Boleslaw Bierut had become president and that fall forced Prime Minister Stanislaw Mikolajczyk to flee once again, fearing for his life and freedom. Mikolajczyk had headed the Polish government in exile in London during the war and had returned after it was over to head a coalition cabinet.

His departure coincided with the death of the Polish primate, Cardinal August Hlond, archbishop of Warsaw and Glieno. Hlond had spent the war in France and only returned in 1945, putting him at some distance from the flock he ruled. Pope Pius XII appointed a different successor with different ties to church and nation—the archbishop of Lublin, forty-seven-year-old Stefan Wyszynski. His advent saw the real start of the war against the Catholic Church in Poland.

The "Barrel" is a meeting room in the Dominican church in Kraków. It got its nickname from the shape of its ceiling. Youth group meetings were held here.

COMMUNIST ATTACKS ON THE CHURCH

Of course, Poland was not the only target of Communist attacks on the church, but it would prove to be the most difficult. Religion was driven out of the Baltic countries, which Russia had incorporated in 1940, with priests barred from performing their religious duties. Most Lithuanian churches had been turned into museums or warehouses. In

(CONTINUED ON PAGE 48)

Light-Life Movement

In the spring of 1972, hiking up a mountain on a camping trip with student youths who belonged to Oasis—a renewal movement in the church designed to foster mature Christian spirituality among high school students through the liturgy and Bible study—Cardinal Wojtyla had this to say to them: "I know three madmen. I'm the first one, the second is my secretary, and the third one is waiting for us at the top of this mountain." In spite of an approaching storm, he kept on trudging to the top of Mount Blyszcz in the Beskids.

Everybody just kept walking behind Wojtyla. After a while, they heard thunder, and it began to rain. This didn't stop the cardinal, and when they all arrived at the top, they gathered around him—and Father Franciszek Blachnicki, the "third madman"—as he celebrated Mass on an improvised altar of stone. Some of those at that celebration of the Mass said their lives were changed forever.

Karol Wojtyla went on many camping trips sponsored by Oasis. Not only did the young people idolize him and want to be with him, he also loved the outings. Often he took bicycle and kayak trips as well, and he enjoyed sitting around campfires, singing with the young people or engaging them in discussions that went on for

Emblem of the Light-Life movement.

hours. He won them over with his enthusiasm, his smile, and his boundless energy, and he was always interested in listening to them.

Father Blachnicki was Karol Wojtyla's friend and founder in the 1950s of Oasis. It spread quickly throughout southern Poland, becoming one of the largest such movements in Europe. Members attended lectures during the school year and went on a three-stage, 15-day retreat in the summer, which was structured around the Mysteries of the Rosary, something Father Blachnicki called an "experiential" format.

Wojtyla supported the movement and defended it against Communist attacks. The party constantly persecuted Oasis, inspecting their camping facilities and frequently telling Father Blachnicki that his permit to host groups was not valid. When Wojtyla became a cardinal, he continued to visit the movement's center in Kroscienko on the banks of the Dunajec, where he celebrated Mass and gave lectures. Wojtyla viewed Oasis as a way of bringing about the vision of Vatican II, and over and over he told the students so.

In 1969 Father Blachnicki presided over the National Pastoral Liturgical Commission, and he achieved most of its

objectives in Oasis functions and retreats. Inspired by Vatican II's *The Dogmatic Constitution on the Church in the Modern World (Lumen Gentium, Light of the World)*, Oasis fostered the idea of the "Church Alive." In 1971 Oasis started a first group for families, and soon after that incorporated some of the experience and methodology of the "Teams of Our Lady" movement in France. Both groups attempted to carry out Vatican II's vision of the Christian home as a "Domestic Church," the domain where the laity lead holy lives.

Light-Life—the name Oasis would later add—adopted the symbols of early Greek Christians for its emblem. A mature Christian is one who has discernment and knows how to combine knowledge (light) with life.

Students remained in Oasis for about three years, somewhat longer if they began membership at a younger age. Early in the 1980s Light-Life spread into Czechoslovakia, and the International Light-Life Evangelization Center was started at the Marian Polish Center in Carlsberg, Germany, in 1983. Members of Light-Life got together in the jubilee celebrations for Christianity's second millennium.

Apart from books written by Father Blachnicki, Oasis has published more than 100 other works, including manuals, liturgical calendars, pamphlets, and religious magazines—*Oasis, Domowy Kosciol (The Domestic Church)*, and *Wieczernik (The Cenacle)*.

Since the mid-'80s, more than 70,000 people have taken part in Oasis each year. The main centers in Poland are in Kroscienko, on the river Dunajec, and in Katowice. The Institute of Pastoral Liturgical Formation in Lublin lends its editorial services to the diverse publications of the movement.

Father Franciszek Blachnicki

Father Blachnicki was born in 1921 into a large family in Rybnik. He attended high school in Tarnowskie Gory and took his final exams in 1938. In September 1939 he joined the underground Resistance movement and fought the German occupation. He was arrested by the Gestapo in March 1940 and spent 14 months in Auschwitz. Two years later he was sentenced to death for his underground activities. After five months on the German "death row," the Nazis commuted his sentence, and he spent the rest of the war shuttling between concentration camps and German prisons. It was while waiting to die that he decided to turn his life over to Christ.

After the war he entered the Silesian Seminary in Kraków and was ordained a priest on June 25, 1950. Between 1954 and 1956, years when

bishops were being deported, he worked with the Curia in Katowice, which had gone underground. When the bishops returned and church repression eased, he helped them adjust to the new conditions in their dioceses. He spent some time in the pastoral department of the magazine *Gosc Niedzielny* while directing a catechism center.

Beginning in 1957, he participated actively in the Sobriety Crusade, a movement to combat alcoholism. In March 1960 the authorities dismissed all the leaders of the Crusade, and in March 1961 they arrested Father Blachnicki. He was detained for four months and then sentenced to three months in jail, but the sentence was commuted to three years of restricted freedom.

In October 1961 Father Blachnicki began his studies at the Catholic University of Lublin, and upon completing them, taught at the Pastoral Theological Institute, where he also did scholarly research. In 1967 he was named national chaplain of the Liturgical Committee, and in that capacity he worked closely with Cardinal Wojtyla, who in 1973 entrusted the Light-Life movement to the protection of the Blessed Virgin.

During the worker revolt in 1981, Father Blachnicki was traveling abroad and never returned home. He set up the Marianum Polish center in 1982 in Carlsberg, Germany, where he died on February 27, 1987. The process of his beatification was begun on December 9, 1995, in Katowice and finalized on August 18, 2002.

Czechoslovakia the church was quickly driven underground after the arrest and imprisonment of the archbishop of Prague, Jozsef Beran. In Hungary, Cardinal Jozsef Mindszenty was accused of espionage and jailed. But in Poland church and state agreed to talk.

They had a prewar "concordat," an agreement between the Vatican and the governments of Catholic countries guaranteeing and defining church rights, as a basis for discussion. Wyszynski was a wily politician. He had spent the war in Poland and had fought the Nazis during the occupation. His anti-Communist leanings after the war were also well known. Still, it took some time to reach an accommodation, and it was never more than that.

Karol Wojtyla moved to this house on Kanoniczna Street in 1951, as noted in the city registry.

TOUGH COMPROMISES

Early in 1949 the Communists accused several priests of "cooperating with Anglo-American imperialism," and prosecution of the clergy was on in earnest. Wyszynski, a tough negotiator, continued to talk to the Communists, and in 1950 they had hammered out a document regulating church-state relations. The Communists agreed that in matters of faith and morals and church jurisdiction, the pope would have the last word, but in other areas of society, the bishops would bow to the edicts of the People's Republic of Poland. When the Vatican accused the Poles of being "soft on Communism," Wyszynski told Pius XII that he wanted martyrdom as a last resort," adding, "I prefer to see my priests in the pulpit and on the altar, not in prison."

In addition to keeping open Lublin's Catholic University, the agreement allowed seminaries to train priests and for Catholic editorials to be published in the press. For a short time the Communists even permitted religious instruction in schools. In return Wyszynski

agreed to have the Communists approve the appointment of bishops and to veto candidates they disliked. But even here, there was compromise. The government opposed the appointment of Eugeniusz Baziak to the Kraków diocese but did not veto it. As a result, he was recognized as archbishop by the Vatican but not by Warsaw.

UPPING THE ANTE

Of course, friction continued. Months after the agreement was signed, the Communists arrested Czeslaw Kaczmarek, bishop of Kielce. He was accused of spying, detained without trial for two years, and given a 12-year prison term. Stanislaw Adamski, the bishop of Katowice, was imprisoned because he had not obtained government permission for his activities. In November 1952 it was Baziak's turn. He was arrested, along with his auxiliary bishop, Stanislaw Rospond. A year later Wyszynski himself was seized and imprisoned, but he never stopped criticizing the Communist regime.

WOJTYLA'S SILENCE

During all this turmoil Father Wojtyla remained silent, even when Father Kurowski, the parish priest of St. Florian with whom he had worked after leaving

Father Wojtyla worked with the young people in St. Florian's parish, where he organized a Living Rosary group.

Niegowic, was arrested. Indeed, he never engaged in open conflict with the Communists or Communism. Apparently, he thought that those with a deep spirituality were immune to the virus of its atheistic doctrine and could resist it more powerfully than others. Nor was he concerned when two of his parishioners in Niegowic told him that the secret police were pressuring them to provide information about Wojtyla's activities in the village. "Don't worry about it. Tell them the truth as you see it," he replied.

Leisure Time in Those Years

—Krysztof Rybicki, a hiking companion

I first met Father Karol Wojtyla on an excursion in the Beskids Mountains with some friends in June 1953. He belonged to a group that was called Srodowisko (The Middle Ground), and we used to call him "Uncle." Our journey took two days, and the route went from Rabka to Kasina. When we passed through towns, Father Wojtyla would celebrate Masses in churches or chapels and open-air Masses out in the fields and on the mountains. From the beginning, he seemed easy to like, and talk to, although he sometimes preferred to walk alone. When he was in his thoughtful mood, he walked quickly, even uphill. I was only fifteen the first time I met him, and all I ever wanted to do was be the first one to get to the top of each slope. One time, on Mount Cwilin, which is a very steep incline, I couldn't reach the top. He must have guessed what I was thinking. He came to a halt, turned around to me, and said, "Run, Krysztof, run."

We knew he always needed time alone. He liked to get in a kayak and sail out into the middle of the lake to pray or meditate. He also took time to meditate on camping trips in the mountains. Then when he came back to the group, he was very friendly, chatty, kind, and even a bit of a jokester. He loved to converse on all sorts of topics, but he liked to listen even more, which he did with much patience. You could say the craziest things and he just listened. After a while he would begin to ask questions, pointing out the weaker parts of our arguments or thoughts.

We realized very quickly that he was an exceptional person. Not just because he was a priest who would go hiking with students in baggy trousers and sneakers but because he was an astoundingly wise, open-minded person and because he was a man of God.

In a letter he wrote to our excursion group (and which he published in *Zapis Drogi*), he told us he had gotten a lot out of those trips because they helped make up for what the war had taken away from him. We got even more out of them than he did. We appreciated the value of these encounters and the chance to talk about various problems with him, even personal concerns. During the kayak trips from 1955 on, he started a custom of walking with a different person each day; this gave each of us the chance to have a private conversation with him. When the group got too big, we had to divide the days, and sometimes he talked with more than one of us at a time. One thing he kept reminding us was that we were creating a modern way of living life as true Christians.

Another of our "uncle's" characteristics was his calmness, how he faced problems very serenely. At the end of one trip to Ustianowa Górna, in the Beskids, we had only one piece of bread left and the nearest store was a day's journey away. In the late afternoon a group of us set off to get fresh supplies. We came back the next day...with nothing. In spite of this, he stayed cheerful and even celebrated Mass. Forty years later, when we remembered this episode, the Holy Father said, "I stopped moving around so I wouldn't waste too many calories and just sat down and read. And I survived."

Another personality trait the Holy Father had was his loyalty to his old friends. At the beginning our group had only a dozen or so members, but later, when our families got involved, we had a couple of hundred people. Many of us kept writing to him, and he always answered us.

I must point out that many things he did in regard to associations and group meetings were against Communist laws. In 1977, when I was older, we were spending a week in Puszcza Notecka. One day a shiny, fashionable automobile pulled into our campsite. Someone had informed on us, and uniformed police had come to get the cardinal. Luckily, my brother and I were the only ones in the camp at that time, and each of us had our two children with us. The police did not have any legal grounds to interfere with us, because this was obviously just a family reunion, but they kept asking why we were there.

"Because it's very lovely."

"You live in Kraków. How did you know that it was so lovely way out here?"

"Because Zygmunt Wrzesniewski told us so."

"And just who is this person?" One of them took out a notebook.

"He wrote the guidebook we're using," answered my brother in all seriousness.

That's what we did to have fun in those years.

Wojtyla did not mount any public opposition to the Communist regime or become directly involved in politics—a reticence that surprised many people. True, he was away on a hiking trip with friends in the Tatra Mountains when archbishop Baziak was arrested, and again he was in the mountains when Cardinal Wyszynski was seized in September 1953. But he clearly felt at the time that politics did not fit into his vision of the priesthood. The Communists, in turn, kept a lookout for priests with moderate views to support for possible promotion. For them Wojtyla seemed a quiet, intellectual cleric without political concerns.

After he was appointed bishop of Kraków, Karol Wojtyla continued with his priestly duties and scholarly research, wrote poetry, and contributed to a number of Vatican II documents.

Chapter 4

A Bishop with Many Missions

In February 1958, Stanislaw Rospond, the auxiliary bishop of Kraków, died. Everybody knew that a Kraków priest would fill his vacant position. Since the church does not divulge the candidates' names, speculation about which priests were nominated went on for months. Even if Wojtyla's name was among them, they projected, it certainly would not have been at the top of the list, because the priest was only thirty-eight. Baziak, Archbishop Sapieha's successor, either went along with Sapieha's wishes for his protégé, or was himself convinced that Karol Wojtyla was ready for more responsibility when he sent his name to the primate in Warsaw.

Pope Pius XII looked at the names of six priests sent from Poland to the Vatican as candidates for the new auxiliary bishop of Kraków. Cardinal Wyszynski, perusing the same list in Warsaw, knew something about five of the priests, but nothing about Karol Wojtyla. When Pius XII chose Karol Wojtyla, Wyszynski sent for him to let him know.

KAYAKING WITH HIS STUDENTS

At that very moment, the priest nominated by the pope to be a bishop was on a kayak expedition in the north of Poland. "We found him! He's with a group of students at Lake Mazuria," Wyszynski's associates informed him.

Kayakers in the *srodowisko,* or lay discussion group, were rowing up the Lyna River. A copy of their schedule for this expedition is now on display in the Curia in Kraków. After a few days' travel by kayak, the group arrived at the Swieta Lipka campsite, nicknamed the "philosophical campsites," run by the Catholic University of Lublin.

Upon the kayakers' arrival at camp, the local parish priest told Wojtyla that he had received an urgent telegram from Warsaw and that he was instructed to tell Father Wojtyla to go to the archbishop's residence in Warsaw at once. The group's "uncle" had to leave them and travel first to Olsztynek in a farmer's milk wagon and from there to Warsaw by train.

MEETING CARDINAL WYSZYNSKI

On the following day, Cardinal Wyszynski received Wojtyla at his residence. The primate observed the tanned, athletic-looking young priest

Above: The archbishop's residence in Kraków is where Karol Wojtyla first studied as a seminary student. He lived there toward the end of World War II and again as archbishop.

Right: L'Osservatore Romano carried the official announcement of Wojtyla's appointment as bishop in 1958.

wearing an old, worn-out cassock with curious interest. A friendly smile seemed forever fixed on the young man's face. Finally the cardinal told his visitor that he had received a letter from Pope Pius XII and that the Holy Father had appointed Wojtyla auxiliary bishop of the archdiocese of Kraków and titular bishop of Antigona.

According to Canon Law, Wyszynski was required to ask Wojtyla if he accepted his nomination. Wojtyla gave his consent. When asked what his immediate plans were, the new auxiliary bishop of Kraków said he had to return to the campsite to finish his excursion with the students.

A NIGHT OF PRAYER

He didn't start back immediately, however. First he went to the train station and bought a ticket for the last train leaving that night. Then he went to a nearby Ursuline Sisters' convent and asked if he could come into their chapel to pray. After he was in the chapel for quite some time, a sister went to check on him and found him lying in front of the altar, his arms stretched out in the form of a cross. She left him alone but came back around dinnertime. She found him still lying in front of the altar, exactly as he was before. When she asked him if he would like to have some dinner with the sisters, the priest asked her to please not disturb him. "I have a lot of things to talk over with God," he said. He stayed praying until it was time to catch the train.

Father Wojtyla was most likely surprised by his nomination. Praying at that altar, he must have been trying to understand God's plans for him. He used to think his future would be in the theater. Then he discovered he had a vocation to be a priest. Now, just as he was getting used to the role of a priest, God was putting him on the road to becoming a bishop. He defined the office of bishop in a letter to friends as "a priceless supernatural legacy from the apostles."

FROM "UNCLE" TO "HIS EXCELLENCY"

The next day, Father Wojtyla passed through Kraków and went to thank Archbishop Baziak for nominating him. Then he told Baziak that he had to finish up at Lake Mazuria before taking on his new duties with the archbishop.

When the new bishop arrived back at the camp, the students received him with wild

(CONTINUED ON PAGE 56)

Archbishop Karol
Wojtyla at a church
celebration.

Karol Wojtyla, Writer

Few readers of the periodicals *Tygodnik Powszechny (Universal Weekly)* and *Znak (The Sign)* realized that the texts published between 1950 and 1970 by Andrzej Jawien, Stanislaw Andrzej Gruda, and Piotr Jasien were written by the same author—Karol Wojtyla, bishop of Kraków.

The crowds that gathered at St. Peter's Basilica on October 16, 1978, probably didn't know that the just elected pope from Poland was a poet. He wasn't the first. In the Renaissance another poet, Enea Silvio Piccolomini, occupied the Throne of Saint Peter from 1458 to 1464 as Pope Pius II.

Soon after Karol Wojtyla's election as pope, *Znak* published a volume of his works, *Poetry and Drama,* for the first time. *Znak* carefully guarded the rights to all of Wojtyla's creative writing. Wojtyla wrote the preface to an anthology of poems written by priests, *Words in the Desert,* published in London in 1971, but he didn't contribute any poems in that volume. Most people knew that the bishop was connected with the literary and theatrical worlds, but only his publishers and closest friends knew what he had actually written.

That the Polish pope would be a writer is easy to understand. Poland has a rich literary heritage bound up with its nationalism. From the first book printed in Wroclaw in 1475, a continuous outpouring of Polish prose, poetry, and drama have flowed—sometimes from Poles in exile. Poland boasts four winners of the Nobel Prize for Literature: Henryk Sienkiewicz, Wladyslaw S. Reymont, Czeslaw Milosz, and Wislawa Szymborska.

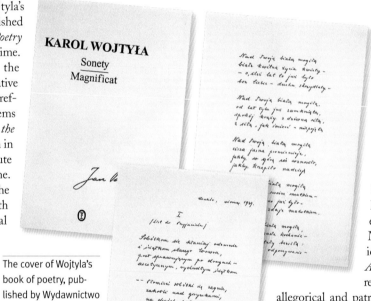

The cover of Wojtyla's book of poetry, published by Wydawnictwo Literackie, is plain and dignified. At right, a copy of his original manuscript, written by hand.

ROMANTIC INSPIRATION

Henryk Sienkiewicz (1846–1916) won his Nobel Prize in 1905. A dedicated nationalist, he wrote mainly about Polish history, but he once toured the United States and delighted his Polish readers with tales of those travels.

He is probably best known for his novel, *Quo Vadis.* Wladyslaw S. Reymont (1867-1925) grew up poor in the Polish countryside and wrote about the life he knew. *The Peasants* was his most popular and critically successful novel. He won his Nobel Prize in 1924. Czeslaw Milosz (1911–2004) won a Nobel Prize for poetry in 1980. He left Poland in 1961 to become a professor of Slavic language and literature at the University of California at Berkeley. Wislawa Szymborska, also a poet, was born in 1923 and has lived her whole life in Kraków. She has written 16 collections of poetry and won her Nobel Prize in 1996.

Karol Wojtyla found inspiration for his poetic style in Polish romantic literature of the nineteenth century. However time-consuming his pastoral duties, Wojtyla always set aside time for reading. He liked the mystical writings of Juliusz Slowacki, a collection of lectures given by Adam Mickiewicz on Slavic literature, and Ignacy Matuszewski's literary criticism, *Slowacki and the New Art Forms.* He also read and reread Stanislaw Wyspianski's allegorical and patriotic dramas. His bedside reading was the *Old Testament Scriptures.*

Wojtyla's first plays were *Job, Jeremiah,* and *David. (David* has been lost.) *Job* takes on a classic theme in Polish literature: The fatherland suffers and represents "Christ for all Nations." The protagonists in *Jeremiah* are romantic heroes in a struggle for independence. They are transformed as they live out tragedy in their fatherland.

Wojtyla used ancient Polish dialect in his first dramas; at the time this was in vogue in Poland's popular theater. Wojtyla's linking of scripture with historic and patriotic themes followed Stanislaw Wyspianski's concept of heroic theater as "the temple of the national spirit."

It is interesting to note that Wojtyla's early dramatic works have hardly any action. Long discourses predominate in *Jeremiah.* The action takes place in the world of the imagination and through the willpower of the characters in the play. These dramas foreshadow plays Wojtyla wrote in later years, described by critics as "dramas of the interior life."

In some of his later dramas, Wojtyla uses the Bible as his sole inspiration. *Brother of Our God* explores his personalist philosophy and its concept of the human person. It is also "hagiography," an inspiring story of the life of a saint—in this case, Brother Albert.

SAINT JOHN OF THE CROSS

After his ordination Wojtyla went back to his doctoral work on the writings of Saint John of the Cross. In an article published in *Znak* in 1951, "On the Humanism of Saint John of the Cross," he wrote that this saint and mystic was characterized "in addition to magnificent coherence and severe logic in the theological tradition, also by truly poetic inspiration." Thanks to his poetic ability, Saint John of the Cross was able to express in a far better way what would have been difficult to put into words in a scientific treatise. Traces of mysticism can be found in Wojtyla's works. His poem, "Song About Reflecting Water," for instance, written in 1950, uses mystical symbolism to reveal the union of the soul with God. Also, in his mystery play *The Overflowing Goodness of Paternity*, there appears the theme of the mystical path on which the soul journeys in search of God.

Karol Wojtyla wrote his mature dramas and poems while he was still heavily involved in priestly pastoral work and in theological study and research. He published *Love and Responsibility* in 1960. Its theme was sexual ethics. An essay, "Encounters with Joy," was published the same year in *Znak* under the pseudonym Andrzej Jawien. Its subject was the sacrament of marriage. In it he suggests the possibility of basing a Christian morality on the ethical system of Max Scheler that Wojtyla greatly admired. The main ideas outlined in both of these works are the same: reflections on human love, the relationship of man and woman in marriage, and the relationship of their love with the love of God.

MATURING INTO A NEW STYLE

Wojtyla's mature dramas underwent a transformation in style. *Brother of Our God*, for example, is written in free verse. Symbols, silences, and complicated metaphors take on major importance. The characters lack individual personalities, and their dialogues, all logically arranged, arrive at general conclusions. The dialogues are not related to particular external events.

The playwright's style in these dramas seems to derive from his particular concept of the theater, the style of the Rhapsodic Theater that restricts the use of all theatrical devices, such as scenery,

actors' gestures, and music. What dominates is the spoken word, delivered in such a way as to bring out the intention of the author to its fullest.

Thanks to his experience as an actor in the Rhapsodic Theater, John Paul II had the astounding ability to reach millions of people whenever he spoke. His poetic language was devoid of any conscious aesthetic concerns. The word is not centered on its own internal beauty but serves to transmit thought. This type of poetry, called "poetry of thought," is born in a creative impulse of thought.

Polish literary critic Jan Blonski attributes Wojtyla's poetry specifically to these experiences:

> *Karol Wojtyla's poetry is strictly religious. Even further, he directs his thoughts to the central religious experience: conversion. Conversion is the exact central theme of his poetry. Conversion is the event his poetry presents, when he meditates on biblical, liturgical, or historic events. To present means above all, to describe, not to give theological explanations for, nor sing lyrical songs about, the subject.*

Karol Wojtyla wrote poems and plays at this desk while he was still very young. The view from the window is Wadowice.

joy. He assured them he would always be their "uncle," not "His Excellency," as some of them had already started to call him.

OFFICIAL BUSINESS BEGINS

The Vatican sent out a correction notice a few weeks later. Karol Wojtyla would be titular bishop of Ombi, not Antigona. Ombi was a newly created diocese in northern Africa. In 1958 Antigona was not available on the Vatican Pontifical Roster that listed dioceses without a titular bishop. This fulfills stipulations that each bishop must have his own diocese and no titular diocese can have more than one titular bishop.

Even before he was consecrated bishop, Father Wojtyla was invited to join other bishops in Jasna Góra, site of the shrine to the Black Madonna, where they were holding the Polish Bishops Conference. As auxiliary bishop, he officially became a member of the Bishops' Pastoral Synod in Kraków.

ORDINATION AT WAWEL CATHEDRAL

September 28, 1958, was the feast day of Saint Waclaw, the patron saint of the cathedral in Kraków. It was cloudy and raining, but not as cold as the day 12 years before, when Karol Wojtyla had been ordained a priest. Now he was to be consecrated as a successor to the apostles, and the ceremony would take place in Wawel Cathedral, not in the chapel of the archbishop's residence. Bishop Franciszek Jopi of Opole and Bishop Boleslaw Kominek of Wroclaw performed the ceremony with Archbishop Baziak. Among the many people in attendance were many of the *srodowisko* students.

The ceremony began in the cathedral, where for centuries the kings of Poland were crowned. First the papal bull was read naming the new bishop. Next Father Wojtyla answered questions from the archbishop, who was seated on his throne. Then the priest made a declaration of faith and pledged to fulfill the duties of his pastoral ministry.

The consecration of bishops contains practices similar to the ordination of priests: The nominee prostrates himself in front of the altar in the form of a cross. The people in the church recite the Litany of the Saints. Then the nominee kneels down and the presiding bishops place a Bible on his shoulders. (Because the Bible contains the Gospels, this action symbolizes a union with Christ.) Finally, the imposition of hands takes place, accompanied by the words of consecration.

Insignia of the archbishops of Kraków are shown at right. First is the *racional*, a gift of Queen Jadwiga, and behind it is the *infula*, which, according to tradition, goes back to the time of Saint Stanislaw.

A PAMPHLET TO TRANSLATE THE LATIN

Since most of the ceremony was in Latin, Father Wojtyla wanted to translate it for the congregation. He thought about doing this in a short introduction he prepared for them, but Archbishop Baziak, adhering to tradition, wouldn't agree to "adding novelties." The ceremony stayed in Latin, though Wojtyla found another way to help his countrymen. He translated the ceremony in a pamphlet that his friends copied and distributed to those present at the Holy Mass of Consecration.

The congregation sang *Veni, Creator Spiritus (Come, Holy Spirit),* and the archbishop anointed the head of the new bishop, Karol Wojtyla. Everybody prayed that the recently consecrated bishop would be zealous in his love of God, that he would reject pride and embrace humility, and be full of truth, never betraying these virtues.

FOLLOWING ANCIENT TRADITIONS

According to the tradition of the time, the new bishop's head was wrapped in a white scarf. (This part of the ceremony is no longer followed.) Baziak anointed Wojtyla's hands and handed him a stole and a pastoral staff. Then he placed a bishop's ring on Wojtyla's right hand to symbolize his loyalty to the church. Finally, he placed the Gospels in his hands and said, "Receive the Gospels. Teach the people what has been entrusted to you." The bishops who performed the ceremony exchanged the Kiss of Peace with the new bishop.

The offering of gifts—lighted candles, bread, and wine—followed. According to Kraków tradition, a representative of the local bakers guild presented one of the bread offerings. Bishop Wojtyla asked some friends from his *srodowisko* to bring the other gifts.

THE NEW BISHOP OFFERS BLESSINGS

At the end of the ceremony, Archbishop Baziak placed the stole on Wojtyla once more and led him to the bishop's throne. The choir sang *Te Deum (To You, God, We Offer Praise),* and then Bishop Wojtyla stood up and walked through the cathedral, blessing people as he went.

Later that evening the new bishop set off for Czestochowa with a group of his young friends; they wanted to pray before the Black Madonna at her sanctuary in Jasna Góra. A few days later he returned to Wadowice to visit Father Leonard Prochownik in his former parish and then traveled on to the Carmelite monastery at Gorka, where he received a scapular of the Blessed Virgin once again, similar to the one he had received when he was ten years old.

A TRANSITIONAL POPE WITH PURPOSE

The Vatican was coming to the end of an era. Scarcely two weeks after Bishop Wojtyla was consecrated, Pope Pius XII died. He had never known Wojtyla personally—they met only once for a few moments when Wojtyla was a student at the Belgian College—but his signature made Wojtyla a bishop.

One month after Karol Wojtyla's consecration, the cardinals gathered for the conclave that eventually elected Cardinal Guiseppe Roncalli, former apostolic delegate to France, to the Throne of Saint Peter. Guiseppe Roncalli, patriarch of Venice, was very popular in Italy but little known in the rest of the world. Seventy-seven years old, he was obviously chosen to be a transitional pope. Taking the name Pope John XXIII, he immediately took steps to bring the church into the modern era. He convened at the Vatican the Second Council of the Universal Church, known as Vatican II.

STRENGTHENING PARISHES

In Kraków the new bishop Wojtyla rapidly assumed his portion of the administrative duties for his diocese. Archbishop Baziak, whose health was failing, needed help. Wojtyla's main task was to visit parishes. This was traditionally a formal event, but Wojtyla took a warmer and friendlier approach.

Bishop Wojtyla instructed the parish priests to get ready for his arrival. He wanted the priests to send him information about their parishes, which he reviewed in minute detail. Then, during the course of his visit to each parish, which might take as long as a week, the bishop compared the information he had received with what he observed and what he learned by asking many questions. The new bishop then celebrated the liturgy and gave forceful homilies in the parishes.

Toward the end of May 1959, his first visit was to the deanery at Sus, where Kalwaria Zebrzydowska, the calvary where his father had taken him after his mother's death, was located. Three months later he returned to Wadowice as "visiting bishop."

APPRECIATING A FELLOW ARTIST

In January 1959 Karol Wojtyla visited the house of the Albertine Brothers in Kraków. The order was founded by Brother Albert Chmielowski, a nineteenth-century artist who gave up painting to become a religious brother and dedicated his life to helping the poor. Wojtyla identified with Brother Albert: "I understand what it means to abandon the world of art. I wanted to be a writer, and now I don't have time to do that. This is a great renunciation," Wojtyla admitted to the brothers.

Bishop Wojtyla celebrated a Mass for the intention of Brother Albert's beatification. He never missed any opportunity to help that cause, and when he became pope, he elevated Brother Albert to the rank of sainthood.

PUBLISHING HIS FIRST BOOK

Besides visiting parishes, the new bishop also organized lecture series, presided when members of religious orders professed vows, and continued to teach at the Catholic University in Lublin, although he went there less often. In March 1959 Bishop Wojtyla started to feel very tired. Blood tests confirmed that he was suffering from

infectious mononucleosis. Since he was forced to take it easy, he spent this downtime editing his first book.

Bishop Wojtyla on a pastoral visit to Dolina Chocholowska in 1963.

While on the kayak trip he was taking when he was nominated for bishop, he had carried in his backpack a typewritten manuscript that he had been working on. When the campers were sitting around and relaxing, he handed out the manuscript and discussed with them one of the most delicate issues that confronts the clergy and the Catholic laity—sex. He published *Love and Responsibility* in 1960. It provoked an uproar because it seemed almost scandalous for a cleric who had been a bishop for barely two years to write frankly about human sexuality. In *Love and Responsibility*, Wojtyla compared the dignified relationship of married spouses, in which the man and the woman were equal partners, to casual sex encounters.

Wojtyla's experience as a confessor and his conversations with students inspired the book. He developed his theme over time as he talked with dozens of people about

We Were Always Important to Him

—Halina Bortnowska, one of his students

I knew Karol Wojtyla when I was a student in his ethics classes at the Catholic University of Lublin. He was a very different type of priest, the kind who presented ideas to young people as he was just mulling them over and they were still in progress, not all "a done deal" or "neatly tied up in boxes" or that were published many years before. The best example of this is his book *Love and Responsibility*, which at that time was an idea that was just beginning to crystallize for him. The style and content of this work matured and developed as he discussed his ideas with us in class. To a certain extent, the reactions of the students in another seminar course he led influenced his ideas, if not the course in which we had to write a paper. We were reading Aristotle's *Ethics* in the seminar.

In addition to teaching, Karol Wojtyla was also a pastoral minister for the students. He took the time to get to know them personally, which permitted him to enrich the theme of his book: the dynamic of being an adult and acting in relationships, such as married partners.

I was a little older than the rest of the students. Actually, most of them were very young. Anyway, all of us were involved in trying to find out "who we were" and choosing a career. The questions for each of us were, "What road do I take and with whom?" Wojtyla's work was based on his own outstanding personal experience, although he never alluded to that directly. He applied the phenomenological method, limiting descriptive anecdotes and just stating conclusions. It is not easy to read *Love and Responsibility*. He explained it more fully during class because we discussed various real-life issues.

Teachers who win over young people are the ones who are truly interested in them, pay attention to them, and respect them. Not too many are like that. Maybe some of them do have this deep respect and interest in young people, but they just don't know how to show it. Father Wojtyla knew how to do that. He was not at all a pushy know-it-all type or "old buddy" type, who try to be just like young people and become

one of them. He always stayed true to himself and what he said came from the serious stance he had toward life. We were very important to him, and he knew how to show that. Maybe that's because he was a person of paradoxes. On the one hand, he treated everybody with reserve, and on the other, he could relate and show feelings toward people. The actor was always acting in him, not in the sense that he always seemed to be "onstage," but in the sense that his gestures let people get a glimpse of who he really was. Karol Wojtyla was very sincere. His gestures and expressions did not contradict his sincerity. He didn't play a role in front of us; he was just simply who he was.

He was no different when we went hiking in the mountains or took kayaking trips in the rivers or lakes. He always did what the situation called for. He seemed a little bit distant in classes, but that was because he was thinking about the subject of the day.

We talked more with him in the seminar course. Sometimes it bothered me that he talked sports so much with the men in the class. That seemed to me to be a terrible waste of time. Sometimes he had to leave class in a hurry to go catch a train, and once again we hadn't finished the chapter, because too much time had been spent talking about who won the latest sports games! He was really interested in sports, especially soccer. I was the only one who kept glancing at my watch, wondering when all the talk about sports would be over. I have to say I really wanted him to keep to the subject of the seminar.

Those sports conversations were not totally boring, but I was more emotionally caught up with the passages from Aristotle that got us around to discussing real-life issues. As I said, he had a profound understanding of people. He was a witness to the interior world and wanted us to discover our own interior world. He never drew attention to himself, never discussed events in his life. Every word out of his mouth was pure poetry.

their intimate relationships, and the book reflected Wojtyla's strong personalist philosophy. He believed that he, as a priest, could not and should not flee from, or make light of, a subject so key to the human condition. Among other things, Wojtyla openly discussed the issue of sexual satisfaction for the woman in the marital relationship and the role the man must play so that sex would be equally satisfying for both partners.

When the book first appeared, reviewers suggested that the author—a priest and theologian—was baldly touching

upon a controversial subject that had no relation to theology. But in fact, Bishop Wojtyla was embarking on paths that other priests and theologians in Western Europe were already following in preparation for the Vatican II Council. Karol Wojtyla, while a student in Rome, had been conversant with these modern currents of thought. Now living behind the Iron Curtain, he was not in contact with them. Nevertheless, he sensed a humanistic crisis and the need for the church to be open to new challenges.

READING THE SIGNS OF THE TIMES

In the spring of 1959, the Preparatory Commission for the Vatican II Council sent out questionnaires to thousands of bishops, rectors of men's orders in the church, deans of theology faculties, and other prominent representatives of the church. Bishop Wojtyla received one, which he returned to the Holy See with his observations in October. His response was in the form of an essay addressed to the church in the modern world.

Bishop Wojtyla's responses to the questionnaire suggested issues that the council fathers eventually took into consideration at Vatican II. Bishop Wojtyla, even from behind the Iron Curtain, had a remarkable ability to read the signs of the times.

In Poland the Communist authorities that controlled passports hadn't yet decided who would be allowed to go to the council in Rome. Pope John XXIII had invited even the auxiliary bishops. The government viewed with suspicion the possibility of a large number of bishops from Poland attending. The party finally decided to restrict passports and allow only the highest members of the hierarchy to go to Rome. Archbishop Eugeniusz Baziak would be the representative from Kraków.

Pope John XXIII surprised everyone when he called the ecumenical council together in January 1959. He admitted later that he even surprised himself; he had acted under the inspiration of the Holy Spirit. By summoning the most prominent clergy in the church to the Vatican, Pope John XXIII set in motion his hope for *aggiornamento*, a term he used to explain the opening of the church to the modern world. He wanted to bring the church up-to-date. No one realized what profound changes would take place.

CONCENTRATING ON HUMAN LIFE

Bishop Wojtyla suggested that the council focus its deliberations on the situation of men and women, rather than just the status of the church. "The various social systems in the twentieth century," he pointed out, "offer humanization by means of things in the material realm, which basically leads to the dehumanization of interpersonal relations. Men and women have to make choices, and they are directing their expectations and their questions to the church and to the clergy." He asked, "How must we respond to these expectations? What do we have to do so that the true humanism Christianity offers will reach even the farthest corners of society, so that human life may be made holy in all its aspects?" The answer would point out the need to educate the clergy with a new focus and to promote a lay ministry, which would enable men and women to go where the clergy could not and influence people not approachable by the church.

THE COUNCIL BEGINS

On October 11, 1962, John XXIII inaugurated the Vatican II Council in St. Peter's Basilica, but Archbishop Baziak was not among the almost 2,000 bishops who attended the first session. The apostolic leader of the archdiocese of Kraków had died in June and was buried in Bishop Zebrzydowski's chapel in Wawel Cathedral. In order to prevent Kraków from going without a leader, the prominent clergy in the diocese immediately elected Bishop Wojtyla as temporary head bishop. For all practical purposes, this meant that the auxiliary bishop would assume the responsibilities of the archbishop, including taking his place at Vatican II.

Although Karol Wojtyla was the youngest of the auxiliary bishops of Kraków, he had been a bishop longer than the others. Julian Grobnicki, Archbishop Baziak's personal secretary, for example, was only consecrated in 1960. And so Wojtyla was present at the ceremony.

DEALING WITH THE GOVERNMENT

Bishop Wojtyla requested a visa so that he could go to Rome. At that time, the Communist authorities carefully

Karol Wojtyla in one of his first official photographs as a bishop.

weighed each visa request and turned down many. Wojtyla, however, had no trouble getting his papers. This probably had something to do with the way he had recently handled a sticky situation with the government.

Just before he was supposed to leave for Rome, the Communist Party in Kraków decided to confiscate the Catholic seminary building and use it for a new State Teacher Training University. Bishop Wojtyla was away on a parish visit when he heard that the seminarians had been evicted. He rushed back to Kraków and went straight to party headquarters to meet with Lucjan Motyka, primary secretary of the region. Wojtyla was the first member of the church hierarchy, in Motyka's memory, to invite discussion on such an issue. As a result of their conversation, a compromise was reached. The

building was divided in two: The ground floor and first story would be occupied by seminarians, and the second story would be occupied by teachers in training. Never before had Archbishop Baziak approached members of the Communist Party in such a way.

Above: Archbishop Wojtyla celebrates Mass in the Dominican church in Kraków.

Right: The bishop's staff is a symbol of his authority.

WOJTYLA AT THE COUNCIL

Other bishops did have trouble getting visas, and the final Polish delegation, led by Cardinal Wyszynski, wound up with just 16 members, including Wojtyla. Once in Rome, it was pure luck and coincidence that Wojtyla, as a low-ranking bishop, would be put in close contact with influential council fathers. Because of his young age and low rank, he was assigned a seat way in the back, near the door of the basilica and far from the main altar. For the same reason, he lived in the Polish Institute on the west bank of the Tiber during the council, while Wyszynski and more prominent Polish bishops were lodged in a neighborhood near the Polish College.

The last time Wojtyla had been in Rome, some 14 years before, he was a new priest. Now he was functioning as an archdiocesan bishop. The council was grappling with matters that affected the entire church. Bishop Wojtyla had his own vision of that responsibility and got involved in the deliberations. He suggested ideas to modify the schemata—that is, issues to be discussed. The Roman Curia had prepared these ahead of time, and Wojtyla spoke with great ease, since the official language of the council was Latin.

BUILDING A NETWORK OF FRIENDS

As a not-too-well-known bishop at the first council session, Wojtyla took advantage of the opportunity to establish new friendships. These contacts were important to his future. On his way to Rome from Kraków, he had stopped off in Vienna to visit Archbishop Franz König. While in Rome, he met with an old friend from his seminary days in Kraków, Father Andrzej Deskur. In 1952, after Deskur finished his studies in Kraków, he attended the Pontifical Diplomatic Academy and became an influential Vatican functionary. During the council he was put in charge of press releases and, thanks to that job, was in contact with all the participants and observers at the council.

Deskur happily shared his information with his old friend from Kraków. He also showed Wojtyla around the Vatican and explained how the Curia operated and what its concerns were. In Deskur's office Bishop Wojtyla met Bishop Krol and Cardinal Rubin for the first time. Of Polish descent, Krol was a bishop from the United States, and Rubin was secretary of the Preparatory Committee

and rector of the Polish College in Rome. Later Rubin became Pope Paul VI's secretary of the Bishops' Synod.

Bishop Wojtyla participated sparingly in the first session of the council, but he took advantage of opportunities to present his ideas. He entered the discussion on the sacred liturgy. After listening to council fathers from other countries, he went up to the podium to share his personal pastoral experience. He proposed reforms for the ceremony of baptism, suggesting the addition of a solemn promise to be made by the child's godparents that they would ensure the child would be educated in the Catholic faith.

Karol Wojtyla acts as a tour guide for Mieczyslaw Kotlarczyk and a friend at St. Peter's Basilica in Rome.

Milan, Cardinal Giovanni Battista Montini, as his successor. Montini became known to the world as Pope Paul VI. The new Holy Father had moderated the first Vatican II session, and he declared that his most important responsibility was to have the council continue its work. He set the date for the second session to begin on September 29, 1963.

VATICAN II'S SECOND SESSION

Bishop Wojtyla left for Rome a few days after the reopening of the council. He had suffered another attack of mononucleosis and needed to rest, but immediately after his arrival on October 7, he got involved in the editing of council documents. His most important contribution was to the discussion on the church in which he emphasized the issue of the universal call to holiness. In his oral presentation, which he later submitted in writing, he said that holiness was not a vocation exclusive to the clergy. All baptized people are called to become saints. "Church" is not just the hierarchy; the entire People of God make up the living church, and their ultimate goal is to participate in the very life of the Most Holy Trinity.

When the second session ended in December, Bishop Wojtyla took a short trip to the Holy Land with others who had attended the council. They were complying with Pope Paul VI's wishes that they go there before his own pilgrimage, which was scheduled for the following year. This first visit to places related to the life of Jesus Christ profoundly impressed Bishop Wojtyla. He wrote his thoughts about it in a long pastoral letter and often spoke of this trip in homilies and conversations.

A MELDING OF SCRIPTURE AND TRADITION

Bishop Wojtyla took part in the discussion on the sources of revelation. The question of revelation brought up the relation between scripture and tradition. Some of the council fathers took a position close to the Protestant view that places emphasis on the Bible. Others emphasized the dominant role of tradition in disclosing the fullness of revelation contained in the Holy Scriptures. Bishop Wojtyla took a position that reflected a theme characteristic of his theology: He united these two ideas into a single formula. He stressed that God desires to communicate himself through both the Bible and tradition. This was the same conclusion Wojtyla had arrived at 14 years before with his mentor, Garrigou-Lagrange, when he explored the difference between Saint Thomas's "Divine Subject," which must be proved with logical mental formulations, and Saint John of the Cross's Living-Personal-Creator God, who must be reached beyond all logic—that is, mystically, through faith.

WINDING UP THE FIRST SESSION OF VATICAN II

With the entire Polish delegation Wojtyla asked the council to draw up a special document dedicated to the Blessed Virgin Mary. Because beliefs concerning the Mother of God were a point of contention in the dialogue with Protestantism, this request went unfulfilled. Finally Bishop Wojtyla presented two interventions in the council's proceedings during the first session. They had to do with the schemata that dealt with the methods of social communication and the role of the church in the modern world.

When the first session of the council came to a close on December 8, 1962, Pope John XXIII was already seriously ill. He died of cancer six months later, just as the second session was about to begin. On June 21 the cardinals in the conclave elected the archbishop of

SEARCH FOR AN ARCHBISHOP

For more than a year and a half after the death of Archbishop Baziak, the palace of the primate and the government offices of the Polish People's Republic exchanged letters on the issue of who would succeed the deceased archbishop. It was a very complicated process. The primate of Poland, Stefan Wyszynski, would send the prime minister of Poland, Józef Cyrankiewicz, a list of three candidates to assume the role of the archbishop of Kraków. If the leader of the government did not

Karol Wojtyla's congratulatory note to an old friend on the occasion of his friend's marriage.

return his veto to the primate within three months, then the list would be sent on to the Vatican for the pope to make his final decision. Cyrankiewicz vetoed the first proposed list from the primate.

In reality, the prime minister had nothing to say about the nominees, because the decision was made by Communist Party leaders, and the government just announced it. In this instance, the decision maker was Zenon Kliszko, a member of the politburo of the Polish United Workers' Party and the person responsible for church-state relations. Kliszko, vice marshal of the parliament, kept in close contact with Stanislaw Stomma, leader of *Znak,* a parliament bloc. Professor Stomma, in turn, dealt frequently with Father Andrej Bardecki, the church-advisory official at *Tygodnik Powszechny,* the Catholic weekly newspaper. Thanks to Father Bardecki, information passed back and forth between the primate's chancellery in Warsaw and church parties involved in Kraków. In October 1963 party deputy Stomma gave out an extraordinary piece of information: Kliszko was going to keep vetoing the lists sent by the primate until the name Karol Wojtyla appeared on one.

The Communist Party officials were indeed making such calculations. The hope that Kliszko and his comrades had of setting parties in the church against one other was, however, unfounded. Their approval of Wojtyla had no effect. Bishop Wojtyla had never given them any reason to believe that he would back down in the face of power. On the contrary, he felt that he was responsible for the People of God and he would never compromise that responsibility.

A case in point was Nowa Huta, a new workers' city built by the Communists as a model of socialist ideals. It was built in fields outside Kraków, according to a plan that allotted no space to build a church. Nevertheless, in 1959 the residents of Bienczyce, one of Nowa Huta's neighborhood subdivisions, managed to construct a small chapel that could be converted into a larger church later on. The authorities refused to grant permission for work to start on the church building. Churchgoers began to attend Masses out in the open air at an altar placed outside the chapel. Bishop Wojtyla decided to help them. He celebrated a High Mass there to commemorate all the births and baptisms from 1959—the date the authorities had permitted the Church of the Ark of the Lord to be built—until the present, which was 1967. The church was given the go-ahead to build.

During the first session of the Vatican II Council, the issue of who would succeed the archbishop of Kraków had been put on a back burner. It resurfaced when the Polish bishops returned from Rome. Cardinal Wyszynski sent another list to the authorities that was also refused. Bishop Wojtyla continued to administer to the archdiocese in the capacity of head bishop. He didn't live in the archbishop's palace, but that did not stop him from doing the archbishop's job.

Left: Archbishop Wojtyla helped Poland celebrate 1,000 years of Christianity in 1966.

THE PARTY WANTS A SPOILER

Cardinal Wyszynski was reluctant to nominate Wojtyla, perhaps because he feared that the bishop was a young philosophical poet, not very interested in politics, whom the Communists would be able to manipulate. He was also inclined to be a liberal thinker in the church. What really worried Wyszynski was that the Communist Party leaders were looking for someone to undermine the primate's unshakable will. The party was hoping, he suspected, that a conflict could be stirred up between two strong personalities that would divide the Polish episcopate and weaken Wyszynski's power.

Right: Church of the Ark of the Lord, in Nowa Huta, was built despite government interference.

POLITICS PLAY OUT

Kliszko's wishes were finally made known to Wyszynski. The primate's third proposed list of nominations for the successor in Kraków contained the name of the head vicar, Bishop Wojtyla. Prime Minister Cyrankiewicz did not oppose this list, so Professor Stomma appeared in the offices of *Tygodnik Powszechny* with the confidential information from Kliszko that the candidacy of

By the turn of the twenty-first century, more than 45,000 students had obtained degrees from the University of Lublin.

The Catholic University of Lublin

In 1918 the Polish bishops founded the University of Lublin, the fourth university established in the recently freed Poland. That first year, 399 students enrolled in the four schools. In 1929 the name was changed to the Catholic University of Lublin (KUL in Polish for *Katolicki Uniwersytet Lubelski*). Six years later Father Antoni Szymanski started the Scientific Society at KUL, a branch of the university that published results of the university's scientific research. A year before World War II started, KUL had 1,400 students and became accredited to award university degrees.

The university suffered heavy losses during the war with the Bolsheviks in 1920 and even more devastation during World War II. Under Nazi rule, the professors had to teach underground classes in Warsaw, Lublin, and Kielce. After the liberation KUL was the first university to start up its educational program again. Under the Communists many departments were closed down, including the Department of Socioeconomic Rights and Systems, the university's most famous one. The Communist authorities confiscated university property, stopped promotions, prevented new appointments, and even arrested some of the professors. But they could not totally destroy the university.

The Catholic University of Lublin had two great protectors during that difficult period: Bishop Karol Wojtyla and Cardinal Stefan Wyszynski, the primate of Poland. Karol Wojtyla began independent studies at KUL in 1954. He taught ethics as chairman of the ethics department up until he left for the conclave that elected him pope in 1978. Wyszynski was secretary of the university from 1946 to 1948.

Karol Wojtyla had been accepted. The primate sent the list with Karol Wojtyla's name on it to the Holy Father, and he then received the papal nomination.

Pope Paul VI was not very well acquainted with Bishop Wojtyla, but he may have noticed his active participation in council sessions. On December 30, 1963, a few days after the closing of the second Vatican II Council session, the pope named Wojtyla as metropolitan archbishop of Kraków. The nomination was made public in Poland on January 19 of the following year, and his installation at Wawel Cathedral took place on March 8, 1964.

A DRAMATIC CEREMONY

Bishop Wojtyla's installation ceremony as archbishop began on the square in front of Wawel Castle Cathedral. Karol Wojtyla waited at the entrance, robed in the vestments of an archbishop. First, the curator of the cathedral's historic museum treasures led him over to the silver reliquary that held relics of Saint Stanislaw, the bishop of Kraków, who died at the hands of King Boleslaw the Brave in the eleventh century. Next, the archbishop nominee went up the stairs and stood at the door of the

cathedral. The members of the cathedral chapter officially welcomed him in. Then, after a welcoming speech, the dean of the cathedral handed Wojtyla its keys. Finally, as administrator of the cathedral, Wojtyla walked through it to the archbishop's throne near the altar, which was specially adorned for this occasion.

Once he was seated on the throne, the secretary of the Curia of Kraków read Karol Wojtyla the papal bull that awarded him the title of metropolitan archbishop. After that, Wojtyla kissed the altar and then returned to sit on the throne, where he received traditional forms of homage that the clergy present to new archbishops.

In preparation for saying Mass in the cathedral, the new archbishop was vested in an antique robe that symbolized how closely the Polish nation was linked to the Catholic Church and its faith. In the early days of the cathedral, Anna Jagiellonka, King Stefan Batory's queen, had commissioned it to be ornately decorated in gold. The bishop's *racional*, embroidered with pearls, was a gift of Queen Jadwiga. Other vestments, rarely used, underscored the exceptional nature of the event, since only four bishops in the world have the right to wear them. The head of the archbishop was crowned with the *infula* of seventeenth-century bishop Lipski. During the Mass Wojtyla exchanged it for another one from the eighteenth century. He wore the ring of twelfth-century bishop Maurus on his finger. In his hand he held a pastoral staff from the time of King Jan III Sobieski and his victory in Vienna. Even the chalice used for the liturgy symbolized unity with the past, since it was a gift of the Jagiellonians. These articles, as well as the content of his homily, spoke to the legacy of Poland's proud history in which the church played a major role.

THE THIRD SESSION OF VATICAN II

The third session of the Vatican II Council was held in the autumn of 1964. Archbishop Wojtyla was assigned a seat closer to the altar and nearer the pope. This change signaled that a closer relationship had developed between the archbishop of Kraków and Pope Paul VI.

Hundreds of council fathers had spoken from the pulpit of St. Peter's; most of them did not draw any special attention. The archbishop of Kraków did get noticed, however. All eyes turned toward him when he rang out the words *"Venerabiles Patres, Fratres, et Sorores!"* (Venerable Fathers, Brothers, and Sisters!) because no one else had addressed the women in attendance at the council as observers.

Always fond of children, Wojtyla makes a pastoral visit to a kindergarten.

Archbishop Karol Wojtyla had chosen to break with tradition and acknowledge the women as he started his address on the apostolate of the laypeople and the dialogue between the laity and the church.

WOJTYLA MAKES HIS POINTS

The "Decree on the Apostolate of the Lay People" that the Roman Curia prepared was criticized right from the start by many council fathers, including Archbishop

Wojtyla. During later sessions he pointed out that the decree was poorly conceptualized. In his opinion, he said, it was directed to the clergy and not to the church as a whole; plus it did not correctly ascribe the source of the laity's apostolate. According to Archbishop Wojtyla, the source of their apostolate was the dignity conferred on men and women at their baptism. Because of this sacrament, they shared the responsibility of every Christian, which was to try to become holy.

Without mentioning his personal experiences, but surely keeping them in mind, the archbishop also took up the subject of the clergy-laity dialogue. According to Karol Wojtyla, both parties ought to be more open with each other because the church's evangelizing mission is strengthened by united effort. Another issue that he raised was the role of young people in the apostolate, one that he would develop during his own pontificate.

ADDRESSING SCHEMA III

During the first session of the council, when Pope Paul VI was still Cardinal Montini, he had promoted Schema III. This council document became the *Pastoral Constitution on the Church in the Modern World.* Its theme was especially dear to Archbishop Wojtyla—he had analyzed it way back in his response to the questionnaire sent by the preparatory committee. In Wawel Cathedral the day he left for Rome, he mentioned that he was hoping to enter the debate at the council on the role of the church in the modern world. Traditionalists in the Roman Curia wanted to eliminate Schema III, and Wojtyla wanted to take up its case and defend it. Paul VI would not allow the document to be eliminated.

On October 20, after a Mass celebrated by Archbishop Wojtyla, the council fathers began their discussions. The next day the archbishop of Kraków spoke on behalf of the Polish bishops and proposed many corrections to Schema III. Over the next few days he submitted others—almost 80 in writing—that would change the tone of the constitution during the drafting stage. In November Wojtyla was appointed to the subcommission in charge of editing the new document.

Paul VI had taken notice of Archbishop Wojtyla, and after the debates on Schema III, he gave him a gift *palio,* a woolen stole decorated with black crosses, symbolizing ecclesiastic power. A bishop wears a *palio* on his shoulders during the investiture ceremony.

THE MEANING OF RELIGIOUS LIBERTY

Archbishop Wojtyla also got involved in the discussion on religious liberty. At the beginning this schema formed part of the decree on ecumenism. Thanks to a council vote, which included that of Wojtyla, it became an independent document. The conflict between the future pope and Bishop Marcel Lefebvre began here. The French bishop supported a traditionalist position. He feared that the council's declaring religious liberty would cause vio-

Above: Bishop Wojtyla blesses a newly married couple.

Right: The cover of Wojtyla's treatise on Christian marriage, *Love and Responsibility.*

lent and profound secularization in society and would change the history of the church. He also suggested that the effects of this decree would be difficult to foresee. For him, "religious liberty" meant "liberalism," and this, in turn, was synonymous with anticlericalism.

The archbishop of Kraków thought differently. He was convinced that faith could neither be imposed nor made obligatory. It must be a free choice for men and women to make. God, through revelation, would make this choice possible. It looked like the votes for this decree were there in the third session, but the conservatives were able to block its progression, and religious liberty had to wait another year for action.

THE FOURTH SESSION OF VATICAN II

In 1965 the fourth session of Vatican II opened. At that point, Karol Wojtyla was no longer the little-known bishop of Kraków who wrote spiritual poetry in the margins of council documents (as he had done during first sessions of the council). Now he was respected as a metropolitan archbishop, whose logical arguments, always enriched by his personalist philosophy, sketched out a new role for the church in the modern world. In 1965 Wojtyla made his greatest contribution to Vatican II—the editing of two documents that had not been voted upon in the previous session.

He spoke about the *Declaration on Religious Liberty* in the final session and stressed the relationship between free will and responsibility. This liberty, Wojtyla argued, was

not only an aspect of human reason but also of the revelation of God. Revelation was linked with human intelligence and logic. Men and women can respond to God freely in faith; they can also reject any forcible pressure to accept this faith. This focus was included in the final text of the declaration. It asserted that the right of men and women to freedom of religion must be reflected in the legal systems of political states. This affirmation, of course, alluded to the political realities of Poland and the other countries in the Soviet bloc. Just as no power should force a person to profess a particular belief, the declaration stated, no power should force a person to deny his faith. Both options are contrary to the dignity of the person.

MODERN-DAY CHALLENGES

One week later Archbishop Wojtyla took up the debate on the church in the modern world once again. The *Pastoral Constitution on the Church in the Modern World* that resulted from the debate was different from other constitutions that treated matters of doctrine. This was the only one written in French—the others were written in Latin—and it was soon translated into other languages. Karol Wojtyla called specific attention to its religious, not doctrinal, character. As one of the editors, Wojtyla took part in all the group meetings and influenced the final form of the document. (Professor Stefan Swiezawski from the Catholic University of Lublin was another editor involved.)

In essence, the document says that given that God, through his son, entered into the history of humanity and the world, the world should not be thought of as something extraneous to the church. Just the opposite: the real history of the world is the history of redemption. Given that the secular world has its own autonomy, open dialogue can exist between society and the church. The church proclaims its truth, and the world reacts to that without closing itself off from the possibility of the transcendent. This truth is based on the conviction that the Christian faith does not enslave or alienate men and women, but rather liberates them to true freedom and dignity.

WE FORGIVE, AND WE ASK FORGIVENESS

In the final days of Vatican II Council in Rome, the Polish bishops tried to mend relations with the German bishops. Archbishops Karol Wojtyla of Kraków and Boleslaw Kominck of Wroclaw kept in daily contact with the German bishops. Cardinal Wyszynski maintained his distance. He finally accepted an initiative made by Bishop Kominck. The year 1966—the millennium of Christianity in Poland—was approaching. Cardinal Wyszynski was the reconciliation. The situation of the dioceses in the north and west of Poland had to be regularized. These areas, which used to be part of the German Reich, were resettled by Poles after the war.

The frontier of the Oder–Neisse Line, established at the Potsdam Conference in 1945, was not officially recognized by any international treaty. For that reason the Vatican also delayed permanent recognition of diocese in the region.

A BAD RESPONSE

The news about the letter written by the Polish bishops and their German counterparts was an unpleasant surprise for Communist authorities in Poland. First Germans and then Poles started dubbing it the "So-called Letter." The Communist Party propaganda machine was in a state of high alert, and the bishops were the object of many accusations and recriminations. The Communists wanted to take advantage of this chance to rouse still strong anti-German sentiment in Polish society and to create a split between the people and the bishops.

The Communists used the employees of Solvay, the factory where Archbishop Wojtyla had worked during the war, to accomplish their goals. The Solvay workers did not have access to the text of the bishops' letter, because the Communists refused to allow its publication in Poland. Many of them signed an "open letter" expressing "their great indignation and astonishment" that their archbishop had written and signed the So-called Letter. His Excellency's actions were criticized as "against the people of Kraków," and his "insolence" offended their "patriotic sentiments."

SMOOTHING THE WATER

The archbishop did not let their critical letter go without a reply. Since it was impossible to publish his response, it was read in all the churches during Christmas Mass. After that, the Polish press did publish it, accompanied by hostile comments.

"If the employees of Solvay had had the opportunity to read the contents of the Polish bishops' letter and the responses of the German bishops to it," said Wojtyla, "they would not have signed their open letter." He also explained the patriotic and religious intentions in the So-called Letter. "Nothing motivated me except the consideration of the truth and good customs of our public life."

That afternoon, the archbishop celebrated a Mass for Solvay employees and their families in his chapel. A month went by, and he celebrated another Mass with the

Above: Vatican II in session.

Right: Reaction in the Polish Communist press to the Letter of Reconciliation drafted by the Polish bishops.

counting on Pope Paul VI and the clergy of the whole world to come to the celebrations in Poland.

The Polish bishops wrote out invitations for the bishops from other countries and delivered them to their representatives in Rome. The invitation to the German bishops contained a special message, since it would be difficult to invite Germans in a Christian spirit of love without having first performed a mutual examination of conscience and expressed a mutual desire for forgiveness.

The text of this letter, edited mainly by archbishops Wojtyla and Kominck, was shown to their German counterparts before making it public. It consisted of a compilation of the damages inflicted by the Germans, as well as damages to Germans caused by Poles. It ended with the words "We forgive, and we ask forgiveness."

There was a pragmatic, as well as religious, reason for

same intention in the new church in Borek Falecki. He prayed for the employees of Solvay who had signed the letter and also for those who had not signed it. He forgave those who signed it, he said, because it brought to mind an incident in the Gospels from which he took counsel. When Jesus was standing accused in front of Annas, the high priest, and a servant slapped him in the face, Jesus said, "If I have spoken wrongly, testify to the wrong. But if I have spoken rightly, why do you strike me?"

EVALUATING THE YEAR

As 1965 came to a close, Archbishop Wojtyla gave a homily in the Church of St. Mary in Kraków. He said that the most important event of the year had been the Vatican II Council, which had just finished its work a few weeks before. This council "took up the great labors of Jesus Christ to unify the church and Christianity," he said, not knowing these words would foreshadow the main objectives of his future pontificate.

Saint Thomas Aquinas

Saint Thomas was both inspiration and challenge to Karol Wojtyla during his years at the Angelicum, the Vatican university devoted to Thomist teachings. The great doctor of the church had enormous influence on the future pope's intellectual development, and an understanding of Aquinas's life and philosophy is integral to understanding the meaning of John Paul II's papacy.

Born to great wealth and position, probably in 1225, Thomas Aquinas was the son of Landulph, count of Aquino and Theodora, Countess of Teano. When he was five, his parents sent him to be educated at the Benedictine Monastery in Monte Cassino, as was the custom of the times. Clearly a gifted child, he had an early bent toward meditation and prayer.

The abbot believed the young boy to be truly gifted and in 1236 insisted that Thomas, not yet twelve, be sent to the University of Naples. There he studied grammar, rhetoric, the natural sciences, mathematics, geometry, and astronomy, blazing a path Wojtyla would follow in his own education. Before the age of seventeen, he decided to become a priest.

His chosen path was not an easy one, however. When he joined the Dominicans as a poor friar, his mother was so outraged that she instructed his brothers, who were soldiers under the emperor Frederick II, to kidnap him. Thomas was kept in the fortress of San Giovanni at Rocca Secca for almost two years, while his family worked to destroy his chances of pursuing a religious life. His brothers went so far as to introduce a "temptress" into his cell, but Thomas would not be seduced. Later in life he would tell a friend that when he fell asleep after the temptress left, two angels came and placed a white girdle around his loins, assuring him of perpetual virginity.

Finally his mother relented, and his superiors sent him to Rome, where Pope Innocent IV interviewed him and ultimately banned any further interference with the young man's decision. Thomas continued his education in Cologne, where he studied under Albert Magnus, the most famous Benedictine scholar of the age, and after five years in Cologne, in 1250 Thomas was consecrated a priest.

Next he went to Paris, where he arrived at the height of a dispute at the city's university, which delayed his getting a doctorate until 1257. By then Thomas Aquinas had become a renowned preacher, teacher, and theologian in demand at all of Europe's major universities and at the Vatican, where he served as the pope's spiritual advisor. Interestingly, he turned down an appointment as archbishop of Naples in order to complete his magisterial masterpiece, the *Summa Theologica*.

As he got older, he was frequently in a condition of ecstasy that grew so strong that he stopped writing altogether, and in December 1273, he began to prepare for death. His reply when asked to continue writing was simple: "I can do no more. Such secrets have been revealed to me that all I have written now appears to be of little value." But that was hardly the judgment of posterity.

During his lifetime Saint Thomas brought the works of Aristotle into Western Europe. After its welcome translation into Latin, he took the Greek philosopher's arguments to their deepest level. Faith and experience, he argued, are compatible and even complementary. Revelation is the only source of some truth, such as the mystery of incarnation. But others, such as what material things are made of, can be found only through experience. Finally, a few truths, notably the existence of God, are made known through both faith and reason.

In the *Summa*, he gave proof of the existence of God "in pure actuality without potentiality" and, going far beyond traditional negative theology, claimed that God's goodness is far more than saying he is not evil. In part two Saint Thomas laid down principles of ethics that have influenced church teaching to this day.

Summing up his accomplishments, one scholar wrote, "His work marks one of the few great culminations in the history of philosophy. After Aquinas, Western philosophers could choose only between humbly following him and striking off in some altogether different direction."

Chapter 5

His Eminence, the Cardinal

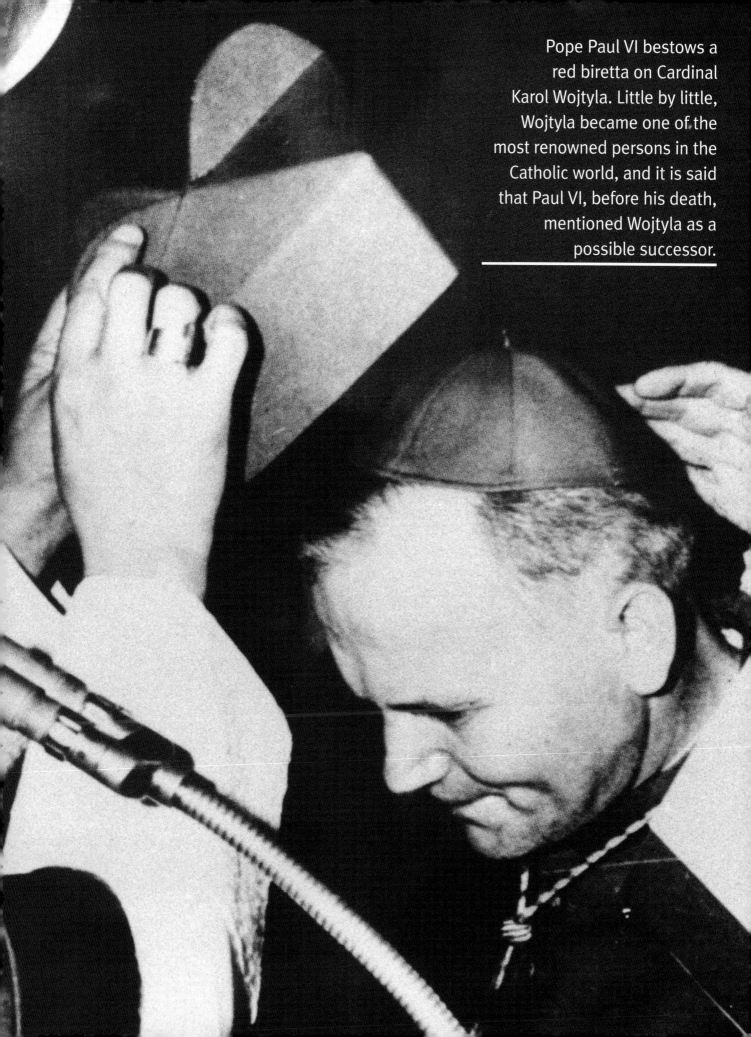

Pope Paul VI bestows a red biretta on Cardinal Karol Wojtyla. Little by little, Wojtyla became one of the most renowned persons in the Catholic world, and it is said that Paul VI, before his death, mentioned Wojtyla as a possible successor.

Cardinal Karol Wojtyla
with Bishop Edward
Head during a 1976 visit
to Buffalo, New York.

At the end of May 1967, Pope Paul VI called a consistory to enlarge the 93-member College of Cardinals by naming 27 new princes of the church. Two Polish names were on his list: John Krol, archbishop of Philadelphia, and Karol Wojtyla, archbishop of Kraków. They would receive their red hats, symbolizing their new office, on June 28, the eve of the Feast of Saint Peter and Saint Paul.

Wojtyla's elevation was a natural progression—nine bishops of Kraków, including his three predecessors, had all been cardinals. Nevertheless, there was some consternation. He was only forty-seven years old, and many in the church thought the pope should have waited a few more years before elevating him to the college.

THE TRIP TO ROME

Archbishop Wojtyla left Kraków for Rome on June 23, after having gone, a few days before, to the monastery at Kalawaria Zebrzydowska. He left a note in the visitors registry: "I came to the Mother of God in this monastery when I was a very young child, and I have been united to her ever since. Once again, I abandon myself to her."

He stopped off in Vienna to change trains and to visit Cardinal Franz König, the archbishop of Vienna, and he celebrated Mass in König's private chapel. The Viennese cardinal had known Wojtyla for several years, having first met him when Wojtyla had spent a few days in Vienna on his way to the opening session of the Vatican II Council in October 1962, but they did not know each other very well.

A year later, a few days after the death of Pope John XXIII, König went to Poland to visit with Polish bishops. A delegation met him at the border town of Cieszyn, but König did not recognize Wojtyla, then still the auxiliary bishop of Kraków—he was named archbishop on December 30, 1963. But they quickly forged a close relationship, mostly during later sessions of Vatican II, when König called his Kraków colleague "a very capable fellow."

A DEEP RELATIONSHIP

History and geography favored the relationship of the two men. The Hapsburg Empire may still live only in the minds of older people, but Galicia and Kraków had been part of that realm for almost 150 years, traces hard to eradicate. Moreover, the distance from Kraków to Warsaw is longer than that to Vienna, and the Austrian capital lies on the shortest road from Wawel Cathedral to St. Peter's Basilica.

Karol Wojtyla would often travel on this road, and he invariably interrupted his journey to see Cardinal König. After Wojtyla became pope, König's influence in his election was often discussed. Certainly Vienna's archbishop was not surprised when the Pole became a member of the College of Cardinals. (König himself was given his red hat in 1958.) König had firsthand knowledge of Wojtyla's talents, abilities, and personality. He had even read his

book, *Love and Responsibility*, which by the mid-'60s had been translated into several languages.

HOT-BUTTON TOPICS

At the time of the consistory that elevated Wojtyla, Pope Paul VI faced a major challenge—defining the church's position on marital and sexual ethics in light of modern sexual mores, and its stand on birth control and the population explosion, all hot-button topics. Like König, Paul VI had read *Love and Responsibility* and found its arguments on family values compelling. He invited Wojtyla to become a member of what was popularly known as the Birth Control Commission, but the group had a more formal title—the Commission on World Population, the Family, and Births.

The cardinal gives a homily in the student chapel of the Catholic University of Lublin during a ceremony honoring Cardinal John Krol of Philadelphia.

The archbishop could not attend the commission's meeting in 1966, because he had passport problems that prevented his leaving Poland. But he managed to participate by setting up his own commission in Kraków to serve as his intellectual base and sounding board. Under the leadership of Bishop Stanislaw Smolenski, the group was to examine the issues and submit its findings to the Vatican II Council.

Over time it became clear that the Poles would come to conclusions very different from those reached in Rome.

The Vatican commissioners would have allowed married Catholic couples to use birth control, and their view became known as the "majority," or "liberal," position. The Kraków commission adopted a contrary "minority," or "conservative," stance, arguing that artificial birth control is immoral and that the "rhythm method"—the use of a

woman's natural reproductive cycle—was the only permitted way to regulate pregnancy.

The church in Osjak, Austria. Legend has it that King Boleslaw the Brave came here to do penance after he murdered Saint Stanislaw.

That may have been the minority view, but it was the one shared by Pope Paul VI, who did not, however, want to turn down the majority option without a thorough discussion. The Wojtyla commission's work gave the pope the basis he needed for formulating the most controversial encyclical of his reign: *Humanae Vitae (Of Human Life)*. Wojtyla, incidentally, had a strong hand in writing that document.

WOJTYLA'S OTHER VIRTUES

But Wojtyla's stand on birth control was not the only reason Paul VI made him a cardinal. His voice was being heard across the church. He became more deeply involved in other projects assigned to Vatican commissions, and most important, the pope thought very highly of him.

Their personal relationship went back to the opening session of Vatican II, during John XXIII's pontificate, when Wojtyla was still the auxiliary bishop of Kraków.

Students at the Collegiate Church of St. Florian had asked their bishop to support a new initiative—new bells for the church. When he met with Cardinal Montini, then archbishop of Milan, he gave him the student petition and asked for his help. Montini had a longstanding interest in Poland dating back to his diplomatic service there in the 1920s. He remembered that the Germans had melted down all the bells during World War I to make cannons and that new ones were hard to come by. He promised to help, and in due course, in 1964, three bells arrived from Milan and were hung in St. Florian's bell tower.

During a private audience with Paul VI during Vatican II, Bishop Wojtyla gave the pontiff a scrapbook with Polish photographs as a present. The pope browsed through the pages with great interest. When he found pictures of the large crowds of Catholics gathered at various holy places in the country, he said to his secretary, "Look, this is only possible in Poland." And indeed Paul VI always thought of the Polish people as a "holy nation." As pope, he blessed the cornerstone of a new church built in Nowa Huta, the workers' housing complex near Kraków.

In another private conversation in the spring of 1967, the pope nominated Wojtyla to the Commission of the

Monsignor Giovanni Battista Montini, the future Pope Paul VI.

Laity and made him a consultant to the group. A month later he announced Wojtyla's appointment as a prince of the church.

THE COMMUNIST PROSPECTIVE

Communist leaders in Warsaw thought the move was politically motivated. A few weeks before, two Vatican prelates, Agostino Casaroli and Andrzej Deskur, both future cardinals, had come to Poland at Cardinal Wyszynski's invitation to help reestablish regular diplomatic relations between Warsaw and the Vatican. Communist propaganda now suggested that the Polish government was behind the nomination of a second Polish cardinal.

That may have been true, but Warsaw clearly did not want the red hat to go to Archbishop Wojtyla. Since he first became a bishop, he had never done anything the Communist regime had wanted him to do, and he had carefully avoided any rift with the primate, making sure to remain in Wyszynski's shadow and never involving himself in Communist politics.

PLEASE SPEAK POLISH

On the morning of June 25, 1967, Karol Wojtyla, still wearing his bishop's garb, climbed down from his carriage at the Stazione Termini in Rome. He was greeted by a group of Polish priests with bunches of crimson flowers in their hands. The next day Cardinal Amleto Cicognani, the Vatican secretary of state, presented him and the other 25 new cardinals with copies of their nomination decrees, and then, in the Sistine Chapel, the pope gave each of them the coveted red biretta. The next day the new cardinals celebrated Mass and received rings from the pope. A few days later, during an audience with Polish pilgrims, the pope remembered his days in Warsaw and asked Cardinal Wojtyla to please speak to him in Polish.

On July 2 Cardinal Wojtyla gave thanks for his elevation in a homily he delivered in the Church of St. Stanislaw in Rome, and what he said would have great resonance in years to come: "Each of us has a vocation to live and a task to fulfill in life. Both are important for everyone because the valor of a person is contained in each of them. I also have to pass the test of valor and run to the finish line along the pathway of my vocation."

On his way back to Poland in early July, he stopped off once again in Vienna to spend a few days with Cardinal König. He went to the church on the Kahlenberg that overlooks the city and then on to the Marian shrine at Mariazell before visiting the site of the concentration camp at Mauthausen.

HONORING HIS HERITAGE

Before returning to Kraków, he celebrated Mass in the church in Osjak, where, according to legend, the tomb of Boleslaw the Brave is located. After the Polish king had killed Saint Stanislaw, the first bishop of Kraków, he fled to this town, where he spent the last years of his life. Legend also has it that he repented for his crime and became a humble monk who dedicated himself to God.

On July 9, during his solemn celebration as cardinal in Wawel Cathedral, Wojtyla said in his homily, "Saint Stanislaw, martyr, was the first to trace the red sign of the cardinal bishops of Kraków in the sand with his blood. He is God's gift to the church."

Father Wojtyla looked very young when he taught at the Catholic University of Lublin. He seemed like just another student.

Cardinal Karol Wojtyla grew closer to Pope Paul VI. He was not only archbishop of Kraków, but he had now become an honorary citizen of Rome. According to tradition, each prince of the church receives a titular church in the Eternal City. Cardinal Wojtyla's church, St. Cesareo, on the Palatine Hill, was not very big, but it was very ancient, dating back to the seventh century. He was to take "canonical" possession of the church in the fall of 1967, not three months after having received his red hat, but Communist politics interfered.

In September Paul VI summoned the first synod of bishops to Rome to discuss ecclesiastical matters. Poland's leading bishops were eager to attend, but the government refused to give the primate, Cardinal Wyszynski, a passport, hoping to provoke conflict among the Polish hierarchy. But those hopes were dashed. Wojtyla and Piotr Kalwa, the titular bishop of Lublin, refused to go in a show of solidarity. Neither prelate would assume

The Church in the Real World
—Cardinal Franciszek Macharski

I have often asked myself a question all bishops ask themselves: "What kind of a church do you belong to?" My answer is anchored in the lives and works of three bishops of Kraków: Saint Stanislaw, Cardinal Sapieha, and Cardinal Wojtyla.

John Paul II named me archbishop of Kraków on December 29, 1978, the third month of his pontificate. When I arrived at the Episcopal residence in Franciszkanska Street after my consecration as bishop, nothing had changed since the cardinal had left for the conclave in Rome.

I arrived late at night. I knew this building well and headed straight for the chapel, groping in the dark for the door keys that I knew would be in his desk. I did the same thing Sapieha and Wojtyla would have done.

In Kraków we are all aware that the church, like any other institution, grows on existing foundations, foundations that in theological terms are laid out according to the wisdom of God.

When I became archbishop, we were just beginning the seventh year of the Pastoral Synod that Cardinal Wojtyla had initiated to commemorate the 900th anniversary of Saint Stanislaw's martyrdom. The work was hard and difficult. Deliberations took a long time and involved many of God's people. But the very fact that our discussions took such a long time and came to such important conclusions left a profound impression on those who believed in faith and the understanding that derives from it.

Thus the first response of the church in Kraków to John Paul II's election was to remain faithful to the task he had entrusted to us.

I remember the month of June 1999. We were at Mass in Blonie, a neighborhood in Kraków. The Holy Father, now ill and feeble, was in Franciszkanska Street. For the millions of people who were present in Blonie Meadow—a vast urban greenery within Kraków's city limits—the physical absence of John Paul II became a spiritual presence.

In the Kraków diocese he informed the conscience of the faithful by teaching his flock how to find religious answers to changing times and the new situations they bring forth, and to do so in thought and deed. Poles were the first and best examples of how to adjust because when he came back to us as pope, everyone in Poland was freshly inspired, especially after the ceremonies held in Blonie in 1979, when he "administered the sacrament of confirmation to the whole nation," transferring to us the Holy Spirit's wisdom and power.

Cardinal Wojtyla taught us that the church, which grows in Christ, has to enter all aspects of the real world in order to bring to people the light of the Gospel of Christ through the mediation of the faithful. He also taught us how to organize the apostolate of the laity and to find the best ways to carry out its mission. Some things he preached were new for us at the time: the dignity of human beings, the holiness of marriage and the miraculousness of family life when love was linked to responsibility, the primacy of the human being over social institutions, and the love of country that did not bar openness to other nations.

When the pope left Kraków in that June of 1979 after a three-day visit, he gave us a copy of his latest poem, "Stanislaw," one he wrote about his predecessor of long ago. It was a new way of looking at what had happened 900 years earlier, when violence and the sword spilled the blood of a martyr:

> On the soil of our liberty fell the sword,
> On the soil of our liberty fell the blood.
> Which weighed the most?

Wojtyla answers these questions about Saint Stanislaw in the last lines of the poem:

> Where did the name come from, received on behalf of the people,
> for the forefathers, for the nation, for Kraków,
> capital of the bishops
> for King Boleslaw, the brave and generous
> for the twentieth century.
> This name…

Everyone who read this poem knew that Karol Wojtyla was born into this world as a gift from the mercy of God.

responsibilities the primate had not given them. For Wojtyla it meant postponing the canonical ceremony of taking possession of the Church of St. Cesareo until February 18 of the following year.

CARDINAL WOJTYLA WENT THROUGH THE BRONZE DOORS
In February 1968, after the ceremonies at St. Cesareo, Cardinal Wojtyla walked through the bronze doors of the Vatican to meet with the Holy Father in a private audience. The subject of their discussion was the imminent publication of the encyclical *Humanae Vitae (Of Human Life)*. The encyclical would end the church debate over use of artificial contraception methods. Wojtyla's Kraków commission had provided the pope with much of the theoretical argument he would use in the document's final formulation. While the encyclical, published in July 1968, did not reflect Wojtyla's personalist mind-set, there is no doubt of the major contribution he and his fellow Polish scholars and theologians made to it.

THE SYNOD OF BISHOPS
Pope Paul VI convened the second session of the Synod of Bishops for the autumn of 1969, and this time the Communists did not put up any obstacles to Wojtyla's attendance. The synod—made up of bishops chosen by other bishops and by the pope—echoed Vatican II Council decrees but also established itself as a new element

in the ecclesiastical structure by clarifying its real purpose.

Derived from principles expounded in the encyclical *Lumen Gentium (The Dogmatic Constitution on the Church)*, which was promulgated in 1964, the synod was an expression of the collegial power exercised by the world's bishops

Cardinal Wojtyla's apartment in the archbishop's palace. Books were always everywhere.

"under the guidance of the Bishop of Rome." It also institutionalized the work of Vatican II—the documents the synod drafted often reflected the differences that had arisen during council debates.

Cardinal Wojtyla was an active participant in the synod from the day he attended its sessions for the first time in 1969. Two years later he was elected to the secretariat, which prepared the issues for synod discussions. He quickly established himself as a powerful force within the group of bishops and indeed within the worldwide church.

U.S. Cardinal John Krol (second from right), with U.S. cardinals Cooke, Deardon, Wright, and Carberry.

The theme of the first session Wojtyla attended in 1969 was the relationship between the papacy and the national conferences of bishops. The new cardinal viewed bishops not only as a group that had come together to solve problems but also as a spiritual community whose goals went far beyond the sociopolitical reality of the day.

CONFRONTING MARXISM
As a member of the Secretariat in 1971, Wojtyla called upon the bishops to pay greater attention to "local churches," including dioceses in Central and Eastern Europe. In 1974 he introduced a new and controversial topic, "Evangelization in the Modern (Current) World." The discussion revealed profound differences among bishops in approaching and confronting the Marxism that had become a powerful sociopolitical reality in the twentieth century.

Latin American and Western European bishops saw Marxism as a serious challenge in countries where poverty and oppression of the faithful were common. While rejecting Marxist ideology, they saw the doctrine as a viable means of combating poverty. The Latin

Americans especially adhered to liberation theology and its emphasis on helping the poor, even though it was linked to the left-wing ideology of "Social Liberation," which accepted armed struggle as a means to that end.

Cardinal Wojtyla and the Polish clergy, with their first-hand experience of Nazi and Communist totalitarianism, saw this position as one of naïve idealism. They remained firmly opposed to the use of force, even if the end seemed to justify the means. But as in the case of birth control, theirs was the minority position, belittled by others as too conservative. The Poles, they argued, did not understand political reality in Latin America. A few Western bishops, however, did take note of the Polish position and especially of the man who promulgated it.

Above: Cardinal Wojtyla talking with parishioners on New Year's Day 1970.

Right: The commemorative medal for the 900th anniversary of the murder of Saint Stanislaw.

HOUSES THAT MAKE ROOM FOR GOD

Wojtyla saw Vatican II as principally a religious and ecclesiastical event, and he never considered its political implications in the life of the church and the world. During the early session of the council in 1963 and 1964, he expressed his feelings through poetry. Later, as archbishop of Kraków, he took a more pragmatic approach, suggesting reforms that would make John XXIII's *aggioronamento* a reality in his archdiocese.

Five dioceses made up the metropolitan archdiocese of Kraków: Kraków itself, and the titular dioceses of Czestochowa, Katowice, Kielce, and Tarnów. Each had suffrage bishops who, as vicar-generals, administered them: Julian Groblicki (Wojtyla consecrated him as bishop while Archbishop Baziak was still alive), Jan

Pietraszko, Stanislaw Smolenski, and Albino Malysiak, all of them older than Wojtyla.

The Kraków Curia was divided into separate departments, along the lines of the Roman Curia, with its different ministries. Three such departments already existed: ecclesiastical governance of the clergy, religious instruction, and pastoral care. As archbishop, Wojtyla added two more: family life and charity. He also set up a pastoral youth center. One of his two secretaries handled administrative and financial affairs, the other ecclesiastical and civil legal matters.

HANDS-OFF ADMINISTRATION

Wojtyla himself was not much involved in the details of administration, which did not greatly interest him. Instead, he spearheaded new initiatives, inspired his coworkers to act, and demanded that they keep him informed of everything they did. He was the archdiocese's spiritual director and is remembered today more for the academic debate that flourished under his rule than for giving orders to others.

He summed up his pastoral feelings in a homily he delivered in November 1967, a few months after receiving the red hat, in Wadowice in the Church of the Blessed Virgin, just across the street from the house where he was born.

"All of us are laying the foundation of a new millennium of faith. As we place each brick, let us think about the house that will be built on that foundation for future generations. Let us think about how we are going to go about constructing this house, the house of God, and from which he will not be thrown out, which sometimes happens in human houses where there is no room for God."

There was one initiative as archbishop he could not complete, however. In 1971 he convoked a Pastoral Synod that was to deliberate until 1979 when the 900th anniversary of Saint Stanislaw's murder would be celebrated. By then Wojtyla had become Pope John Paul II, and the Communists were not about to let him return on so patriotic a day. He arrived a month later and was greeted by 3.5 million people.

IN AMERICA AND KANGAROO COUNTRY

In 1969 Cardinal Wojtyla made his first journey to North America, visiting Canada and the United States over a period of five weeks. The trip was something of an accident. Polish communities in the two countries had issued the original invitation to Cardinal Wyszynski, but the primate did not speak English and was uncomfortable at press conferences, so he suggested that Wojtyla go in his stead.

Wojtyla flew to Rome on August 26 and then on to Montreal. Several close friends accompanied him on his first transatlantic flight—Bishop Szczepan Wesoly; Father Stanislaw Dziwisz, his personal secretary in Kraków; and Father Franciszek Macharski, who would succeed Cardinal Wojtyla as archbishop.

Representatives of the local archbishop, the mayor, and the Polish-Canadian community were on hand to greet them when they arrived at the Dorval airport. For three weeks it was a symphony of receptions, excursions, cocktails, and conversations. From Montreal Cardinal Wojtyla flew to Quebec to meet the primate of Canada, Cardinal Maurice Roy. Ottawa was next, and then Wojtyla traveled across central Canada, ending his tour in Toronto. Given his tight schedule and his meetings with Polish-Canadian groups, he had little opportunity to get a taste of real life in Canada.

Crossing into the United States, he first visited Niagara Falls and then began his tour from Buffalo. Again he met mostly Polish-Americans, although he did touch base in major U.S. cities that had cardinals in place, including Boston, Chicago, Baltimore, St. Louis, New York, and Philadelphia, where he already knew Cardinal John Krol, a prelate of Polish descent who had been elevated to the College of Cardinals at the same consistory as Wojtyla.

BONDS OF POLISH TRADITIONS

The two men had another bond. Polish tradition demands that new Polish cardinals make a solemn entrance into their family's hometown. Although Krol was born in Cleveland, he decided to honor that tradition with a visit to Siekierczyna, a small town in the Tarnow diocese. However, Polish authorities refused him a visa, so in December 1967 Wojtyla went in his stead, delivering a homily stressing that he was in town as Krol's surrogate.

At the end of September 1969, Wojtyla returned to Rome to participate in an extraordinary session of the synod. Back in Poland, he talked about his trip during a homily in the Church of St. Mary:

Being among our compatriots thousands of miles from here, I realized that Poland is not just a geographical place. It's a spiritual community in the larger human family in which we Polish people have a particular contribution to make. We have Polish values to share, and they are special values. I realized this when I listened to

the Canadian and the U.S. bishops. They gave witness to what Polish people have brought to the church in Canada and the United States. Polish people continue to make a contribution.

Karol Wojtyla's philosophical work, *The Acting Person*, is published in 1969.

Fiftieth-anniversary celebrations at the Catholic University of Lublin in 1968.

He would visit the United States again in 1976 at the head of an 18-man delegation during the American bicentennial celebration and remain for seven weeks. It would be a busy time. Cardinal Krol took him to the Eucharistic Congress in Philadelphia and traveled across the country with him, visiting the seminary at Orchard Lake in Detroit, where priests ministering to the Polish community were educated. He also traveled to Catholic universities in Washington State, Wisconsin, and California.

He lectured at Harvard about "Engagement or Alienation" and met with Zbigniew Brzezinski, who would become President Jimmy Carter's national security adviser. Brzezinski even interrupted his vacation to come to Cambridge to see him, although the Polish-born scholar-diplomat usually avoided Polish bishops. When Wojtyla was elected pope, Brzezinski represented the United States at his inauguration ceremonies, and the two men met often during the Reagan administration.

Between these two trips to the New World, Wojtyla traveled to Asia and Australia. In 1973 he visited Manila in the Philippines—where Cardinal Sapieha had been in 1937—New Guinea, and New Zealand on his way to the Eucharistic Congress in Melbourne. There he met Mother Teresa, and wherever he went, he saw and spoke with local Poles.

Let Martyrdom Come Later

Stefan Wyszynski was primate of Poland during the church's most difficult years. As the cold war intensified, Soviet bloc countries stepped up their propaganda barrage against the Vatican and the church. Individual Communist countries chose different approaches in their efforts to annihilate church influence on society, but they always acted under the Kremlin's overall direction.

Wyszynski, the forty-seven-year-old bishop of Lublin, became primate in 1948 when church-state relations were most tense. The Communists accused the church of "meddling in the affairs of the state" and of "cultivating a reactionary political attitude among the faithful."

Many workers took part in the Communist May 1 parade. The consequences of not attending this "spontaneous movement" are easy to imagine.

Trybuna Ludu, the official Communist newspaper, wrote: We will react only against this one act of insurgency, which any progressive person would judge to be harmful." The words "only against this one act of insurgency" were meant as a Communist act of "kindness and generosity." But it quickly became apparent that anything could be interpreted as "an act against the state," including religious ceremonies and large church gatherings.

From the day he took over the primate's office, therefore, Wyszynski had to defend his church and his faith. He began the battle with "little steps" that would give him final victory in 30 years' time.

IT'S BETTER TO KNOW HOW TO LIVE THAN TO LEARN HOW TO DIE

It wasn't easy to lead the church in the midst of Communist terror. The church had been cowed in Hungary, Yugoslavia, and Czechoslovakia. But Wyszynski adopted a different tactic than the one his fellow bishops in Eastern Europe had used. He posed a basic question: How can we take care of the physical existence of the nation nearly destroyed by the war and at the same time protect its spirituality from totalitarian absolutism? He would ask himself that same question from the beginning to the end of the struggle.

Wyszynski's answer was this: "If God is asking us to become martyrs again, we will shed our blood unstintingly. But I think that the ideal for our times is to know how to live for the church and for Poland, rather than learn how to die. We have already shown that we know how to die for the church and for Poland. We proved that in Dachau and the Warsaw Uprising. Martyrdom is a grace and an honor. But when I think of the great challenges and the needs of Catholic Poland today, I prefer that martyrdom be delayed for as long as possible."

Political trials and harsh sentences became a common occurrence.

THERE'S STRENGTH IN TRANQUILLITY

Wyszynski knew that the struggle would last for a long time, and that was the secret of his victory. He chose the slow road of operating within the law and in political reality. He did not negotiate vague agreements with the Communists. What concessions he made were limited, and what rights for the church he achieved were clearly laid out in the terms of any agreements that he concluded.

From the beginning the regime wanted the support of the church in order to increase its popularity, and it was willing to compromise to achieve that end. Teaching of religion was permitted in public schools. Catholic schools and organizations were allowed to operate, as was the Catholic media.

When the first such agreement was signed in 1950, some in the clergy opposed it. But Wyszynski felt strongly that the church needed a political and legally documented agreement that would provide a basis for discussion whenever new church-state conflict arose.

The agreement did ease the situation of the Polish church for some time, and it gave the government what it wanted—a declaration that said, "The Polish bishops affirm that economic, historic, cultural, and religious rights, as well as historic justice, require that the Reclaimed Lands will belong forever to Poland."

This was a major political issue at the time, since Poland had acquired vast German territories after the war and the government went all out to prevent the Germans from ever getting the ceded land returned.

But the declaration was not enough. The Communists wanted the primate to persuade the Vatican to establish Polish ecclesiastic administration over the Reclaimed Lands. And they also wanted to create a rift between the Polish church and the Holy See as well as between the church and the people. They underestimated the primate, however. He knew how to play this game masterfully, and he used the strength of his tranquillity to outfox his opponents.

The Communist press ridiculed the church and the Vatican, often in vulgar ways. (Cartoon: *Sztandar Ludu,* 1954)

He began to pay a lot of attention to the church in the new territories, frequently visiting the faithful in the western dioceses, thus crossing Communist propaganda that the Polish bishops and the Vatican were ignoring the area. He also explained his tactics to Pope Pius XII, who was reluctant to go that far but was willing to appoint a provisional administration and to tolerate the primate's efforts to coexist with the Communist regime. Wyszynski finally persuaded Pope Paul VI in 1972 to install a permanent Polish ecclesiastic administration. The move, he argued, was supremely important for the universal church and for Poland.

WE WILL NOT ACCEPT THIS!

Wyszynski's calm political realism did not always suit his own clergy. Some did not understand his "increasingly conciliatory" behavior. Was it, for example, really necessary to congratulate President Boleslaw Bierut on his seventieth birthday, given all the troubles the church faced in 1952?

Wyszynski understood the widespread confusion his policies were causing, so he went all out to convince people he was on their side and to fully explain his actions.

On August 15, 1952, on the feast of the Assumption of Mary, an immense crowd of Catholics gathered at the monastery of Jasna Góra in southern Poland, the site of the Black Madonna of Czestochowa, the country's most revered Catholic icon. Cardinal Wyszynski delivered a visionary homily about human dignity and human rights.

Despite open and covert reprisals against the church, the government authorities tried to keep up appearances.

Among other things, he talked about "the right to live, the right to believe in God, the right to know the truth, the right to love and the right to freely choose a form of government, the right to choose one's path and career in life, the right to peace in family life, the right to freedom of the homeland, and the right to be loyal to the homeland, and the right to struggle in the homeland."

For the Communists this was incendiary, a call to renewed Catholic opposition to their rule.

Open warfare followed quickly. In early 1953 false accusations were routinely fired at the church. Priests were arrested on the flimsiest pretexts. Bishop Czeslaw Kaczmarek of Kielce had been held for two years and still was not put on trial. He would be sentenced to 12 years later that year. Churches were raided. A new propaganda blitz was launched against the hierarchy. The regime tried to overturn church decisions—refusing to recognize new parishes the bishops had set up, for example, and blocking nominations to church offices.

The government confiscated church property and wealth. They intensified campaigns to close down churches, banned religious instruction in schools, and closed the Catholic press. The archbishop, named to the College of Cardinals the month before, was harassed and scoffed. On February 16, 1953, officials stopped him in the street. "What's your name?" one of them asked scornfully, and rudely demanded to see his papers. Respectfully the prelate did as he was asked.

Conversations with high government officials grew more and more confrontational, but they were unable to goad Wyszynski to reply in kind. He stuck to his polite stance but refused to compromise on basic principles. Efforts to divide the Catholic clergy enjoyed some success. Priests did join the Patriotic Priests movement, but those who did were promptly excommunicated.

Finally, on May 8, 1953, Wyszynski struck back. Speaking on behalf of the Conference of Polish Bishops, the primate defiantly declared, *"Non possumus!"* (We will not accept this!) Inevitably his defiance led to his arrest. "People in the nation were waiting for this moment," he wrote in his *Notes from Prison.* "More than once I found people crying in their churches." Clearly, peaceful co-existence between the church and Communism was becoming impossible.

The explosion would come in September, just six months after Stalin's death. On the eighteenth Wyszynski had again gone to Jasna Góra, where he spoke at the plenary session of the Conference of Polish Bishops, saying, "I prefer to be in prison than being someone who is privileged, because suffering in prison brings me closer to those who are suffering. Being well off encourages people to abandon the straight path the church must tread, the path of truth and love."

After saying Mass in St. Anna's Church a week later, on September 25, 1953, he told students, "Please say the Rosary for me." He knew trouble was imminent, and so did many people who had heard his sermon. Many stayed out in front of the church until way into the middle of the night, as if they knew what would happen, as if they knew about the decision the government had made the day before.

In the middle of the night, the secret police entered the primate's residence. Wyszynski was calm, asking only why they had come so late to visit him. His dog, Baca, was less friendly. He bit one of the intruders. Wyszynski assured the policeman that his dog had been vaccinated against rabies and tended his wound.

DON'T BELIEVE THEM!

The police allowed him to pack. He didn't have much, never having received the cardinal's red biretta or ornaments. (He would only get them years later.) He took his breviary, his Rosary beads, and a thick overcoat. Six automobiles escorted the primate to "isolation quarters."

As a prisoner—he was held in several monasteries under "house arrest"—the cardinal protested against his illegal confinement, but he did so in his calm fashion and he continued to feel free and strong. He had prepared well for his incarceration. Days before the secret police came for him, he had said, "When I am in prison and they say that I betrayed the works of God, don't believe them. If they say that my hands are dirty, don't believe them. If they say your primate is intimidated, don't believe them! If they say your primate acted against his nation and his fatherland, don't believe them!"

PRISON IS THE BEST PLACE FOR ME

Wyszynski bore his imprisonment with equanimity and without anger, though he did chafe at being cut off from his flock. Prison, he believed, did not exempt him from his responsibilities toward the church and the nation, and he wrote to the government over and over, demanding to know why he had been jailed. His letters were never answered.

The three years he spent in jail may have removed him from control of outside events, but they were not lost years. They would

A large crowd gathers in Jasna Góra in 1966 for the National Day of Prayer.

become an integral part of his biography and that of the history of Poland. His detention had political reverberations in his own country and throughout Europe, and there were political consequences.

In his *Notes from Prison,* he would write, "Every day I see more clearly that the best place for me at this time in my life is to be in prison." He knew how to take advantage of his incarceration and eschewed self-pity. He did not seek fame, and he didn't consider himself a martyr. He prayed, meditated, and worked.

He also took time to think about a new pastoral program for his captive nation and how to create it. In his "Act of Abandoning Myself to the Most Holy Blessed Mother," written on December 8, 1953, Wyszynski petitioned the Blessed Mother: "I beg you to have me forever as your servant and son. Be my help in all my physical and spiritual needs, as well as in my priestly labor for others."

In 1956, while the cardinal was still imprisoned, preparations were under way to celebrate the 300th anniversary of the oath King Jan II Kazimierz took on April 1, 1656, in the Lemberg Cathedral to celebrate a Polish victory over Sweden. In that oath he put all the lands of his kingdom under the protection of the mother of God and declared her to be the patron saint and queen of Poland.

When news of the preparations reached Wyszynski, he buckled down to draft a new text for the king's oath: in effect a new Marian program for the nation. "The idea of rethinking Jan II Kazimierz's Oath on his tercentennial celebrations," he would write, "was born in my soul in the place where 300 years ago the king and the primate at the time thought about how to liberate the nation from a double disgrace: foreign invasion and social misery."

He completed the text of the new Oath of Jasna Góra early in 1956, and in it he was already looking ahead to the millennium of Catholicism in Poland 10 years hence, which "The Abandonment of Poland to the Servitude of the Most Holy Mother, for the Liberty of the Church in Poland and in the Whole World" would serve. The oath would be part of his conception of a Grand Novena to celebrate the millennium, renew the nation's spirituality, and achieve for the church the victory of faith and freedom.

A THREAT TO THE REGIME

On August 26, 1956, more than a million people came to Czestochowa for a solemn renewal of the oath at the shrine of Jasna Góra—"Queen of Poland, we pledge our allegiance to you"—and to pray for the primate's early release. On October 26, 1956, their prayers were heard. The primate was freed as part of Poland's "spring in October" defiance of Moscow under the leadership of Wladyslaw Gomulka, the new party leader. It marked the beginning of a new church-state relationship in Poland.

Komancza, the abbey of the Sisters of Nazareth, is the last place where Cardinal Wyszynski was held prisoner.

HIDDEN EXAM

During the winter of 1953, three researchers at the Nuclear Physics Institute of the Jagiellonian University invited Father Wojtyla to go skiing with them. They had met during a seminar on Saint Thomas Aquinas that he had organized for science students, and they wanted to get to know him better, although the purpose of this invitation was to see if he could ski, but Wojtyla did not know this.

He hadn't gone skiing since high school, but nevertheless he gladly accepted their invitation. He had one problem, however. His shoes did not fit the ski bindings. So one of the young physicists took the bindings to a university workshop and had them adjusted. Once on the slopes, Wojtyla had no trouble remembering his school-day skills, and the outing was the start of a close friendship between the priest-philosopher and the physicists.

Future ski trips turned into fruitful seminars, where Wojtyla satisfied his long-held scientific curiosity about the material world that dated back to his childhood, while the physicists were able to add a transcendental dimension to the exact sciences. These discussions continued for many years while both the priest and the physicists rose through the ranks of their chosen professions—one became a bishop, the others renowned scientists with degrees and titles.

Above: Cardinal Wojtyla among a gathering of U.S. and Polish cardinals in Rome on the 25th anniversary of John Krol as bishop.

Above, right: a note inviting the Polish bishops to visit Canada in 1976.

Eventually the physicists moved closer to the archbishop's palace, where they often met, bringing engineers and other scientists with them. As archbishop, Wojtyla did not limit these informal seminars to the sciences but brought in historians and philosophers to join their discussions. It was a habit he took to the Vatican, where he continued his conversations with scholars.

THE INSTITUTE OF HUMAN SCIENCES

In the spring of 1981, he put his support behind the idea one member of his circle, Krzysztof Michalski, had of putting this seminal exchange of ideas on a more organized basis and to include people from other countries. The pontiff enlisted Vienna's cardinal König, who helped found the Institute of Human Sciences in Vienna, shortly after martial law was declared in Poland.

Over the years, the institute has developed along the lines the pope laid down—meaning no clearly defined political or religious orientation—and thus allowing a free exchange of ideas among participants. Since 1983 the institute has organized conferences in the pope's summer retreat at Castel Gandolfo, which brings together scientists and other scholars from East and West, with John Paul II often taking a direct part in its deliberations.

THE LENTEN RETREAT SERVICES

In 1976 Pope Paul VI invited Cardinal Wojtyla to direct the Lenten retreat services in the Vatican. Retreats were held each year behind closed doors, and the Holy Father and his most important colleagues in the Roman Curia attended them. The invitation was a great distinction, but the month it was issued—February—didn't leave Wojtyla much time to prepare. He went to the Polish winter resort in Zakopane for a week to plan the retreat.

There he started his days with Mass at the Ursuline Sisters' convent, where he was staying, as he always did, and then he buckled down to work with Father Tadeusz to outline the 22 conferences he had to organize in the Papal Palace.

After returning to Kraków for a Conference of Polish Bishops, the cardinal resumed work at his residence after the conference concluded. In Rome he settled into the Polish College to put in four more days of labor. The day before the retreat began, he went to pray at the Marian Seminary of Mentorelli, outside Rome.

Cardinal Wojtyla delivered his first presentation on the evening of March 7 in St. Matilda's Chapel in the Papal Palace, with the Holy Father and the highest dignitaries of the Roman Curia in attendance. The themes for the 22 conferences in the Lenten cycle that Wojtyla had chosen were close to his thoughts and very familiar to him: the mystery of humanity in the presence of the mystery of the Incarnate Word. In developing his theme, Cardinal Wojtyla used theological writings, his own observations, and his experience as a confessor.

He hoped to describe the greatness and dignity of humanity and the human aspiration to encounter God by means of conversion, or a turning toward God. The retreat made an excellent impression not only on those who attended but also on those living beyond the walls of the Vatican, since his presentation found a wide readership upon publication. After the retreat Wojtyla met once more with Paul VI—it would be their last meeting—and then went back to the seminary at Mentorelli.

THE HOLY FATHER KEPT AN OLD POLISH ALARM CLOCK

Paul VI died on the night of August 6, 1978, in his summer residence at Castel Gandolfo. By his bedside was an old alarm clock he had bought in Warsaw when he served there as a Vatican diplomat 55 years before. When the pope received Holy Communion for the last time and commended his soul to God, the old alarm clock began to ring and no one knew whether to stop it or let it ring itself out. Finally it fell silent, and the secretary of state, Cardinal Jean Villot, certified that Paul VI, eighty-one years old at the time, had died.

On August 7, 1978, Cardinal Wojtyla was on vacation with friends when he heard the news of the pope's death on the radio. He left at once for Kraków and then for Rome, with Cardinal Wyszynski and a Polish government delegation. Paul VI was buried on August 12, and for the first time services were held not in St. Peter's Basilica but in the vast plaza outside it, where an altar had been set up for the funeral Mass. The conclave began two weeks later, on August 25.

HE NEITHER AFFIRMED NOR DENIED

The archbishop of Kraków's name had been mentioned more than once as a possible future pope. Both Italian and American media speculated about his chances for election, but Wojtyla never did. He never talked or joked about it; nor did he seem terribly interested in the prospect. But it was clear that the speculation made him uncomfortable.

His old friend Stefan Swiezawski, the professor at the Catholic University in Lublin who had persuaded Wojtyla to teach in the school's ethics department when he was a young priest and a promising theologian, brought up the subject while listening to a homily the cardinal gave at an International Thomist Congress in the Abbey of Fossanuova in Italy (where Thomas Aquinas had died). "He's going to be pope," Swiezawski told his wife, and then he repeated his prediction to his friend. Wojtyla looked him straight in the eye and then moved away without saying anything. For Swiezawski the reaction seemed to say, "I neither affirm nor deny the possibility."

Since Paul VI had been sick for some time, his death was not unexpected. He had talked about a number of possible successors, and of course speculation mounted after he died. But no one really expected that the centuries-old tradition of electing one of the Italian cardinals to the Throne of Saint Peter would be broken.

A few cardinals—Archbishop König of Vienna was one of them—did suggest that it might be time to pick a non-Italian, but the idea was not taken seriously. The consensus was that the new pope would again be an Italian, even though no one candidate emerged as a favorite. Speculation centered on the next pontiff's ideological position—would he be a conservative or a progressive?

The press mentioned several cardinals as *"papabili,"* meaning they might be viable candidates. Cardinal Giovanni Benelli of Florence was one prominent candidate. He had been one of Paul VI's closest collaborators

Cardinal Wojtyla visited Australia in 1973, where he stopped off at Melbourne, Sydney, and Canberra.

and served as undersecretary of state. But he had only been cardinal for a year, and at fifty-seven he was considered too young. Many in the college favored Cardinal Giuseppe Siri, a critic of Vatican II. But the late pontiff had introduced reforms to the conclave likely to block Siri's path to the papal throne.

The winner would need two-thirds of 120 votes—the full complement of the College of Cardinals. But only 111 were in attendance. Some were too sick to come; others were over eighty years old and barred from voting under Paul VI's reforms. Under the circumstances Siri could not rally enough opponents of the changes the council had approved. The new rules would favor a centrist candidate who would be able to bring together both sides of a deeply divided college.

THE SMOKE WAS GRAY

At five thirty on August 25, 1978, Cardinal Wojtyla walked into the Sistine Chapel as one of the papal electors. He expected a long conclave, telling his personal secretary, Father Stanislaw Dziwisz, and the other person on his staff, (future) Bishop Stanislaw Ryla, that he might be gone for some time. They went on vacation, while Wojtyla began his long march to a new destiny, no matter how remote it seemed at the time.

Popular opinion believes that the deceased pontiff exercises great influence in the election of his successor, holding that in their declining years, popes give indirect signals pointing to their choice for the papacy. And in fact, the language cardinals and bishops use has room for allusions, euphemisms, symbols, and allegory. As a rule, therefore, it is possible, after the election, to point to some secret signals the late pontiff had given. Paul VI, it was said, had given his dying voice to two cardinals. One of them was Cardinal Albino Luciani, patriarch of Venice and thus successor to Pope Pius X (later declared Saint Pius X) in the metropolitan diocese of Venice.

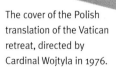

A RELUCTANT POPE

The conclave elected Cardinal Luciani on the fourth ballot of the first day. He accepted the election, but not gladly, and more as an act of humility for the church. (Humility was this bishop's motto.) He clearly felt that the conclave had not made the best selection.

The cover of the Polish translation of the Vatican retreat, directed by Cardinal Wojtyla in 1976.

A photograph of the funeral of Pope Paul VI (1897–1978). During his pontificate he wrote the encyclicals *Ecclesiam Suam (On the Church), Populorum Progressio (On the Development of Peoples),* and *Humanae Vitae (On Human Life).*

Before his fellow cardinals asked him if he accepted his election, he said, "May God forgive them for what they have done." Then he announced that he would take the name of John Paul I.

Perhaps he was not the only one to express doubt—smoke coming from the chimney of the Sistine Chapel seemed to do the same thing. Traditionally it belches white smoke upon the election of a pope, black smoke to signal that the cardinals are still deliberating. This time the color of the smoke was gray, and it stayed gray four times. The vast crowd that gathered on St. Peter's Square had no idea what this smoky ambiguity meant.

The Pope and His Ties to *Tygodnik Powszechny*

The first edition of *Tygodnik Powszechny (Universal Weekly)*, the liberal Catholic magazine, was published on March 24, 1945, and it has been going strong ever since, despite its decades-long opposition to Poland's Communist regime.

The editors first ran into serious trouble when they refused to publish a full-scale article about Joseph Stalin's death in 1953, limiting coverage to a short obituary. The incensed Communists shut the weekly down and only allowed it to reopen when Wladislaw Gomulka became party leader in 1956 and inaugurated a period of relaxation between church and state. Jerzy Turowicz, the founding editor, returned and stayed at the magazine's helm until 1999.

The weekly's close ties to the future pope began in 1949 when it published his first article, "Is France a Missionary Country?" based on Wojtyla's experience with the worker-priest movement in that country. He continued to write in the weekly, publishing his first poetry in 1950 and an article about his mentor, Jan Tyranowski. Interviews, homilies, and open letters to the editor followed. He even reported on Vatican II for *Tygodnik Powszechny* because the government refused to give Turowicz a passport, and he collaborated with the editor on the Press Study Commission.

As a cardinal, Wojtyla often defended the weekly against Communist attack. In 1977 he had the magazine publish a sermon he delivered after the tragic death of Stanislaw Pyjas, a student who worked with the Committee in Defense of the Workers. During his Corpus Christi Mass that year, he praised both *Tygodnik Powszechny* and the Catholic literary magazine *Znak (The Sign)* for the contributions they had made to the church. And of course, *Tygodnik* gave extensive coverage to Wojtyla's election as pope.

After martial law was declared in 1980, the periodical was shut down again but was revived in 1982. Things changed after Communism fell in 1989. *Tygodnik Powszechny* began to adopt a more liberal line that did not please the church or the magazine's one-time defender, the pope.

On the weekly's fiftieth anniversary in 1995, the pontiff wrote Turowicz a letter summing up his feelings about what had once almost been his house organ:

The year of 1989 brought many profound changes in Poland because of the fall of the Communist system. Liberty came back to life, but did so in a paradoxical form. Liberal and leftist lay groups intensified their attacks against the church, the bishops, and the pope. I had warned about this in my last visit to Poland in 1991.

Everything was now geared to blotting out the memory of what the church had meant in the life of the people during Communist rule. The church was accused of plotting to govern Poland or to put brakes on the political emancipation of Polish society. Tygodnik Powszechny *reflects the influence of these currents of thought.*

At this difficult time, the church does not find in Tygodnik Powszechny *a defender and supporter, which, to a certain degree, it has the right to expect. The church does not feel it is well thought of. I write this in sadness because the fate and future of* Tygodnik Powszechny *is dear to my heart.*

Inaugural ceremony of the third session of the Ecumenical Vatican II Council in Rome on September 14, 1964.

The Holy Father criticized *Tygodnik Powszechny*, but he always respected the weekly magazine and greatly admired Jerzy Turowicz.

Confusion grew in St. Peter's Square until the Holy Father appeared, surrounded by his retinue, on the balcony of the basilica. Cardinal Pericle Felici stepped forward to proclaim the traditional words, *"Habemus papam"* (We have a pope), and he gave the name of the cardinal who had just been elected, as well as the name he had taken, John Paul I.

The solemn inauguration took place on September 3.

John Paul I declined the traditional coronation ceremony that emphasized the power of the pope as an absolute monarch. Instead of the pomp and circumstances, he opted for a solemn religious ceremony. He had done that before. When he was named patriarch of Venice in 1969, he had declined to lead the sumptuous parade of gondolas during his installation. Now, as pope, he wanted to simplify Vatican protocol.

Cardinal Wojtyla celebrates a solemn Mass in honor of Saint Waclaw in Wawel Cathedral on his twentieth anniversary as a bishop in 1978.

UNCLE WILL ALWAYS BE THEIR UNCLE

Karol Wojtyla arrived back in Kraków on September 6, after a private audience with John Paul I. Two weeks later he joined a delegation of Polish bishops, including Cardinal Wyszynski and the bishops Jerzy Stroba and Wladislaw Rubin, for meetings with West German prelates. They traveled first to Cologne to meet with its archbishop, Cardinal Joseph Häffner, president of the Conference of German Bishops. Then they moved on to Munich, Maguncia, and Dachau. In Fulda Wojtyla spoke at the tomb of Saint Boniface, apostle of Germany, before the assembled German cardinals and bishops: "I stand next to this stone which symbolizes the advancement of the Gospel in the first millennium. Let us ask the Immortal King of the Centuries and the Savior of Our Souls, in the shadow of the third millennium after Jesus Christ, to open new roads to the future, so that the hearts of all persons, nations, and races will bear fruit and receive life which is stronger than death."

He would express his thoughts in the same way once he became pope, although no one could then imagine just how close his pontificate was.

Upon his return from Germany, he celebrated the twentieth anniversary of his consecration as bishop in a Mass at Wawel Cathedral on September 27.

"In a strange way, the holy martyrs unite in a single

fountain of spirituality, the example of Christ," he said during his homily, referring to Saint Waclaw and the bishop Saint Stanislaw, patrons of the cathedral. At seven in the evening, he officiated at the opening of the cathedral museum and then went to the home of some friends who wanted to celebrate his 20 years as bishop and spiritual guide in their own way. The theme for the evening was "Uncle will always be our uncle."

GOD'S DESIGNS ARE INSCRUTABLE

The next day before noon, Archbishop Wojtyla was scheduled to take part in the Council of the Pontifical Faculty of Theology, an institution that continued the tradition of the Theology Faculty of the Jagiellonian University. He got up early, as usual, said his prayers, and worked for a while before breakfast. As he was eating in the dining room, he heard noises coming from the kitchen. His chauffeur was talking about some astounding news, but Wojtyla's house staff didn't want to disturb him. Finally one of them came in and said, "Your Excellency, it seems incredible, but they just said it on the radio. The Holy Father just died." Cardinal Wojtyla was speechless for a moment; then he said, "God's designs are inscrutable. Let's bow our heads before them." Not waiting to finish his breakfast, he went to the chapel and prayed.

Earlier that morning in the Vatican, the sister who brought John Paul I his coffee every day, noticed that the cup she had put on the table next to his door had been left untouched. She knocked on the door, but there was no answer. Worried, she knocked again. Still no reply. She opened the door a little and saw the pope lying motionless

Pope John Paul I with Cardinal Wojtyla, who would succeed him as pope and take the name John Paul II.

in bed, holding a bunch of documents in his hand. She immediately went to tell his secretary, Monsignor John Magee. When he arrived in the pope's bedroom, he realized that the Holy Father was dead.

Jean Villot, the secretary of

state, immediately put together an "official" version of what happened for the media—Magee had found the deceased pope. Villot wanted to hide the fact that a woman was the first one to see the Holy Father in bed that morning. Although well intentioned, this was an anachronism, even for the Vatican, and the "official story" didn't last very long. Two years later, after John Magee had become a bishop, he let it be known that Sister Vincenzina was the first person to enter John Paul I's room. Also uncovered was the little white lie that the pontiff was holding a copy of *The Imitation of Christ,* written by the mystic Thomas à Kempis (380–1471), in his hands as he was dying.

John Paul I loved simplicity and hated artificiality. He probably would have resented the image cleansing his Vatican colleagues had undertaken. No one knows what documents the pope was reading when he went to sleep. Villot ordered all the pope's personal effects taken out of the papal apartment. Only Villot and two other persons knew what was in those documents, and they have kept the secret. Some people say they had to do with changes in the Roman Curia the pope was going to announce the following day, but no one can be sure.

REACTION IN KRAKÓW

Back in Kraków that day, Cardinal Wojtyla did not change his plans. When he left his chapel after praying for the deceased pontiff, he attended the Council of the Pontifical Faculty of Theology. Later in the day he traveled to a parish in Bielsko-Biala and did not return to Kraków until October 1, when he celebrated a Mass for the pope's intention. In his homily he said, "John Paul I was born to be a pope…and thinking of him, we find strength to face death."

I Should Have Been in Jail

—Albin Malysiak, Retired Auxiliary Bishop of Kraków

The Communist government put up as many obstacles as it could to prevent priests from doing their work. The red tape was incredible. The flow of mail and phone communications among the cardinal, the Curia, and the government's department of religion was incredible.

It was even worse before 1956 when for a time priests were forbidden to teach religion in schools and held catechism classes in churches instead. Bureaucrats from the Ministry of Education and secret police agents would ask us priests for the names of parents whose children attended. We were told to keep records and draw up lists of names. They even gave us special forms to fill out. Of course we never gave out such information.

As a result, I was interrogated very forcefully and even threatened with jail, down to being told to report to prison for my refusal to conform. But I was saved by a government amnesty. Father Wladyslaw Kaiser, the parish priest of Wroblowice, near Kraków, was not as lucky. Nor were some others who were also jailed with him. This was after Wojtyla had become a cardinal, and when he heard about Father Kaiser's arrest, he went out to Wroblowice to celebrate Mass several times, and he spoke out forcefully in Father Kaiser's defense.

"I gave the order. The priest was just obeying me. So I'm the one who should have been put in jail and not him." His stand impressed the people of the diocese very much because it seemed to be an open provocation of the Communists. But it worked. After that, Communist persecution eased up a little bit.

In postwar Poland new neighborhoods sprang up in many cities, and of course, the Communists forbade building new churches in them. They never told us why. In such situations Cardinal Wojtyla was a good tactician. He would order placing crosses or other religious symbols in any place people might congregate. Priests would gather to say the Rosary or celebrate Mass, and gradually more and more of the faithful came—at first it was only 5 or 10, but soon the number was up to 200.

The police would move in and make the worshippers leave, but they would just come back. That kind of open-air religious celebration continued for several years until priests built a roof above the site. Those who celebrated Mass risked persecution, fines, even jail. But they persisted, and after more time passed, people began to build little chapels where the roofs had been.

The authorities harassed them, of course. They levied fines. Sometimes they tore down what had been built—something the police did in Karniowice, a little town near Chrzanow. The local faithful wanted to enlarge the small chapel they had, and they did so without bothering to get an official permit. The Communists moved in with 400 soldiers and heavy equipment, destroying everything.

When I went there on a canonical visit, I found the people crying over what had been destroyed, but we celebrated Mass amid the rubble and under the open sky.

Two days later Cardinal Wojtyla and the Polish bishops were bound for Rome for John Paul I's funeral. Before leaving, Wojtyla took the time to arrange the handling of all his pending projects. Those who said good-bye to him at that time remember that he was unusually calm.

Maybe he knew that the second cardinal that Paul VI had discreetly signaled as his successor was Cardinal Karol Wojtyla.

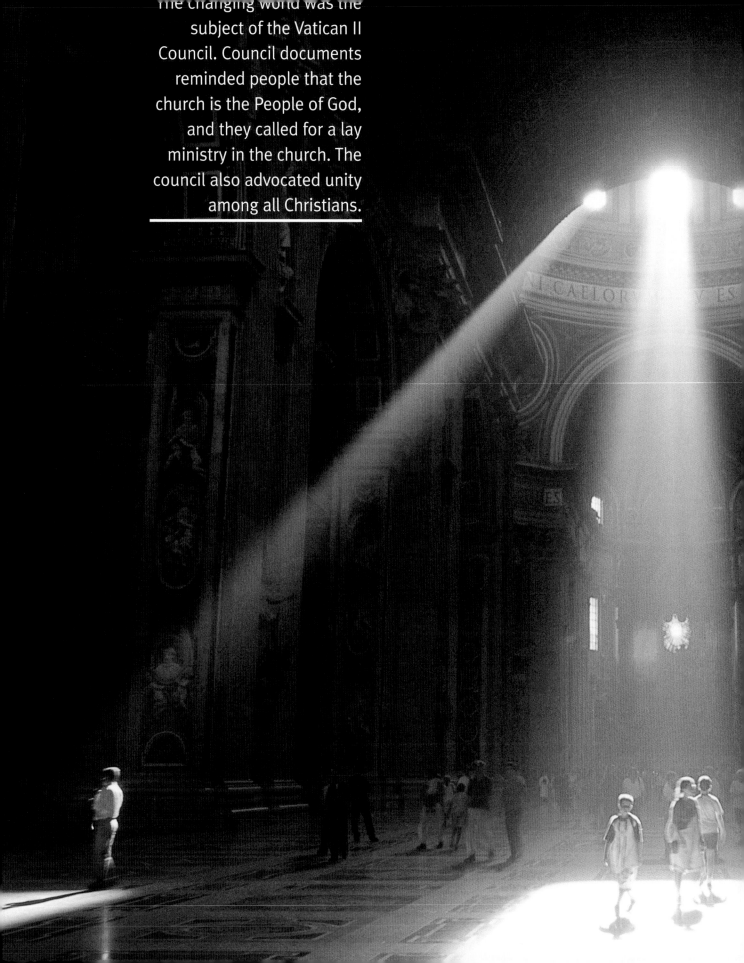

The changing world was the subject of the Vatican II Council. Council documents reminded people that the church is the People of God, and they called for a lay ministry in the church. The council also advocated unity among all Christians.

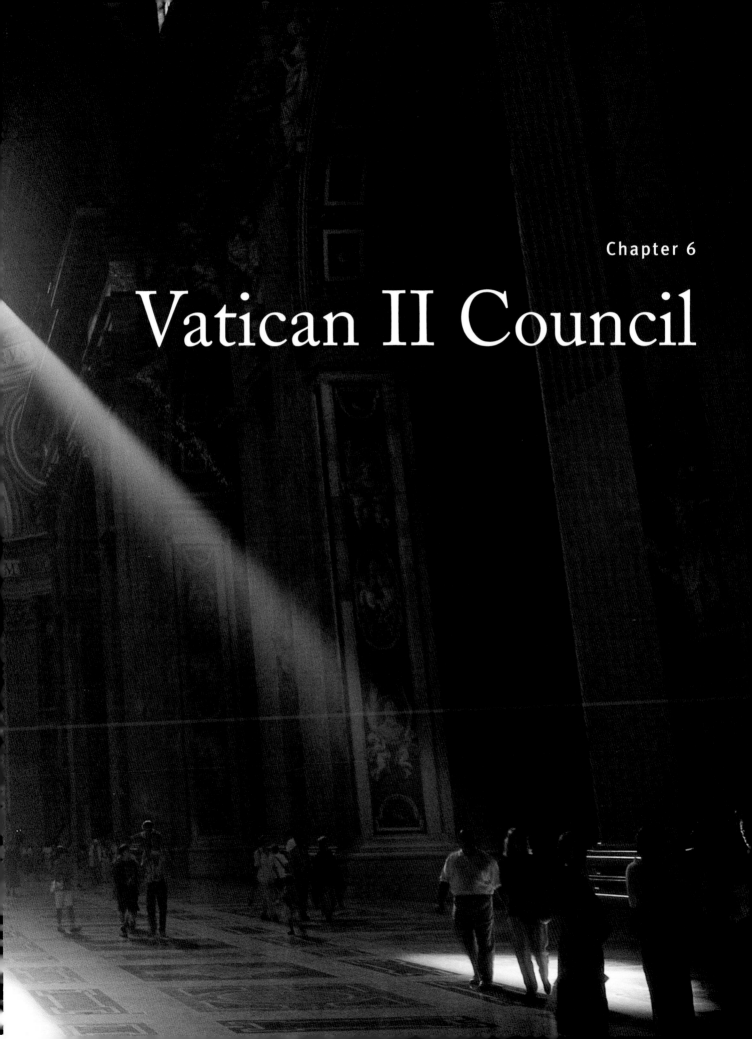

Chapter 6

Vatican II Council

A procession of Roman Catholic cardinals and bishops passes through crowds in St. Peter's Square in the closing ceremonies of the Vatican II Council in 1965.

In the more than 2,000 years that the Roman Catholic Church has existed, it has convened councils only 22 times. The first was the Council of Jerusalem, called in AD 49 and mentioned in the *Acts of the Apostles*. Some apostles, as disciples of Jesus Christ, were proclaiming the Good News of the savior beyond the confines of the Jewish world. An urgent problem arose: Church leaders had to meet in Jerusalem to resolve the issue of whether or not pagan men who wanted to become Christians had to be circumcised before they could be baptized. All the apostles were Jewish, and they believed that circumcision, practiced in Judaism as a purification rite, was a prerequisite to becoming Christian. Amid heated discussions, Saint Paul fervently defended his contrary position: "We ought not to impose unnecessary hardships on pagans who want to convert to Jesus Christ." In the end, the other apostles accepted his position and sent written epistles, or letters, to the earliest Christian communities to confirm this belief. These epistles are the first council documents of the church.

The Council of Jerusalem became the model for later councils. Bishops from around the world gathered together; no specific dates were set for subsequent councils. The first council after apostolic times was called in AD 325 at Nicea, and the next took place 50 years later. Pope John XXIII called for a church council in 1962. At this council bishops, "together with the Bishop of Rome, the Successor of Saint Peter and Head of the Church" (exact wording of the Vatican II Council declaration), were to reflect on how Christians should live in the world and in what ways the church needed to be reformed.

Both Pius XI and Pius XII had considered calling a council. During Pius XI's pontificate (1922–1939) the atheistic totalitarian systems of Nazism and Communism came into being. They caused violent social and political upheaval throughout the world—both inside and outside the church. The church needed to take a stand. Pius XI, although he did not convene a council, addressed these matters by publishing two encyclicals in 1937. The first, *Divini Redemptoris (Promise of a Redeemer: On Atheistic Communism)*, dealt with the Communist threat; the second, *Mit Brennender Sorge (With Intense Sorrow)*, dealt with the dangers of Nazi socialism. During Pius XII's pontificate (1939–1958) Fascism caused devastation before coming to an end, but Communism continued to gain strength and exert its influence all over the world. This represented both a threat and a challenge for the church because

A daytime view of the crowds that gather in St. Peter's Square for important services or events.

Communism became a political and ideological option for millions of people struggling to survive in harsh economic conditions. Pius XII did not call for a council to face the situation.

Each of these popes may have faced powerful opposition from the Roman Curia, whose members were firmly set against innovation or change. In 1870 the pope's authority had been declared infallible; he ruled as the successor to Saint Peter. The Curia believed that the pope just had to take his stance; he did not have to take the bishops' opinions into account.

When Pope John XXIII became the leader of the church in 1958, there was still a nineteenth-century mind-set in the Vatican. The church went by rules laid down by the Vatican I Council. Pope Pius IX had called for Vatican I in 1868 (a preliminary commission spent three years preparing for it); it officially opened in December 1869 with 700 council fathers—bishops and cardinals—representing the worldwide church in attendance. The majority of the representatives were European and Caucasian.

THE POPE, PRISONER OF THE VATICAN

Vatican I Council sessions took place during a time of enormous tension in Europe. Prussia, under Premier Otto von Bismarck, was uniting the German states into a single powerful nation. From the Vatican's point of view, Protestant Prussia had incorporated Catholic territories won from Austria and France to form a Protestant German Empire in 1871.

While the Austro-Prussian and Franco-Prussian wars were going on, revolutionaries in Piedmont, a province in northern Italy, were trying to unite the states in the Italian peninsula. They attacked states under Vatican control, which were under the protection of the French at that time. When the Franco-Prussian War began, however, the French had to retreat and Piedmont troops entered Rome. Pius IX rejected the new government's proposal that the Vatican recognize the extraterritoriality of Rome and pay an annual rent. The pope became a self-imposed "Prisoner of the Vatican" and decided not to leave the Papal Palace. The pope no longer ruled the papal territories; they were annexed to the newly unified Italy. Vatican I Council had no official ending, since some bishop's left when the Franco-Prussian War started. In the end, Pius IX just suspended it.

Faced with this difficult political situation, the bishops decided to go along with the Roman Curia in strengthening the pope's power inside the church. This became known as the "ultramontane," or "beyond the mountains," policy. Ultramontane referred to France and Germany, countries over the Alps from Italy. The Roman Curia declared the absolute power of the pope over and above national authority. After Vatican I the Catholic Church structure became centralized and highly authoritarian, run by a compact bureaucracy.

Actually, Pius IX was a dominating power in the church long before 1870. The council fathers just confirmed this. They did embellish his power by proclaiming that he and other popes were infallible. According to the doctrine of papal infallibility, the pope is not subject to error; but this applies only when he proclaims matters of faith and morals while speaking *ex cathedra* (from the throne).

Little by little, the church turned inward and functioned behind a wall of mistrust, pitting itself against whatever was new or outside the church. (To the Roman Curia, this meant beyond Rome.) The Holy See rejected and condemned any innovations in Christian community life in a world that was changing rapidly. Trends the church condemned most of all were "moderns" in the church who advocated renewing the liturgy, and "liberals" who stressed the validity of applying critical reason and rational thought to experience and who had democratic tendencies, the opposite of centralized bureaucracy.

The world in which priests and the faithful lived was steadily undergoing transformation, and many Catholics began to move away from the rigid rules of the Roman Curia, petrified as it was in nineteenth-century attitudes. The Curia kept its ultramontane mind-set for many years, perpetuating a big split between clergy and laypeople in the church. The people who sat in the pews were thought of as just clients of the priests—passive participants in Masses celebrated in Latin. They did not realize their own call to participate in the Eucharistic liturgy. Strict authoritarianism in the church dictated who was capable of reading the Bible, for fear the sacred scriptures would be misunderstood. Very few "ordinary" Catholics thought the Bible had the power to reveal God. Finally, the Catholic Church's mistrust of, if not outright hostility toward, other denominations, even Christian ones, made ecumenism virtually impossible.

John XXIII

Angelo Guiseppe Roncalli was born on November 25, 1881, in Sotto il Monte, near Bergamo, Italy. His father was a tenant farmer. Young Roncalli was an intelligent boy and began studies for the priesthood at an early age. After finishing his seminary studies, he earned a doctorate in theology. Ordained to the priesthood in 1904, he was assigned as secretary to the bishop of Bergamo and also taught at the local seminary. During World War I he was conscripted as a hospital orderly and later became a military chaplain. Pope Pius XI consecrated Roncalli as bishop in 1925 and sent him as apostolic delegate to Greece and Turkey. At the end of 1944, he took the post as papal nuncio to France. He stayed in Paris until 1952, when he was nominated to become archbishop and patriarch of Venice, and it was at that time that he received his cardinal's red biretta.

Elected pope in 1958, he took the name John XXIII. His most important accomplishment was convening the Vatican II Council. His successor, Pope Paul VI, brought it to a close. John XXIII's other important accomplishments were the encyclicals he wrote: *Mater et Magistra (Mother and Teacher: On Christianity and Social Progress)* in 1961 and *Pacem in Terris (Peace on Earth: On Establishing Universal Peace in Truth, Justice, Charity, and Liberty)* in 1963. He laid out his thoughts very clearly. *Pacem in Terris* was a call for peace, justice, and liberty among all nations of the earth. It was widely read not just in Christian circles but also in Soviet-ruled countries and beyond.

Pope John XXIII's openness to dialogue bore fruit in the closer relationships he established between the Vatican and the governments in Communist-ruled countries. The pope received the daughter and son-in-law of the Soviet Union's First Secretary of the Communist Party, Nikita Khrushchev, in a private audience. He maintained close ties with Polish bishops (nominating 27 of them)—above all, with Cardinal Stefan Wyszynski.

John XXIII was the first pope to travel outside the Vatican. He visited Loreto and Assisi to pray for the success of the council. After opening the council in 1963, however, he was diagnosed with cancer. He died on June 2, 1963, not living long enough to see the second session of the council convene.

Catholics and other admirers from all over the world remember him as "Good Pope John." Everyone who got to know him loved him. He left a diary, *Il Giornale Dell'Anima (The Journal of a Soul),* which has been published in many countries.

John XXIII's diary, shown in its Polish translation, was well received around the world.

BRINGING THE CHURCH NEARER TO WHATEVER WAS "BEYOND THE MOUNTAINS"

Almost 90 years later, many clerics within the Catholic Church felt a need to change the ultramontane policy and look for ways to renew the church. When John XXII became pope, following a week of prayer for unity among Christians, he declared on January 25, 1959, his intention to convene a worldwide council in the church. This came as a great surprise. Organizing a council is an enormous and complicated undertaking that requires years of careful planning. The pope had just turned seventy-eight. No one suspected he would initiate such an enormous project.

Since John XXIII was also bishop of Rome, he first called a synod in Rome before the council would begin. No new proposals came out of the Synod of Rome. Of all the dioceses in the world, Rome clung most tenaciously to the "beyond the mountains" tradition and reacted least well to change. Compared with the church in Rome, the worldwide church had changed dramatically since the previous council. The number of priests ordained had quadrupled since Vatican I, and the pastoral works of missionaries throughout the world had produced a growing number of new clergy. Indigenous peoples now had their own priests and bishops. Two thousand five hundred priests and bishops attended the opening session of Vatican II. Only one-third of them were from Western Europe. A little more than that—35 percent—were from the Americas, and more than 12 percent of this group was from Latin America. One of every five bishops was from Asia, and one in ten was from Africa. Almost 100 of the bishops from Africa were Black. Nearly 100 bishops were from countries in the Arab world (although they barely made up 4 percent of the total number of participants). The number of bishops from Central and Eastern Europe was small in relation to the total number of bishops who attended. Communist governments were loathe to let bishops leave their countries. So usually only 50 to 80 representatives from Communist countries attended any particular council session.

Twelve commissions were appointed to work on preparations for the council, which took four years. Nine of them were set up to match the nine congregations at the Vatican, so they related either to ministries in the church or to the Vatican Secretariat. The tenth commission worked on liturgy, the eleventh

John XXIII delivers an address over radio and television from his private library in the Vatican on September 11, 1962.

A session of the ecumenical Vatican II Council fills St. Peter's Basilica in Rome.

addressed the apostolate of the laity, and the last one coordinated the work of all the other commissions.

By way of these commissions, the Roman Curia produced 72 documents, or schemata, in over 2,000 pages, to be treated at the upcoming council. These schemata perpetuated a vision of the church as a centralized monarchy, pyramidal in structure, with the pope at the top, operating as its sole authority.

John XXIII saw the bureaucrats in the Curia who wrote up these schemata as the greatest obstacle to opening the church to a broader vision. He was hoping that bishops coming from around the world would render decisions that would renew the rigid structure that the Roman Curia had created and wanted to maintain.

He was right about the bishops from around the world. On the opening day of the council, October 11, 1962, the Holy Father, seated on his *seda gestatoria*, the chair that raised him above the throng, was carried with great pomp into the huge nave of St. Peter's Basilica. He mounted the throne prepared for him and opened the first session of the Vatican II Council. As this first session progressed, the council fathers rejected all the schemata the Roman Curia had spent four years preparing by a majority vote. The council fathers had to start over practically from scratch, but ultimately, they produced forward-looking documents after working on them until virtually the last days of the council.

The council went on for three years. Those who participated met in four sessions that varied in length, according to the number of weeks it took to deliberate different topics. The sessions took place at yearly intervals, and in between sessions, members of the commissions edited and refined the final texts.

In simplified terms the bishops were divided into two main groups—progressives and conservatives—that faced off against each other. The progressive, or liberal, group of bishops shared Pope John XXIII's viewpoint, and they hoped to make profound changes in the church to open it up to the world. The conservative group of bishops wanted to block any and all changes. The progressives formed the largest group of council fathers, and despite the obstacles the Roman Curia put in their way, they were able to begin to modernize the church (*aggiornamento* in Italian). Following the directives of many of these council documents, the church embarked upon new routes to the future.

A post-Vatican II missal has the Mass in both Latin and the native language—in this case, Polish.

Cardinal Alfredo Ottaviani, Head of the Holy Office of the Inquisition, elderly and almost blind, was the standard-bearer and spokesperson for the conservative group. Bishop Marcel Lefebvre, among others, was also

Above left: The Vatican II Council introduced substantial changes in liturgical rites. Formerly, priests celebrated Mass facing the altar. *Above right:* After Vatican II, priests began celebrating Mass by turning toward the people.

on that side. After the council Lefebvre became a severe critic of new developments in the church and, later, of the direction Pope John Paul II would take. As a consequence, Lefebvre led a breakaway church, and John Paul II eventually had to excommunicate him.

The Belgian Cardinal Leo Józef Suenens and Cardinal Giovanni Battista Montini, of Milan, among others represented the progressive group. These two cardinals moderated the first session of the council in 1962. John XXIII asked Suenens to deliver the opening address for the discussion about the church in the modern world. Cardinal Giovanni Battista Montini later became Pope Paul VI, the next successor to Saint Peter when John XXIII died.

There was an important innovation in this council's procedures. Council fathers were allowed to bring their own professional theological advisers, or consultants (*periti* in Latin), with them. They were theologians who were drawn from both the clergy and laypeople in the church. Some of the most famous advisers were Jesuits Henri de Lubac and Jean Danielou and Dominican Yves Congar—all three would later become cardinals—and the German theologian Father Hans Küng. During Pius XII's pontificate in the 1950s, they were among the many Catholic intellectuals who were severely criticized by Rome because of their opinions. Professor Stefan Swiezawski from the Catholic University of Lublin acted

Why Worry?

—Bishop Tadeusz Pieronek

I remember one of the trips I took with Archbishop Wojtyla to this very day. During a break in council sessions, we took a trip to Sicily on All Saints' Day and All Souls' Day at the beginning of November. I went straight to Sicily by train with Bishop Pietraszka, and the archbishop met us there. We visited many places, from Palermo to Catania. We even took a cable car up to see the volcano at Mount Etna. It had snowed, and walking was difficult and dangerous. We spent a while there, but then it was getting near the departure time of our airplane flight to Rome. Wojtyla, however, didn't seem anxious about that, and on our way back he took even more time at the foot of Mount Etna to stop to pray, reading his breviary.

Getting a little nervous, we went up to him and said, "Your Eminence, the plane is going to take off soon, and you're here praying." He didn't seem to notice us and kept on praying. We started worrying among ourselves. "We're not going to make that plane. We're going to miss it." And of course, we did arrive 15 minutes late at the airport, but it looked like the plane was waiting for us. The archbishop of Catania knew Archbishop Wojtyla was scheduled to take that flight, and he made the pilot wait for us. Wojtyla turned to us, smiling, "You see? Everything is fine. Why were you so worried?"

He attended all the council sessions. I was one of the support people and never got to attend a session. Father Jurek Chmiel from Kraków and I helped Wojtyla in minor matters: We typed his texts, took care of chores, bought whatever he needed, kept his calendar, and arranged meetings for him—things like that.

Sometimes we got the chance to meet visitors, especially people from other countries, usually at restaurants. Wojtyla had the habit of inviting some of his students to Rome. This was an extraordinary opportunity for us because we didn't have any money and we couldn't have gone to eat in restaurants on our own. He didn't have any money either but always managed to meet up with some patron, like Father Deskur or someone from the West, who did.

During the last sessions Wojtyla was a member of several commissions, and at times, he arrived home very late. I remember he got home so late one evening that the sisters

had closed the kitchen, so he came to my room and asked me if I had anything to eat. He was never demanding about food and always ate what was placed in front of him. He never paid attention to restaurant menus; we had to choose what he would eat.

As soon as Archbishop Wojtyla took part in Commission XIII at the council, people in Rome started talking about him. The commission was working on the *Pastoral Constitution on the Church in the Modern World.* Unfortunately, I couldn't stay in Rome until the end of the council. Two months before, in September 1965, Archbishop Wojtyla called me to come see him. A rightist professor was slinging offensive attacks at the church, and the archbishop said to me, "I'm sorry, I have to send you back to Kraków, but I'll try to make it up to you if I can. Tell me what I can do for you." I asked him if I could come to Rome again when they awarded him his titular church, and he agreed. In 1967, when that announcement came out, we were all together in my uncle's rectory. (He was a parish priest.) My uncle reminded Cardinal Wojtyla of his promise to me, and he replied, "I have kept that in mind for a long time. Of course I will take Tadeusz with me when I go to my titular church in Rome." He kept his word.

When memories of those days come back to me, I recognize in Pope John Paul II the same Karol Wojtyla I knew for years. I was lucky to have met him in my life. He was always accessible to everyone. You didn't have to request a private audience to come see him. He didn't even know what the word "audience" meant. If it had not been for the dignity of the papacy and diplomatic protocol requirements, I'm sure he would have been as he always was before he became pope.

As pope, John Paul II never refused to see any of his old friends. It did not matter if a friendship could be embarrassing for him, or if someone wanted to see him who had lost his way in life, or even if someone had a bad reputation. For him, in the final analysis, what was always important was each person.

as adviser for Karol Wojtyla, the archbishop of Kraków. Wojtyla consulted him and others at various stages of the council.

Actually, distinctions in discussions between conservatives and progressives were not always simple or clear-cut.

Divergent opinions surfaced regarding practically every one of the important issues discussed at the council. For example, several bishops from Eastern Europe accepted profound changes in the liturgy but wanted to draft a separate document dedicated to the Blessed Virgin Mary,

For the first time, a pope traveled to the Holy Land. Pope Paul VI wanted to promote mutual understanding between religions.

while other bishops who also pushed for liturgical reforms proposed to include a text on the Blessed Virgin inside other constitutions drafted by the council. Their proposal won the debate.

Conflicts between factions have always arisen at church councils. In the final analysis, controversies in the church are the motivating force for calling bishops together so they can express their ideas at council sessions. An outstanding difference in the results of the Vatican II Council from previous councils was evident, however. Neither John XXIII nor Paul VI was upset by the need for change in a changing world, and neither condemned nor corrected anyone or anything.

In 1864, well before the Vatican I Council, Pius IX proclaimed a *Syllabus of Errors*—that is, a document that listed 86 errors that Catholics could not accept. Vatican I appropriated this document and stated, as the last *error* on the list, "The Holy Father may and should accept progress, liberalism, and modern civilization." One hundred years later that Vatican I thesis statement became very relevant at Vatican II Council, only this time the council did not intend to condemn it as an error.

Vatican II produced 16 documents, which taken together formed a volume of several hundred pages: four constitutions that were doctrinal in character and dealt with fundamental theology for the church, nine decrees that outlined the position of the church on particular issues whenever these issues were not treated elsewhere in constitutions, and three declarations that dealt with the church's positions on general (nondogmatic) themes.

The constitutions were the documents with a dogmatic, or teaching, character on matters of faith. Whenever topics came up for discussion that were not specifically matters of dogma but were thought important by the council fathers, new ways had to be found to express these ideas. That's how the topic of *Gaudium et Spes (Joy and Hope)* was handled. It was incorporated into the *Pastoral Constitution on the Church in the Modern World,* which dealt with the role of the church in the modern world. To differentiate this constitution from other specifically dogmatic constitutions, it was called a *pastoral* constitution. Another document, *Sacrosanctum Concilium (The Sacred Council),* had to do with the liturgy and was incorporated into the *Constitution on the Sacred Liturgy. Lumen Gentium (Christ Is the Light of Humanity)* was a dogmatic constitution that dealt with the church, and another, *Dei Verbum (The Word of God),* spoke about revelation from God.

These documents wrought profound changes in the church. *Lumen Gentium* did away with the traditional division of the church into hierarchy, priests, and people. Henceforth, the entire church—the Body of Christ and gift of God for the salvation of all humankind—was thought of as a single body, the People of God and all members of the church participating in the priesthood of Jesus Christ. There was a universal call to holiness; all the People of God, by virtue of their baptism, were called to be saints. This vision allowed people to find a new place in the church or to recover an ancient one they once filled in the earliest centuries of Christianity. The last part of this constitution dealt with the relationship between the hierarchy and priests in the church and the responsibilities they have in service to the faithful.

Since laypersons now had a new place in the church, the liturgy needed to be modified so that the people could fully participate in it. In order for the prayer of the church to be the prayer for all the sons and daughters of the church and not just a select few, the language that priests spoke to the people during the liturgy had to be one they could understand—their own language. The *Constitution on the Sacred Liturgy* introduced these changes for the Latin rite and also stressed equality of all liturgical rites in the church, including the Eastern rites.

END OF THE BESIEGED FORTRESS

Dei Verbum, the dogmatic constitution that spoke of divine revelation, reestablished the proper place of the sacred scriptures. Until that time it was thought that there were two sources of revelation: the Bible and tradition, and that the Bible was within the overarching shadow of tradition. Very few "ordinary" Catholic people were familiar with the Bible. The council fathers resolved the dilemma over which of the sources of revelation was the most important. They recognized that there is only one source of revelation—the Word of God—and that is manifested both in sacred scriptures and in tradition.

The most innovative document of the council was the *Pastoral Constitution on the Church in the Modern World.* This text spelled out the role of the church in the contemporary world. John XXIII first mentioned this idea, and Paul VI took it up. The vote on the final text was taken the day before Vatican II closed, and thanks to the pope's firm support, this document was finally completed and adopted. It doesn't contain dogma. It describes what the church receives from the actual world in which it is immersed. Conversely, it shows what the world can hope for from the church, since the church serves as inspiration in the world. The church, having the saving power of Jesus Christ, is an exceptional "offering" for the world. With this document and its application, the Catholic Church abolished the image it had of being a "besieged fortress" and opened itself up to dialogue with other Christian denominations, other religions, and nonbelievers alike.

Another constitution that was accepted after much debate was the *Pastoral Constitution on the Church in the Modern World,* which was approved on December 7, 1965. It contained the documents *Gaudium et Spes (Joy and Hope)* and *Humanae Personae Dignitatem (On the Dignity of the Human Person: On Dialogue with Unbelievers).* This constitution spoke about freedom of religion and, after being edited in the third and fourth sessions (which Paul VI also insisted upon), was finally

approved by 97 percent of the council fathers.

It decisively ruptured the union between the church and the throne, which in the past brought about many abuses in the propagation of the faith. This constitution established the belief that no one should be forced to either receive or reject faith. That is a decision for each person to make according to his or her conscience. This document defends religious liberty and the dignity of every person. When governments separate individuals from their religious faith, or when they make living in religious communities difficult, that is a violation of human freedom.

Many representatives of other Christian churches that had separated from Rome participated in the council as observers. One of them was Athenagoras I, the Orthodox patriarch of Constantinople. On one of the final days of the council, Pope Paul VI and Patriarch Athenagoras I, by mutual agreement, annulled the excommunications that each church had declared against the other in the eleventh century

Meeting in Jerusalem in 1964, Paul VI and Patriarch Athenagoras I of the Greek Orthodox Church end a 900-year rift between their two churches.

by the ancestors on both sides. (That was the cause of the schism between the church in Rome and the church in the East at that time.) By their gesture, these two leaders opened the road to reconciliation among all those who believe in Jesus Christ, which was an important goal of Paul VI's and of his successors on the Throne of Saint Peter, including Pope John Paul II.

When the eminent cardinals
elected the new bishop of Rome,
they summoned him from a far-off
country, distant in miles but close
in the community of faith and in
the Christian tradition.

Chapter 7

Habemus Papam

The year 1978 was the year of three popes: Paul VI died in midsummer; John Paul I was elected August 25; and after his death just 34 days later, the College of Cardinals was reconvened to elect a third pope. The date prescribed by Canon Law to start the long election process again fell on October 13. The cardinals at the conclave drew lots for their rooms, the monastic-like cells that they would occupy during its duration. Cardinal Karol Wojtyla pulled out the paper with 91 written on it. This directed him to a tiny room with a cot, a bedside table, and a small desk. As a member of the Sacred College of Cardinals about to vote for the new pope, he and the other cardinals would be out of contact with the rest of the world until the name of a new pope was announced.

Just before the voting procedure started, news arrived at the Vatican that Karol Wojtyla's dear friend, Bishop Andrzej Deskur, had suffered a stroke and had been taken to the Gemelli Clinic. Cardinal Wojtyla left immediately to go see his friend. He found Deskur almost totally paralyzed and hardly able to speak.

MORE THAN A FRIEND

Bishop Deskur and Cardinal Wojtyla had been friends since their seminary days. They had renewed their friendship during the Vatican II Council in Rome, where Deskur was living at the time. In 1978 he was president of the Pontifical Council on Social Communication. In the days leading up to the conclave, he organized an intense campaign to convince members of the College of

After Karol Wojtyla was elected pope, Father Edward Zacher recorded this information in the parish baptismal records at Wadowice.

Cardinals that Cardinal Wojtyla was the best candidate to be elected pope. Many influential persons passed through Bishop Deskur's office and living quarters in those few days. Deskur also attended meetings that other dignitaries organized and where they spoke in off-the-record conversations. He tried to gather information on what other cardinals were thinking and form alliances for his own candidate. Before the conclave officially started, he had already gathered about 10 votes for Cardinal Wojtyla, and so it seemed his candidate was being considered. A minimum of two-thirds of the cardinal electors plus one had to be convinced, however, before Cardinal Wojtyla would be the new pope.

The cardinals weren't sure the time had come to elect a non-Italian pope. The totally unexpected death of John Paul I caused them to stop and think. Barely a few weeks had gone by since they had elected the Patriarch of Venice to be Pope John Paul I and then buried him so soon after in the crypt of St. Peter's Basilica. How were they supposed to interpret that sign? Who should be the next Holy Father?

AN ITALIAN ROUND

As the conclave began, the cardinals prayed to the Holy Spirit to help them elect the head of the church. They believed that each of their individual votes would lead to a group decision that would reveal God's will. But the means by which the will of God would be made known was subject to democratic choice. Cardinals would vote by writing names on pieces of paper and putting them into a chalice. Once the votes were collected and tallied, if there were not the required majority of two-thirds plus one of the votes, the process would begin again.

Giuseppe Siri, archbishop of Genoa, was confident the council would clear the way to the papal throne for him. For some time he thought of himself as defending the church against chaos, which he thought came about after the Vatican II Council. He divulged his thoughts in public appearances and could count on the support of some conservative cardinals. He had not garnered enough support at the previous conclave, such a short while before, in August. This time, however, he could hope for more votes. He faced an important adversary, however, in Archbishop Giovanni Benelli of Florence. Benelli had many supporters, and he thought the church should not abandon the road it had taken in implementing reforms called for by the council. Six weeks before, Benelli had given his support to Cardinal Luciani, who became the consensus candidate, a bridge candidate between the conservative and progressive groups. Now he set himself up in direct opposition to Siri. Neither of these candidates, however, had enough support from a majority of the cardinals.

ATTRIBUTES OF A GOOD CANDIDATE

Given this situation, Cardinal Franz König thought that it might be possible to elect someone from outside the

Cardinal Karol Wojtyla, at the conclave that elected him pope in October 1978. He wears his red vestments for the last time.

Italian group of cardinals—they comprised almost one-fourth of the College of Cardinals. If any candidate were to break the 400-year-old domination of Italian popes, he would have to be accepted by both the conservatives and the progressives. In addition, the candidate could not be from a powerful country. So the Americans, the Germans, and the French didn't stand a chance. This was a nonwritten tradition that originated in the fear of Italian prelates that a pope from those countries would bring foreign bureaucrats along with him and chase Italians out of the Roman Curia, which would be a disaster for those who belonged to this institution. So only someone from a small country could be considered. Also, it was hoped that the candidate would have a good deal of pastoral experience and be well informed about the world scene.

The Austrian cardinal König had a candidate in mind who possessed these attributes: Karol Wojtyla. Cardinal Wojtyla knew what the Austrian was thinking. One day, when they were taking a taxi together in Rome, König said to the driver, "Please drive carefully. The next pope is in your cab." Wojtyla could also count on the support of Cardinal Krol from the United States, although for different reasons. The Austrian was sure that Wojtyla as pope would continue along the new paths that Vatican II Council had opened up for the church. The United States cardinal clung to tradition. To him, Wojtyla signified a pope who would defend doctrines that had been eroded over the past few years by "leftist" persons in the church. Karol Wojtyla was generally inclined to synthe-

The cardinals enter the Sistine Chapel as the conclave is about to begin. In the chapel, separated from the outside world, their mission was to elect a person who could guide the future of the church.

The 111 cardinals are gathered in the Sistine Chapel to elect the successor to John Paul I. They chose Karol Wojtyla on October 16, 1978.

size opposite poles in philosophy, theology, or politics and that turned out to be an attractive point in his favor. As a *papabile* (someone with a good chance of becoming pope), he could count on the support of both moderate conservatives and progressives.

IT WASN'T A JOKE

The archbishop of Kraków didn't enter these discussions or make suppositions. During a meeting that Bishop Deskur arranged, one of the guests, Mario Rocca, an influential cardinal at the Vatican, openly stated that Cardinal Wojtyla was his candidate for pope. Wojtyla looked at him and replied, "Perhaps we'd better leave this to God's providential decision."

After John Paul I's funeral, Cardinal Wojtyla left to visit the Marian shrine at Mentorelli, near Rome, which he cherished, and then to tour Castel Gondolfo, the summer residence of the popes. A week before the first session of the conclave, he went to Lake Vico with Bishop Deskur, and he spent the last few days just prior to the Friday start day for the conclave with some friends in Rome. He stayed at the Polish College as he had when he was a bishop. Cardinal Wyszynski stayed at the Polish Institute because it was closer to the Vatican. They didn't see each other on a daily basis, and Wyszynski had no knowledge of the campaign Deskur was orchestrating—until one day, after hearing something said in a conversation with Cardinal König, he invited Andrzej Deskur and another Polish bishop, Wladislaw Rubin, to come see him. When Wyszynski asked them who would be the next pope, he heard them say "Karol Wojtyla." Bishop

Deskur had the reputation of being the most informed person in Rome about such matters, so what he said was taken seriously. Bishop Rubin, secretary of the Synod of Bishops in Rome, also had firsthand information and concurred. It was only two days away from the beginning of the conclave.

THE LORD IS CALLING YOU

After visiting his friend Bishop Deskur at the Gemelli Clinic that Friday afternoon, Cardinal Wojtyla went back to the Polish College. The next morning he offered Mass for the intention that Deskur's health would be restored, and then he went on to St. Peter's Basilica for the Mass said for the intention of the conclave, celebrated by the Vatican secretary of state, Jean Villot. After a quick meal he entered the Sistine Chapel for the last time as archbishop of Kraków. Walking toward the basilica, he passed by the Gemelli Clinic once again. On his previous visit the day before, he had been told Bishop Deskur might not survive the stroke. This time he learned that although Deskur was still in a precarious state of health, he was much better already. Strengthened by this news, the cardinal went on to the conclave.

As a member of the conclave for the second time in seven weeks, he again climbed the staircase to the Sistine Chapel. The master of ceremonies, Cesare Tucci, had already erected a huge cross. After finding cell 91 and dropping off his suitcase, he went to the chapel where the cardinals were singing *Veni, Creator (Come, Holy Spirit).*

One hundred and eleven cardinals sat by order of seniority in two rows perpendicular to the altar, down both sides of the chapel. Above their heads was Michelangelo's fresco of the creation of the world and, in front of them, his painting of the final judgment. The cardinals were about to determine the future of the church. Whoever was elected would surely take Christianity into the third millennium.

The cardinals were not in contact with the outside world. All technical means of communication were forbidden, so they could communicate only among themselves. The one piece of information that would leave the Sistine Chapel—a signal that revealed whether or not a pope had been chosen—was relayed to the outside world by the color of the smoke that rose from the stove that stood behind a curtain in a corner of the chapel.

The cardinals met twice a day during the conclave. Normally two votes were taken in each of these sessions. After morning Mass on Sunday, October 15, the cardinals, writing tablets at hand, took their seats. In deep silence each of them voted by writing the name of a candidate on a piece of paper, then folding it in half, and dropping it into the chalice. A voting commission of three cardinals supervised by three other cardinals read out the names that were placed in the chalice. The first vote count showed that the two main Italian candidates had more or less the same number of people voting for them, but each

of them had less than the required majority. The same thing happened on the second vote except this time, a few new names were mentioned as the votes were called out. A third vote that afternoon also failed to conclude the election. On the fourth vote the name Karol Wojtyla was called out for the first time.

Cesare Tucci put a handful of wet hay and some black coloring agent into the stove. The smoke traveled through a long chimney pipe that led to the open air through a window near the ceiling. When a cloud of black smoke rose above the Sistine Chapel, the world knew the cardinals still had not reached a decision.

Above left: Some thought that Giovanni Benelli, archbishop of Florence, would be a worthy successor to John Paul I. *Above right:* Austrian cardinal Franz König knew Karol Wojtyla very well and insisted someone other than an Italian should be elected to the Throne of Saint Peter. *Above:* Jean Villot, Vatican secretary of state, was also in favor of the archbishop of Kraków.

Since it was impossible to elect an Italian, the vote Monday morning would include someone who was not from Italy. Candidates mentioned were from the Netherlands, Argentina, and Brazil. In the second vote on Monday, a large number of electors let it be known that they would support the cardinal from Kraków. After that session Cardinal Maximilian von Fürstenberg, rector of the Belgian College when Wojtyla studied in Rome, came close to his former protégé and said to him in Latin, *"Dominus adest et vocat te."* (The Lord is here, and he is calling you.)

Moderation and Enthusiasm in Poland

At first the official news media in Poland reported John Paul II's election with cautious restraint. *Slowo Powszechne*, the periodical of the Pax Association, published the only full account. *Trybuna Ludu* gave this story equal space and importance as the report on the end of the harvest season in Poland. On the other hand, for *Zycie Warsawy*, the most important news was Polkolor's success…. However, the Politburo's opinion appeared soon after: "With warm friendship we wish to express our joy for the honor that has been bestowed on a great son of the Polish nation."

The telegram Polish authorities sent to the pope read, "On the occasion of the elevation of his eminence to the dignity of the papacy, in the name of the whole Polish nation and of its highest authorities, we send cordial congratulations and best wishes." The telegram was signed by Edward Gierek, Henryk Jablonski, and Piotr Jaroszewicz. Official press releases published the entire telegram, stating with satisfaction that "for the first time in history, a son of the nation of Poland sits on the pope's throne, which is edifying for all the citizens who are united and cooperate toward the greatness and prosperity of their socialist homeland."

How did people in Poland react to the election of a Polish pope? They poured into the streets, holding flowers and lighted candles. They sang. They said prayers out loud. Among them were people who knew Karol Wojtyla, but also others who had never met him or hardly even knew who he was. Church bells rang all over Poland, and hordes of people flocked to churches. In the pages of *Tygodnik Powszechny*, one of the few authentic Catholic publications, Jerzy Turowicz wrote: "It's three o'clock in the morning. I hope our Holy Father John Paul II is lying down in the cell assigned to him during the voting. I am not sure he's sleeping, however. The 'yes' he answered when they asked him if he would accept his election as pope must have been the most difficult answer he ever had to give in his life."

The Zygmunt bell in the tower of Wawel Cathedral proclaimed the new Polish pope. The bell is rung only for historic Polish events.

A Mass to offer thanks to God for John Paul II's election as pope was celebrated in the courtyard outside Wawel Cathedral in Kraków the day the news came out.

THE NEW POPE WILL BE CALLED JOHN PAUL II

The world could not have known what Karol Wojtyla was thinking. After lunch, he went to Cardinal Wyszynski's cell. The tension was enormous. Anyone could see that Wojtyla had tears in his eyes while Cardinal Wyszynski was holding him in a fatherly embrace. Cardinal

Above: The crowd in St. Peter's Square waits patiently for the election results of the conclave.

Right: White smoke above the Sistine Chapel informs the world that the cardinals had elected a new pope.

Wyszynski felt in himself a sudden and complete change toward Wojtyla. Back in the Sistine Chapel, he went up to the candidate who was vacillating before the Throne of Saint Peter and said to him, "If they elect you, please do not refuse." The seventh vote did not bring a solution either. Some cardinals were still not convinced they should vote for someone from behind the Iron Curtain. Nevertheless, during a recess the cardinals who were for Wojtyla managed to convince a few German bishops and some undecided Italian ones.

During the reading of the names on the papers in the eighth vote, Cardinal Wojtyla sat up straight for a moment and then lowered his head into his hands. He, along with everybody else, realized that so far, he had received almost 100 votes. After the last vote was read, when the final tally assured Wojtyla the required number of votes, Cardinal Jean Villot walked over to Cardinal Wojtyla and asked him the prescribed question, "Do you accept?" The cardinal just elected pope did not vacillate. He had already prepared a few words to formalize his consent, "In obedience

to faith in my Lord Jesus Christ, placing my confidence in the Mother of Christ and in the church, and being fully aware of the enormous difficulties involved, I accept." Cardinal Villot asked him a second question: "What name will you take?" The new pope answered that out of fondness for Paul VI and John Paul I, he would like them to call him John Paul II. There was a round of applause. Cesare Tucci put a new handful of dry hay into the stove. It was cloudy outside in St. Peter's Square, but the official person on watch duty for the white smoke signal informed the crowd that a new pope had been chosen.

The master of ceremonies led the Holy Father up a stone staircase to a small room where Karol Wojtyla would leave his red cassock behind forever and would put on the robes of his new office, the white vestments of a pope. (There was a selection of sizes laid out, small, medium, and large, so one of them would fit the stature of the new pope.) He had already been through great emotional turmoil. Actually, the small room was called the "room of tears," since new popes often let the flood of their emotions out here. After a few moments, wearing white, he returned to the Sistine Chapel. An armchair was placed in front of the altar for him to sit while he received the homage of the cardinals. When the master of ceremonies mentioned to the Holy Father that he could sit down, he answered, "No. I will receive my brothers standing up." One by one the cardinals came to him, and he embraced them. While all this was going on, the fire in the stove was consuming the little pieces of paper with the cardinals' handwriting on them.

The crowd of 200,000 people in St. Peter's Square already knew a pope had been elected, but no one knew who it was. They waited anxiously for the Holy Father, who was simultaneously bishop of Rome, metropolitan archbishop of the province of Rome, and primate of Italy, to appear. At about seven o'clock in the evening, Swiss Guards were the first to enter the square to the sound of music; then Cardinal Pericle Felici appeared on the middle balcony of the basilica, where he announced, *"Annuntio vobis gaudium magnum…. Habemus papam!"* (I have a great joy to announce to you…. We have a pope!) After the cheering stopped, the time came for him to reveal the name he had written on a piece of paper (along with a close approximation of how to pronounce it): *"Carolum Sanctae Romanae Ecclesiae Cardinalem*—he took a glance at the paper— *Wojtyla."* (Karol Cardinal of the Holy Roman Church…Wojtyla.) He then announced that the new pope had taken the name John Paul II.

FAREWELL TO THE FATHERLAND

Some people in the crowd knew who the new pope was, but the rest of the crowd was bewildered. They realized the pope was not an Italian but were wondering what country he did come from. News spread quickly among Polish groups that the new pope was one of their countrymen, the cardinal from Kraków. John Paul II didn't keep the people waiting. After blessing the crowd in Latin and politely stepping aside from the master of ceremonies, he took hold of the microphone and spoke to the crowd in Italian, "My dearest brothers and sisters! Praise be to Jesus Christ!" When the Italians heard their own language, they broke out in wild applause. He continued, "We are all still in deep mourning after the death of our beloved Pope John Paul I, but our most eminent cardinals have elected a new bishop of Rome. They summoned him from a far-off country, distant in miles but forever close in the community of faith and in the Christian tradition."

Everyone listened very carefully to the reasons he gave for accepting the papacy. He repeated what he had told the cardinals after Cardinal Villot asked him if he agreed to become pope. "So then, as I stand before you, I proclaim our common faith, our hope, and our confidence in the Mother of Christ and in the church, as we start out once again down the historic road of the church, with the help of God and along with people of goodwill."

SMALL BREAKS WITH TRADITION

Pope John Paul II walked this new road from the very first moment of his pontificate, as he moved away from traditional conventions and gently broke rules that had kept popes who had gone before him in bondage. As in previous days, he woke up the next morning in cell 91. Other members of the College of Cardinals were also sleeping in their cells because he had asked them to remain, as if the conclave had not ended. That morning all the cardinals celebrated Mass in the Sistine Chapel, and he gave his blessing. He delivered a homily he had written out the night before in Latin. In it, he affirmed that his main "responsibility" was to finish implementing the goals of the Vatican II Council, "the most important event in the almost two-thousand-year history of the church."

He also spoke of continuing the work of ecumenical unity: "How many times have we conjointly thought about Christ's wish, when he asked his father for the gift of unity among his disciples?" At the end of the homily, the pope gave an answer that revealed the core of his pastoral mission: "What will our pontificate be like? What will the future hold for the church in the years to come, with the will of God? What path will humanity take as this century draws to a close? There is just one answer to these questions—only God knows."

CHECKING IN WITH FRIENDS

That afternoon he decided to go visit his friend Bishop Deskur at the hospital. He didn't ask anyone's permission to do so. His chauffeur could drive him there. He was now the vicar of Jesus Christ on earth, a successor to Saint Peter who was the leader of the apostles, patriarch of the church in the West, and apart from those titles, he was also head of the Vatican State. So he went to the hospital in the black Mercedes always at the pope's disposal, as any head of a state would do.

That evening he invited some close friends for his first private papal audience. They called this little gathering his "farewell to the fatherland."

The eyes of the whole world turned toward him on October 22, 1978, during his solemn inauguration to the highest level of the priesthood of the Word made Flesh. Here he was acting on a scene that hovered between the temporal and the infinite. He began the inauguration ceremony by stopping to pray at the tomb of Saint Peter the Apostle, to whom Jesus Christ had entrusted the care of his kingdom. Meanwhile, 300 bishops, plus heads of state and their representatives, as well as a crowd of 300,000 of the faithful were waiting outside the basilica under the autumn sun for him to appear in St. Peter's Square.

LITERALLY IN THE EYES OF THE WORLD

At the same time, millions of eyes the world over were fixed on television screens. For the first time in history, Holy Mass was broadcast on television. Everything came to a standstill all over Poland.

The three popes who had gone before John Paul II in the twentieth century began their pontificate by placing a tiara on their heads, which popes had done for 12 centuries. This headdress with three crowns, the *triregnum*, resembled crowns worn by Oriental sovereigns. The crowns symbolized the three powers of the pope. John XXIII received it from the hands of the major cardinal deacon: "You are father to

The day after he became pope, Karol Wojtyla visits his good friend Bishop Andrzej Deskur in the Gemelli Clinic.

(CONTINUED ON PAGE 110)

An Important Event for the Whole World

When white smoke finally rose from the chimney in the Sistine Chapel during the late afternoon of October 16, 1978, and announced that a new pope had been chosen, nobody knew it really was smoke from cannon fire," wrote André Frossard, a French journalist and writer.

The smoke signaled the "breaking of the tradition of Italian popes and the election for the first time in history of a pope from behind the Iron Curtain.... Those who were standing near the recently elected pope say that for a brief moment he stood motionless, pale, and somewhat terrified. Afterward, when he announced that he agreed to accept and would take the name John Paul II, and when he was taken to the sacristy of the Sistine Chapel and robed in the white vestments of the pope, he looked as if he always had been pope."

On October 18, 1978, Robert Sole asserted in the French newspaper *Le Monde:*

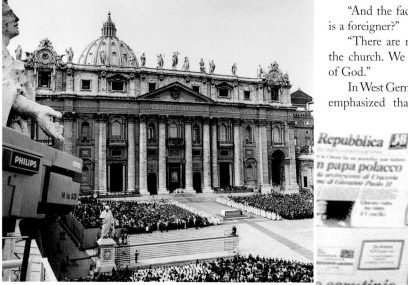

In the space of two weeks we went from one John Paul to another, from the countryside outside Venice to the fresh air of Kraków, from a country parish pope. Even a nation as flexible as Italy, because it always has to adapt to the most surprising events, was in shock.... The only thing anyone could truly predict was the name the new pope might take. It seems that for the first time in the history of the church, in taking the name John Paul II, he was evoking the memory of the three popes who had immediately gone before him. Anyone who would have been elected pope would have had to emphasize this continuity. But in Cardinal Wojtyla's case, the significance of the name he chose passed by almost unnoticed. The only thing that seemed to matter was the fact that the pope is Polish.

Angelo Rossi, Brazilian director of the Congregation for the Evangelization of People in the World, said with a broad smile, "I wasn't expecting that.... I thought it was going to be an Italian, but then it all changed. This is a big surprise, and we are all very happy."

Giovanni Benelli, archbishop of Florence, was also smiling. "It was a very well thought-out election. The right man was chosen at the right time." And he answered a question as to whether this was a historic turning point. "I don't think about historic turning points. The pope himself said he wanted to continue along the lines of John Paul I and Paul VI."

"And the fact that the pope is a foreigner?"

"There are no foreigners in the church. We are all children of God."

In West Germany, newspapers emphasized that the German

papal electors had voted for the candidate from Poland.

The *Berliner Morgenpost* commented that the new pope was "a force propelled toward reconciliation with the German nation."

An article in *Der Tagespiegel*, "Commotion in Rome," affirmed that the election of the archbishop of Kraków, Karol Wojtyla, brought great fame to the Polish nation.

AMERICANS APPLAUD ECUMENISM

In the United States, a country in which the majority of Christians are not Catholics, the mass media directed its attention to the issue of unity among diverse religious denominations.

The Associated Press stressed that the pope met with representatives of Protestant denominations and with members of the World Jewish Congress. It emphasized that the election of the new pope was a great opportunity for agreement among various denominations and religions.

On the other hand, the Swiss did not see the new pope as a good choice for agreement among churches. *Neue Zürcher Zeitung,* the liberal magazine, was of the opinion that the pope was too embedded in Catholic tradition and doctrine and would not be able to achieve significant progress in the ecumenical movement.

COMMUNIST REACTION

The Soviet news agency *Nowosti* asserted that "ascending the Throne of Saint Peter for the new pope will awaken peoples' interest. They will ask what stance the new administration will take about the most important facts of our time; that is, how to promote peace, control the arms race, put an end to tensions all over the globe." In conclusion, the agency wrote, "the need for détente today corresponds with the interests of all people, whether they are Catholic, Orthodox, Protestant, or nonbelievers. The pope is the spiritual guide of millions of Catholics throughout the world. He can help solve many international problems and help to increase understanding between believers and nonbelievers."

The Soviet weekly *Novi Vremia* stated, "Wojtyla's election caused a big stir. For the first time since 1523, the pope is not Italian. The new leader of the Catholic Church is from a socialist country. Why was he elected? Some Western commentators seem to think the cardinals elected Wojtyla *on purpose* because of his personal experience. He knows Socialism and Communism firsthand, and how to fight them. It seems those commentators are confused. They can't tell dreams from reality."

Bernard Margueritte, Warsaw correspondent for the French weekly *Le Point,* wrote, "Poland will never be the same since the election of Pope John Paul II, the ex-archbishop of Kraków, Karol Wojtyla."

The Guardian said, "As of today, no one can foresee the consequences of Cardinal Wojtyla's being elected pope, but it will surely have an enormous influence on the situation in Poland and Eastern Europe, on the future of the various branches of the Communist Party, and relations between the East and the West."

kings and princes, guide for the whole world, and our savior's representative." In 1964, during Vatican II Council sessions, Paul VI informed the council fathers and the world that he would donate the proceeds of the sale of his tiara (given to him as a gift from the people of Milan) to the poor and needy, so he came down from his throne and placed it on the altar. John Paul I declined being crowned with a tiara. For John Paul II, only the white pallium embroidered with little black crosses, symbols of his ecclesiastic power, was set aside for him. This was the gift Paul VI had given him when Wojtyla was archbishop of Kraków.

John Paul II raises a chalice during his inauguration ceremony in St. Peter's Basilica on October 22, 1978.

After saying the prayer at the Tomb of Saint Peter, the pope went outside the basilica, preceded by 111 cardinals, to ascend to the throne and receive the pallium from the hands of Cardinal Pericle Felici, who pronounced the prescribed formula: "Blessed be God who chose you to be pastor of the whole church and entrusted you with the apostolic mission of service."

With this power now conferred on him, the time came for the cardinals to pay homage to the new successor of Saint Peter. The whole College of Cardinals lined up behind Deacon Carlo Confalonieri to kneel in front of the pope and kiss his ring. They lined up by order of age

and seniority, but John Paul II disregarded this custom in one instance. He wanted to show special respect for Cardinal Stefan Wyszynski, the primate of Poland, so when Wyszynski began to kneel down close to the Holy Father, the pope stood up and embraced the old cardinal instead for a long time.

A WORLDWIDE MASS

To emphasize that this event in St. Peter's Square was not just for Rome and Italy but for the whole world, the first reading of the Mass was given in English. For the second reading, the world heard Polish, the language of the new pope's native land, which filled the Polish people with pride. The third reading was read in Latin and Greek. It was an extract from the Gospel according to Saint John and referred to the foundation of the papacy and the church. The Holy Father called to mind the words Christ spoke to Saint Peter after his resurrection—"Feed my lambs, feed my sheep"—symbolizing his handing over the keys of the kingdom of heaven to Peter.

A few minutes later he spoke the words that would sum up his pontificate: "Have no fear! Open the doors to Christ. Open them ever wider. Open the borders of your countries, your economic systems, your political systems, your current customs and civilizations to his saving power. Do not be afraid! Christ knows all about humanity and who each of you is. Christ is the only one who really knows."

He found the exhortation "Open the doors to Christ," when he read the treatise *True Devotion to the Blessed Virgin*, written by Saint Louis-Marie Grignon de Montfort, while he was studying at the Solvay plant in Borek Falecki during the 1940s. John Paul II also found the motto that he adopted as bishop and kept as pope: *Totus tuus* (All yours) in that work as well.

PROFOUND SILENCE BEFORE GOD

After John Paul II summoned the world to open itself to salvation, he added a request: "Anyone who wants to serve Christ, please help the pope and everyone else who serves other human beings in his saving power." Then the pope made it clear that just like Saint Peter, he came to the Eternal City, led there in obedience to give witness to the truth and ready to sacrifice his life. He arrived as the son of the Polish nation to become a Roman, although in a certain sense he had been in Rome from the beginning, because his nation had never separated itself from the faith of Saint Peter; it was always faithful to it. Finally, after expressing his gratitude to the people in many languages, he said to his Polish compatriots, "Anything I could say pales in comparison with what I feel in my heart at this moment. And also in comparison with what you feel in your hearts. So let's leave words aside and place ourselves in profound silence before God, the silence of pure prayer."

On October 23, the day after his inauguration, instead of starting to study documents given to him by the secretary of state, Pope John Paul II met with some Polish friends who had to leave Rome. Cardinal Wyszynski was in the departing group, and John Paul II embraced him affectionately once again. "You did not shrink in the face of prison and suffering. Without your deep faith, your heroic hope, your trusting yourself to the Holy Mother of God at Jasna Góra, this Polish pope would not be occupying the seat of Saint Peter. Today he is full of the fear of God, but also full of trust in the Lord, as he begins his new pontificate. I am indebted to the whole history of the church in our fatherland, which is tied to your service as bishop and primate." He asked his compatriots to oppose "all that is contrary to the dignity of the human person and all that debases conditions of a healthy society." For John Paul II, Poland, always faithful to Rome, would not be just a wellspring of incurable nostalgia, but also the redoubt of resistance to systems that oppose Gospel values—and over time everyone in the Vatican would come to realize this.

ANOTHER SMALL BREAK WITH THE PAST

The day before, at the end of the inaugural Mass, John Paul II approached people who were standing nearby, behind a wooden barrier. If he were to follow protocol, at this precise moment he should have gone back inside the basilica. He decided to break the tradition the Roman Curia had established. He walked firmly and steadily along long lines of people who were applauding him. He greeted them directly and blessed them. He grasped hands that were stretched toward him and kissed a little boy who ran up to him with a bouquet of flowers.

When he finally wound up at the front door of the basilica, he turned around and made the sign of the cross several times over the crowd with his silver bishop's staff.

When Cardinal Stefan Wyszynski knelt to kiss the new pope's ring, John Paul II bent over to kiss the hand of the primate of Poland; then the pope embraced him for a long time.

Over the course of its uninterrupted 2,000-year history, the office of the papacy has been constantly redefined. Throughout, papal influence has been viewed as a major political force in history.

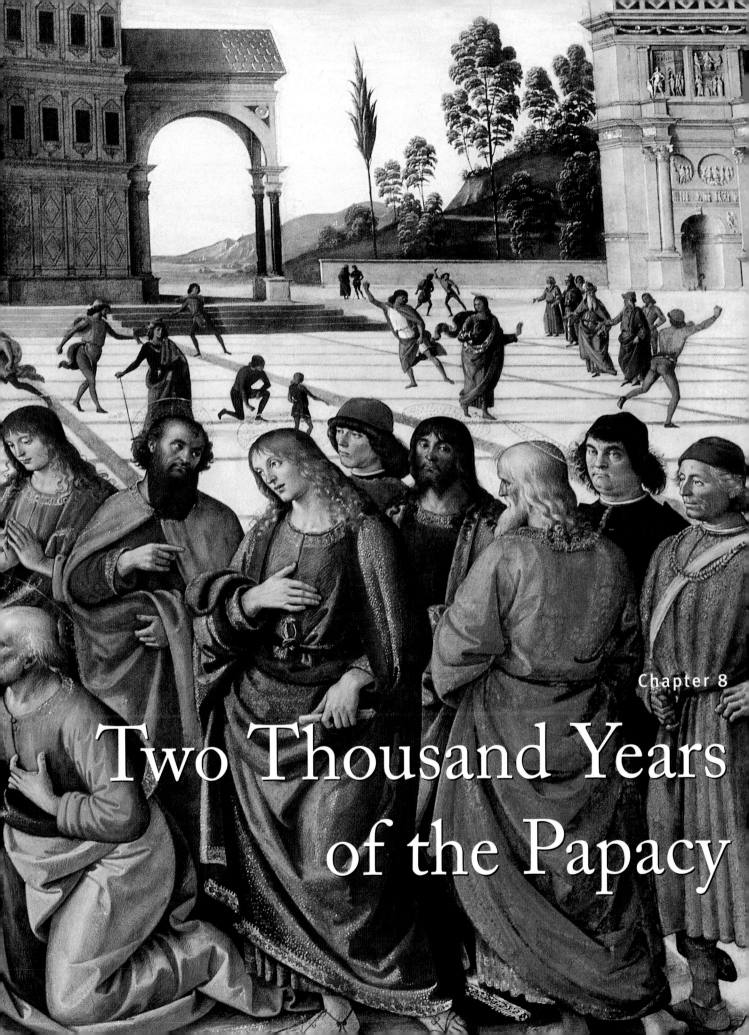

Chapter 8

Two Thousand Years of the Papacy

*Y*ou are Peter, and upon this rock I will build my church and the gates of Hades will not prevail against it (Matt. 16:18). Jesus spoke these words to Simon, a plain and simple fisherman, at Gennesaret, on the shores of the Sea of Galilee. Simon, from then on to be called "the Rock" (*Petrus*, in Latin), may not have understood that the history of the papacy began at that moment, a history replete with sanctity and sinfulness, accomplishments and failures, and around which the entire past, present, and future of the church would be centered.

When Jesus called Simon Peter, he wasn't the disciple who had the deepest or strongest faith in Jesus; nor was he the most beloved of the disciples. Quite the contrary, he had little faith and was weak in character. The Teacher from Nazareth reprimanded Peter more than once: *Get behind me, Satan. You are a stumbling block to me, for you are setting your mind not on divine things but on human things* (Matt. 16:18). When Jesus asked Peter to climb out of his boat and walk toward him on the water, Peter became frightened and Jesus had to go and rescue him. Peter's serious betrayal of Jesus happened the night before Jesus died on the cross. Despite his failures, after the death of Jesus, Peter reappeared as the leader of the apostles. He was the first person to enter the tomb where the body of Jesus had been placed and to give witness to the fact that it was empty. After Jesus rose from the dead, he reaffirmed that Peter was the pastor of the infant church: *Feed my sheep* (John 21:17).

PETER AS POPE

The timid Peter became another person. He never wavered when preaching what Jesus taught. He became an itinerant apostle and visited cities where Jewish communities had settled in order to start new Christian communities. He finally arrived in Rome, and although disciples of Jesus had already established the church there, he is considered its founder.

Peter died a martyr's death during Nero's persecutions in the first century, as did Saint Paul, the second great apostle. According to legend, Peter asked to be crucified upside down and buried on Vatican Hill. In the fourth century Pope Sylvester I commissioned St. Peter's Basilica to be built in his honor at his burial site. It has been rebuilt several times and has come to symbolize the Vatican in our time. The Papal Palace, residence for the successors of Saint Peter, is located next to the basilica.

WHO ARE THE POPES?

Until 1978 Italians have occupied the See of St. Peter most frequently; others elected to the papal throne have come from Syria, Greece, Spain, France, and Germany, among other countries, and from all social classes, professions, and occupations.

One pope in the history of the papacy was descended from an influential Roman Jewish family. A majority of the cardinals elected him pope in 1130, and he took the name Anacletus II. A minority group of cardinals caused a schism when they concurrently elected Pope Innocent II. Saint Bernard of Clairvaux, an imposing church figure at the time, supported Innocent II, while the king of Sicily, Roger II, endorsed Anacletus II. When Anacletus II was murdered, the problem of who was the rightful pope was resolved and Innocent II was recognized as pope. Historians still dispute which of them was the legitimate successor to Saint Peter.

Popes practiced many trades and professions before they were ordained priests and eventually became popes. Nino Lo Bello, author of *The Vatican Without Secrets* mentions some of them: Pope Eusebius (fourth century) was a physician and a historian, Boniface VIII (fourteenth century) was a lawyer, and Pius II (fifth century) was a poet. Clement IX (ninth century) was a playwright who continued to write dramas after he became pope. There was one banker among the popes, Innocent IX (sixteenth century), and one soldier, John XXIII (fifteenth-century antipope).

CHANGES TO THE OFFICE

The nature of the holy office of the papacy and its corresponding dignity has been constantly redefined over the course of its uninterrupted 2,000-year history. This developmental process was influenced by both church teachings and historical events. After Saint Peter was martyred, and despite the fact that some of the other original apostles of Jesus were still alive, the position of the bishop of Rome assumed a great deal of importance. In his *Adversus Haereses (Against Heresy),* written in the second century, Saint Irenaeus stressed these words: "Thanks to the primacy of the church in Rome, all other communities in the church, that is, all the faithful from all over the world must remain in accord with the church in Rome."

During the earliest centuries of the church, popes intervened in local church affairs all over the Christian world, stemming from ecclesiastic duties as bishops of Rome. In his *Epistle to the Corinthians,* Clement I (end of the first century) admonished the Christians in Corinth regarding their shortcomings and called them to Christian unity. This epistle has been given the same reverence and respect as Saint Paul's Epistles.

Biographical facts regarding the earliest popes are scarce. The main source of information about their names, dates of their reign, and what they did during their pontificate can be found in the *Liber Pontificalis (The Book of the Pontiffs),* an early collection of biographies of the bishops of the Eternal City. Many of these popes died a martyr's death. The anti-Christian emperor Maximus Thrax, for example, sentenced Saint Pontian, who was pope from 230 to 235, to forced labor in Sardinian mines, where most convicts died due to the harsh conditions. Pope Pontian abdicated because he did not want the church to be without a leader. The date of his abdication is the first recorded date in the history of the papacy.

Crucifixion of Saint Peter by Caravaggio hangs in the Church of Santa Maria del Popolo in Rome.

EARLY UPS AND DOWNS

Frequent internal problems caused the church to fall into decline. At the beginning of the third century, a theological controversy arose concerning the nature of the Holy Trinity. Hippolytus, a well-known theologian of the time, asserted that Pope Callistus I (217–222) was aligned with a heretical group and caused the first severe schism in the history of Christianity. Hippolytus refused to accept Callistus as pope, and a rival group of bishops elected Hippolytus as the first antipope.

Actually, there have been many struggles between opposing factions, as more than 40 antipopes have been elected by discontented cardinals, groups of clergy, rulers, and aristocratic Roman families—even by the people of Rome. During the Great Schism of the Western church, three popes reigned at the same time, and each of them was thought to be the legitimate head of the church. The last antipope was Felix V, whose papacy reigned from 1439 to 1449.

When Emperor Constantine the Great proclaimed the Edict of Milan in 313, he recognized Christianity as a legitimate religion and granted freedom of religion to all the people in the Roman Empire. The status of the church and the popes changed dramatically. Constantine gave Pope Melchiades (311–314) the Lateran Mountain and ordered a basilica, a baptistery, and a papal residence to be built on it in honor of Christ the Savior. From that time on, the Lateran Basilica was thought of as the mother church and the Foundation for other Christian churches in the world. The Lateran Palace served as residence for the popes for almost 1,000 years and also as the venue for five ecumenical councils. The only thing that remains of this ancient papal palace today is its chapel with a holy

The ornate design on the fourth-century *Codex Calixtinus* shows the creative work of the monks who performed this type of manuscript illustration in modern book form. Earlier manuscripts were copied on rolled sheets of papyrus.

This bust shows the Roman emperor Constantine I, the Great (280?–337), son of Saint Helena.

relic—the Holy Staircase leading to its entrance. Saint Helena, Constantine's mother, had these steps transported to Rome because, according to legend, Jesus once walked on them.

Through the ages Christian emperors constantly tried to exercise power in the church, even if only informally. They influenced church politics and even influenced the formulation of doctrines when they convoked councils with the purpose of presiding over them. Pope Sylvester I (314–335) was so subject to Constantine's power that he did not even take part in synods or councils convened by the emperor.

In 380 Gratian, the emperor in Rome, and Theodosius II, the emperor in Byzantium, elevated Christianity to a new rank: The church was placed on a par with the state because any deviation from orthodoxy (correct belief) was considered a violation of the laws of the state.

SOME OF THE GREATS

In the fifth century Pope Leo I, the Great, who reigned from 440 to 461, strengthened the authority of the papacy when he saved Rome, twice, from barbaric invasions by Huns and Vandals. According to church historians, Leo I was the first pope who reigned in the capacity of sovereign in Rome, the capital city of Saint Peter. The *Book of the Pontiffs* emphasizes that he made decisions as a head of state, without conferring with the emperor. Actually, it was during his pontificate that popes started to be called the successors and heirs of Saint Peter.

Another pope who earned the title Great or Magnificent was Gregory I (590–604). He was descended from an eminent patrician family in Rome and compiled the Latin missal that set the standard for liturgical rites followed by churches in union with Rome. (These rites remained in use until the Vatican II Council introduced rites in the vernacular.) Out of humility, Gregory I would not allow himself to be called the ecumenical patriarch—highest ecclesiastical position in the church in both the East and the West—and denied the patriarch of Constantinople that title as well. He ordered that he be called the "Servant of the Servants of God." This title was added to the list used in connection with popes, and all of Gregory's successors have adopted it. Gregory I administered church goods and finances so well that along with receiving the territories of Sicily, Sardinia, and southern Italy as donations, he became the wealthiest landowner on the Italian peninsula and, *de facto*, the political sovereign of Rome. He also administrated profits from the sale of wheat and so became, as church historian M. David Knowles describes him, "the banker and loan officer of the emperor."

Leo I, the Great

Leo I, the Great, was pope from 440 to 461. His main task was to fight heresy. To do this, he convened synods and asked rulers of states for help. He also wanted to strengthen the primacy of the bishop of Rome.

At his insistence Emperor Marcellus convened the first Ecumenical Council of Chalcedon, presided over by his own functionaries. Although the pope's representatives were able to present his position prior to the others, and although his pontificate was the first to carry through the decisions made at the council, in reality they carried no authority. That's why they could not stop the council from declaring that the patriarch of Constantinople had the same status as the bishop of Rome.

In 451 Attila the Hun invaded the north of Italy, destroying much of the countryside. Leo I went on a peacekeeping mission to Attila's military encampment (at right). Attila stopped the invasion by withdrawing beyond the Danube.

In 455 Vandals under the command of Genseric were outside the walls of Rome. As he had done previously, Leo went to the camp of the invading forces. This time he was not able to prevent Genseric from sacking the city, but he was able to save its people from being massacred and the city from being burned.

He was recognized as Italy's saving hero, and posterity called him "the Great."

Leo I was an imposing figure in the church at that time. He died in November 461 and was buried in St. Peter's Basilica. In 1754 Benedict XIV bestowed on him the title of Doctor of the Church. He is now venerated as a saint.

EAST-WEST CONFLICT

During the eighth century Lombards from the north threatened to attack Rome. When the Byzantine emperor Constantine V would not come to the aid of the city of Rome, Pope Stephen II (752–757) sought the help of Pépin le Bref (Pippin the Short), king of the Franks. Pope Stephen bestowed the title Patrician of the Romans on him. The principality of Rome and the duchy of Ravenna were added to the papal territories, thus forming the foundation of the Papal States that remained unchanged for the most part until the middle of the nineteenth century.

Once the church asked for support and protection from the Frankish kingdom, the church in the West broke with the church in Byzantium. Stephen II was succeeded by his younger brother, who took the name Paul I.

This East-West Schism in the church grew wider because of various episodes over the centuries, such as the issuance of a Roman coin bearing the image of Pope Hadrian I on it, not the Byzantine emperor, as had been

the custom. Hadrian reigned from 772-795. The bishop of Rome became the sovereign ruler of the Papal States. Church communities in the East and West were then still united, as the Great East-West Schism between the Orthodox Church in the East and Roman Catholic Church in the West had not yet taken place. In the meantime, the bond between the papacy and the Frankish kingdom continued to grow stronger. Stephen IV, who reigned from 816 to 817, wanted to consolidate his spiritual supremacy over the emperor, so he anointed (that is, validated) Louis the Pious as emperor. This was a reversal of the centuries-old tradition whereby emperors validated papal elections. From that time on, popes proclaimed the right to anoint the Holy Roman emperors.

THE DARK CENTURY

Dark clouds were approaching, however. Europe was divided into rival kingdoms, and these further subdivided into principalities, duchies, and fiefs of other lower ranks of nobility. Those who came into power in fiefdoms appropriated church properties and assumed control over the local church. Whoever ruled awarded privileges and decided who would fulfill ecclesiastic offices in dioceses and parishes. Due to this increasing secularization, whole regions and at times even dioceses found themselves subject to rival rulers, and Christian unity was broken. The Throne of Saint Peter became a pawn to be shuffled among diverse enemy factions in their wars and skirmishes.

The dukes of Spoleto opposed Pope Formosus, who reigned from 891 to 896. Formosus then sought the protection of Arnulf, king of the Franks, whom he anointed as emperor. The Spoleto army captured Rome, and the pope died soon after that. Following Pope Formoso's death, Boniface VI, who reigned in 896, was pope for a very brief period. The people of Rome had elected him despite the fact that he had been defrocked twice because of the immorality of his life. Actually, Boniface VI died two short weeks after his election, perhaps poisoned by the beautiful and cruel Agiltruda, a princess of the Spoleto family.

PAPAL NADIR

Pope Stephen VI (897–897) was elected to the Throne of Saint Peter, thanks to the support of the House of Spoleto. He became famous because he called for the infamous Cadaver Synod, one of the most repulsive events in the history of the papacy. Stephen VI, on Agiltruda's orders, demanded the body of Formosus be exhumed in order for the deceased pope to be brought to (a mock) trial. The corpse, in a badly decomposed state—Formosus had been dead for nine months—was vested in full papal robes and propped up in front of the papal tribunal. A deacon answered the judge's questions on behalf of the cadaver; Formosus's defense was weak, of course, and he lost the trial. The synod declared that all Pope Formosus's official papal acts and ordinations that he had performed were null and void. To add to the ignominy, Stephen VI ordered three fingers of Formosus's right hand be cut off (fingers he used to give blessings when he was alive), that they strip him of his papal robes, drag him through the streets of Rome, and throw his body into the Tiber.

The Cadaver Synod was held in the Lateran Palace. When it was just finishing up its proceedings, an earthquake struck, and the whole building caved in upon itself. The people of Rome interpreted this as a sure sign that God was angry. Stephen VI was deposed soon after, put in prison, where he was strangled to death. Over the next eight years, eight new popes occupied the Throne of Saint Peter.

Thus began the dark century in the history of the papacy. Bishops of Rome led immoral lives, and more than once their papal reigns were terminated by assassination.

A MORAL VACUUM

During Pope Sergius III's reign, from 904 to 911, the pope appointed Theophylact, a local senator, in charge of the papal treasury and in command of the local army. Theophylact's daughter, Marozia, became the pope's mistress, and she acted as if she were queen of Rome. She managed to have their illegitimate son elected Pope John XI. John's half brother Alberic II, absolute ruler of Rome at the time, revolted against their mother and had John deposed.

Gregory I, the Great

Gregory I was born into an aristocratic Roman family about the year 540. He was a prefect in the city administration of Rome when he was thirty. Two years later he renounced his wealth and its privileges and transformed his home into a Benedictine monastery. From that time on, he lived as a monk. In 590 he was consecrated as bishop of Rome, which he protested because he preferred the contemplative life of a monk. He was the first monastic to occupy the Throne of Saint Peter.

His priorities were to improve relations with the Eastern church and to reaffirm the primacy of the bishop of Rome, since at that time the patriarchs of Constantinople were claiming to be "ecumenical patriarchs." In 592, when Lombards were once again

poised to attack Rome, Gregory I went on a diplomatic mission to the Lombard king, paid him a large bribe, and promised yearly tribute to him. The emperor in Byzantium criticized him for this solution, but nonetheless Rome was spared and these negotiations ended the war with the Lombards. Gregory I also sought to maintain contact with Germanic tribes.

Another of his accomplishments was the Christianization of England. He sent a Benedictine prior, Augustine (later prior of Canterbury), and 40 monks to England in 596. As a result of this evangelizing mission, King Aethelberht was baptized. In 597 Gregory installed Augustine as archbishop of Canterbury, establishing the foundation of the church in England.

His pastoral letters, widely read, influenced religious life at the time. His 33-volume *Commentary on the Gospel of Saint John* became the basic moral theology text during the medieval era. Gregory I died in Rome on March 12, 604. The church venerates him as a saint.

Some say Alberic arrested Marozia and had her incarcerated in a convent. Others say he locked her up together with his brother, Pope John XI. Alberic seized full power in Rome, ending decades of what the Catholic historian Baronius called the "pornocracy" of the papacy. Although Alberic managed to bring about reform of monastic life in the Eternal City, he was never able to restore the papacy to its former splendor.

When Alberic's son, Octavian, was elected as Pope John XII, he reigned from 955–964 and inaugurated a new political era. This young pope, a talented politician, anointed Otto I, establishing a long line of Holy Roman emperors. Unfortunately, as one historian put it, the final analysis of his pontificate is that it was profoundly corrupt. After several ups and downs, John XII was finally deposed and convicted of assassination, the sale of church property, perjury, and sexual immorality.

John XIII (965–972) began moral reform in the church. He belonged to a reformist group that had originated in the Abbey of Cluny, in Burgundy, who were reforming the church in France. The inhabitants of the Eternal City did not readily accept his measures. The Romans revolted against his strict discipline and put him in prison. When news arrived in Rome that Otto I was coming to rescue the successor of Saint Peter, the people of Rome let the pope go free, asked him for his pardon, and handed him complete authority over their city.

GREATER SCHISMS

During the pontificate of Leo IX (1049–1054), rivalry between factions in the church precipitated the Great East-West Schism between the Roman Catholic Church in the West and the Orthodox Catholic Church in the East that has continued even into the present. The patriarchs of Constantinople, the capital of the Byzantine empire (a more civilized kingdom than the European one at the time), did not want to be subject to the power of Roman pontiffs who always seemed to be claiming greater prerogatives and who interfered more and more in the local affairs in the Eastern church. The church in the East granted that the bishop of Rome could exercise some authority over other church groups, or at least that each priest could appeal to the pope if he ran into conflict with local church authorities,

Pope Steven III (768–772) limited the influence of civil power in the election of popes.

Hadrian I (772–795), an aristocratic Roman, started the custom of dating papal documents in agreement with the dates of the pontificate.

but on the other hand, the Eastern church rejected the notion of the primacy of the pope—that is, the supreme power of the pope over all of Christianity.

This controversy between Rome and Constantinople began not only because of the authority problem but also because of slight differences in theological formulations. The two church divisions had been embroiled in a theological dispute ever since the seventh century. When it reemerged in the eleventh century, it was one of the main causes of the schism. In obedience to decrees promulgated by the Council of Toledo, Roman missionaries in Bulgaria were teaching that the Holy Spirit, the Third Person of the Holy Trinity, proceeds from "the Father *and* the Son." According to theology in the Eastern church tradition, preserved in the Creed of Constantinople formulated in the fourth century, the Holy Spirit proceeds from "the Father *through* the Son."

Pope Leo IX sent a special diplomatic envoy to Byzantium. He did this in response to an offensive letter he had received from another Leo, a bishop in the Bulgarian church who was subject to the ecclesiastic authority of the church in Constantinople. In his letter Bishop Leo criticized Christians in the Western church for using unleavened bread during Mass. Two proud and inflexible men— Patriarch Celularius of the Eastern church and Cardinal Humbert, the diplomatic envoy from the Western church—met in Constantinople, and their encounter ended with the mutual excommunication of the two church communities. Pope Leo IX died shortly after that. At any rate, this tragic rupture came about as a result of growing political enmity between East and West and culminated in the ignominious sacking of Constantinople during the Crusades.

THE CRUSADES BEGIN

Gregory VII reigned from 1073–1085 and called for the First Crusade. The goal of this Crusade was to take Jerusalem back from Muslim control. He received no response. Nevertheless, Gregory

EXPENSIVE CONQUESTS

Pope Urban II, who reigned from 1088–1099, took up Gregory VII's unfinished business, the First Crusade. Urban II called for a Holy War against the Turkish Ottoman Empire, which was occupying the Holy Land and persecuting Roman Christian pilgrims. He received a response way beyond his expectations. He placed a white cross on the right shoulder of many crusaders, promising them that their sins would be forgiven. "God wills it" became the motto of those who enlisted in the Holy War–pilgrimage led by Bishop Puy Ademar. In this way, the pope became the undisputed Christian leader of the church in the West, and the crusaders' army conquered the Holy Land. Urban II died two weeks before the Christians took Jerusalem. The crusaders slaughtered the populations of Jerusalem, Damascus, Sidon, and many other cities on their route. They maintained power in the Holy Land for less than five years.

The notion of the Crusades stayed alive in Europe over the next two centuries. Crusading knights and warriors took up arms seven times in defense of the faith. The final judgment on the Crusades, however, is negative. The Fourth Crusade (beginning of the thirteenth century)

VII is famous in history as the pope who settled the issue of lay investiture (civil rulers interfering in the appointment of bishops and abbots): At the core of this issue was the question of

A portrait of Pope Gregory VII (1020–1085) from a wood engraving by O. Knille.

who held supreme power—church or state, pope or emperor. Gregory VII opposed the fact that popes were approved by emperors and that bishops were approved by princes and kings. He wrote in his *Dictatus Papae (Pronouncements of the Pope):* "Only the pope's feet are to be kissed by all princes. The pope shall not be judged by anyone. Only the pope in Rome, who is at the highest level of the priesthood, is worthy of the supreme title of ecumenical bishop (bishop that could exercise universal rule over all Christendom)." His inflexible stance provoked wars between those who supported him as pope and those who supported the German princes. Before Gregory VII's pontificate the German king Henry IV had been excommunicated and later repented, but he insisted that the pope renounce some privileges in the civil domain.

Gregory VII's main objective was to reform the church and centralize its spiritual power. He opposed simony (the buying and selling of church offices) and enforced mandatory celibacy for priests. The Synod of Rome pronounced decrees that chastised bishops who allowed priests to live with concubines in exchange for money. Priests in France and Germany took a long time to accept celibacy. Gregory VII managed to unify liturgical rites throughout the church in the West.

Saint Francis of Assisi (1182–1226) founded the Order of Friars Minor, commonly known as the Franciscans. With Saint Clare he established the Franciscan Order of the Poor Clares. He also established a related order for laypeople in the world, now known as the Secular Order of Franciscans.

sealed the division between the Eastern and Western churches. Instead of going to conquer the Holy Land, the crusaders turned toward Byzantium to support Alexis IV, the pretender to the imperial throne. Eight months after Alexis took power, civil war broke out in the city. The crusaders attacked and sacked Constantinople again, totally destroying it. Historian M. David Knowles has written, "This Crusade ended with a crime that destroyed relations between the church in Rome and the Greek Orthodox Church for centuries. It's a crime that lives on like a bad dream in the minds of many Christians in the East."

For all of that, the Fourth Crusade took place during the pontificate of Innocent III, an outstanding successor to Saint Peter, whose reign lasted from 1130 to 1143. The greatest flowering of medieval culture took place during his pontificate. He approved the founding of the Franciscan order. He called the Fourth Lateran Council, the largest assembly of clergy in medieval times, to initiate church reform. Twelve hundred bishops, priests, and theologians took part in it. Decrees promulgated at this council mandated Catholics to confess their sins and receive the sacrament of Holy Communion at least once a year.

Innocent III

Born Lotario di Segni in about 1160, Innocent III came from the same aristocratic family as Pope Gregory IX and Alexander IV. He was elected pope at age thirty-seven. He had a solid and rigorous theological education and a thorough knowledge of Canon Law. He was convinced that he was elected pope by God's Providence. Right from the start he took on a task that lasted almost his entire pontificate: Two rival candidates fought for the imperial crown in Germany, and there was constant strife. In one of his letters, Innocent III decreed that the pope alone should decide this matter because he was the one who crowned the emperor. Because of his powerful influence, Frederick was finally chosen emperor of Germany.

Innocent III gave his approval to Saint Francis of Assisi to start the Order of Friars Minor. The friars preached and gave witness to evangelical poverty and became a reform movement in the church. Innocent III called the Fourth Lateran Council in 1215 with a view toward reforming the church and restoring peace. The council decrees emphasized the importance of evangelization and the pastoral work of bishops, defined articles of faith regarding the sacraments, and imposed the requirement that all Catholics make an annual confession and receive Holy Communion during the Easter season.

He failed in instigating a successful new crusade. The Fourth Crusade, which took place during the first years of his pontificate, ended disastrously with the sacking of Constantinople, and it aggravated the hostility that already existed between the churches in Rome and Constantinople.

Innocent III died in Perugia on July 2, 1216. He was a dedicated patron of the arts, and his pontificate contributed to the grandeur of the papacy in medieval times. He also added the duchy of Spoleto, the March of Ancona, and the Ravenna district to the Patrimony of Saint Peter, the Papal States.

THE HORRORS OF THE INQUISITION

On the other hand, the darkest pages of church history were written during the reign of Gregory IX (1227–1241). Although the Inquisition had already been in existence for some time, it was Gregory IX who included the proceedings of the Holy Office of the Inquisition in Canon Law, along with detailed descriptions of its punishments. Execution of these punishments was left to civil authorities, even though the most serious penalty—being burned at the stake—was introduced by the German emperor. The Inquisition extended throughout France, Italy, Germany, the Netherlands, and northern Spain, and it soon instilled fear throughout the whole world. Although Pope Sixtus IV (1471–1484) left a legacy of magnificent works of art, among them the Sistine Chapel, it was due to his orders that the persecution of Jews and Muslims began in Spain. Many Jews in Spain became nominal Christians under this forceful pressure but continued to remain faithful to their former beliefs.

In Andalucia, Spain, Inquisitor General Tomas de Torquemada condemned about 2,000 people to be burned at the stake from 1483 to 1498. Persecution of heretics became more severe under Pope Paul IV (1555–1559), since he was an inquisitor before he became pope. He is infamous in history as the one who drafted the *Index of Forbidden Books.* Although the Spanish Inquisition was less active in later years, its activities were not actually prohibited until the beginning of the nineteenth century.

THE "BABYLONIAN CAPTIVITY" OF THE POPES

The era of what has been called the "Babylonian Captivity" of the popes began with the pontificate of Clement V, which lasted from 1305 to 1314. Avignon, France, became the Holy See of the papacy for 70 years. Clement V, elected by French cardinals, was totally subject to the French king. He brought the papal court and the Roman Curia to Avignon, where many of them lived a luxurious life. Deprived of income from the Papal States, he imposed an unusual form of taxes: He made

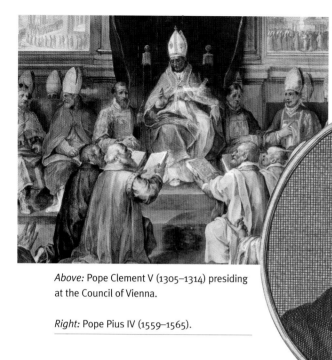

Above: Pope Clement V (1305–1314) presiding at the Council of Vienna.

Right: Pope Pius IV (1559–1565).

Neither the successors to Clement VII nor Urban VI obeyed the council's orders. Alexander V died a year after he became pope, and Cardinal Deacon Balthasar Cossa, a soldier and sailor, succeeded him. He took the name John XXIII and was the antipope from 1410 to 1415. King Sigismund of Luxembourg convinced John XXIII to convene the Council of Constance at the beginning of the fifteenth century. The council fathers demanded that the three popes abdicate. Initially John XXIII fled the city and did not present himself at the council. Afterward he accepted the council's decision and so did Urban VI's successor. On the other hand, Benedict XIII (antipope from 1394 to 1417), who succeeded Clement VII, did not want to renounce his papacy. In spite of his refusal, Martin V occupied the Throne of Saint Peter from 1417 to 1431 and was accepted by the majority of the European rulers. The Great Schism that divided the Western church ended with the death of Benedict XIII.

THE CHALLENGE OF THE REFORMATION

One hundred years later the Roman Catholic Church would face another crisis. Martin Luther, a German priest, protested when Leo X (1513–1521) announced the sale of "indulgences" to raise funds for the construction of St. Peter's Basilica. When Luther refused to renounce those teachings deemed to be against the teachings of the church, the pope signed a papal bull that threatened him with excommunication. When Luther set the bull on fire, the situation grew more intense, and reformers like Luther gathered new adherents among the German princes.

Hadrian VI (1522–1523) realized that the salvation of the church, menaced by this new schism with the protestors, or Protestants, as they were called, depended upon internal church reform. He began reforming the Roman Curia and also reduced the size of the papal court and administration. Hadrian VI was the first pope to make a public confession of guilt, an unprecedented event in the history of the papacy, when he wrote, "We know that for many years abominable things have taken place in the Holy See, betrayal of spiritual values, breaking the commandments…. All of us prelates and priests left the path of law and since that time nobody has been doing what is right."

Pope Paul III (1534–1549) called the Council of Trent in the middle of the sixteenth century as a counter-reformation to the Protestant reform movement. The reforms decreed by Trent spread throughout much of the

everyone—administrators and visitors alike—who entered the buildings of the Curia pay an entry fee. Anyone who avoided paying this tax was punished with fines, admonitions, and even excommunication. Due to pressure from King Philip IV, who wanted to confiscate their property, Clement V disbanded the Order of the Knights Templars. Clement's successors, also French, did not want to return to Rome. Urban V, although he did eventually move to Rome for three years, returned to Avignon despite pleas from Saint Bridget of Sweden and Saint Catherine of Siena for him to stay in Rome. Gregory XI (1371–1378) was the last French pope on the Throne of Saint Peter, and he returned the papacy permanently to Rome.

The hasty election of Urban VI (1378–1389) as the successor to Gregory XI started the Great Schism of the Western church. Europe was divided into factions that supported two, sometimes three popes, each of them considered to be the legitimate representative of Christ on earth.

The crisis started when the cardinals elected Urban VI, and then afterward he began to reign without consulting them. They rebelled against him, declaring they had elected him under pressure from the people of Rome, and then unanimously elected another pope in 1378, who took the name of Clement VII and reigned from Avignon with French support. Historians today still debate which of them was the legitimate pope.

None of the popes who succeeded these two popes agreed to renounce their pontificate, and they resisted all attempts to resolve the conflict. Finally the Council of Pisa deposed both rival popes and installed a third one, Alexander V, who reigned as antipope from 1409 to 1410.

European continent and accomplished many improvements in the church. The work of this council continued for 20 years; it was interrupted on several occasions, but each time, it took up the job again. Four popes died during its duration; Pope Pius IV (1559–1565) brought the council to a close. The legacy it left shaped the church until the middle of the nineteenth century. The council fathers redefined the teachings of sacramental theology and also the confession of faith as expressed in the creed promulgated by this council. It approved decrees on the doctrines regarding purgatory, indulgences, and the saints. It commanded bishops to create seminaries for proper formation of priests and confirmed the celibacy requirement for priests in the Western church of Rome.

THE COUNCIL OF TRENT AND CHURCH REFORM

Pius V (1566–1572), successor to Pius IV, was characterized both by his humility and his firmness in implementing the reforms of Trent. During his pontificate the Roman Cathechism, a compendium of Catholic doctrines of faith that has been passed down over the centuries, as well as the missal that standardized the Latin liturgy throughout the church in communion with Rome, were issued. Pius V, a former inquisitor, introduced strict discipline in Rome. He firmly chastised anything that was sacrilegious with respect to the liturgy, blasphemy, and immorality. A Venetian diplomat wrote, with some exaggeration, that this pope had changed the whole Eternal City into a monastery.

After the death of Pius V, Gregory XIII (1572–1585) and Sixtus V (1585–1590) continued council reforms. Sixtus V founded the Vatican library and a Vatican publishing operation.

END OF THE PAPAL STATES

The church under Pius VI (1775–1799) experienced difficult times. The Holy Roman emperor Joseph II suppressed monasteries and expected to appoint clergy himself. He encouraged rulers in Spain and Italy to help him assert the supremacy of the state. The leaders of the French Revolution ordered priests to swear an oath to the new French constitution, and the pope objected. The French authorities were merciless; three bishops and 300 priests were shot to death in Paris, and 40,000 other

Pope Gregory XVI (1831–1846) actively promoted reading the Bible. His pontificate coincided with an era of revolt by liberals in the church.

priests were sent into exile. Next Napoléon occupied the Papal States, and Rome declared itself a republic. The Holy Father was exiled to Siena and beyond. He died in Valence, France.

His successor was Pius VII (1800–1823), who also suffered at the hands of Napoléon, losing both the Papal States and Rome to him. After Napoléon's downfall Pius VII returned to Rome and rebuilt the church in Europe. The Papal States were returned at the Congress of Vienna. His dignity during Napoléan's brutal treatment and his gracious benevolence toward the fallen emperor's family later made him a popular figure in Rome.

Pius VII was succeeded first by Pope Leo XII (1823–1829) and then by Pope Pius VIII (1829–1830), who were not well attuned to the political changes astir in Europe. Pope Gregory XVI (1831–1846) was a conservative in both theology and politics. He called in the Austrians to help him suppress revolutionary Carbonari outbreaks in Rome.

THE LONGEST-REIGNING POPE

Pius IX, who reigned from 1846 to 1878, succeeded Gregory XVI in the middle of the nineteenth century, witnessed the dissolution of the Papal States, and became the "prisoner of the Vatican." The people of Rome had received him with enthusiasm; he was known to have a sense of humor, and many hoped he would reclaim the Papal States. But Pius IX opposed the unification of Italy and fled when revolutionary troops captured Rome. When the Republic of Rome was declared, he excommunicated those who had advocated it. He returned to Rome with the help of the French army. He never liberated the Papal States, and he was hostile toward democratic ideas.

Pope Pius IX convoked Vatican Council I, which never officially ended, because Rome was annexed to the newly unified Italy and the Papal States ceased to exist. In the face of this bleak outcome, the council fathers accepted the doctrine of the infallibility of the pope, which in itself almost provoked a new schism. During the pontificate of Pius IX, Roman Catholicism developed with unusual intensity—above all, in the United States and Canada. The dogma of the

Immaculate Conception of the Mother of the Savior, proclaimed by this pope, inspired an increase in devotion to Mary.

Of all the popes in the history of the church, Pius IX was the one most blessed with longevity; his pontificate lasted 32 years. Perhaps his longevity was due to playing billiards with cardinals and members of the Swiss Guard. Pius IX, according to Nino Lo Bello, was the last pope who organized sumptuous receptions in the Vatican. One of the banquets, with 300 invited guests, took place under the roof of the Basilica of St. Peter. The pope did not forget about the less fortunate; he invited 100 of Rome's poor to dine with the other guests.

Right: Pope Pius X, watching tensions rise before World War I, said, "I would gladly offer up my life, if by that means I could preserve peace in Europe."

PRISONERS OF THE VATICAN

Leo XIII, who reigned from 1878–1903, was the next "prisoner of the Vatican." He never left Rome. His successors also stayed behind Vatican City walls, until the pontificate of Pope John XXIII. (He took this name because that name was struck from the list of popes after the "first" John XXIII was dethroned.) The name Leo XIII is connected with *Rerum Novarum (On the Condition of the Working Classes),* the first encyclical in history to address problems of social justice. He described Christian principles that bear on the relationship between capital and labor.

Leo XIII's successor, Pope Pius X (1903–1914), became famous for his encyclical *Pascendi Dominici Gregis (Feeding the Lord's Flock)* in which he condemned modernism as "the résumé of all heresies." The modernists believed that doctrines of faith ought to be in dialogue with the ongoing historical situation of the church. Pius X was a tireless promoter of peace in the world.

Pope Benedict XV reigned from 1914 to 1922 and succeeded in producing the Code of Canon Law in a single volume. Pius XI, who reigned from 1922 to 1939, began his career in Poland, where he was the apostolic nuncio in the newly resuscitated Republic of Poland. He was courageous in the face of danger: When the Bolshevik army was advancing toward Warsaw and its occupation seemed imminent, Achille Ratti (his name before he became pope) remained in Warsaw while others fled the danger. This experience most likely influenced his strong repudiation of Communism. This Holy Father also understood the danger of Nazi socialism and condemned it in his encyclical *Mit Brennender Sorge (With Burning Concern),* which seems to be the only encyclical ever to have been written in German. Pius XI died some months before the beginning of World War II.

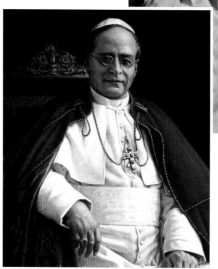

Above: Pope Pius XI. During his papacy an agreement was signed between Poland and the Holy See.

His successor, Pius XII (1939–1958), seemed to be somewhat conflicted about Nazi socialism. He was aware that Europe was on the brink of war, and immediately after he became pope, he stated that promoting peace was his primordial concern. Vatican diplomacy had direct dealings with Hitler and Mussolini, and after the invasion of Poland, the pope did not stop his entreaties for peace. But he never made any public statements condemning the extermination of Jews. Pius XII managed to maintain the sovereignty of the Vatican against Hitler. The culminating point of his pontificate was the proclamation of the doctrine on the Assumption of the Blessed Virgin Mary into heaven. He also wrote important encyclicals on Catholic doctrine and was the first to use a typewriter to compose his preliminary drafts.

Pius XII was also the first pope to appear on television. Nino Lo Bello describes Pius XII as a person obsessed with thrift, since he used to go about the papal apartments turning off lights in order to save money on the electric bill, and he wouldn't let people seal envelopes, so they could be used again. In fact, his last will and testament was written on the back of a used envelope.

A COUNCIL FOR MODERN TIMES

After being elected pope, Angelo Guiseppe Roncalli, who reigned from 1958 to 1963, took the name Pope John XXIII. Perhaps he wanted to undo the shame connected with this name in the fifteenth century, or perhaps he wanted to break the chain of bad luck of the other popes named John. Both were assassinated. If that was what he intended to do, he succeeded. Roncalli not only overcame the bad luck that weighed on his predecessors, he radically changed the image of the papacy in the Roman Catholic Church. Italians loved him; they even called him "Good Pope John." This pope's great contribution was convening the Vatican II Council to start church reform.

More than 2,500 bishops gathered in Rome in 1962 at its opening session. For the first time in history, 18 representatives of other religious denominations accepted the invitation to attend sessions. John XXIII drew up an active political strategy toward Communist-controlled countries. An example of this was the private audience he gave to the daughter and son-in-law of the premier of the Soviet Union, Nikita Khrushchev. He had critics, however, who said that he contributed to the spread of Communism's popularity in Italy. Although the Holy Office at one time had investigated him for his tendency to favor new approaches to things, he actually held traditional religious beliefs. John XXIII may have been chosen to be a pope of the transition, but he changed forever the image of the church.

After the death of John XXIII, Pope Paul VI (1963–1978) continued his reform work. During his coronation, which was televised, he donated his papal tiara to help poor people. This particular event predicted a new governing style in the church. Paul VI had taken part in council proceedings while he was still a bishop and cardinal, and he immediately resumed the sessions. The constitutions and decrees produced by the council revolutionized the church. There were notable changes in the liturgy, since after hundreds of years when Latin reigned in the Western church, the use of the vernacular in various countries was reinstated.

In another surprising event Paul VI met with Patriarch Athenagoras I of Constantinople at the council. To conclude the council in December 1965, the mutual excommunication between Roman Catholic and Greek Orthodox churches was annulled. The pope retracted the excommunication imposed on the Orthodox Church 900 years earlier, and the patriarch of Constantinople annulled the excommunication proclaimed against Catholicism. The difficult road toward reconciliation between the two churches of the East and West lay ahead, but an optimistic beginning had been made.

Paul VI changed the structure of the Roman Curia, and he also internationalized it; he introduced reforms in the election of successors to the pope and mandated that bishops retire when they reached the age of seventy-five

Pope Paul VI was both faithful to tradition and open to trends in the modern world.

and that cardinals who reached the age of eighty could not vote in the election of popes.

After 100 years of popes being "prisoners in the Vatican," Paul VI began to take trips to foreign countries, and since he was also a bookworm, he collected dozens of cartons of books to read on each trip. He also gave audiences to high-ranking Soviet government officials and spoke at a General Assembly of the United Nations. He attempted to unite openness to reform with respect for tradition. Underneath his papal vestments he wore a penitential garment, which constantly caused him pain. He died in 1978.

John Paul I, who reigned in 1978, occupied the Throne of Saint Peter for scarcely 33 days. This pope wanted above all to be a good shepherd of souls; he rejected being crowned as pope and also the lavish enthronement ceremony. His sudden death gave rise to rumors of a suspected assassination, which historians agree were false.

The French cardinal Jean Villot blessing the cardinals at the conclave in the Sistine Chapel that would elect the new pope, John Paul II, on August 25, 1978.

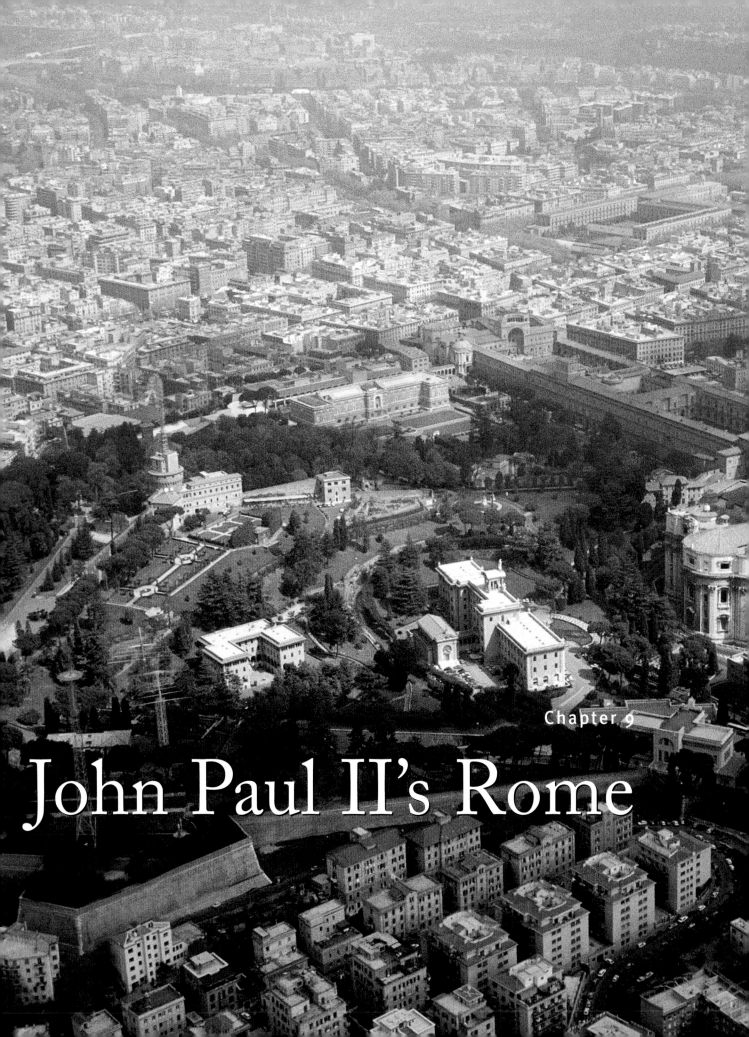

Chapter 9

John Paul II's Rome

Now it was no longer the Rome of his student days at the Angelicum or the Rome of Karol Wojtyla, archbishop of Kraków. It was the Rome of John Paul II.

The windows of the private apartment of the popes on the top floor of the Papal Palace face out over St. Peter's Square. From his bedroom window John Paul II, the new pope "from a faraway country," has a panoramic view of the old Rome that was once the capital of the Roman Empire. As pope, he would have to regard the Eternal City from a new perspective. He was no longer just His Excellency Cardinal Karol Wojtyla, the archbishop of Kraków, who inherited the spiritual legacy of the bishop and martyr Saint Stanislaw and a 1,000-year-long tradition of the Catholic Church in Poland. Now he was also His Holiness, John Paul II, Supreme Pontiff of the Universal Church, the bishop of Rome and successor to Saint Peter. In the past John Paul II's contact with Rome revolved around the small Polish enclave he visited over the years. Once he became pope, these places blended into Italy for him.

The pope could glimpse the Quirinal, one of Rome's seven hills across the Tiber. In times past, John Paul II's predecessors used to spend summers in the palace built on its summit. But after 1870, when Rome became the capital of the new Italian kingdom, the king and his descendants took up residence there, and after the republic was established in 1946, it became the home of Italy's presidents.

The Italian monarchy was reestablished in 1861 with Victor Emmanuel II as the first king. His family was descended from the ancient dukes of Savoy, the region on the French-Italian border, and he had been living in Piedmont and Sardinia. When the Papal States ceased to exist as of September 1870, the king moved his court from Florence to Rome and took over the Quirinal Palace.

PAPAL LOSSES

Loss of the palace was one of the many historic changes Pope Pius IX could not accept, and so, by his own choice, he became a prisoner for life inside the Vatican. He wouldn't even entertain the thought that the Papal States had once and for all become part of the kingdom of Italy, thus marking the end of an era for the church.

The Papal States were the legacy of Saint Peter and had been in existence since the beginning of the Middle Ages, when powerful Italian families gave territories to the bishops of Rome. They grew in size in 754 when the Frankish king, Pépin le Bref (Pippin the Short),

The papal throne in St. Peter's Basilica is under a stained-glass window that depicts a dove, a symbol of the Holy Spirit.

bequeathed more land to the pope. For many centuries it seemed as if the Papal States would go on forever, but they came to an end after nearly 2,000 years.

When Italy came into being as a sovereign national state, the status of the papacy changed radically. The pope always believed that Rome—the city surrounding St. Peter's Basilica—belonged to him, but it was now ruled by another power. Leo XIII, who reigned from 1878 to 1903, witnessed the dissolution of the Papal States, but he never really accepted their loss.

WHEN THE OLD ORDER DISINTEGRATED

It was a time of euphoria, when everyone felt the exhilaration of a new national identity. Even the pope's subjects were becoming more and more "Italian." Many had high hopes that the pope would lead the battle to unite the Italian peninsula and liberate its people from foreign occupation and Austrian domination. The pope, however, perceived his mission in an entirely different way. He did not appreciate the nationalistic hopes of the Italians. In the end, the old political order gave way, and in the wake of its destruction, the church and the papacy experienced rebirth in a spiritual reign. The papacy was stripped of its temporal power, but it had the power to unite people in a common faith.

Nevertheless, tensions between the papal tiara and the royal crown never abated during the first 60 years of a united Italy's life as a new nation. It was only in 1929 that a new modus vivendi between church and state was achieved, through the Lateran Treaty, solving the long-festering "Roman problem" and ending papal isolation.

THE LATERAN TREATY

The Lateran Treaty set up Vatican City as a separate state, fixed its boundaries, set the area within it at 44 hectares, or 108 acres, and determined what buildings outside the Vatican's physical confines were still under papal rule. These included the patriarchal basilicas of San Giovanni in Laterano, Santa Maria Maggiore, and San Paolo Fuori le Mura, "the edifice of San Callisto, adjoining Santa Maria in Trastevere," and the Papal Palace of Castel Gandolfo, the pope's summer retreat.

The treaty guaranteed the Vatican's sovereignty and independence. The Italian government also agreed to furnish public service and to protect the new state. And insult to the pope would be punished as harshly as one to the sovereign. Foreign diplomats were to have unfettered access. The Vatican, in turn, finally recognized the

Each year on Good Friday the pope led a procession of the stations of the cross in the Coliseum in Rome.

kingdom of Italy under the House of Savoy as the legitimate ruler of Italy.

A POLISH PERSPECTIVE

When Karol Wojtyla became pope, he had lived in Poland for 58 years—years when millions of his compatriots had shown him much love. Now he faced living in a new country with different history, language, geography, ideology, and politics. He had to win the approval of the Italians, and that would not be easy.

Romans were accustomed to popes who thought the way they did and who handled national problems alongside them. John Paul II was a foreigner who had a Slavic mind-set. For him history involved the vicissitudes of Poland first, before other nations, because Poland was the bulwark of Christianity, with its great romantic tradition and its heroic resistance to foreign occupation.

He lacked the ingrained understanding of the conflict between the papacy and the Italian state that Italian cardinals, with their personal, familial, or social experience, brought to the papacy. Now he

The Quirinal Palace, which used to be the pope's summer residence, is now the official home of Italy's president.

The Popemobiles

Throughout his papacy John Paul II traveled widely across the world and, of course, throughout Italy. He first used a limousine to ride around the Holy City, but traffic jams drove him into the air. He would fly in a helicopter that would take off from and land at a heliport at the edge of the Vatican gardens. The landing pad is still used by visiting heads of state.

He used other means of transportation as well—jets, ships, gondolas, trolleys, and even trains. But it was the "popemobile" that drew the widest popular interest. He inherited his first one from John Paul I—a truck painted white. It was not the first papal motorcar. Pius X started the trend in 1909 when he was given an Italia 20–30 limousine as a gift. In 1930 a

The pope had several automobiles at his disposal, ranging from limousines to convertibles. He even had an all-terrain vehicle manufactured specially for him.

would have to learn the intricacies of a problem he knew only from a distance, having observed it while a student in Rome in 1946.

EARLY DAYS IN ROME

As a young priest, the pope had lived in the Belgian College, a building not far from the Quirinal Palace, which he could now see from his Vatican windows across the Tiber. The college had moved in the 1960s. Only a plaque reminded passersby that Belgian priests had once lived there.

At that time, Wojtyla had walked past the Quirinal on his way to the Angelicum, the Thomist University from which he had graduated as a doctor of theology without a diploma because he could not afford to have his thesis printed. When he passed the palace, Italy's kings no longer lived there. Just before he arrived in Rome, a majority of Italians had voted for a republic.

Umberto II, Victor Emmanuel III's son, was forced to abdicate only months after mounting the throne. His father had abdicated in May 1946 and at once moved to Portugal. Umberto II went into exile in Egypt in 1947, and the president of Italy followed him into the palace on the Quirinal Hill.

IN MEMORY OF VICTOR EMMANUEL II

The view from the papal apartment is sweeping, but John Paul II could not see the Angelicum, where he had studied, from his windows because of the giant monument built in memory of Victor Emmanuel II, which was completed in 1911 (during the pontificate of Pius X). Its mammoth size dominates every neighborhood around it for miles.

A dining table set for 10 could fit into the belly of the horse the king is mounted upon, and his achievements are noted on each step. And yet the monument is not the only place dedicated to his memory. A nearby palace bears his name, as does a subway station. And the Corso Vittorio Emmanuele II winds its way from the monument through ancient Rome, inside a bend of the Tiber, and ends at a bridge where the road leads into the Via della Conciliazione (Avenue of the Reconciliation), a majestic street that goes to the square outside St. Peter's.

Victor Emmanuel II and his son Umberto I are buried in stone sarcophagi in the Pantheon, the only intact Roman temple in the city. It was designed by the emperor Hadrian, an amateur architect, in the second century AD and given to Pope Boniface IV in 608 when it became a Christian church—Santa Maria ad Martyres—located on

(CONTINUED ON PAGE 137)

French automaker gave Pius XI the most famous vehicle of that lot—a black Lictoria Six C6 Citroën, complete with a throne-like seat upholstered in purple and gold. The Vatican finally bought its first automobile a few years later—a black Mercedes Neuburg 460. Pius XII rode in popemobiles almost every day. But it was Pope John Paul I who began the practice of driving around in white automobiles.

Security was tightened after the pope was shot in an attempted assassination in 1981. Since then, the pope rides only in specially equipped automobiles, behind bulletproof windows. John Paul II protested this separation from his flock, calling his armored car the "glass trap," but his protests went unheeded. He never traveled alone; someone was always at his side.

Several days before he left on his extensive travels, the pope's automobiles were shipped ahead by special air transport. Before shipping, the cars underwent a thorough going over by experienced mechanics, and only authorized chauffeurs were allowed to drive the pontiff.

Below: John Paul II in a red Cabriolet Ferrari Empress—an unusual automobile for a pope (1988).

Below, right: A Lancia, designed for the exclusive use of the head of the church (1999).

Colleagues

Pope John Paul II was able to surround himself with some of the most intelligent, trustworthy, and competent men of his time. These close and very important colleagues managed the details of his pontificate, offered support and friendship, and, most significantly, enabled the pope to tend to the people and the problems of the world.

CARDINAL JOSEPH RATZINGER

Joseph Ratzinger, perhaps the most trusted papal adviser among the Roman Curia, used to meet the pope every Friday evening. They talked in German and without an agenda, sitting down at a table after shaking hands. They briefly discussed personal matters and then would get down to official business. The pope usually asked a lot of questions. What interested him most were issues of morality, bioethics, ethics in society, philosophy, and theology.

The German cardinal received his red hat in 1977 and first met the future pope shortly before his election in 1978 at a bishops' synod. They got to know each other at their first conclave in August 1978. "What brought us together most of all was his spontaneity," Wojtyla said of his friend. "He was free of any

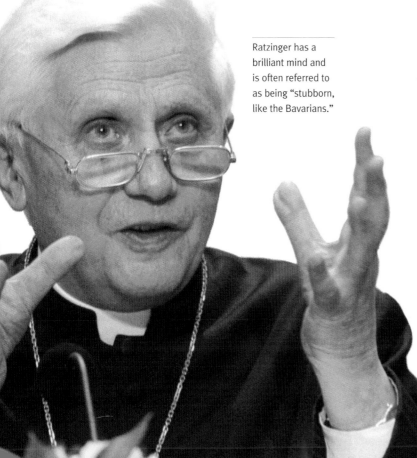

Ratzinger has a brilliant mind and is often referred to as being "stubborn, like the Bavarians."

personality complexes, and his friendliness radiated naturally to others."

Soon after becoming pope, John Paul II asked Ratzinger to move to Rome. The cardinal demurred, citing business in the archdiocese of Munich, a post he had held only for about a year. "We'll think about this later," the pope told him. The "later" came after the failed assassination attempt in 1981, and Ratzinger pulled up stakes and went to the Vatican.

The tiara and keys in the papal coat of arms symbolize the supreme pontiff's authority.

Ratzinger is the Vatican's prefect of the Congregation for the Doctrine of the Faith (once known as the Inquisition), in charge of safeguarding the integrity of the Catholic faith. His focus, therefore, is on some of the most important and troublesome issues in today's church: liberation theology, priestly celibacy, women's ordination, and divorce. The congregation he leads is not there to judge or condemn but to search for answers and help those who have fallen by the wayside. He often stressed that the best way to defend the faith is to spread it.

As prefect, Ratzinger is assisted by a secretary, an undersecretary, a promoter of justice, and a staff of 33. He has another 28 "consultors" working for him. The staff is divided among four divisions: an office for priests, another for disciples, a third for doctrine, and a fourth for matrimony. The staff stays in touch with theologians around the world, maintains close contact with bishops, and evaluates reports from national conferences of bishops.

The cardinal is also a member of five other congregations: for the Bishops, for the Evangelization of Peoples, for Catholic Education, for Liturgy, and for the Church in the East. In addition, he participates in the work of two advisory councils and a Commission for Latin American Affairs. As prefect of the Congregation for the Doctrine of the Faith, he was the principal editor of the long-awaited Catechism of the Catholic Church, the first published since the catechism promulgated by the Council of Trent in the sixteenth century.

In 2000 Cardinal Ratzinger published the Vatican declaration *Dominus Iesus (The Lord Jesus)*, in which he reaffirmed that "the pilgrim church is necessary for salvation because Jesus Christ is the only intermediary with God and he alone is the sole road to salvation" and that "the church of Jesus Christ, despite the division between Christians, exists in its fullness only in the Roman Catholic Church."

Joseph Ratzinger was born Holy Saturday, April 16, 1927, in Bavaria—"a beautiful day, which in a sense foretold my vision of history and my own situation that is in the eve of an Easter still to come." He was the youngest of three brothers who grew up in a poor and very religious rural family. He reveled in his poverty, saying that "it's precisely in such conditions that joy is born, a joy that people who are well off may never experience."

During the war he served in the Flak, an antiaircraft corps. He was a deserter from the Wehrmacht, but the Americans took him prisoner during the last days of the war. He was released in July 1945 and entered a seminary the following year. He was ordained a priest in 1951 and, while pursuing advanced theological studies, taught catechism in Munich. Later he became a professor in several German universities, among them Bonn and Munich.

With Hans Urs von Balthasar, Henri de Lubac, and others he launched *Communio*, a Catholic theological quarterly review that adopted a highly critical attitude toward the Congregation for the Doctrine of the Faith. Ratzinger was a *peritus*, or theological adviser, to the German bishops who attended Vatican II. He was one of the theological experts who drafted the *Dogmatic Constitution on the Church*. Pope Paul VI named him archbishop of Munich and Freising in 1977 and elevated him to the College of Cardinals three months later.

Ratzinger loves classical music. He plays the piano and wrote poetry in elementary school. His interest in liturgy and theology dates back to his youth, although clearly he never thought at the time that he would become one of the leading theologians of his age.

JOAQUÍN NAVARRO-VALLS

Joaquín Navarro-Valls has been director of the Holy See's press office since December 4, 1984, and he is the first layman to hold so high an office in the Vatican. He has revolutionized the Vatican's media relations, which in the past were based on a "no comment" approach to issues of the day, through frank and open dealings with the press.

He has a direct phone line to the Holy Father and is therefore in a position to clarify the pope's stand on any controversial issue. He reviews the Holy See's official communications before they are sent out, holds and oversees press conferences, and is the spokesman for the Vatican's official positions. He was the first man in the Vatican to use a computer and to access the Internet. In 1991 he launched the Vatican Information Service that issues daily news bulletins.

The pope thought very highly of him and appreciated his openness to the world, which reflected a new vision of the church in modern times. One of Navarro-Valls's most important and difficult tasks was informing the world about the pope's health, something he was well equipped to do, since he is a physician by training. But the pope used him for media relations as well, and he entrusted him with delicate diplomatic missions.

Navarro-Valls is handsome, gracious, loves sports, and always wears well-tailored suits. His colorful and often unconventional remarks about the pontiff have become legendary. A couple of examples: "He's a fantastic person, but sometimes he forgets he is carrying a cross," and "Karol Wojtyla ended October 16, 1978, and Pope John Paul II began."

For a press spokesman his background is eclectic: He has been a psychiatrist, a professor at the University of Madrid, a newspaper columnist, and Rome correspondent for the Madrid newspaper *ABC*. He also reported from Israel and from Poland in the 1980s, where he was impressed by the Polish people's strong, solid, and well-rooted faith.

He loves to read, especially contemporary philosophy, travels a lot, and plays tennis in his free time. He often accompanied the Holy Father and Bishop Stanislaw Dziwisz on hiking trips in the mountains. But despite popular belief, Navarro-Valls was never a bullfighter, although he often attended corridas as a student. "Somebody invented that idea, but it is not true."

Navarro-Valls is a member of Opus Dei (The Work of God), one of the most influential organizations in the church. He spends most of his time on the job, which

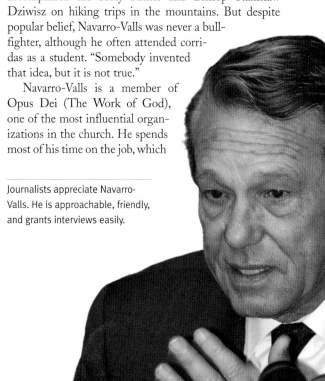

Journalists appreciate Navarro-Valls. He is approachable, friendly, and grants interviews easily.

often forces him to change plans.

He is unmarried and celibate. His vocation, he asserts, is to live in the secular world as a single person. He adds, "Thank God, in Christianity, each person gets to choose the path that suits him or her best."

BISHOP STANISLAW DZIWISZ

John Paul II's private secretary, Bishop Stanislaw Dziwisz, hails from the same region of Poland as the pope—Raba Wyzna in the Beskids Mountains. Their relationship goes back to 1963 when then archbishop Wojtyla ordained Dziwisz a priest. Years later the pope called him back to Kraków from Maków Podhalanski, where Dziwisz had served as a vicar, to become a chaplain.

In effect, however, he was soon the prelate's secretary, who took care of all the administrative details and other practical matters that did not much interest the archbishop. The role made Father Dziwisz indispensable; so did his sense of humor, which dovetailed with Wojtyla's. They communicated using few words, and they shared a love of hiking and skiing in the mountains.

Once in Rome, Father Dziwisz became one of the Holy Father's closest and most important aides. At official events he was always the man in the second row—behind the man in charge. He oversaw the pope's daily schedule, traveled with him, helped him with his overcoat, held an umbrella over him, and handed him the text to read at public events. Those who know him well call him "Lord Stanislas."

The pope fell into Dziwisz's arms when he was shot in 1981, and in the hospital the priest anointed the pontiff with holy oil. He remained by his side during John Paul II's entire hospital stay, as he did when the pontiff returned for follow-up treatment. He is exceptionally intelligent and is blessed with a phenomenal memory. In many ways he was the pope's "right hand" and confidant. The pope completely trusted his discretion and loyalty, perhaps one reason Dziwisz never granted interviews. He is one of seven persons authorized to confirm the authenticity of the pope's signature.

John Paul II consecrated him a bishop in 1998. "From the beginning of my pontificate, he has remained faithfully at my side as my secretary, sharing the hard times and joys, the worries and hopes linked with the office of Saint Peter," the pope said during the moving ceremony. "Today it is with joy that I give praise to the Holy Spirit, that with my hands I consecrate you a bishop."

At the same time, the pope made him auxiliary prefect of the papal household. His duties included scheduling meetings, handling requests for audiences, and arranging the Holy Father's travels in Rome and Italy.

Born on April 27, 1939, he was named Stanislaw in honor of the patron saint of his parish, Saint Stanislaw, bishop of Kraków and martyr, someone the Holy Father much admired. As the pope's secretary in 1981, he defended his doctoral dissertation on the Polish saint.

One of six brothers, Dziwisz was nine years old when his father was killed in a train accident. His mother died many years later. After finishing high school, he was admitted to the seminary in which the future pope was a professor.

Shortly after the pope chose Dziwisz—breaking with a centuries-long tradition of Italians in the papal household—he named a U.S. priest, Father James Harvey, as prefect of the papal household. Both choices provoked much comment at the time, which the pope dismissed with this ironic response: "A prefect from North America. . . Impossible! An auxiliary prefect from Poland . . . Worse yet!"

BISHOP PIERO MARINI

In the past, popes took part in

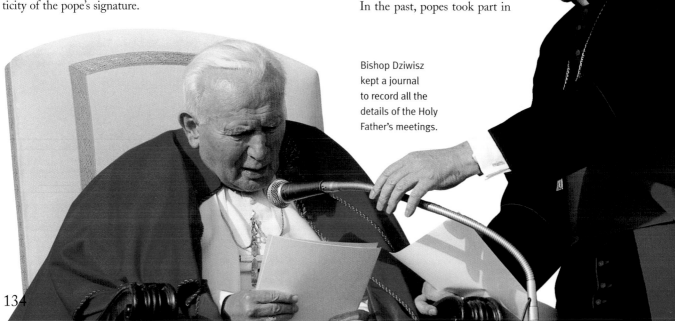

Bishop Dziwisz kept a journal to record all the details of the Holy Father's meetings.

only a few liturgical ceremonies every year. John Paul II celebrated liturgies every week and sometimes more often than that. He needed someone he could trust, who could direct the liturgy during his travels abroad and during apostolic visits to Italian dioceses, parishes in Rome, or liturgical celebrations in St. Peter's Square.

In 1987 the pontiff chose Piero Marini as master of ceremonies, the man charged with implementing liturgical principles on the large stage, created whenever and wherever the pope appeared. The Italian press has called him both "Mister Vatican" and the pope's "guardian angel" because he always stood at his side in public ceremonies. He handed the pope his pastoral staff and the pages of a talk, and when called for, he put the miter on the pope's head.

More important, he choreographed the pontiff's Masses wherever he went, and he accompanied John Paul II on 70 of his trips. Millions around the world have watched the Masses staged by Marini, which, his critics contend, too often resembled a Broadway musical. He managed everything down to the most meticulous detail—the number of chairs and vestments needed for Masses concelebrated by several priests, for example. He did not allow too many or too few chairs, important when, on some occasions, hundreds of priests were gathered around the altar.

Marini prepared readings in several languages and decided which celebrant would read what. He picked priests to distribute Holy Communion at papal Masses and determined just how many of the faithful would receive the Host from the pontiff himself. He monitored the pacing of each program and tried to make sure it hewed to the liturgy. And of course, he consulted with the pope on all the details.

Charming and well educated, the pope could be inflexible at times and would resist changes in Marini's carefully laid-out plans. Marini had to be ready for the ad hoc changes the pontiff, famous for his volatile nature and unpredictable behavior, decided to make. Often there were last-minute switches—even in introductory remarks before Mass began—and John Paul II frequently even dropped the homily that had been prepared for him by the Office of Celebrations so that he could talk about something else.

A key feature of Marini's job was to act as the advance man on the pope's foreign journeys. He visited the chosen country well ahead of time to plan every detail of the trip, down to decorations used and locating the altar and cross. He worked together with the local clergy to make sure everything went off seamlessly. That meant supervising rehearsals with priests and acolytes, inspecting sites where the Holy Father would appear to celebrate Mass or take part in other ceremonies, and making sure that everything complied with the liturgy. Marini also prepared official liturgies for bishops or cardinals who act as papal surrogates. This was a frequent occurrence during the pope's

Year 2000 Jubilee, when so many ceremonies had been scheduled, the pope could not possibly officiate at all of them.

Piero Marini is Italian; he was ordained a priest in 1965 and a few months later began to work in the Roman Curia in the commission charged with liturgical reform to implement recommendations made by Vatican II. After he joined the Congregation for Divine Worship and for the Discipline of the Sacraments, he continued to work on liturgical issues, writing widely about the liturgy and pastoral theology. In 1985 he was named undersecretary of the Congregation for Divine Worship and for Discipline of the Sacraments. Two years later he became master of ceremonies.

Bishop Marini's office staff includes three priests and three sisters, and he is also assisted by four other priests who work in various Vatican institutions. Marini speaks French, German, English, and Spanish, besides his native Italian. He was consecrated as bishop in St. Peter's Basilica on March 19, 1998. The Holy Father thanked him for his dedication and the help he had given during the entire pontificate.

Marini always stood beside the pope, or just behind him, during liturgical ceremonies.

A Day in the Life of John Paul II

—Father Konrad Hejmo, O.P. (Dominican priest from Louisiana)

Despite age and illness, John Paul II worked at a hectic pace and disliked hearing about changes in his tight schedule. Nor was he willing to rest for long unless illness and his infirmities forced him to do so. His already full schedule seemed to get more crowded with new commitments each passing year. But he always had time for prayer—his breviary, the stations of the cross, and the Rosary. Despite pleas from those around him to save his strength, he spent more time on his knees than sitting down.

The Holy Father rose at about five thirty or six o'clock each morning. After bathing, he prayed alone in his private chapel. Sisters of the Sacred Heart arrived about eight o'clock, and he celebrated Mass. The only change that those who attended the pope were able to make in his schedule was the time set for morning Mass; up until the middle of 2000, the pope celebrated Mass at six thirty.

Those who attended Mass with him were usually guests invited by the Holy Father or persons chosen by Bishop Stanislaw Dziwisz. The pope used to distribute Holy Communion himself, but later Bishop Dziwisz or one of the others attending the Mass took over. Some guests stayed for breakfast—a relaxed and friendly affair in which differences in status between the Holy Father and the invited guests disappeared.

John Paul II celebrating Mass in his private Vatican chapel.

John Paul II worked in his office from nine thirty to eleven o'clock in the morning. He read and signed documents—the most important of which were signed with a special gold pen—attended to correspondence, and prepared homilies, which he dictated or wrote in longhand. Sometimes he used a computer. He wrote most of the rough drafts in Polish and then translated them. Magazines in different languages were piled on his desk: Italian, French, Polish, German, and Spanish. When he was in the Vatican, he read them himself; while traveling, he scanned summaries of articles in local and Italian periodicals that were prepared for him.

After his office duties, the pope received guests: ambassadors, heads of state, church leaders, and members of the faithful. His library was large enough to accommodate up to 10 groups at once. Even though he had trouble walking, he went up to each group and personally greeted each person. Audiences always ended with a souvenir photograph taken by Arthur Mariego, the official photographer.

The pope held general audiences every Wednesday in St. Peter's Square or in the Paul VI wing of the Papal Palace. Thousands of pilgrims from all over the world attended them. On one occasion, during a private audience with pilgrims from Poland, a sister came up to him and introduced herself as the person in charge of finances in her religious order. Smiling, the pope remarked, "So you are never short of money, are you?" John Paul II liked to joke with his visitors.

His schedule became even more crowded during his Jubilee Year, when he met with pilgrims on Saturdays and Sundays in addition to his regular Wednesday audiences. He used to stand among his visitors for photo sessions, but later he remained seated while the faithful crowd surrounded him.

He always loved to talk and joke, and he came alive in each audience, radiating warmth. When he talked to Polish visitors, he loved to reminisce about his childhood and his life in Kraków, and sometimes he would ask Poles detailed questions about their lives and where they came from. The pope noticed everything.

In one audience where more groups than usual jammed the library, Bishop Dziwisz, his private secretary, asked people to gather around the pope for a group picture—there were simply too many groups for him to pose with each one. A priest called out that he had brought his mother and could he bring her closer to the pope.

John Paul II asked about the priest, but only after the man had left the audience hall, so he called me and said, "One of the priests asked if I would receive his mother. Go find him." I immediately went looking for him, but unfortunately, the priest had left and I caught up with him two days later. Of course, the pope met with the priest and his mother.

On a day when there were no audiences, the pope met with members of the Curia, theologians, or philosophers. He prayed the *Angelus* at noon on Sundays. The midday meal was set for one thirty in the afternoon, and almost always, invited guests joined the pope. One of his coworkers joked that "with the pope, there are two things that no one knows until the last minute: what time he is going to eat and with whom."

But Bishop Dziwisz always knew because he invited the guests. The pope preferred simple meals but often gave his guests a choice of foods. The Sisters of the Sacred Heart were fond of Italian dishes, but he still prefered Polish cuisine. After lunch the Holy Father relaxed for a short while by going out for some fresh air, where he prayed or meditated. He returned to work after a brief stroll. His afternoons usually started out with meetings with his co-workers, the prefects of various congregations, and office heads in the Vatican secretariat. He was always busy and never complained about being tired or not feeling well.

The Church of St. Stanislaw, where Wojtyla celebrated Mass as a bishop and a cardinal.

During summer vacations at Castel Gandolfo, John Paul II set afternoons aside for reading. Often he selected up to 10 or 12 books to read in one day. He knew which ones to skim through and those worth special attention, especially works his friends or people he knew had written.

The evening meal usually began at seven thirty. Dinner guests were rare, and those who did come were usually close friends. The meal always ended with a prayer. Sometimes Bishop Dziwisz turned the television on so that the pope could watch an important world event or a soccer game.

After dinner the pope would go back to his personal apartment to write or read, and he spent the last minutes of his day in his private chapel. The light in his rooms went off around eleven o'clock at night. Once someone asked him how he could sleep with so much on his mind and so hectic a schedule. He replied without hesitation, "I sleep as I have always slept, any way I can, and I leave the rest to God's Providence, because God is the one who chose me and who gave me a job to do."

the Piazza della Rotunda, about three blocks up from the Corso Vittorio Emmanuele II.

SAINT CATHERINE OF SIENA

Down the street from the Pantheon stands the Church of Santa Maria Sopra Minerva, Rome's only Florentine Gothic church, perhaps built, as the name suggests, atop an ancient temple to the Goddess Minerva. Saint Catherine of Siena, Italy's patron saint, is buried here. She was proclaimed a Doctor of the Church for her wisdom and intelligence and was instrumental in bringing the "Babylonian Captivity" of the papacy in Avignon to an end by persuading Pope Gregory XI to return to Rome.

Saint Catherine of Siena had the same significance for John Paul II as Saint Stanislaw, archbishop of Kraków and patron saint of Poles did for Cardinal Wojtyla when he was archbishop of Kraków. During his days in Rome as a young priest and later as an archbishop, Wojtyla stopped often at the lovely church with its Michelangelo statue of the Risen Christ and the Filippino Lippi frescoes.

A WALK FROM STUDENT DAYS

When he lived at the Belgian College, it took Father Wojtyla about 20 minutes to walk to the Angelicum, the Pontifical University of Saint Thomas. He would stroll along the Via del Quirinale past the Church of Sant'Andrea al Quirinale, a church dear to his heart because it holds the tomb of Saint Stanislas Kostka, a young Polish Jesuit who died during a malaria epidemic in Rome in 1568. He was canonized in 1726 and proclaimed the patron saint of youth. More than a century later Pope Leo XIII would celebrate his first Mass as a priest in that church.

At the Quirinal Palace Wojtyla would turn into the Via XXIV Maggio and then walk across the large Angelicum past the Via Nazionale to where the Catholic University was located. It had moved several times over the centuries but found a permanent home in a monastery that an order of nuns had ceded to the Angelicum in 1932. Father Wojtyla strode through the main gate, up a steep staircase, and into the inner courtyard that was often the site of heated discussions among students and their professors. Before, Vatican II priests never wore business suits or informal clothing. Today such attire is as common as the white habits of the Dominican Fathers.

Beyond the Foro Romano and on the slopes of the Palatine Hill, south of the Angelicum, stands the Church of St. Cesareo, dating back to the eighth century. It is the

The Roman Curia

The Roman Curia dates back to the third century, but it was not until Pope Sixtus V issued his decree *Immensa Aeterni Dei (Almighty Eternal God)* on December 22, 1588, that the Curia, as it is known today, was put in place. Nine congregations, twelve pontifical councils, three tribunals, three offices, and two dicasteries (basically, judicial courts) operate within its overall framework.

When a non-Italian pope was elected, the tension that had built up over 400 years between pontiff and Curia, already high during the reigns of the popes before him, heightened even more. John Paul II knew very well how much this petrified structure would resist changes, so he wasted no time in introducing them to his simple policy: Make changes and make them stick.

He presented to the Curia new ways of doing things and scrapped old ones. He put new people in charge of accomplishing new tasks, and many of those he recruited came from outside Italy, including, understandably, a number of Polish priests whom he had known at home. He worked

more closely than his predecessors with the Secretariat of State, the Vatican's governing body, introducing important reforms.

The Secretariat was divided into two bodies: General Affairs handles the Holy Father's dealings with the universal church, the Roman Curia, and the formulation of key church documents. The "Foreign Office" deals with other countries, international organizations, and the nomination of bishops, since their names must be acceptable to national governments.

Nine congregations comprise the Roman Curia:

- The Congregation for the Doctrine of the Faith concentrates on church doctrine. Its duty is to watch over the integrity of the faith and clarify Catholic moral norms. Cardinal Joseph Ratzinger is the prefect of this congregation, and he collaborates with local bishops in other countries.
- The Congregation for the Oriental churches maintains contact with Eastern churches that recognize the authority of the pope and the Holy See. Cardinal Achille Silvestrini presides over it.
- The Congregation for Divine Worship and the Discipline of the Sacraments is dedicated to the liturgical

rites and sacramental life of the church. Cardinal Jorge Arturo Medina Estevez heads this congregation.

- The Congregation for Causes of Saints is the most recently formed congregation. It has been in charge of the process of beatification and canonization of saints since its inception in 1969. Archbishop Jóse Martins Saraiva is in charge.
- The Congregation for Bishops is one of the oldest in existence and takes care of everything connected with bishops: their nomination, changes in their assignments or duties, and the determination of boundaries of dioceses and the formation of new dioceses. Cardinal Lucas Moreira Neves heads this congregation.
- The Congregation for the Evangelization of Peoples is the principal agency in the Vatican in charge of missionary activity. Cardinal Józef Tomko is its prefect.
- The Congregation for the Institutes of Consecrated Life and Societies of Apostolic Life takes care of both men's and women's religious orders in the church. Cardinal Eduard Martinez Somalo directs it.
- The Congregation for the Clergy is responsible for all clerical affairs. Cardinal Dario Castrillon Hoyos is its prefect.
- The Congregation for Catholic Education is responsible for teaching in Catholic schools. It oversees schools that train church administrators, Catholic universities, and seminaries. Cardinal Pio Laghi is its prefect.

Pontifical councils support the work of these congregations that were created to handle such diverse church affairs as the laity, the family, social communication, culture, interfaith dialogue, and justice and peace issues.

These councils are responsible for the promotion of Christian unity, legislative texts, pastoral care of health-care workers, pastoral care of migrants and itinerant people, and Cor Unum (With One Heart) is the council in charge of charitable works.

In addition, a dicastery, the Apostolic Penitentiary, is an internal-affairs tribunal of the church in charge of handling serious misconduct with regard to morality, heresy, and apostasy.

A new regulation introduced in July 1999 was designed to bring younger people into the Curia. Only clerics under forty-five years of age may work there. Congregation prefects are the exception, since they are generally older than forty-five and bring long experience to their positions. Laymen, on the other hand, must be at least thirty-five. People who work in the Curia may not talk to the press without permission or accept gratuities, and they must respect church laws, even in their private lives, at all times.

The Holy Staircase, leading to the entrance of the private chapel of the popes in the Lateran Basilica. According to legend, Christ climbed these steps to enter Pontius Pilate's palace in Jerusalem.

century, it is known as the "mother of all churches" and is the cathedral of the pope as bishop of Rome. From the beginning it was central to the life of the church, caught up in the upheavals and misfortunes that struck the city after the decline of the Roman Empire.

WHEN IT SNOWED IN AUGUST

In AD 896 an earthquake reduced the Lateran Basilica to a pile of rubble, but it was rebuilt in all its splendor. A renovation ordered in 1650 gave the basilica its current baroque façade with gesturing and gyrating saints staring down at the faithful. Inside, the cloister has retained its thirteenth-century Cosmatesque. The popes lived in the Lateran Palace until 1309 (when they removed to Avignon for almost 70 years) and were crowned pontiff in the basilica well into the nineteenth century.

Relics kept in the church add to the basilica's prestige. In its altar are the heads of Saint Peter and Saint Paul, the true founders of the Catholic Church. An ancient Latin description—*omnium urbis et orbis ecclesiarum Mater et Caput;* that is, the mother and foundation church of all church communities in Rome and throughout the whole world—give it added cachet. On the Feast of the Assumption, popes follow established tradition in bestowing a special blessing from its balcony.

The Basilica of Santa Maria Maggiore lies to the north, between the Via Nazionale and the main railroad station. After John Paul II was shot in May 1981, he greeted the people of Rome via a message he had recorded in the hospital and which was broadcast from the balcony of this basilica.

Legend has it that Pope Liberius had a dream in AD 353 in which Mary told him that if it snowed in August, he was to build a church on the place where snow fell. It did snow, and the pope did as he was bid. Archaeologists, however, have found nothing to corroborate the legend. The fact is that the basilica was built on Cisipian Hill under the reign of Pope Sixtus III between 432 and 440, shortly after the Council of Ephesus, held in 431, proclaimed Mary to be the mother of God.

titular church given to Archbishop Wojtyla after he became a cardinal. When he took canonical possession of the church in February 1968, Cardinal Wojtyla became an honorary citizen of Rome. As cardinal, he would often visit this church, celebrate Mass, and preach homilies to the gathered faithful who were mostly Polish. Once he became pope, however, the church was given to someone else. John Paul II now presided over Rome's four patriarchal basilicas—vast St. Peter's, inside the Vatican walls, and three others in Rome proper.

San Giovanni in Laterano sprawls across a large square just inside the old city walls and south of the Esquiline Hill. Founded by the emperor Constantine in the fourth

On August 5 the Feast of Our Lady of the Snows takes place at the Basilica of Santa Maria Maggiore. To celebrate, white flower petals are strewn from the church balconies.

The basilica was the first "great" *(maggiore)* church dedicated to the Virgin Mary. Mosaics in the nave of the basilica date from the fifth century and depict scenes from Mary's life. The church blends various architectural styles from the fifth century on—Byzantine, Romanesque, a Renaissance ceiling, and a baroque makeover.

HE LEFT SOME ENVELOPES BEHIND

The Polish College on the Valentine Hill can also be seen from the papal windows, though far in the distance. A tree-lined avenue that runs up steeply past the Circus Maximus below the Palatine Hill ends at the small Remuria Square. The college is set back from the road and surrounded by a garden. Karol Wojtyla used to stay there when he visited Rome. He occupied a small, modestly furnished room that had a copy of the icon of the Black Madonna of Czestochowa in it. He would receive guests in a small adjoining room.

When he left the Polish College to attend his first conclave as a cardinal in August 1978, he returned after the election of John Paul I. When he left for his second conclave a month later, he did not come back.

In Kraków Father Stanislaw Dziwisz picked up Cardinal Wojtyla's personal belongings. He had left behind a packet of white envelopes in his apartment; the heading on them in purple letters read, *"Carolus Cardinalis Wojtyla Archiepiscopus Metropolita Cracoviensis."* As for the Polish College, the Holy Father did return 20 years later when he was celebrating the Jubilee Year of his pontificate.

THE FOURTH BASILICA

Near a bend of the Tiber, a couple of miles south of the Campitelli, stands the last of the Roman basilicas, that of San Paolo Fuori le Mura (St. Paul Outside the Walls). It was built by the emperor Constantine in the fourth century beyond the wall constructed during Marcus Aurelius's reign and on the site where Saint Paul was martyred. For 400 years it was the largest church in Europe until the Saracens sacked it in 846. It was rebuilt—several

times—and is still the second-largest church in Rome. A fire destroyed the basilica in 1823, but thanks to generous gifts from benefactors who included the viceroy of Egypt and the Russian tzar, it was rebuilt according to its original design.

THE SUMMER PALACE

Some 14 miles south of Rome in the Alban Hills overlooking Lake Albano stands the pope's summer residence, Castel Gandolfo. Built in the seventeenth century, the palace affords the pontiff an escape from the hot and humid Roman summers. Two months before he was elected pope, Cardinal Wojtyla and Bishop Deskur toured the residence and admired the gardens. But it would be a while after his election before John Paul II found time to relax in his new getaway home.

Northeast of Rome is another place the pope visited often, the monastery at Montorella, which is staffed by the Polish Fathers of the Resurrection. Indeed, one of his first trips as pontiff, taken on October 29, 1978, took him to the rocky outpost where a church to the Blessed Virgin was built in the fifth century.

The Holy Father's private map of Rome also includes the Pallottine College, housed in a building near the Tiber. It was the residence of a missionary priest, Father Vincent Pallotti, who founded the Society of the Catholic Apostolate, dedicated to encouraging laypersons to take a more active role in the church and who was canonized by John XXIII.

Father Wojtyla spent a few weeks here in the autumn of 1946 before moving to the Belgian College. No souvenirs remain to document his stay, but he confirmed this episode in his life when he returned to visit the Pallottine Fathers in June 1986 and prayed in front of the tomb of Saint Vincent Pallotti.

THE CROWN JEWEL

The Pallottine College is about a 20-minute walk away from the Vatican and St. Peter's, the crown jewel among the pope's Roman basilicas. The square outside the church was designed by the seventeenth-century architect and sculptor Lorenzo Bernini and is defined by curving colonnades that enclose the oval ellipse. The square has an Egyptian obelisk in the center and can hold several hundred thousand people who gather regularly on Sundays to sing the *Angelus* prayer and, of course, to wait for announcement of a new pope's election.

The wide modern avenue that leads to St. Peter's Square, the Via della Conciliazone (Avenue of the Reconciliation), was laid out during the 1930s. This part of Rome is densely populated, and St. Peter's Square lies at the end of a labyrinth of narrow streets, typical of an ancient city layout.

PETER WAS HERE

The Tiber flows by one end of the square while the other is dominated by St. Peter's. From his windows John Paul II could see the imposing cupola designed by Michelangelo that rises above the basilica, the extension of the Corinthian colonnade leading to the entrance of the church, and the huge sculptures of Christ and the apostles looking down from the façade. According to legend, St. Peter's Basilica is built over the Tomb of Saint Peter, the apostle Christ named "the Rock" and to whom he entrusted the keys to the kingdom of heaven.

Archaeological excavations begun by Pope Pius XII during the war and that were ongoing while Father

Wojtyla was studying in Rome have proved that the legend was not a myth: Near an obelisk dating from the second century and bearing the inscription "Peter Is Here" in Greek, the archaeologists found bones of a tall man about sixty years old that can be dated to the first century. After further specialized scientific examinations, Paul VI confirmed in 1968 what Pius XII believed to be true in 1950: The relics belong to Saint Peter.

During Nero's time a circus (a round, open area) for blood sports stood there. In the fourth century it was replaced by the first basilica built in Byzantine style in the belief that Saint Peter had been crucified on this spot in AD 64 and buried nearby. Construction was completed under Constantine II, son of Constantine the Great. And it was here in the year 800 that Pope Leo II crowned Charlemagne as Holy Roman Emperor of the German Nation. His Carolingian successors would be crowned there for a long time to come.

The popes moved from the Lateran Palace to the Vatican after Pope Gregory XI brought the papacy back from Avignon to Rome in January 1377. He did not want to return to the Lateran Palace, because during the 70-year "Babylonian Captivity" of the papacy in France, the area around the palace had decayed and become depopulated. So he moved into the Vatican, where the papacy has stayed ever since.

The Byzantine basilica in honor of Saint Peter lasted almost 1,000 years before it fell into ruin. Gregory XI, who died in 1378, did not have time to repair the church. Reconstruction, therefore, had to wait until the middle of the fifteenth century, when Nicholas V launched the Renaissance in Rome, becoming one of the most illustri-

St. Paul's Basilica was one of the most beautiful churches in Rome. It was rebuilt after a fire but lost much of its beautiful interior.

ous popes of that era. His reign ranked as the "Golden Century" of Italian culture when the Eternal City shone beauty designed to strengthen the faith of pilgrims.

He beautified Rome in order to make it a worthy capital of the Christian world and, in doing so, "to strengthen the weak faith of the populace by the greatness of that which it sees." He employed leading artists and architects to refurbish ecclesiastical and secular buildings, giving the city a beauty and splendor it had not had for a thousand years. He also engaged in more prosaic works—reconstructing the Roman aqueducts

Above: Avenue of the Reconciliation, the main Vatican thoroughfare, is named to commemorate the agreement signed between the Vatican and Italy in 1929.

that supplied water to the city and strengthening Rome's fortifications. Both had deteriorated badly in the preceding centuries.

An agile diplomat, he navigated the troubled waters of church politics in the fifteenth century. He played a leading role in the Council of Basle, one of the longest in church history. It lasted from 1431 to 1449 and was brought to an end on the verge of Nicholas's becoming pope. In a sense, he cleaned up much of the mess the quarrels of the fourteenth century—the western schism and the second papacy in Avignon—had left behind. He even persuaded the antipope, Felix V, to resign.

But the culmination of his work was founding the Vatican library, one of the shining treasures of western civilization. True, popes had always had personal libraries but never anything on the scale Nicholas envisaged. He gathered three major collections—the secret library and the Latin and Greek libraries—and he envis-

aged them for the "common convenience of the learned." His love of books and learning earned him the sobriquet of the Humanist Pope.

When he died in 1455, work on St. Peter's Basilica was halted, not to be resumed until Julius II mounted the papal throne some 50 years later. He moved with great speed and determination. The old walls were torn down, and a new basilica rose on the foundation of the old—this one built in the classic Roman and Greek style.

Julius II was another pope who changed the face of Rome. He was, first of all, a soldier who reestablished the powers of the Papal States and ended French dominance over the church. He heard Mass daily and often celebrated it himself. He extended the reach of the church across the Atlantic by setting up dioceses on the islands of Santo Domingo and Puerto Rico, and he fought against clerical and ecclesiastical abuse,

Below: Interior view of St. Peter's Basilica as seen from the gallery. The cupola entrance is next to the baptistery, near the statue of Marie Clementine Sobieska, granddaughter of King John III Sobieski.

convening the Lateran Council to codify his reforms.

As a patron of the arts, Julius II gathered the best painters, sculptors, and architects of his age into an artistic stable unmatched in history. Michelangelo painted the ceiling of the Sistine Chapel and sculpted the statue of Moses outside the papal mausoleum at St. Pietro in Vincolo. Raphael completed the stunning Camera della Signatura in the Vatican, and he hired Bramante to link the Vatican with the Belvedere.

Before the Papal Throne

—Father Konrad Hejmo

Every Wednesday some 15,000 to 30,000 pilgrims would gather in St. Peter's Square (in Holy Years the number often reached 50,000 people) in the hope that they would be granted a general audience with the pope. During winter these audiences were moved inside and took place in the Paul VI assembly hall, which can hold about 10,000 people. In his Jubilee Year John Paul II also received pilgrims on Saturdays in special jubilee audiences.

Passes for the general audiences could be obtained any day of the week before every Wednesday directly from the apostolic prefecture or from the Swiss Guards at the bronze gate. They could also be obtained by mail or fax. A signature from a parish priest or bishop facilitated the proceedings.

Up to 200 people were allowed to approach the papal throne during the course of a general audience. A dozen or so were allowed to kiss the pope's hand. A short curriculum vitae had to be attached to the letter applying for a pass to admit these privileged visitors. The letter had to be signed by the parish priest or the bishop of the applicant's home diocese. The signature was a guarantee that the person in question deserved the privilege.

At the beginning of the general audiences, a spokesman for each linguistic group present would read the names of the organizations and of the individuals who belonged to each one. Later the Holy Father would salute the most numerous groups and resume the sermon in their language. The groups of pilgrims were required to register with the prefecture in advance.

Every Sunday and Holy Day of Obligation, the pope would appear at the window of his library at noon sharp. Then he would speak a few words in various languages to the faithful gathered in St. Peter's Square.

The distinction of a private audience with the pope is reserved for heads of state and government, for ambassadors, scientists, or renowned artists. Anyone can ask for a private audience, however, no matter what his occupation. It is enough to write a letter to the prefect of the pontifical house. In each case, a recommendation from a church functionary must be included.

Finally, only a very few people were allowed to participate at Holy Mass celebrated by the Holy Father in his private chapel.

As for the future shape of St. Peter's Basilica, Julius II's successors moved even further afield, changing the basic design to fit the reigning baroque fashion. Even the floor plan was altered, the classic Greek cross design by Donato Bramante, Julius II's chief architect, was replaced 100 years later by the Latin cross, which was designed by Carlo Moderno, Pope Paul V's architect. Ultimately, this new floor plan made the basilica much larger and more spacious.

None of these changes affected the location of the Saint Peter's Tomb, however, which remained in the center of the church, visible from any site in the central nave. Today the tomb is placed underneath the main altar, together with the remains of earlier pontiffs.

Many of the popes who ruled the church after the emperor Constantine established Christianity as the state religion were the great builders of Rome. John Paul II belongs to that tradition even if his edifices are not built of stone and brick. He has changed the church and the city of Rome by making the church more global. Italians ruled both church and city for centuries and kept them from broadening their scope. During his pontificate John Paul II has made Rome international with clergy and pilgrims from all over the world.

Chapter 10

New Style, New Approaches

John Paul II led the church
out of the past and into
the twenty-first century. He
created a new style of pastoral
teaching and changed the
image of the papacy.

When the news came out that the new head of the Roman Catholic Church was not an Italian but a Pole from Kraków, it caused an uproar in Rome. Roman citizens were astonished but in time warmed up to the pope from a foreign country. An atmosphere of nervous apprehension, however, hung over the Roman Curia because most of its members were Italian, and for many of them, a foreigner on the Throne of Saint Peter meant job uncertainty. Although the Roman Curia was held in high regard for many centuries, it had become inflexible and entrenched in its own bureaucracy. Now a pope from a foreign country would rule it without being familiar with how it worked from the inside. The pope also lacked support from directors of the curial offices, who felt he could easily be dominated.

John XXIII had wanted to reform the Curia, but neither he nor Paul VI managed to bring about any of the needed changes. John Paul I also had plans to restructure its administration and probably would have if he had lived longer. The task of reform fell to John Paul II.

Karol Wojtyla had faced a similar situation when he was nominated bishop of Kraków, but the scope of the Vatican problem was much greater. Members of the Curia in Kraków had been chosen first by Cardinal Sapieha and next by Archbishop Baziak, who was even more severe and less approachable than Cardinal Sapieha ever was. Wojtyla had known for a long time how the Curia in Kraków worked, and all its members also knew what he was like. The personality of the bishop in charge always influences the behavior of the bureaucrats in the diocesan office. All Bishop Wojtyla had to do to introduce a new style and mind-set was to present new ideas that would inspire the Curia and to elect auxiliary bishops who would be up to the task.

A TOUGH BUREAUCRACY

The situation in the Roman Curia was different. This ponderous bureaucratic machine held sway over the church in Rome and throughout the world. In addition, it wielded great power over the pope. The Vatican II Council reestablished the collegial process of handling church affairs and

allowed national bishops' conferences much independence from Rome. The Roman Curia functioned as a kind of central government for the entire church, and this collegiality took away some of its functions. Bureaucrats in the Curia grudgingly relinquished responsibilities and resisted handing over power. After a time of post–Vatican II Council "experiments," they were hoping that a pope would be elected who would bring back the old order.

Prior to both conclaves held in 1978, the bureaucrats were hoping Cardinal Giuseppe Siri of Genoa would be elected. The newspapers called him the "Curia's candidate." Siri was a traditionalist. He never went as far in his criticism as the French archbishop Michel Lefebvre, but he was in the habit of openly joking about the principles of collegiality elaborated by the council and post-council synods of bishops. In an interview he gave on the opening day of the conclave, a journalist asked him to comment on collegiality, and he responded, "I don't even know what that means."

That afternoon, just before the conclave was about to start and after the doors of the Sistine Chapel were locked to shut the cardinals off from the outside world, someone distributed the draft text of that newspaper article to each cardinal's room at the conclave. (Siri had made an agreement that the article would appear in the newspaper only after the conclave began.) Whoever distributed the article dashed the last hope—in the person of Cardinal Siri—of those who were against post-council change. Cardinals who were undecided, who perhaps might have supported Siri in the end, didn't feel they could after they read what he told the reporter.

AN OUTSIDER'S ADVANTAGE

John Paul II had an advantage over Paul VI and John XXIII, who also wanted to modernize the central administration of the church. They and the popes who reigned prior to Vatican II Council were in a certain sense graduates of the Roman Curia. John Paul I was not a member of the Curia, but he couldn't take advantage of his outsider status, because his pontificate was so short. Earlier popes had worked in congregations of the Curia. They came up through the ranks of Vatican bureaucracy convinced that the routine in the Curia, although it was a heavy burden, enabled the church to function properly. Finally, despite reform measures that were implemented to a greater or lesser degree, members of the Curia still stuck to the old routine "because that's the way it has always been done in Rome," even when that routine defied common sense.

The first time the pope kissed the ground was in 1948, when he arrived as a newly ordained priest at his parish in Niegowic. Thereafter, his health willing, he kissed the ground wherever he traveled in his pastoral ministry.

John Paul II always believed that it was very important to have direct contact with the faithful; it energized him in his pastoral work.

Although the papal court professed the principle of absolute obedience to the pope (also true for other members of the church's hierarchy), the popes' actions were so limited by rigid protocol that far from acting like kings, they seemed more like prisoners of the Curia. For many centuries ordinary bureaucrats, along with their superiors, acted as if they were taking care of a golden cage wherein they locked up the pope.

Over the centuries the papal court became a complicated network of interdependencies in which each person knew his place and the duties he had to do or not to do in order to maintain the stability built up over many years. Paul VI wanted to reduce the size of the court he inherited from his predecessors so that he could become more independent. He began by eliminating outdated job responsibilities. From the Vatican roll, he eliminated employees whose functions were overly specialized, such as serving the pope wine during meals or helping him to put on liturgical vestments. Paul VI also dismissed employees with outdated jobs, such as the horse groom in a Vatican that no longer had stables. When John Paul II became pope, he scrutinized the household staff list. When he had finished, he dismissed everyone except a private chauffeur.

The Vatican started an Information Service during John Paul II's pontificate. Here travelers can obtain information about how the Holy See functions and how to tour all its facilities.

THE ADMINISTRATIVE STRUCTURE OF THE VATICAN

The Roman Curia currently consists of 28 sections called "dicasteries," which are similar to government ministries or secretariats. They are not all equal in the overall Vatican structure. The Secretariat of State has the most important function, since it is in charge of both the internal and external affairs of the Holy See and also coordinates the functions of other dicasteries.

The most important dicastery is the Congregation for the Doctrine of the Faith, created by Pope Paul III in 1542, then known as the Holy Congregation of the Roman and Universal Inquisition and later called the Holy Office of the Inquisition. Eight other congregations currently handle church affairs: the Congregation for the Oriental Churches; the Congregation for Divine Worship and the Discipline of the Sacraments; the Congregation for the Causes of the Saints; the Congregation for the Clergy; the Congregation for the Bishops; the Congregation for the Evangelization of Peoples; the Congregation for the Institutes of Consecrated Life and Societies of Apostolic Life; and finally, the Congregation for Catholic Education. Councils are another type of dicastery; two of them have Latin names: Iustitia et Pax (Justice and Peace) and Cor Unum (With One Heart). The administration also includes three offices: the Camera Apostolica (Vatican Archives), the administration of the Patrimony of the Holy See, and the Prefecture of the Financial Affairs of the Holy See.

The cardinals who preside over these dicasteries form a kind of cabinet of ministers, specifically for the Vatican

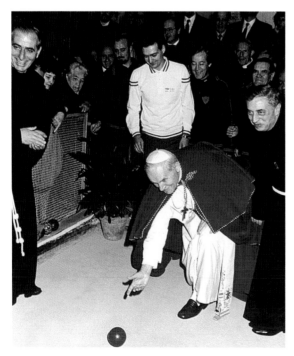

After celebrating Mass, John Paul II plays skittles with parishioners at the fiftieth anniversary celebration of the parish of St. Tarcisio in Rome in 1985.

political regime. This group functions somewhat differently from cabinet ministers in other countries, and they do not make collegial decisions. At meetings the cardinals just inform the Holy Father about issues that happen in the institutes under their care. The pope has the power to decide what to do; then the secretary of state implements the decisions.

CHANGE IN THE CURIA

On his road to the highest office in the church, John Paul II had not climbed the ladder of the curial structure. He found himself at the top all at once, and since he was free of ties and influences, he could go about things in his own way. Once he exerted his power over the administrative machinery, everyone had to go along with him whether he wanted to or not. The pope started at the very beginning of his pontificate. Immediately after he was elected and newly vested in white papal robes, he remained standing as he received the homage of the cardinals. Previously, popes used to sit down at this point in the ceremony. This was the first sign that he wished to break tradition.

He did not want to be a monarch to whom the cardinals were subject; he preferred acting like a brother who would work with them as they together realized the tasks and objectives outlined by the Vatican II Council. But this did not mean that he would just be first among equals, different from the cardinals because he wore different vestments. In his very first homily, which he gave to the cardinals in the Sistine Chapel, he made it clear that although he wanted the church to function in a collegial manner, his role and their roles were distinct. His was to determine the objectives of the church; the cardinals' function was to carry these out in accordance with the pope's instructions.

ANOTHER CONCLAVE OF CARDINALS

John Paul II set the pattern for his governing style during his first meeting with the cardinals in a conclave at the beginning of November 1979. This was a rare event; for the first time in four centuries, 120 princes of the church were in Rome at the same time, not to elect a new pope, but to give John Paul II advice about three important issues for the Vatican and the entire church. The pope was mainly interested in what they had to say about restructuring the Curia. He asked their opinions on how

The Dignity of the Person

In *Redemptor Hominis (The Redeemer of Man)* John Paul II wrote, "Humanity is the path the church travels…as chosen by God's plan for all eternity." The classic definition of the human person is that "man is a rational animal." The pope adopted another one, in which he says that the human person is "an indivisible subject who has a rational nature." He separates himself distinctly from Marxist philosophy, since he believed it was subject to society and social-class theories. He also disagrees with theories that define man as a being unto himself, because the individual is not the object of human rights, the person is. That's because the "person is more that just an individual substance"; he wrote in his volume *The Acting Person* that "to be a person is to be a 'someone.'" And "someone" evokes, by way of contrast, "something."

Human beings are called to develop within the framework of interpersonal relationships and human development an interdependence with the development of societies of nations. Man enters the world as a creative force and is capable of transforming the world of nature and culture in societies. Thus he reveals himself as both the subject and center of the developmental process.

Nevertheless, society cannot be based on rights demanded by separate, concrete individuals, because then society would just be a conglomeration of individual egotists. It's necessary to construct political and social structures so that they can effectively bring about progress. "Concern for the well-being of the individual entails, therefore, serving the common good," he wrote.

Citing "The Declaration of the Rights of Man," John Paul II stated that "the recognition of the inherent dignity, as well as the equal rights of all members of the human family, is the foundation of liberty, justice, and peace in the world." He applied whatever advice he gave bishops and priests in his own daily life. He wanted the clergy to be "a critical (discerning) conscience in society," and he constantly stressed that "we cannot ignore anything that harms human dignity, no matter what the reason, what concrete form it takes, nor where harm takes place."

to support the work of the Pontifical Academy of Science (created in 1937 by Pope Pius X) and for recommendations on how to take care of the Vatican's deficit. He also wanted to hear about any problems the cardinals wished to bring to his attention.

It was a purely deliberative assembly. Discussions went on for four days. The pope listened but did not feel obligated to do anything that the cardinals suggested. The Curia would in time have fewer and fewer Italian members, since foreign cardinals would be asked to direct congregations and councils, and various foreign languages would be spoken in curial establishments. This first conclave with the cardinals was the forerunner of a new type of church government: First the pope would consult with the cardinals, and then he would make his own decisions.

HE DIDN'T ASK ANYONE'S PERMISSION

During the first days of his pontificate, John Paul II displayed his main personality trait, which was well known in Kraków circles. He listened attentively to everyone,

(CONTINUED ON PAGE 152)

Science and Faith

Ever since he was young, Karol Wojtyla was certain there was no contradiction between faith and science. He had learned this in his high school religion classes taught by Father Edward Zacher, who was a catechist and also the parish priest in the Church of the Presentation of the Blessed Virgin Mary in Wadowice. Father Zacher incorporated the facts of astronomy and other natural sciences into his lectures so that his students would become aware that the revelation of faith and scientific knowledge coexists without any conflict. This was the priest who presented the future pope with the events in Galileo's life: The Holy Office of the Inquisition brought a case against him and forced Galileo to publicly retract his statements about the order of the planets in the universe.

Conflict between the scientific and religious points of view had its origins in theological attitudes in the Middle Ages. Medieval scholastic theology and its decrees weighed heavily upon theologians. They didn't know how to interpret new scientific discoveries, and so they looked upon that kind of knowledge with mistrust and hostility. This situation lasted into the nineteenth century, and both scientists and theologians made mistakes. Theologians blurred knowledge learned in astrophysics with truths of the faith, and scientists questioned truths of faith in areas of the natural sciences. Some scientists even gave up their faith, and those who remained faithful to church teachings had conflicts of conscience.

Charles Darwin's theory of the evolution of the species through natural selection is still contested by those who defend Bible texts on the creation of the world; fundamentalist believers understand the biblical account of creation according to a literal interpretation of Bible texts. Today the theory of evolution is taught in seminaries, and Catholic scientists are permitted to hold the opinion that man, in the physical aspects of his nature, rose out of the animal world.

Theologians have taken a long and difficult path to accepting scientific discovery. Roughly 100 years after the French Revolution, in some of the documents issued by the Vatican I Council between 1869 and 1870, human reason was considered a means to help us prove that God exists. This meant that rational thought could be a path to

Background: Scientists still have not determined the origin of the Shroud of Turin.

Inset: This telescope at St. Peter's Basilica was presented to the Holy Father in 2000 as a gift from scientists.

the Creator, and not just a way to deny the existence of God. In 1879 Leo XIII in the encyclical *Aeterni Patris (Eternal Father)* agreed with the theological propositions of Saint Thomas Aquinas concerning the synthesis of reason and faith. Since then neo-Thomistic interpretations of the theology of Saint Thomas have became the official philosophy of the Roman Catholic Church. "Truth cannot...deny truth," Leo XIII wrote. Facts discovered through scientific inquiry and interpreted correctly with the help of God's gift of human intelligence cannot negate the revelation of God.

One of the main centers of neo-Thomistic theology is the Angelicum College in Rome, taught by Dominicans. This is where Father Wojtyla studied for his doctorate in 1948. Later, when he was a parish priest and did theological research, he befriended a group of scientists, mostly physicists, and was able to reaffirm his conviction that theology and science complement each other.

Nevertheless, relations between theology and science remained under the dark cloud of the Holy Office of the Inquisition that ordered Galileo to retract his theory of a heliocentric universe. Copernicus had earlier posited this theory, which was condemned by the church. In 1981 John Paul II created a commission to study Galileo's case while he was recuperating from the assassination attempt. The commission, supervised by Cardinal Paul Poupard, director of the Pontifical Council for Culture, worked on it for 11 years before handing in a report. Finally, 350 years after Galileo's death, on October 31, 1992, John Paul II held a meeting in the Papal Palace with members of the Pontifical Academy of Science. The purpose for the meeting was to restore the reputation of the great scientist in the presence of the diplomatic corps, cardinals, and other dignitaries of the church, as well as members of the Pontifical Council for Culture. The commission delivered its report, and the pope commented on the subject. The work of the commission encompassed theological, biblical, scientific, historic, and legal aspects of the case. After this protracted study, Cardinal Poupard was able to unequivocally state that the judges who condemned Galileo were in error; they did not know how to distinguish between truths of the faith and astronomical observations.

The pope recognized that he had to admit the judges' error and to express regret for the wrongful sentence imposed on Galileo. There was a lesson to be learned from this experience, however. No one could be sure that a similar situation would not happen again in the future. In order to solve conflicts of this nature, scientists and theologians must enter into dialogue, be aware of the limits of their respective competencies and also of their ability to enrich one another's understanding. John Paul II's conclusion regarding the relationship between science and faith is contained in his encyclical *Fides et Ratio (On the Relationship Between Faith and Reason)*, promulgated in 1998. In it he expressed his conviction that the twenty-first century would witness a synthesis of faith and reason after they were set apart for several centuries, with tragic results. The pope affirmed that faith and reason are two

Galileo

Galileo Galilei was born in 1564. He was a physicist, astronomer, and one of the scientists who devised the scientific method based on observation and experimentation. He also taught mathematics in the universities of Pisa and Padua. Galileo gained fame when he publicized the results of his scientific experiments and formulated the laws of inertia and of falling bodies. He built his first telescope in 1609, which enabled him to observe craters on the surface of the Moon and Jupiter's satellites. With it he also discovered the existence of sunspots. Using his telescope, he confirmed the theory of Copernicus that the earth revolved in an orbit around the sun and that the phases of Venus were analogous to the phases of the Moon. (Copernicus arrived at his conclusions by mathematical calculations; he did not have access to a telescope.)

When Galileo supported this heliocentric theory of the universe, inquiries against him were initiated by the Holy Office of the Inquisition. The Inquisitors passed judgment against him, and he was forbidden to postulate in public that the earth revolved around the sun. In 1633 he was again summoned before the Inquisitors regarding his *Diologo Sopra i Due Massimi Sistemi del Mondo, Tolemaico e Copernicano (Dialogue Concerning the Two Chief World Systems, Ptolemaic and Copernican)*. It was placed on the index of forbidden books.

In order to avoid being tortured, Galileo was forced to publicly renounce the Copernican theory and also not publish the *Dialogue*. It is said that after he recanted his theory in a loud voice for the Inquisitors to hear, very softly, under his breath, he added, "Nevertheless, it really does revolve...." For the rest of his life, the Inquisitors scrutinized his scientific studies. He died in 1642.

Galileo readily believed in revealed truths of the faith, but he did not resort to them to determine the laws that govern nature and the universe. Since he was a scholar, he based his findings on the results of his experiments, but he did not overestimate their importance in the discovery of the truth about the world. He valued the basic scientific procedures in logic and mathematics because they led to the discovery of relationships between facts, and he knew that science is not made up of isolated facts.

wings of flight that let humanity rise to contemplation of the truth. If theologians do not appreciate the importance of human intelligence to get to know the truth, and if scientists and philosophers do not admit the possibility of revealed truths, it will be impossible to arrive at the truth of the human condition.

letting each person speak at length and express his or her opinion on an issue. Then Karol Wojtyla would take what the person said into consideration, but when he made his final decision about something, he would do it alone.

People also noticed that when someone didn't think the way Karol Wojtyla did, he kept talking, trying to convince the person of his way of looking at the issue. He was not always successful. John Paul II talked for a long time with the rebellious archbishop Marcel Lefebvre; Paul VI had forbidden Lefebvre to ordain priests, because the archbishop insisted loudly and openly that the reforms introduced by the Vatican II Council were sacrilegious. When Archbishop Lefebvre later consecrated as bishops four priests who agreed with him, there was nothing left for John Paul II to do but excommunicate him.

THE REBEL POPE

As far as the Roman Curia was concerned, John Paul II was a "rebel." His rebellion was a post-council reform. He always did what he thought he should. The day after he was elected pope, for example, he got up from the papal

Pope John Paul II holding a press conference in the sky with journalists on his flight to the United States on April 10, 1995.

throne and walked over to the journalists gathered for a press conference without asking the permission of the master of ceremonies, an expert in papal protocol. No doubt, the expert would have said no. This press conference was an unprecedented event in the history of the Roman Curia. Without hesitating, John Paul II sidestepped the cardinal who wanted to block his path and walked directly toward the journalists. He circulated

The pope appears at the window of his private library and prays the *Angelus* prayer along with the crowd below.

among news correspondents from all over the world, answering their questions in their own language. (Formerly the Curia selected questions and prepared the pope's answers.) "The church and all of humanity value your work," the pope said, speaking to the journalists. When they asked him how he envisioned his future life at the Vatican, he answered that if things continued as they were going at the moment, he would probably survive.

No other pope had been so frank and spontaneous, so John Paul II immediately conquered the news media with his quick responses. Before long, the press corps realized what a media star the Holy Father was turning out to be and how he made use of his public relations talents to spread the Gospel message.

BETTER THAN A POP STAR

Familiar with the theater and gifted with a tremendous ability to modulate his voice, Pope John Paul II rapidly became an easily recognized figure on television. He used his personal magnetism as no one before him had ever done. Perhaps popes in the earliest centuries of Christianity were like this, but their voices could not project much farther than the Catacombs of Rome. When John Paul II evangelized, he was often standing before masses of people, and because of the technological miracles of the mass media, his words and image reached the farthest corners of the world.

Not one to waste an opportunity to spread the Gospel, John Paul II also taught religious education lessons during his general audiences on Wednesdays. Pius IX started these at the end of the nineteenth century to keep in contact with the faithful when he was the "Prisoner of the Vatican." He met his congregation inside the walls of the Vatican. The Wednesday audiences were called "general" audiences to distinguish them from private audiences in which the pope received people inside the Papal Palace.

John Paul II, whose popularity with the people grew day by day, used the Wednesday audiences to teach the faithful who gathered in St. Peter's Square. He was innovative in his choice of topics, which he covered in thematic cycles. Many of these lessons were very frank—some would say daring—as when, for example, he dedicated his religious instruction to the theology of the human body.

A POPE WHO WAS APPROACHABLE

No pope before John Paul II ever granted interviews to journalists. He did away with the image of the pope as unapproachable, out of the reach of the mass media, a person who revealed his thoughts only in encyclicals, exhortations, or apostolic letters, all carefully prepared by the secretary of state. John Paul II's interviews with journalists and his memoirs that were published in book form became literary best sellers and were translated into many languages. When speaking about himself in official statements, he stopped using the traditional "royal we," speaking of himself in the first person plural as kings used to do. (Pope John Paul I had already given up this anachronism.) John Paul II continued to simplify the formulas of speech. If saying "I" seemed awkward to him, he used the third person and simply spoke of himself as "the Pope."

John Paul II also broke the tradition of eating papal meals according to formal rituals. He sat at the table with the poor people that Mother Teresa of Calcutta and her group of sisters serve. He also shared a meal with the fishermen of Fano and workers he visited on Saint Joseph's Day. When eating in the Papal Palace, he served himself and any guests present quite easily and gracefully without the help of a waiter.

Strict protocol in the life of the popes had been a long tradition. When John Paul II dropped protocols, many members of the Curia were very disturbed. The pope's simplicity embarrassed members of the papal court who were accustomed to dignified, albeit artificial, ritual. At the beginning of the eighteenth century, for example, Pope Pius VII dined with guests, but he sat at a separate table under a canopy. Cardinal Braschi stood beside him and took his skullcap off every time that the Holy Father of Our Lord (a title that popes had used from the time of John XXIII in the fifteenth century until the pontificate of Paul VI in the twentieth century) took a sip of wine.

CANARY AT THE TABLE

During the difficult times when the Papal States were being incorporated into the kingdom of Italy, popes stopped the custom of eating with guests. Pope Pius X ate only with two of his secretaries. Pope Pius XII ate alone, served by nuns from Bavaria. He loved his canary very much, so he placed its cage on the dining table. No pope

John Paul II's Renovations at the Vatican

Each pope leaves his mark on the Vatican. John Paul II is no exception. One of the first physical changes he ordered was the renovation of St. Matilda's Chapel, part of the pope's personal living quarters on the third floor of the Vatican Palace. Now it is known as the Chapel of the *Redemptoris Mater* (Mother of the Redeemer). At Castel Gandolfo, John Paul II added a swimming pool to the sauna, solarium, and gymnasium housed in a building donated by the Polish community in the United States.

After the attempt on the pope's life in 1981, the Papal Palace added some safety features. Bulletproof glass panels were installed on the roof of the palace, around the pope's private terrace garden, and protective windows were installed on the top floor, where John Paul II looked out upon the crowds that gather in St. Peter's Square.

St. Peter's Basilica had its façade restored during this pontificate. Other renovations were motivated by concern for people attending ceremonies in the basilica. During the wintertime and on big feast days, huge television screens were installed in the nave of the basilica to let people see what's going on at the main altar. An elevator was also installed in the basilica. Until that time tourists who wanted to view Rome from the dome of the basilica had to climb 520 steps. Now they can take the elevator if they wish. John Paul II also commissioned the renovation of the Sistine Chapel. He dubbed it the "Sanctuary of the Theology of the Body" because of Michelangelo's famous frescos that adorn one wall and the ceiling.

Farther along the walls of the Vatican, just beyond the Palace of the Holy Office, is a building marked with the number 9. A plaque over the door reads, "Royal House of Mary, Missionary of Love," and another, next to the intercom near the front door, reads, "House of the Poorest of the Poor." The pope built this house in 1988, after he met with Mother Teresa of Calcutta and she proposed the idea. A house of hospitality, it has room for 70 people, an infirmary, and a dining hall that can accommodate up to 100 people.

John Paul II was not afraid of innovative technology and knew how to use it effectively. In the spring of 1995, Joaquín Navarro-Valls, director of the Vatican's public relations office, suggested that the pope open a Vatican Web site, and on December 24 of that year, the Holy See used the Web site to broadcast the customary *Urbi et Orbi* (To the City and to the Whole World) Christmas message from the pope.

would entertain guests in his private living quarters. Kissing the foot of the pope while kneeling in total silence was still part of papal audiences.

Many customs and archaic court procedures fell into disuse during the era of the council, although not all. Even Paul VI, who traveled and dined with other people, kept the separation between the pope's public and private apartments in the palace, and the Roman Curia carefully guarded the secrets of the Holy Father's private life. During the Renaissance, between the time of Nicholas V, who built the Papal Palace until Alexander V, the private apartment of the pope was located in the middle of the second floor. Julius II succeeded Pope Alexander Borgia, whose infamous lifestyle brought disgrace to the church,

(CONTINUED ON PAGE 156)

153

Responding to God's Call

—Bishop Wiktor Skworc

The teachings of John Paul II regarding the value of human labor are in line with the scriptural affirmation *Be fruitful and multiply, and fill the earth and subdue it* (Gen. 1:28), a fundamental message in the Judeo-Christian tradition. This message needs to be interpreted in light of the complex context of the modern world. The pope's words are a response to forces in society that threaten man's existence and do not allow him to develop his full spiritual potential and improve himself through work. In his encyclical *Laborem Exercens (On Human Work)*, written on the ninetieth anniversary of Pope Leo XIII's encyclical *Rerum Novarum (On the Condition of the Working Classes)* in 1981, John Paul II wrote that it is precisely thanks to man's labor that he "in a certain sense becomes more human." Work provides for his bare necessities but also creates other benefits. Man,

then, responds to the call of God to transform the earth, which is a gift from God. Through his labor, man acts and interacts with others, and when this activity is directed toward the common good, it allows men to grow in their understanding of what it is to be human.

As I would like to demonstrate in this brief analysis, many thoughts about the phenomenon of work can be found throughout the teachings of John Paul II. Without a doubt, labor is the activity through which man defines himself as a created being called to be fully conscious of his duty to do what is good, many times over.

I suppose it is possible to wonder why John Paul II dedicated his first encyclical to the subject of human labor. Does this mean he was departing somewhat from the traditional teachings of the church about this subject?

If it could be said that there were changes in his way of thinking, they would only be in the general sense, because our times call for change. But this is not a question of something new in the absolute sense, just a better and deeper understanding of the essence of the Christian message.

The social changes that

Left: The pope holds a steel cross made by Italian workers at a Castellammare di Stabia shipyard.

came about in Europe during the nineteenth century were the result of the spread of capitalism. In the twentieth century we resented the negative results of those changes because they did not take the "fundamental value of human labor" into account. Both capitalism and Communism became threats for man because in both of these systems, human beings were degraded and became tools to make others rich and to build utopias.

Pastoral ministers in the church were quick to recognize the danger, and they passed judgment on the inequality built into social organizations. Pope Leo XIII pointed out dangers in his encyclical *Rerum Novarum* in 1891 and so did Pius XI in his encyclical *Quadragessimo Anno (On the Fortieth Anniversary of Leo XIII's Rerum Novarum)*. Leo XIII showed a penetrating intuition as to the direction social changes were taking. When he promulgated *Laborem Exercens (On Human Work)* in 1981, John Paul II reminded people of the personal dimension of work. It's enough to recall the number of times his words have been cited and how they helped many of us chase away the ghosts of the Communist past.

John Paul II's thoughts about human labor have influenced current history in Poland. He was always concerned about the difficult situation of the workers under the Communist system. It is most important to reestablish ethical values in order to renew social relationships.

Because of these thoughts, John Paul II's teachings have universal value. His understanding of the worth of human labor is based upon a certain anthropological vision; that is to say, upon a concept about what man is and what the meaning of his existence is. It is very important to stress here how very relevant the issue of the individual is. When a person works, then it follows that another person is his employer and that the product of the work is for the purpose of serving someone else. It's obvious that globalization processes are frequently criticized because

Opposite: The pope was closely involved with the problems of workers. On Labor Day in 1995, John Paul II met with Italian workers.

Man and His Work

John Paul II promulgated his encyclical *Laborem Exercens (On Human Work)* on September 14, 1981. He published this document on the ninetieth anniversary of the first encyclical that treated social issues, *Rerum Novarum (On the Condition of the Working Classes)* that Leo XIII had written in 1891. In *Laborem Exercens* John Paul II stressed that work—as an element that constitutes the human being—is worth more than capital or property. Therefore, capital should be at the service of labor. The worker cannot be treated as merchandise, because he has personal characteristics, both from the point of view of what he creates with his labor as well as the product of his labor, which is destined to be received by someone else. In this way, a person-to-person relationship is established. According to John Paul II, economics should focus on the person. Perhaps this could be accomplished if some of the profits were used to create and improve better working conditions, if profits were divided, if family circumstances of workers were taken into account, and if some private wealth could be shared and used to help the common good.

John Paul II also spoke about the problem of workers who are handicapped and the problems of immigrants. He stressed that the right to work belongs to each person, and he is opposed to discriminating against handicapped persons, whether it be a case of letting them work (according to their ability), paying them fair wages, and respecting their rights as workers. He reminded people that the human rights of citizens of any given country should be shared with those who were forced to leave their own country. It is not acceptable to treat immigrants as a cheap labor source and deny them a safe haven in society.

Work molds the body and soul of man. It is not a curse, but a participation in the very work of the Creator and contributes to the work of salvation. Christ himself is an example of the workingman.

John Paul II clearly stated that "above all, 'Work is for man,' not 'Man is for work.' "

they wipe out the importance of the individual. The one who employs another is no longer a concrete human person but an abstraction created by the owners of companies and their shareholders. As a result, the employee becomes just one more element in a complex organizational structure and cannot identify with that because the laws of economics are of the utmost importance for the corporation.

The pope always had a great capacity to show empathy. With young people, he was young; with those who were suffering, he also suffered; and with workers, he was one of them. He always had something to say to them, not as a stranger, but as the vicar of Christ who understands those who work hard and the fatigue that comes from their hard work.

Vatican II Council Continues

On October 16, 1978, cardinals from all over the world elected Karol Wojtyla as pope, and many analysts predicted he would implement decisions of the Vatican II Council. They were not wrong: Since the beginning of his pontificate, John Paul II was faithful to the legacy of the council in his encyclicals, exhortations, and many of his homilies.

The second day after he was elected pope, in his *Urbi et Orbi* message *(To the City and to the World)*, he said, "Above all, let us all keep in mind the ongoing importance of Vatican II Council and consider it our duty to implement its teachings in the life of the church. Isn't this ecumenical council the foundation stone? Isn't it an important event in the history of almost two thousand years of the church, and consequently in the religious history of the world, that shows the way to live a truly human life?"

In the fourth year of his pontificate, when the church celebrated the twentieth anniversary of the opening of the Vatican II Council, the pope was praying to the Holy Spirit while he was in the Vatican catacombs: "We pray to ask you that the work of this council…be carried out in faithful perseverance, so that day by day and year by year, it will be realized."

In his apostolic letter *Tertio Millennio Advenente (As the Third Millennium of the New Era Draws Near)*, he referred to the council as "a providential event, which the church began to prepare for during the Jubilee of the second millennium." In this document he noted the examination of conscience that all the members of the church are urgently required to make. He stressed that all have to ask themselves how the call of the council is reflected in the life of the church, in its institutions, and in the way it carries out its obligations.

Everything John Paul II did was a reflection of the Vatican II Council, since it called upon all Christians to bring Christ and his Gospel message closer to the world. The pope complied with this directive in his many apostolic visits. He succeeded in bringing the church closer to the actual world and enlivened the dialogue between the church and the world, which the council so frequently mentioned. Everything he did to strengthen unity among Christians and on behalf of peace carries out the council's teaching.

In 1985 and 1987 the pope convened sessions of the Synod of Bishops, which were called for by the Vatican II Council. The goal of the 1985 synod was to "honor, confirm, and implement" the council. This synod discussed council topics: collegiality, responsibility, the pledge to work for ecumenical unity, and dialogue with nonbelievers. The fruit of this synod was the initial work on the *Catechism of the Catholic Church*, an indispensable reference for catechesis in various regions of the world, as the council fathers had stressed. The catechism was produced in a relatively short period of time. The second synod in 1987 was dedicated to the vocation and mission of laypeople ministering in the church and evangelizing in the world.

In his book *Crossing the Threshold of Hope*, John Paul II asserts that "the Holy Spirit who spoke through the medium of the Vatican II Council wasn't speaking to the wind. After all the experiments and over the course of these last few years, new openings to the Word of God can be seen, truths which the church must proclaim now and forever. Whoever is a servant of Gospel values must thank the Holy Spirit for the gift of the council and constantly feel indebted to the council. And this debt of the legacy of the council ought to be paid for many years to come and by many generations."

and he did not want to live in the same accommodations as Alexander, so he moved his quarters to the floor above.

In later centuries the papal apartment kept being moved up one floor and to the right until, during the pontificate of Pius X, it was located in the corner of the fourth floor, where it was easier to slip away from the members of the court. The way to get to his apartment was by a staircase next to the public apartment on the third floor. Only the pope and his secretary were allowed to go up those stairs. John Paul II broke with the tradition of secrecy and brought guests into his private living quarters.

John XXIII and Paul VI were carried in the *seda gestatoria,* a chair attached to poles and on which the pope is carried—a special privilege to perform—by functionaries. It remained in household use during the time of Pope John Paul I. He used it only once, though, at the request

of the people of Rome. Because he was small in stature, they could hardly see him during public appearances. During the papacy of John Paul II, known for his humility, the *seda gestatoria* was no longer used.

It didn't take long for the archbishop of Kraków to win over the Romans and people from all over Italy. In the first few days of his pontificate, he traveled to the monastery at Mentorella, where many Italians go on pilgrimages. The pope, still not yet used to the idea of being pope, explained to everyone at Mentorella that this was one of his favorite places to come to pray, and once he became a Roman, he wanted to go there as soon as possible.

AN ITALIAN AMONG ITALIANS
The Sunday after that, John Paul II visited places of worship connected to the patron saints of Italy. First he went

John Paul II changed many papal customs. Here he is seen sharing a meal with guests at the Hospital of St. Martha in 1988.

to the Basilica of St. Francis of Assisi, where he would later invite the religious leaders of the world to an ecumenical prayer service. Thousands of people were in Assisi, and the pope reminded them of what everyone already knew: He wasn't born in Italy, but his arrival in Assisi symbolized a desire to be born there spiritually. On his return to the Vatican, he passed by the Church of Santa Maria Sopra Minerva in Rome, where he prayed at the Tomb of Saint Catherine of Siena, another patron saint of Italy. A week after that, the pope took possession of his titular church in Rome, St. John Lateran, and he met with the people of Rome on this occasion as well.

If he had won the hearts of the Italian people, he had not yet conquered the goodwill of the Italian bishops. John Paul II's situation was rather complicated. Italian popes oversaw the work of Italian bishops. This new pope was from Poland, and although he was the bishop of Rome and primate of Italy, he was not a citizen of this country.

If he had to intervene directly in the affairs of the church in Italy, he would be in an uncomfortable situa-

tion. After seven months John Paul II asked the bishops of Italy which of them they would like to see in the post of president of their Conference of Bishops. When the majority of them chose Anastasio Ballestrero, bishop of Turin, the Holy Father approved his nomination. This was his skillful way of not violating Pope Paul VI's decision that the pope must choose the president of the Italian bishops. John Paul II left Italian church affairs in Italian hands.

YOUNG PEOPLE WERE FOR HIM

At the end of November 1978, the pope met with a large group of Roman Catholic youths for the first time. When they cheered him, he responded, "The pope is counting on young people." Nobody knew at the time how important his encounters with the youth of the world would become in later years of his pontificate. Many times during the following months, he stressed the importance of keeping in contact with young people. During Lent in Rome, he repeated what he had done in Kraków: He met with students.

About the same time, he spoke in front of 10,000 members of the *Communione e Liberazione* (Communion and Liberation) movement that was connected to the Christian Democratic Party in Italy. That autumn he

(CONTINUED ON PAGE 160)

157

Working with the Mass Media

"The Roman Catholic Church and modern means of mass communication work alongside each other to perform their service to the human family" John Paul II said on June 4, 2000. The media were observing him right from the start of his pontificate and he, more than any other pope who went before him, recognized the importance of the mass media. In Poland he always kept informed about what the press and certain other mass media controlled by atheists and Communists were doing, especially the Communist propaganda service, which was on the side of the party and not society as a whole. He also was familiar with the council document *Inter Mirifica (Decree on the Media of Social Communications),*

Journalists at the Vatican television broadcasting station inform the world about important events at the Vatican and about the pope's activities.

about the mass media of social communication. More than anything else, the council fathers appreciated the undeniably positive aspects of the mass media, but at the same time, they warned that some people "can use them against God's plans and even thwart them." But from the moment of his election as pope, John Paul II had high hopes for the mass media in the free world. He was convinced that they were "a modern-day Aeropagus that influences people's thoughts and behavior and that they are actually shaping a new culture."

THE POPE ANSWERS ALL THEIR QUESTIONS

During his first interview with journalists, which took place October 21, 1978, John Paul II suggested that they

come to an agreement. When they report on the life and the activities of the church, they should try to capture the real, profound, spiritual motives of whatever is going on. The church, for its part, should listen very attentively to the objective witness that journalists give about the hopes and needs of this world. This did not mean to say that the church would shape its mission in the light of the actual world, since the Gospel is what always ought to inspire the church's stance.

This first interview with the mass media made history. After his opening address to the journalists and dismissing the protests of his entourage, the pope moved among the reporters and spoke with them in their own languages. They asked many questions: "Would the Holy Father still go skiing?" "I don't think they'll let me," he responded. He became enormously popular even among the most skeptical journalists. The following day the journalists wrote in their articles, "The pope answered all our questions."

In 1979, during his first apostolic visit overseas to Mexico and the Dominican Republic, John Paul II had long conversations with journalists during the flight. He continued the custom of Paul VI, who also traveled with journalists and met with them during the trip. But there was a difference. Paul VI never gave press conferences; he just inquired about their families, their health, and loved to bestow blessings on them, and—in keeping with protocol—these representatives of the media were not allowed to ask him any questions. John Paul II broke that rule and began a new one: He intended to answer all their questions.

For the journalists and, through them, all the people in the world, these apostolic voyages were a perfect opportunity to find out about the Universal Church and the culture and events in local churches. Journalists became witnesses and participants in unique events. They were the first people to receive a copy of the pope's speeches and homilies, and they were responsible for broadcasting what the pope said and re-creating the ambiance of his encounters with the faithful.

IN MEHMET ALI AGCA'S PRISON CELL

Pope John Paul II realized that the mass media facilitated spreading his message to multitudes of the faithful.

"Today's means of social communication have great possibilities. The church sees in them a sign of the creative and salvific work of God, and we are called to add our contribution to that. The media can therefore become a powerful means of spreading the Gospel," John Paul II wrote in 1985 in his letter on the nineteenth anniversary of the World Day of the Media of Social Communication.

Every time John Paul II met with representatives of the media, he recalled the ideas of the council decrees. He stressed that when they inform people, they should be "honest and correct"—that is, they should abide by moral principles and the rights and dignity of humankind. The responsibility in the first place belongs not only to those who are active in the world of communication but also to everyone in society, meaning those who read what journalists say should not just be passive receivers of information.

John Paul II showed that he greatly understood the work of journalists. On December 27, 1983, he went to visit Mehmet Ali Agca, his would-be assassin, in his prison cell in Rome, and the press became very worried about covering it. They didn't think they would be allowed to take photos of the pope inside a prison cell. The Holy Father calmed their concerns. He assured them that anything that helped to spread the Gospel message was fit to print.

DANGER AND RESPONSIBILITY

John Paul II was aware of possible danger involved with the mass media, such as a lack of sensitivity toward fundamental problems in the world and the exaggeration of petty details that obscure the real truth.

"Freedom of the press allows it to publish ideas, and this is a great social benefit, but it does not guarantee freedom of expression. Freedom to say whatever you want doesn't help if the words spoken are not free, if they are full of egocentrism, lies, fraud, or even hatred, and if they disparage persons of other nationalities, religion, or philosophies," John Paul II said while visiting in Olszyn, Poland, on June 6, 1991. "Responsibility for the words expressed is extreme because words have the force of witnessing, they testify to the truth and become a moral good, but can also be offered in such a way that they turn away from the good. We call this the manipulation of truth."

RADIO, NEWSPAPERS, AND TELEVISION

The pope approved using the mass media and hoped

those who worked with him would to do the same. He wanted information about every important event in the church to be disseminated.

The Pontifical Council of Social Communication (under various titles) has been in operation since 1948. There is also Vatican radio, television, filmmaking, and the daily newspaper *L'Osservatore Romano*, whose weekly and monthly editions come out in various languages. The Office of the Internet has been in existence since 1995; it maintains the Vatican Intranet, a local network system that connects diverse institutions of the Holy See and also the Extranet that facilitates communication with apostolic nuncios and bishops' conferences all over the world. More than 30 million people access the Vatican Web site each year. Journalists receive daily up-to-date information about the pope and the Holy See from the Vatican Press Office. Traditionally, cardinals who head the various congregations discuss new and important church documents produced by their Vatican offices in press conferences.

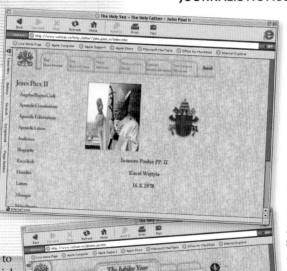

The Vatican and John Paul II Web sites.

JOURNALISTIC ACCOUNTABILITY AND THE TRUTH ABOUT HUMANITY

On June 3 and 4, 2000, during the Jubilee of the Journalists, John Paul II said: "Since journalism exerts such a great influence…on public opinion, it can not be directed simply by criteria of economics, effectiveness, or special-interest groups. On the other hand, in a certain sense, journalism can be thought of as a holy endeavor, one that is carried out with the notion that powers given to the media are for the common good, especially for whoever is disenfranchised, from children to poor people, from invalids to those who are discriminated against and shunted to the fringes of society. Programs written just to get good ratings should not be broadcast, since they are neglecting their primary job, which is to inform the public. The right to disseminate information cannot be invoked without taking into account all other rights. No freedom is absolute, including freedom of the press, because its freedom encounters the limits placed on it due to its responsibility for respecting the dignity and freedom of all. Programs that falsify truth should not be written, produced, or broadcast. I am referring not only to the truth about facts that inform but also the truth about human dignity in all its dimensions."

In 1986 the Holy Father visited the Jewish synagogue in Rome, where he met with Rabbi Elio Toaff.

participated in a meeting with the members of the Sant'Egidio community, which had come into being in the turbulent year of 1968, when a majority of students in the world were active in leftist groups and even extreme leftist groups. Linked with the Catholic left in Italy and in the spirit of the Gospel, this group helped the needy and the marginalized at home and in third world countries as well. These meetings were the seeds of World Youth Day rallies that were regular events in the life of the church in years to come.

HE WON THE HEARTS OF THE ROMANS

On December 3, before the Christmas festivities began, Pope John Paul II visited the parish of St. Francis Saverio in the Garbatella neighborhood of Rome. This was the first of his parish visitations in Rome. (The following month he visited the Church of Santa Maria Liberatrice, and by the end of 1979, he had visited 17 parishes.) For the Holy Father this was just the continuation of what he had done once before in Kraków. He also visited the

Church of Santa Ana inside the Vatican confines that was the local parish church of the Vatican.

News of the pope's spontaneity quickly spread around Rome. On the second day of Christmas, a crowd in St. Peter's Square began to shout the pope's name, asking him to come to his window. The window opened at noon, and John Paul II came out and said the *Angelus* prayer with the people. After that, he spoke a few words with them. Joking, he said, "You must be checking to see if the pope is at home on the second day of Christmas." And then he added that he could not have done anything else, because he was waiting to see if the Roman people would come to visit him.

The pope's wish to get closer to the people of Rome came true two months later. It all began one day in January, when the pope left the Vatican to go see the traditional Christmas crèche the street cleaners of Rome had set up near the walls of the Vatican. He spoke with them for a few minutes, and a daughter of one of the street cleaners courageously asked if His Holiness would marry her and her fiancé. To everyone's surprise he said yes. And at the end of February, he blessed the marriage of Vittoria Janna and Mario Maltese at a Mass that was celebrated in St.

The Pope and His Jeep

—Bishop Jan Chrapek, travel companion

When Pope John Paul II began his catechetical lessons, which were later incorporated into a full-length volume, someone asked him whether he thought they were too difficult for people to understand. He answered, "I realize that perfectly well, and that's exactly why I move around the crowd in a jeep."

At the beginning of his pontificate, everyone noticed that the pope rode around St. Peter's Square in a jeep. That was an unheard of event at the Vatican. The Holy Father mingling with crowds! Anyone present could look into his eyes, shake his hand.

How are the jeep and the difficult language of the pope's catechetical instruction related? This is how the pope clarified the point: "The jeep is a media event. Anyone who likes to see me do that may also want to go look into the contents of my catechesis."

The pope's extraordinary sense of presence in front of the mass media was not due to hype and hints from the experts; he had a natural gift. His ability to operate in front of a crowd of onlookers most likely came from his pastoral experiences and his acting days in the theater. The Rhapsodic Theater used a method of simple forms and Karol Wojtyla learned how to be the servant of the spoken word. It was precisely in the Rhapsodic Theater of Kraków, directed by Mieczyslaw Kotlarczyk during the occupation, that the future pope acquired a profound respect for the style and the text to be communicated.

Many people believe that the pope's appearances were staged, but this is not true. I accompanied the pope on some of his pilgrimages to Poland, and I can say in all certainty that we never thought about using media tricks.

The pope cut himself during one of his trips to Poland, and reporters asked him if those who organized his trip made him wear a bandage to add a little interesting note in the pilgrimage. Let me assure you, we never resorted to tricks like that.

On the tenth anniversary of John Paul II's pontificate, researchers in the art of communications at the Center for Culture and Communication of the University of Toronto investigated why he was so compatible with the mass media. They determined that John Paul II was the perfect type of person to do well with them because he made good use of space and time. He moved about a wide-open space such as St. Peter's Square as if it were a theater stage, and thanks to his sense of presence, he made good use of time, even if he was dealing with a large crowd. He didn't use his talent to act like a media star. And he didn't look as if he were following a script. His supporters did not see an actor in him. He was a witness to the divine human reality, and he shared his own experiences with his audience.

John Paul II realized the need to change the way the church operated in the modern era of mass media. He knew that if he could not broadcast the truths of the faith, he would not be able to move the hearts of men and women. He cited the observation Paul VI made in his encyclical *Evangelium Nuntiandi (On Evangelization in the Modern World)* in which he wrote that the church would stand guilty before God if it failed to make use of the marvelous new means of communication to spread the Gospel.

For this reason John Paul II motivated the church to cooperate with the mass media, especially in huge productions, such as the youth rally during the Year 2000 Jubilee that was organized with a view toward being televised. John Paul II thought highly of the media as being able to help with evangelization, though they would never be more valuable than the Gospel. He did not believe that the church could spread the faith using only the influence of the media. The most effective means is the personal and immediate experience of faith. Personal encounter was most important for John Paul II because he wanted to reach everyone, everywhere, and touch people heart to heart. Perhaps he realized that the imaginary world of the media only gives an illusion of authenticity and keeps man apart from actual experience. This is fatal for spreading the Gospel message that is the foundation for private life. In spite of their effectiveness, the media are no substitute for person-to-person contact, for exchanges between man and man, or man and nature, and of course, the media are not intermediaries between man and God.

Paul's Chapel. The press immediately picked up the event, and Vittoria and Mario became the most famous newlyweds in all of Italy.

Everyone realized that this pope would not be hiding behind the walls of the Vatican, one who would meet with the faithful only on special occasions. John Paul II simply liked to meet people, and this gave him a chance to evangelize by direct contact. It also seemed to give him strength to carry on in his work. The difference between John Paul II and Paul VI was very clear, since Paul VI avoided this type of situation. He was also different from John Paul I, who knew how to greet strangers but was shy among crowds.

STILL INVOLVED IN SPORTS

John Paul II's private apartment in the Vatican was furnished as simply as the one he occupied in Kraków. This apartment in the Papal Palace was renovated at the beginning of his pontificate while the Holy Father took up temporary residence in St. John's Tower, which is located in the Vatican gardens and serves as the official residence of the Holy See's invited guests. Once the construction of the new apartment was completed, it accommodated both public and private functions. John Paul II's office, next to that of his secretary, had many Polish details. The first was the icon of the Black Madonna of Czestochowa, and the second was the photograph of Cardinal Adam Sapieha on his desk. A personal detail was his parents' wedding photograph, which the Holy Father kept on a small desk in his bedroom.

His bedroom had closets, a large table, and a bed that was covered with a bedspread and separated from the rest of the room by a folding screen.

When Cardinal Wojtyla became pope, the news media in the Western world began to publish photos that were out of the ordinary for average readers who were accustomed to a different image of the vicar of Christ. The photos showed him beside a campfire, playing soccer, rowing a kayak, and skiing. When he moved to the Vatican, Karol Wojtyla, now the pope, was the same person he had been as a child and young man because he was still involved in sports, which confused people at the Vatican. No other pope had ever gone ski-

John Paul II loved to go mountain climbing. Here he hikes during his visit to the Valle d'Aosta region of Italy on September 7, 1986.

ing high in the Alps, and the Holy Father didn't just slalom down the slopes at great speed; he also climbed the Alps, played soccer, and went swimming. It took the Vatican some time to get used to this new image of a pope. While other daily newspapers published photos of the pope on skis, *L'Osservatore Romano* just included a short announcement about it. John Paul II decided to have a swimming pool built in 1979 at the summer residence of Castel Gandolfo, and he was immediately criticized for the high cost of building it. He countered this by saying it would cost a lot more to convene a new conclave.

LOOSENING SOME PROTOCOLS

At the end of the nineteenth century, a few decades before the pontificate of John Paul II, the future Saint Thérèse of Lisieux had the honor of kissing the feet of Pope Leo XIII and managed to speak a few words with him when two Swiss Guards motioned to her to be quiet and leave. When they saw that she wasn't paying any attention to them, they took her by the arms and escorted her out of the room. The pope did not react to the situation. In former times women were also threatened with excommunication if they dared to go down into the Vatican catacombs.

John Paul II never encouraged anyone to kiss his ring, although he never prevented anyone who wanted to show him this traditional form of respect. He preferred to chat with each person who came up to him. At audiences and meetings he was capable of kissing a child, patting someone on the cheek, or kissing him or her on the forehead—actions which in the beginning clashed with the exaggerated sense of dignity of older cardinals in the Vatican.

His ability to throw off the straitjacket of protocol, carefully supervised by the Curia, was possible because of Father Stanislaw Dziwisz, his private secretary from his Kraków days. Dziwisz's presence was felt from his first day at the Vatican. The pope's other secretary was Father John Magee, the same man who served both Paul VI and John Paul I. But Father Dziwisz was the sole person charged with reorganizing the daily life of John Paul II, and he made sure everything went the way the pope wanted.

THE DOOR TO THE POPE

Father Dziwisz soon became known in Rome as "Lord Stanislas." He was the person closest to the Holy Father and had the most influence perceptually, more than what corresponded to his actual rank in the Vatican hierarchy. But this opinion of him was false. The Polish bishop Thadeusz Rakoczy, who worked at the Vatican for many years, described Father Dziwisz's job very well: "He is just a door. He isn't someone who bars the door to people; he is the door through which countless people who love the pope get to see him. And since the number of them is immense, someone has to decide which persons the pope will meet in an audience and those who have to wait until a later time. Stanislas is a kind of spiritual son to the pope and is totally dedicated to him. He also protects him from the enormous pressure of the Curia because these functionaries think they know what's better for the pope than the pope himself."

Since John Paul II ended the strict separation between the private and public papal apartments and entertained guests in both places—to the indignation of some members of the Curia—it was established that Bishop James Harvey, prefect of the papal household, would oversee the third floor, where the public apartment was located, and the private secretary of the pope, Father Dziwisz, would supervise the fourth floor. Of course, things got confused because many guests went from one floor to the other accompanied by the pope. This problem was solved in 1998 when Father Dziwisz was made subprefect of the papal household, and he became an auxiliary prefect under Bishop Harvey, who supervised the entire household. This illustrates how the Vatican administration functions, and in order for this arrangement to go into effect, the Curia had to approve of it, not just the pope.

HEAD OF THE PAPAL STATE

When Wojtyla decided to spend his first Christmas as pope in Bethlehem, the birthplace of Jesus, he created an earthquake in the Secretariat of State, directed by Cardinal Jean Villot. The pope may have had a wonderful idea, but it was impossible to carry out. Because he was the head of a state that did not maintain diplomatic relations with either Israel or Palestine, he was in no position to make arrangements. He didn't drop the project; he just postponed it until the year 2000.

Two days before Christmas, it was confirmed that the pope would not be going to Bethlehem in 1978. The cardinals were informed, however, that the Holy Father would be flying to Mexico in January because he had decided to attend the general assembly of the Latin American Bishops' Council, and he would also visit the sanctuary of Our Lady of Guadalupe.

After Christmas the pope reminded everyone that the cardinals elected him not only as head of the church but also of the Vatican State. In this function he planned to enter into the arena of international politics. His first intervention was in Latin America. The pope received a request to resolve a regional conflict that threatened to spark a war between two Catholic countries: Chile and Argentina. The Holy Father thought he could not remain passive in this situation and sent a special emissary, Cardinal Antonio Samore, whom he entrusted with the authority to mediate the dispute. It was settled, and no blood was shed. The secretary of state then understood that the pope was going to act in untraditional ways in the political arena, too. This was very different from his predecessors, who depended on the Curia for foreign-policy advice. Archbishop Sodano was asked to perform the duties of an apostolic nuncio in Chile. A

Every Good Friday John Paul II would hear confessions in St. Peter's Basilica.

few years later he succeeded Cardinal Agostino Casaroli as Vatican secretary of state.

FIRST VISIT TO MEXICO

Archbishop Casarolli, director of international affairs at the Secretariat of State, arranged this visit. It was not an easy task. Although the Holy Father had received an invitation from the Mexican bishops, represented by the archbishop of Guadalajara, it was not an invitation from the government. The Vatican did not maintain diplomatic relations with Mexico, even though the religion of the country was predominately Roman Catholic. Relations had been severed as a result of the Mexican Revolution that took place between 1911 and 1917. When the

John Paul II's Documents

The pope is the principal guardian of the faith. He presides over the Office of the Magisterium of the Church and safeguards matters of faith in his homilies, catechesis, and occasional discourses, as well as in official documents such as encyclicals, exhortations, manifestos, apostolic letters, and apostolic constitutions.

Encyclicals are the most important documents. Written for the benefit of everyone in the church or at times for specific groups in the church, they explain the doctrines of the faith, clarify controversial issues, and direct the ongoing development of Roman Catholic doctrine.

His first official document, the encyclical *Redemptor Hominis (The Redeemer of Man),* stressed the essential points of his pastoral program and was promulgated March 4, 1979. In it he pointed out, "Man is the road on which the church travels, and man is the key to understanding the nature of its teaching." Here the pope stresses that owing to the fact that we are saved by the Redeemer, the inherent dignity and worth of humanity and the value of each individual person is confirmed, no matter what the person believes or which culture nurtured him. The church's duty is to proclaim Jesus Christ, to establish a dialogue with the world, and to respect the rights of the human person.

These truths of the faith were contained in other encyclicals: *Dives in Misericordia (On the Mercy of God),* promulgated on November 30, 1980, and *Dominum et Vivificantem (On the Holy Spirit),* promulgated on May 18, 1986. Along with *Redemptor Hominis,* these documents comprise a kind of triptych on the subject of the Holy Spirit. John Paul II developed his very insightful thoughts on the Holy Spirit during a series of talks he gave in Wednesday audiences; the Liberia Editrice Vaticana (the Vatican publishing house) published the encyclicals as a series.

John Paul II analyzed practical pastoral issues in several encyclicals. In *Redemptoris Mater (Mother of the Redeemer),* promulgated on March 25, 1987, he reflected on the role of the mother of the savior in the life of the church; in *Redemptoris Missio (On the Church's Missionary Mandate),* promulgated on December 7, 1990, he spoke of the church's duty to evangelize; and in *Ut Unum Sint (That They May Be One),* promulgated on May 25, 1995, he called for unity among all Christians; in *Evangelium Vitae (On Evangelization),* promulgated on March 25, 1995, he emphasized the holiness and inviolability of human life from the moment of conception to the point of death.

John Paul II taught about the value and truth in the process of acquiring human knowledge in his encyclical *Veritatis Splendor (Splendor of Truth),* promulgated on August 6, 1993, and about the relationship between faith and human reason in *Fides et Ratio (On Faith and Reason),* promulgated on October 14, 1998. In these encyclicals, apart from dogma, John Paul II touched upon themes that were related to concrete problems in the modern world. In *Laborem Exercens (On Human Work),* promulgated on September 14, 1981, he also wrote about the role work plays in the life of modern man. He presented the problem of ever increasing poverty in *Sollicitudo rei Socialis (On the Social Teaching of the Church),* promulgated on December 30, 1987. In *Centesimus Annus (On Rerum Novarum),* promulgated on May 1, 1991, he did an analysis of the world situation after the fall of Communism.

On June 2, 1985, many years before the European Union was opened toward Eastern Europe, the pope, who came from this region, promulgated his encyclical *Slavorum Apostoli (On the Apostles to the Slavs),* in which he reminded people of the Christianization of the Slavic people by Saints Cyril and Methodias. In it he also emphasized the spiritual unity of Eastern and Western Europe.

John Paul II also published legal documents, among them the outstanding apostolic constitutions *Sacrae Disciplinae Leges,* promulgated on January 25, 1983, which inaugurated the new code of Canon Law, as well as *Fidei Depositum,* promulgated on October 11, 1992, which announced the publication of the *Catechism of the Catholic Church.* Both of these constitutions are the realization of the decision to modernize the church according to the spirit of the Vatican II Council.

The pope also published various apostolic letters—some were addressed to the clergy concerning Holy Thursday, and others dealt with preparations for the celebration of the Year 2000 Jubilee (in which John Paul II called for everyone to make an examination of conscience). These letters were a novel event, since compared to documents of other popes, they were written to specific individuals.

John Paul II's exhortations are documents of a lesser rank and contain proceedings of bishops' synods, as well as instructions to several congregations dispersed by the Holy Father. Papal bulls are documents that carry a lot of weight. They are written on parchment, in Latin, and then sealed. John Paul II's bull, *Totus Tuus Poloniae Populus* ("The People of Poland Are All Yours"), established a new territorial division in the church in Poland.

In summary, documents authored by John Paul II cover thousands of pages and, along with his published discourses, constitute a large volume of published works.

revolutionaries seized power, they banished the church from public life, and the postrevolutionary regime not only separated itself from the church, it passed laws forbidding priests from wearing cassocks and nuns from wearing religious habits out in public. José López Portillo, president of the Institutional Revolutionary Party (PRI), which had been in power in Mexico for some time, was not able to extend an invitation to the pope, since that would have violated the Mexican constitution.

Vatican diplomats had to come up with a clever solution, and they took advantage of the fact that López Portillo's mother and sisters were Catholics who had remained in the church. They had ordered a small private chapel to be built in the president's residence and were able to convince him to allow the pope to come to Mexico on a private visit. The Holy Father could enter Mexico on a tourist visa. Vatican diplomats were offended by these terms, but the pope—inflexible in matters of doctrine but open to other ideas—accepted them. Since the pope would be treated like any other tourist, the president did not have to honor him as a visiting chief of state.

The compromise was accepted, and from January 25 to February 1, 1979, Pope John Paul II embarked on his first pilgrimage to a foreign country—and never looked back. From that time on, his international politics centered on renewing evangelization and pastoral work in all nations and securing recognition of the Vatican State as a political entity in the world. As head of the Roman Catholic Church, he considered these activities to be his job.

When López Portillo realized the enormous interest this visit had provoked among the Mexican people, he decided to greet the visitor in a personal capacity, not officially. When the pope landed at the airport, there were no national flags flying, no military bands playing, and no politicians in sight. But the pope wasn't upset by this lack of official recognition. Thousands of ordinary people had come to the airport, and they were waving Mexican, Vatican, and Polish flags. Church bells rang all day long all over Mexico City.

When the Holy Father stepped off the plane, he knelt down and kissed the ground. When he got up again, he listened to the president's greeting (his wife was standing beside him): "Sir, you are welcome in Mexico. May your mission of peace and harmony, as well as your efforts to bring about justice, bear fruit. Your hosts here are the leaders of the church and all of its people." Then, after a short response from the pope, the president left.

A REAL MEXICAN WELCOME

While this conversation was taking place, the Mexicans were going wild with joy about the pope's arrival in their country. The crowd at the airport broke through the security gates, a child kissed the pope, people threw flowers, someone put a sombrero on John Paul II's head, and the cheers kept coming.

The trip from the airport to the center of Mexico's capital city, about 10 miles away, took two hours. People

Above: John Paul II attends a soccer match at the Olympic Stadium in Rome in October 2000.

Left: John Paul II taking part in the washing-of-the-feet ceremony at the Lateran Basilica on Holy Thursday, a yearly tradition.

all over the city waved the Vatican flag, and in return the pope blessed the Mexican people with a large smile on his face. A million people lined the route. Priests and nuns ignored the prohibition and went out into the streets wearing their religious clothing. When he arrived at the Plaza de la Constitution to celebrate Mass at the cathedral, he immediately won over all the Mexican people when he said in his homily, "In my country, we are in the habit of saying of ourselves, *'Polonia Semper Fidelis'* (Ever Faithful Poland), and now let me say, "Mexico is also ever faithful." The next day the pope spoke to 300,000 people in the Basilica of Our Lady of Guadalupe.

(CONTINUED ON PAGE 168)

Music and the Pope

Popes before John Paul II thought that rock music was diabolical, possibly the work of Satan, and a waste of time to listen to. John Paul II paid attention to rock music. He challenged the Woodstock rebels who were for "free love," anarchy, and drug use, and Generation X after them, who were brought up listening to the captivating rock of the older generation.

Through the years the pope had met many popular musicians. One of his guests was Bono, lead singer of U2, one of the most successful rock groups. U2 has fought for the respect of human rights and the environment. Bono gave as a gift to John Paul II a pair of sunglasses that he usually wore onstage.

The Holy Father also met with Bob Geldof, a British musician who started Live Aid, a charity organization set up for African relief. Other artists who have performed for the pope are singer-songwriter-guitarist Lou Reed, master of electronic music Jean Michel Jarre, and 1980s pop group the Eurythmics. B. B. King, the legendary blues artist, not only sang for the pope but also gave him his guitar "Lucille" as a gift—the guitar King had played for almost 50 years.

Bob Dylan sings for John Paul II and those at the 1997 Eucharistic Congress in Italy.

Bob Dylan, a symbol of the 60s generation, gave a concert at the Eucharistic Congress in Bologna, Italy. Soon after that, the pope thought about the words of his famous song, "Blowing in the Wind." "You're asking me, 'How many roads must a man walk down, before they call him a man?' "

The Holy Father receives Bono, lead singer of U2, in a private audience at Castel Gandolfo in 1999.

The pope's answer, "Only one. There is only one road for man, and that road is Jesus Christ."

Karol Wojtyla always loved to sing—at Mass, walking in the country, or sitting around a campfire. During a visit to Castel Gandolfo, he and an old school friend played the piano and sang all evening long. Perhaps that's why the Holy Father liked the idea of recording his own album. In *Abba Pater* his homilies, prayers, and reflections combine harmoniously with the musical compositions of Leonardo de Amicis and Stefano Mainetti, creating a unique effect. In this album the pope's voice also went along perfectly with the choirs of the Roman Academy and Pablo Colino's. Twenty-seven million copies were sold, making it one of the best-selling albums in the history of the recording industry.

John Paul II liked vocal concerts; one of his favorite artists was Andrea Boccelli, the blind tenor who blends pop and classical music. The pope made Boccelli's rendition of "Glory to You, Jesus Christ" the official hymn of the Year 2000 Jubilee, a singular honor.

The Old Man and Young People

In 1984 John Paul II organized the first World Youth Day, but many thought that young people would not want to listen to him. The Western press suggested that the pope's conservatism would discourage youngsters. Something unexpected happened, however. As the pope grew older and weaker, more and more young people wanted to attend his conclaves. He met with 4 million young people in Manila, 1 million in Paris, and 2.2 million in Rome.

The young people's enthusiastic response to the pope's invitations got the attention of psychologists and sociologists who felt obliged to find out what the younger generation—brought up in a culture of visual imagery and moral relativism, computers, and CD players—is all about. Why would they want to make a long, difficult pilgrimage when they could find something a lot easier to do nearer to home? Journalists called these young people "papa-boys," meaning the generation of the pope. According to sociologist Edmund Wnuk-Lipinski, "The pope helped young people to organize their ideas, to put things in proper order; he helped them distinguish between what's important and what was not relevant." Father Adam Schulz thought that "values the world preaches, as in Communism, liberalism, and permissiveness, do not satisfy young people. In a way, many skeptics cannot understand, young people are searching for deep spiritual values…. The pope perceived that young people have a profound desire to encounter God and he helped them live according to the Gospel." Father Jan Gora, a Dominican, commented, "The pope is a father, and he sets boundaries. He is not just an old pal, some guy on the TV who slaps them on the shoulder."

The pope knew that although youth is a precious time, it's not without its worries. "Young people, you are at the beginning of a lifelong project, one undertaken with a sense of values. You have to ask yourselves at this stage of life, where am I headed?" That's why it's important for young people to build strong moral character that will allow them to be people who have a good conscience.

The pope's method for building this strong spiritual spinal column is prayer. "They are learning how to pray and are praying. They are opening their heart and their conscience to find out more about themselves, which may be more than you know about them," the pope taught. Sports and good physical health are also important. Because of them, "man feels the joy of self-mastery, of overcoming obstacles, and resisting bodily urges. What the world needs is new men who are strong, have very well defined objectives for their lives, in order for a new civilization to be built. You are building this civilization and are basing it on love!" the pope said at a youth rally in Buenos Aires, in 1987. "The youth are courageous in facing difficulties in life and unjust conditions. They are promising to fight for justice, solidarity, and peace in the world."

The pope did not avoid difficult subjects: contraception, premarital sex, abortion, and euthanasia. He was not afraid of being rejected, and to the surprise of skeptics, his inflexible stance was being accepted. This happened in Denver, Colorado, when he stressed the need to defend life. He categorically opposed abortion and euthanasia as ways to resolve personal and social problems. He asked forceful questions: "Why isn't the conscience of youth rebelling again this?…. Why were so many of them silent in the face of ideologies and behaviors that offend human dignity and deform our vision of God?" He urged them, "Young people…do not stifle your consciences!" In a reflective meditation during a rally at Monte de Gozo, in Santiago de Compostela, Spain, he asked, "Are you ready to defend human life with deep convictions? In all circumstances? Even the most difficult ones? Are you ready…to live with love and defend life in indissoluble matrimony to protect the unity of the family, which helps you to bring your children up in peace and harmony? Under the shelter of the combined love of the father and the mother? This is the Christian witness that the world is hoping most of you will live."

The pope also reminded the young people that each person has a proper place in the church and that is the vocation they should follow. In order to find out what that is, they have to be strong and work hard, but that's the way people grow. In the manifesto for the seventh World Youth Day in 1992, he observed, "The Christian vocation also implies a mission…. It consists in making the presence of Christ evident in your personal lives, in fulfilling your daily duties, and in making concrete decisions that are consistent with the Gospel." The pope told them that they are called to evangelize their contemporaries most of all. "It's not time to be ashamed of the Gospel; now is the time to openly proclaim the good news, out in public. Let go of fear, leave an easy life aside, and answer Christ's call."

During the rally at Rome's Tor Vegata, the pope put down his staff and picked up a wooden beam that he blessed and symbolically placed on the shoulders of the young people gathered there.

During World Youth Day celebrations in Paris in 1997, the pope meets with young people under the Eiffel Tower.

At that time, Mexico was a country ruled by a single party, but the party was not totalitarian in the Soviet style. The press was relatively free. Newspapers influenced by the government had been criticizing the pope and the papacy the day before his arrival. They changed their tune once they saw the enthusiasm of the people. One of the daily newspapers printed a huge headline the day after the pope arrived: "He Came and He Conquered." Two days later newspapers were filled with welcoming greetings, paid for by Mexican businessmen. The good feeling was contagious, and the president and his whole family met with the pope for more than a half hour in the president's private residence.

HE SPEAKS TO THE BISHOPS

Enchanting the Mexican people was easier than winning the hearts and minds of Latin American priests who had revolutionary ideas. The crucial reason for the pope's visit was to confront the new liberation theology (see Chapter 15) that was spreading through Latin America as a way for clergy and lay Catholics to help relieve the poverty and violence suffered by the continent's poor. John Paul II, for all his concern for the poor and abused of the world, had been advised that liberation theology had Marxist overtones. He wanted to discourage its practitioners in his speech before the Latin American Bishops' Conference in Puebla.

The drive to Puebla was like the trip from the airport. Once again, millions of believers turned up. They didn't mind spending the whole night at nearby parishes in bad weather just to get a glimpse of the Holy Father and to welcome him. In Puebla there were balloons and fireworks and thousands of waving flags. Handel's Hallelujah Chorus could be heard from a plane flying low overhead. Church bells rang out all over the city, and bands played at every corner. Mass was held in the open air at an altar set up next to the wall of a seminary because it could not be legally celebrated in a public place.

The bishops' conference took place in the Palafoxiano Seminary. John Paul II addressed these church fathers, who represented all the faithful from Tierra del Fuego to the Río Brava (Rio Grande north of the border), on injustice in society and violent means of combating it. He had studied this problem in Poland for more than 40 years. What he emphasized to the bishops was that the truth contained in the Gospels is the truth about the living Son of God; he was not someone who fought a war in Palestine against the Roman occupation and for the cause of political and social liberation. The true liberation that Jesus offers is a liberation of love, forgiveness, and reconciliation, and that liberation leads to salvation. Any other interpretation of the Gospel is contrary to the teachings of the church, the foundation of which is Christian humanism, and it is the church that contains the full truth about humanity. Faith teaches that man is the image of God and not just a product of nature or social forces. This was the only truth that the bishops ought to be proclaiming, because the church does not need any other ideology to help it defend the dignity of the human person and religious freedom. The church does not demand participation in public life. It is founded on Jesus Christ and proclaims Gospel truth. The rest remains in God's hands. He did not mention liberation theology; nor did he allude to the widespread murders and torture that dictatorial regimes had carried out on their opponents—including the clergy—in Latin America.

Everyone except the pope was afraid of what might happen on his visit to Mexico from January 25 to February 1, 1979.

HE SPEAKS TO THE INDIANS

Before he left Mexico, John Paul II met with the Zapotec Indians, ancient inhabitants of Mexico. He flew in a helicopter to Cuilapa, Oaxaca, where half a million Zapotec Indians were waiting for him. In the afternoon he sat under a canopy among the ruins of an ancient cloister, wearing a sombrero. One Zapotec, chosen to speak to the pope, told about the difficult living conditions of his people. The Holy Father took up this topic in his homily and said that he wanted to be the voice of those who were not able to speak and those to whom nobody was listening.

"The worker who waters his distress with his own sweat, can no longer wait for his dignity to be recognized.

He has the right to be respected and must not be deprived of this right and of the little bit he does have—by maneuvers that are usually robbery…. He has the right to receive effective help, which is not just charity, nor mere crumbs of justice." Here the Holy Father was speaking to politicians. "Profound changes have to be made and urgent reform has to begin without delay."

The speeches to the bishops and Zapotecs may have seemed contradictory, but they illustrate two repeating themes: the liberation and dignity offered to humans through Christ and the need to help the poor.

On this first foreign trip, the pope wanted to show the world a new style of pastoral teaching, and he succeeded. The Mexicans loved him. When his plane departed from Mexico City, people flashed thousands of mirrors in the sun to say good-bye to the pope.

The Reason for the Total Gift of the Self

John Paul II was a powerful defender of human life. He stressed the value of human life right at the beginning of his pontificate. He took a stance on advocating the repeal of death sentences and urged ending armed conflicts in various parts of the world. He expressed his thoughts on the value of human life in his encyclical *Evangelium Vitae (The Gospel of Life),* which he promulgated on March 25, 1995.

Respect for human rights is central to all of John Paul II's writings. His fundamental criterion is the well-being of the person. The pope directs this message not only to Roman Catholics and other Christian denominations but also to

everyone in the world. He based his thoughts on the unique value of human life, grounded in the life of the transcendent Living God—the source of life of all human beings.

For the Holy Father human beings come first, ahead of whatever they produce by their labor, and solidarity among workers is better than competition among different social groups. Persons mature in their physical spiritual nature when they are loved; they form their selfhood within the framework of the married life and love of their parents.

John Paul II introduced a theme into this discussion that could be thought of as a discourse on the body. He pointed out that the purpose of the conjugal act is to form an exceptionally strong bond between the husband and the wife, in a union that entails a profound spiritual and corporal gift of self. Devaluing the marital act, by divorce or annulment, always has tragic effects on the persons involved.

Everything the pope says in *Evangelium Vitae* derives from his thesis that marital love is both unitive and procreative. While he was still a cardinal, he highlighted the unifying aspect of conjugal relations, in contrast with the prevailing opinion that the procreative aspect was most important.

"Christian morality regarding human sexual relations frees them from falling into the pitfall of lust—it does not prohibit the bodily expression of love *(Eros).* Quite the contrary, it frees it to become a complete and mature expression of love."

John Paul II affirmed and distinguished the unifying and procreative aspects of marital love. On the one hand, he agreed with the opinions expressed in Pope Paul VI's encyclical *Humanae Vitae (On Human Life),* which condemned artificial birth control, since it violated the purpose of the conjugal act. According to the pope, spouses who resort to birth control act like "judges" who question God's will and "manipulate" and devalue human sexuality, and along with it their own personal worth and that of their spouse, thereby falsifying the value of the total gift of self to the other person. On the other side of the issue, he was also opposed to in vitro fertilization. Just as it is not right to exclude procreation in the conjugal act, it is also wrong to exclude conjugal union by in vitro fertilization used to procreate. Marital partners are not free to decide the number of children they want to conceive or the time for them to be born. This decision should be made in the context of the natural law that God embedded in human nature, especially with respect to the woman's body and human nature. According to John Paul II, following the natural law, the couple develops in mutual respect and moderation. That way, spouses are not turned into slaves of sexual desire, and the purpose of marriage is not reduced to sanctioning pure biological instinct.

Meetings at Castel Gandolfo

Above: John Paul II gives a blessing from an upper porch at Castel Gandolfo in the summer of 1996.

Left: Castel Gandolfo is a palace built in the seventeenth century by Pope Urban VIII.

John Paul II went to Castel Gandolfo during the first days of his pontificate, but he spent only a few hours there. He returned to it in the autumn of 1979 and stayed longer. These were the first two times Karol Wojtyla went to Castel Gandolfo to take a vacation after being elected as pope, and he wanted to spend them with some of his friends. He asked Jerzy Janik, a physicist he had known in Kraków, to come visit him and to bring his wife and family. Janik thought that his old friend would just spend an hour or two with them, at most, but that's not what happened. The pope spent his whole summer vacation with him and his family.

Janik was one of the scientists who organized annual interdisciplinary seminars in Kraków. Karol Wojtyla took part in them while he was cardinal and archbishop. The last seminar had to be suspended when John Paul I died and Cardinal Wojtyla left for the conclave.

During their vacation at Castel Gandolfo, the pope and the scientist decided to reactivate this old tradition,

Toward the end of July and beginning of August, the inhabitants of Rome flee their city because of the summer heat and humidity that make life unbearable. The pope also left Rome to spend the hot spell in his summer residence, the Castel Gandolfo. This palace, located in a more temperate climate and nestled between the slopes near Lake Albano, afforded him a place to take a relaxing vacation.

right there in the summer residence of the pope. The first session on the theme of "Science, Religion, History" was set up for August 1980 and was attended by Polish scientists and researchers working in various social science and applied science disciplines.

Another meeting was held at the end of the winter of the following year, this time with the professor-priest Father Józef Tischner and Professor Dr. Krzyszt of Michalski, who also had organized sessions in Poland. These meetings were later transferred to Vienna. Cardinal Franz König, the pope's friend, supported the establishment of the Institute for Human Sciences with Michalski as its rector. Thus began the Sessions of the Scientific Council of the Institute in Vienna, which met every two years.

In August 1983 the topic was "Man and Modern Science." At other sessions the contradictions between science and faith were discussed. Although many participants at these early meetings were Polish intellectuals, eventually delegates from other European countries and the United States were included. John Paul II always took an active part in the sessions whether he entered the discussions or joined the scientists at their workstations.

Above: Every two years for many years, international scientists met at the pope's summer home. The gatherings were known as "Conversations at Castel Gandolfo."

Left: Fabiola Moroni, the cook and pastry chef at the summer residence of Castel Gandolfo.

Above: Brother Matthew Timmers and Father Walter J. Miller use the telescope in the observatory at Castel Gandolfo.

171

Chapter 11

New Political Policy toward the East

John Paul II did not believe that the
political boundaries set by the Yalta
Conference were permanent. He was
hoping for a free, united Europe that
would be founded on the great
Christian tradition.

In October 1978 news of the election of a Polish cardinal as pope arrived at the Kremlin, the seat of the Soviet government in Moscow, and Yuri Andropov, first head of the Committee of State Security (KGB), summoned the head of the secret services in Kraków to come to Moscow immediately. Betraying anger in his voice, he asked, "How could you have let them elect a citizen of a Soviet country as pope?" The secret services agent immediately responded that their comrades in Rome were at fault.

Andropov could not get it into his head that something like that could happen without the knowledge of the KGB. He called for a special investigation. The Information Office came up with the answer he was waiting to hear: Karol Wojtyla was elected because of a plot hatched by antisocialists and led by Polish people in the United States—namely, Cardinal Jan Krol of Philadelphia and Zbigniew Brzezinski, national security adviser for President Jimmy Carter. They wanted to cause trouble in Poland to weaken the Warsaw Pact and the entire Soviet bloc.

Cardinal Krol did indeed back Wojtyla for pope, organizing the North American cardinals in his behalf, but the KGB Information Office was wrong about Brzezinski's having a role in the papal election. Brzezinski, who was born in Poland, did know the pope. They had met in 1976 when Brzezinski was a professor at Harvard and Cardinal Wojtyla gave a speech there. They had been correspondents ever since. Later, as President Jimmy Carter's security adviser, Brzezinski kept a close watch on Poland and the other Soviet satellite countries and their struggles against Moscow. He represented the United States at Pope John Paul II's accession to the Throne of Saint Peter.

UNHAPPY ALLIANCES

In 1978 Russia described its satellites as a socialist community, but they were more like an empire ruled out of Moscow. The Communist governments of Bulgaria, Czechoslovakia, the German Democratic Republic, Poland, Romania, and Hungary had some autonomy in running their countries' internal affairs, as spelled out in their constitutions, but they were subject to Moscow when it came to international affairs. Loyalty and friendship toward the Soviet Union were also written into their constitutions. And they were all part of the Warsaw Pact, a mutual-defense treaty set up by the Soviets to counter the West's North Atlantic Treaty Organization.

Four of these satellite countries had revolted unsuccessfully from Soviet rule. Workers in East Berlin rioted in 1953, but Soviet tanks moved in quickly to quash

Soviet foreign minister Andrei Gromyko attends the United Nations in New York in 1982 after several trips to the Vatican.

that rebellion. Hungarians in Budapest made a bid for freedom in 1956 under a coalition led by Imre Nagy. Soviet tanks again brutally crushed the insurrection, Nagy and some of his ministers were executed, and nearly 200,000 refugees fled the country. The "Prague Spring" of 1968—a move toward democratization in Czechoslovakia under party leader Alexander Dubcek—also brought harsh reprisals. This time Moscow sent in the Warsaw division of the Warsaw Pact standing army. Poland rebelled several times, but it was not invaded by foreign troops. In 1956 and 1970 the Communist-controlled Polish army and police force put down uprisings at the cost of many lives. Special military forces also were called upon to restore order in 1968 and 1976.

By the end of the 1970s, Resistance movements were still active in the most rebellious Soviet-bloc countries: Czechoslovakia, Poland, and Hungary. In Hungary Laszlo Rajk, son of the Communist Party leader and foreign minister Laszlo Rajk, who had been executed in 1949 for conspiring to overthrow the government, led a relatively small group. Czechoslovakian intellectual activists formed an opposition group called Charter 77. Its best-known dissident was the dramatist (and later president of the Czech Republic) Vaclav Havel. Poland's best-known group was the Workers' Defense Committee (KOR) led by Jacek Kuron and Adam Michnik. Other movements also sprang up in Poland: Young Poland, the Movement for the Defense of the Rights of Man and Citizen, and later, Solidarity, the trade union movement officially called the Organization of the Independent Self-Governing Trade Unions, led by Lech Walesa.

Poland was the only country in which opposition movements could count on the Catholic Church for help. Severe Soviet policies in Czechoslovakia had sent the Catholic Church underground in Stalin's time. The church in Hungary suffered a similar fate.

A NOT-SO-DIPLOMATIC EXCHANGE

After the Communist Party's initial shock at the pontificate of John Paul II, it saw that the Holy See's policy of ongoing dialogue with the East—begun by John XXIII and continued in the *Ostpolitik* of Paul VI and his secretary for the Council for Public Affairs of the Church, Archbishop Agostino Casaroli—might become troublesome under Wojtyla.

Watching the Vatican's moves, the party foresaw problems in Poland. Their instincts were correct. Although the policy seemed the same on the surface, there was one distinct difference. John XXIII and Paul VI assumed that the Soviet satellite countries, awarded to Russia in the Yalta

During his second trip to the United States in 1987, John Paul II talks with President Ronald Reagan; the president mobilized support for Solidarity in Poland and kept the pope informed of USSR military moves.

agreements after World War II, would stay under Moscow's thumb indefinitely. They worked for small concessions. John Paul II, in contrast, believed that a strong, devoted church could mobilize Catholics to bring down Communism.

Above: In 1949 a demonstration organized by the Catholic Youth Organization and the Boy Scouts in front of St. Patrick's Cathedral in New York City protests Cardinal József Mindszenty's incarceration in Hungary.

In January 1979, after Karol Wojtyla had been pope for only four months, Soviet foreign minister Andrei Gromyko, a veteran of the Soviet diplomatic corps, took a trip to the Vatican to get to know the pope personally. The Holy Father greeted him with Archbishop Agostino Casaroli, a veteran of the Vatican diplomatic corps, at his side. Gromyko behaved as he would have on any routine diplomatic mission. In line with the Kremlin's diplomatic tactics, he spoke about "working together for peace" and ways to accomplish this. He mentioned what the Soviet Union was doing for peace and disarmament and acknowledged that the church was also active on these issues.

John Paul II, for his part, preferred to discuss his concerns about religious freedom, a topic the Kremlin didn't want to hear about. Resorting to a diplomatic speech, John Paul II wanted Gromyko to understand that people in the Soviet Union seemed to be finding obstacles when it came to freedom of religion. To which Andrei Gromyko replied that the Soviet constitution guaranteed the people the right to believe in God, and he assured the pope that people in his country could practice their religion without any trouble. He even cited Byelorussia, where he once was

a deputy, as proof of this. The pope thought that what Gromyko said belied the facts.

Gromyko had met with other popes on previous occasions: once with John XXIII and five times with Paul VI. The theme of their conversations was always about "strengthening the peace." This time he was dealing with John Paul II, who had lived under Soviet rule in Poland. John Paul II had no intention of starting an anti-Communist crusade. He believed that the evil of totalitarian systems could not be fought with violence, because violence creates more evil. The only defensive weapon was Gospel truth. Once people changed according to the spirit of the Gospel, then they could better resist any evil they met in the Communist ideology.

Below: Cardinal József Mindszenty, primate of Hungary, was sentenced to life imprisonment in 1949 for opposing Communist rule and declaring himself a Catholic.

A POLITICAL STRATEGY OF TAKING SMALL STEPS

When Archbishop Casaroli met with Soviet foreign minister Gromyko, he was secretary of the Council for Public Affairs of the Church. His duties at the Holy See were equal to those of a minister of foreign affairs in any other country, and the Vatican's political policy toward the East was mostly of his making. His tactics were typical of Vatican diplomacy. Members of the Vatican diplomatic corps characteristically accomplished their objectives with complicated negotiations, often secret, and during private meetings with people at the cabinet advisory level in their country. Progress came in small steps. Casaroli was a master at this diplomacy. The strategy he had followed for many years, however, was based on the presupposition that the way Europe was divided at the Yalta Conference would be permanent. Casaroli accepted things as they were and tried to secure as many benefits as he could for the church in the East. This differed from the *Realpolitik* of Pope John XXIII.

During the Vatican II Council John XXIII proclaimed that the church was becoming more open to the world, including territories governed by Communists, but this still meant accepting a divided Europe. To let the world know that the church had just started a new chapter and was willing to openly discuss issues in the global political forum, on March 7, 1962, John XXIII received the daughter of Nikita Khrushchev (he was general secretary of the Communist Party at that time) and his son-in-law, Alexis Adzubey, at the Papal Palace.

Neither this audience nor a later one with Gromyko changed the Kremlin's policy toward the church. Internal politics of the Soviet Union also did not change; citizens who professed a belief in God were not allowed to take part in public life. Any improved contacts between the Union of Soviet Socialist Republics and the Vatican during the 1960s and early 1970s resulted only in political benefits: Moscow would not openly criticize the papacy, and the Vatican would not condemn the atheistic regime, as Pius XI and Pius XII had done. In addition, thanks to the new "normalization" of the relationship, Communist regimes in Central Europe freed important members of the Catholic hierarchy from prison and allowed them to go to Rome. Greek Catholic cardinal Josyf Slipyj of the Ukraine was freed from a Soviet gulag and went into exile in 1963; Cardinal Josef Beran was allowed to leave Czechoslovakia in 1965; Cardinal József Mindszenty left Budapest in 1971. To fill these vacant ecclesiastic posts, the Vatican nominated apostolic administrators who had a more conciliatory attitude toward Communist governments. Also, as a result of this thaw in relations, high Communist officials visited the Vatican during Paul VI's time: Josip Tito of Yugoslavia, Nikolai Podgorny of the Soviet Union, Todor Zivkov of Bulgaria, and Edward Gierek of Poland.

HE DIDN'T AGREE THAT EUROPE SHOULD STAY DIVIDED

The arrival of a pope in Rome from the other side of the Iron Curtain upset the balance his predecessors had maintained. Shortly after he became pope, John Paul II requested to see the documentation of Paul VI's policy toward the East. As soon as he understood that Paul VI's *Ostpolitik,* he openly challenged its premises. The pope from Poland could not agree that the division of Europe established at Yalta was permanent.

Archbishop Casaroli, faithful to the directives of former popes and convinced that the postwar changes in Europe were fixed, found himself in a difficult situation. He couldn't agree with a public policy that labeled the Soviet system evil, because he feared making the situation worse for local bishops in Communist countries.

Agostino Casaroli

Agostino Casaroli was born on November 24, 1914, in the town of Castel San Giovanni, near Piacenza, Italy. After finishing his studies in the Collegio Aberoni in Piacenza, he entered the Pontifical Lateran Athenaeum in Rome, where he obtained a doctorate degree in Canon Law. He was ordained on May 27, 1937, in Piacenza and began working in the Vatican Secretariat of State in 1940. He received his first ecclesiastic nomination on January 4, 1945. He became privy chamberlain to the pope, making him a high-ranking priest, and entered the service of the Vatican foreign affairs office.

In 1961 he was named undersecretary of the Congregation of Extraordinary Ecclesiastical Affairs. In March of the same year, he was chief of the Vatican delegation to the United Nations Conference on diplomatic relations held in Vienna; he also took part in many other international meetings and conferences as a representative of the Holy See. As Vatican representative, he signed agreements with Tunisia (1964), Hungary (1964), and Yugoslavia (1966).

Paul VI named him titular archbishop of Cartagine, Italy, and ordained him 12 days later in St. Peter's Basilica. The newly ordained bishop was appointed secretary of the Council for Public Affairs of the Church and president of the Pontifical Commission for Russia. As representative of the Holy See, he signed the Nonproliferation Treaty in Moscow on February 25, 1971, and the Charter of the Conference on European Security and Cooperation in Helsinki, Finland, on August 1, 1975. John Paul II named him pro-secretary of state and pro-prefect of the Council for Public Affairs of the Church on April 30, 1979.

John Paul II made him a cardinal on June 30, 1979, and, at the same time, secretary of state and prefect of the Council for Public Affairs of the Church, as well as President of the Pontifical Commission for the State of Vatican City. As cardinal, Casaroli was active in many meetings of the Synod of Bishops and was often sent on special diplomatic missions. On May 31, 1981, he represented the Holy Father at the funeral of Cardinal Stefan Wyszynski, since the pope was convalescing in the hospital from his bullet wound.

Cardinal Casaroli died in Rome on June 9, 1998, and was buried under the main altar of the Church of the Twelve Apostles.

Despite their differences over political policy toward the East, when Vatican secretary of state Cardinal Jean Villot died in March 1979, John Paul II appointed Casaroli to take his place and made him a cardinal. The new political policy for the East was going to be carried out by the same diplomats who served John Paul II's predecessors. The Holy Father had nothing against cabinet meetings held in secret or with making diplomatic headway in short steps—but that would not constitute the Vatican's main diplomatic strategy. The new pope's goal was not to maintain the way Europe was divided, but to build, or to put it better, rebuild a united Europe based on a Christian foundation. The Christian cultures of the East

(CONTINUED ON PAGE 180)

The Silent Church

In November 1978 John Paul II attended a celebration in honor of Saint Francis of Assisi. During the ceremony someone suddenly shouted, "Don't forget the silent church." The pope reacted immediately, answering, "The church is no longer silent, because it has my voice to speak for it." At that point, Catholics in Central Europe had been living under Communist governments for 30 years. These governments persecuted religious institutions because they wanted to spread their own atheistic beliefs without interference.

During the 1920s Bolsheviks carried out a campaign of brutal repression that destroyed an already weakened church structure in the USSR. Following that example, other Communist countries began to wage war against "religious superstition." Communists thought the Catholic Church was especially dangerous because of its international scope and the fact that its center of power lay outside the Soviet sphere.

Although Stalin looked down on the Vatican territory of the Holy See—he famously joked, "How many army divisions does the Vatican command?"—his secret service advised infiltrating the church to thwart its activities. Authorities in totalitarian systems were suspicious of bishops because bishops are obligated by Canon Law to maintain direct contact with the Roman Curia.

At the end of World War II, Catholics were living in all of the countries occupied by the Soviet Union. The majority of them lived in Poland, Hungary, Czechoslovakia, East Germany, and Lithuania—a country that the USSR had annexed in 1940. The church in Poland was certainly hounded, but the church in these other countries suffered more severe and lengthy persecutions at the hands of the Communists.

LIFE IMPRISONMENT FOR THE PRIMATE OF HUNGARY

At the end of World War II, about 60 percent of the Hungarian population declared they were Catholic. Their primate, Cardinal József Mindszenty, was arrested in December 1948 for his categorical opposition to Communist rule. After being detained in prison, he faced a "show trial" designed to humiliate him and was sentenced to life imprisonment. A large number of Hungarian clergy, especially members of religious orders, shared his fate. An alternate collaborationist Committee of Catholic Priests for Peace, known as Pax, was created by the Communist government to replace the authentic institution of the priesthood.

Cardinal Mindszenty was liberated in October 1956 during the Hungarian insurrection. After the uprising failed, he took refuge in the United States Legation in Budapest and remained there—a virtual prisoner—for the next 15 years.

After 1956 the church's situation in Hungary improved little by little, but the church was never as autonomous as the church in Poland under Gomulka. The Hungarian government signed an accord with the Holy See in 1964 in which it made a concession regarding the nomination of bishops to dioceses that had no bishops. This agreement was a result of the Vatican's policy toward the East, started by Pope John XXIII and carried on by Paul VI. In essence, their policy was an attempt, after Stalin's death, to gain some freedom for the church, but it resulted only in a partial improvement in the church's situation.

The agreement struck by the Vatican with Hungary in 1967 achieved a few additional positive results: Children were allowed to attend religion classes, and two years later another agreement allowed *ad limina* visits by all the Hungarian bishops to the Vatican. (Bishops are required to meet with the pope every five years.) When John Paul II began his pontificate, the church in Hungary still had limited freedoms, but apart from Poland it was in a better situation than churches in other countries in the Soviet bloc.

THE PRIESTS' CONSPIRACY

The situation of Catholics in Czechoslovakia was much worse. The church underwent persecution soon after the Communist coup d'etat in February 1948. The majority of Catholic schools, hospitals, and charitable organizations were closed. Catholic Action, an organization of the laity, was infiltrated by secret police agents, and many priests were arrested. In June 1949 Bishop Josef Beran, primate of Bohemia and a Dachau survivor, was arrested after he preached a forceful homily in defense of the church's rights.

By 1951 more than 3,000 priests—a third of the Catholic priests in Czechoslovakia—had been imprisoned. Members of religious orders were all interned in so-called "reeducation camps." Seminaries were replaced by "schools for priests" that were controlled by state authorities. Faced with this situation, the church in Czechoslovakia was forced to go underground. With the special authorization of the pope, nine bishops were secretly consecrated to replace the bishops who were in prison. Pastoral ministry soon resumed underground, thanks to hundreds of brave priests who were ordained clandestinely by those bishops.

After many negotiations by the Holy See, Bishop Beran was released in 1965, on condition that he go to

Rome and stay there. Solving the problem with Beran made it possible for John Paul II to name Bishop Frantisek Tomasek as the new ecclesiastical administrator for the diocese of Prague. But neither that nor the brief thaw of the 1968 "Prague Spring" made any substantial change in the difficult situation of the church in Czechoslovakia. At the beginning of the 1970s, more than half of the parishes in Moravia had no priests, and in Slovakia there was not one officially recognized bishop. Although the government gave its consent for three Slovak bishops to be consecrated in 1973, they belonged to Pax, a Czech organization directed by the secret police similar to the Catholic Priests for Peace organization in Hungary.

CATHOLICS SPIED UPON BY THE EAST GERMAN STASI

In contrast to Poland, Hungary, and even Czechoslovakia, the German Democratic Republic (East Germany) had a minority of Catholics. The million and a half Catholics who lived there were kept under strict surveillance by the Ministry for State Security, also known as the Stasi. Spies and informants were everywhere, and authorities in the German Democratic Republic never had to put bishops in prison in order to subjugate the Catholic population. In the spring of 1990, after the fall of Erik Honecker's regime, Klaus Gysi, who was the minister of culture in charge of church-state relations for many years, openly declared, "The Catholic Church adopted a policy of distancing itself from the regime, of not getting involved, a policy of absolute loyalty."

REBELS IN LITHUANIA

Catholics in Lithuania were less docile, even though this country formed part of the Soviet Union. The Soviet secret police had destroyed the underlying church structure in the 1940s, and whatever remained of it was infiltrated by secret agents. For the more than 2 million Lithuanians who were Catholic, clinging to the faith of their forefathers was a question of national identity and pride. Lithuanian Catholics managed during the 1970s to publish underground Catholic periodicals and documents. An Open Letter to the Secretary General of the United Nations was produced protesting the lack of religious freedom in their homeland. This treasonous document was signed by 17,000 Catholics.

CONTINUITY, CONFLICT, AND CHANGE

Hansjakob Stehle, an expert in Vatican politics in Central and Eastern Europe during the pontificate of John Paul II, described his political strategy in three words: continuity, conflict, and change. This Slavic pope rejected starting an all-out anti-Communist crusade without taking into account the possible costly outcome to members of the clergy behind the Iron Curtain. Cardinal Josyf Slipyj, who had spent many years in a Soviet gulag before he went into exile in Rome in 1963, might have preferred a crusade. On the other hand, John Paul II did not share his predecessors' illusions about the mendacious nature of Soviet regimes—illusions to which some members of the Vatican diplomatic corps had succumbed more than once.

Poland was at the core of John Paul II's policy toward the East. This was not only as a consequence of the Holy Father's love for his country but also because he was convinced that Poland, because of its strong Catholicism, was the "weakest link" in the Soviet system. The church worked with Solidarity for workers' rights. After the *perestroika* program began in the Union of Soviet Socialist Republics, along with the beginning of a process of liberation of Soviet satellite countries that ended with the "autumn of the nations" in 1989, the church found itself freer to act, and the Holy See adopted a program of peaceful democratization and transformation of the individual countries in the former Soviet regime.

"The Catholic Church sees, with enormous respect and love, how powerful and vital is the legacy of the Slavic peoples of the East," John Paul II wrote in his letter to Mikhail Gorbachev in 1988, in which he asked the Soviet leader to find a solution to the difficult situation of Christians in parts of the Soviet Union. Events that happened in the ensuing years to come proved that his efforts to reestablish full human dignity and rights for the faithful in Central and Eastern Europe paid off handsomely. The majority of the information on how he accomplished this, however, remains a closely guarded secret in the Vatican archives, and he admitted he didn't do it alone.

In the Church of Our Lady of Victory in Prague, Carmelite Sisters change the vestments of the infant Jesus several times a year to reflect the liturgical season.

Angelo Sodano

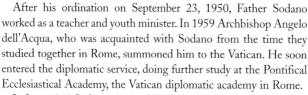

Angelo Sodano was born on November 23, 1927, in the rural Piedmontese town of Isola d'Asti. He was the second of six children in a family that was very active in the church. His father, Giovanni, belonged to the Italian Christian Democratic Party and was a member of parliament from 1948 to 1963.

After finishing his seminary studies, Sodano continued his education in Rome at the Pontifical Gregorian University, where he earned a doctorate in theology, and at the Pontifical Lateran University, where he earned a doctorate in Canon Law.

After his ordination on September 23, 1950, Father Sodano worked as a teacher and youth minister. In 1959 Archbishop Angelo dell'Acqua, who was acquainted with Sodano from the time they studied together in Rome, summoned him to the Vatican. He soon entered the diplomatic service, doing further study at the Pontifical Ecclesiastical Academy, the Vatican diplomatic academy in Rome.

In June 1962 Sodano obtained his first assignment as secretary in the nunciature in Ecuador, and he was assigned later to Uruguay and Chile. Upon returning to the Vatican in 1968, he worked for almost 10 years in the Council for Public Affairs of the Church.

Pope Paul VI appointed Sodano as apostolic nuncio in Chile and named him titular archbishop of Albano, near Rome. He occupied this post for almost nine years, until May 23, 1988.

John Paul II appointed him secretary for the Council for Public Affairs of the Church and promoted him to Vatican secretary of state on December 1, 1990, when he replaced Agostino Casaroli, who had retired. In the consistory of June 28 of the following year, the Holy Father made him a cardinal. Cardinal Sodano usually accompanied the pope on his trips overseas and represented the Holy See at various meetings and conferences. He was the personal representative of the pope at the funeral of former president Ronald Reagan on June 11, 2004.

and the West—Byzantine and Latin—were going to be two lungs of the same body.

Moreover, in clear, straightforward words, the pope interjected a Gospel approach into the political arena. He defended the inherent dignity of men and women as human beings and their right to live their lives in conditions that guaranteed freedom of conscience and freedom of religion. Secret negotiations did not serve this purpose very well, so the pope decided to take direct action with those he could influence with his political approach. He would proclaim Gospel truths in a loud voice, and this would be a spark to enflame immense regions of the world where the Marxist-Leninist ideology supported a false vision of humanity. He believed that Gospel truths had the power to change Europe and the whole world.

A CHALLENGE FOR MOSCOW

Moscow framed its response to John Paul II's policy toward the East after a year of watching what he did.

During this time the pope launched three challenges to "real socialism." During his first papal pilgrimage to Mexico, he criticized liberation theology. He feared it was infiltrating the Latin American church, which he thought was too closely aligned with Marxist ideology. Proponents of liberation theology proposed to replace the Gospel message with armed struggle in order to bring about a change in social structures. Then, on his first pilgrimage to his native Poland, John Paul II questioned the terms of the Yalta agreements and advocated respect for the rights of nations to govern themselves. Also, in a speech he gave to the United Nations General Assembly in New York, he criticized government systems that violated fundamental human liberties and the right to freedom of religion.

Another of John Paul II's challenges was the moral support he gave Cardinal Frantisek Tomasek, bishop of Prague. He sent a pastoral letter to be read loud in all the churches of Bohemia and Slovakia on Christmas. March 1979 was drawing near, and that would mark the 250th anniversary of Saint John Nepomucene's death. At the end of the fourteenth century, King Wenceslaus IV of Bohemia and Luxemburg ordered this priest to be assassinated because he would not break the seal of confession. So John Paul II wrote a letter to Tomasek on this occasion, and in it he presented Saint John Nepomucene as a Czech martyr and an example of someone who had great Christian faith. Tomasek was eighty years old and had formerly criticized Catholics who were active in the Charter 77 opposition movement. John Paul II's letter changed Cardinal Tomasek's conciliatory politics. With this support from the Holy Father (they had met at the Vatican II Council), Tomasek became an implacable critic of the Communist regime.

The pope also sent a letter to Cardinal Josyf Slipyj, who lived in exile in the United States, to mark the occasion of the millennium of the acceptance of Christianity by the Kievan Rus. (The Rus people founded Kiev.) They were a prime symbol of the Christianization of the Eastern Slavic peoples before the schism between the Roman Catholic and Greek Orthodox churches. The pope took advantage of this opportunity to remind everyone about the right to freedom of religion, a fundamental human right, clearly alluding to the extremely difficult situation of Greek Catholics in the Ukraine who were in union with Rome and who, despite suffering many years of persecution, never broke off contact with Rome.

In the beginning the new pope's tactics made people in the Kremlin nervous, but he created an all-out panic when his words of hope—"Don't be afraid. Open the doors to Christ"—were publicized in Poland, Czechoslovakia, and the Ukraine, regions under direct control of the Soviet Union.

THE KREMLIN'S COUNTERATTACK

In November 1979 a special commission of the KGB drew up guidelines on how to stop the Vatican's influence in socialist countries. The Communist Party, as well as the Communist-controlled press and television, was ordered to intensify propaganda against the Vatican in Soviet countries with largely Catholic populations: Lithuania, Latvia, the Ukraine, and Byelorussia. Communist parties in Western Europe and Latin America were also given the same directive. From then on, party members had to inform the Soviet embassy staff in each country about any sign of support they detected that was given to John Paul II's stratagems. The Soviet Foreign Office and the KGB mounted an intense media campaign to insinuate that any political moves by John Paul II would harm the church.

In the United States, Zbigniew Brzezinski became national security adviser for President Jimmy Carter in the late 1970s. It was the height of the cold war between the United States and the Union of Soviet Socialist Republics. Carter and Brzezinski met with the pope in Rome and kept close watch on the satellite countries. President Carter supported efforts to smuggle anti-Communist publications into these countries. In 1981, when Ronald Reagan became president, he kept Brzezinski on as a special adviser on Poland.

A SIMILAR VIEW OF COMMUNISM

President Reagan and the pope shared the idea that Communism was evil and that it could be brought down. Reagan believed that it would implode of its own inadequacies; the pope saw it falling in the face of Christian truth. Reagan, a Protestant, saw the Catholic Church as an important ally in the fight against Communism and successfully worked on legislation reestablishing diplomatic relations with the Vatican.

Reagan and the head of the Central Intelligence Agency (CIA), William Casey, wanted to help the rebels in the Soviet-bloc countries. They saw Solidarity, the independent labor movement in Poland led by an out-of-work electrician named Lech Walesa, as a potent weapon in undermining Communist power in Poland and, possibly, beyond Poland. Solidarity was supported both financially and materially by U.S. labor unions through the AFL-CIO. The role of the CIA was to get the money and supplies into the country. Casey also saw to it that the pope was kept informed of Soviet troop movements. The CIA and the Vatican shared intelligence on Poland. The United States prepared to put economic pressure on the Soviet Union, if necessary, to keep it from invading Poland.

MANY ROADS TO FREEDOM

Other forces were also conspiring to bring change to Poland. The Communist leadership in Poland, principally General Wojciech Jaruzelski and Stanislaw Kania, did not want the Soviet or the Warsaw Pact armies to invade their country. To hold off Moscow, they imposed martial law on Poland in 1981, arresting many members of Solidarity and putting Lech Walesa under house arrest.

The pope is greeted in Washington in 1979 by Zbigniew Brzezinski, national security adviser to President Jimmy Carter.

This action brought economic sanctions from the West, which caused great hardship for the Poles. Partly because Jaruzelski could not bring himself to negotiate directly with Solidarity, martial law lasted five years. Finally, with another

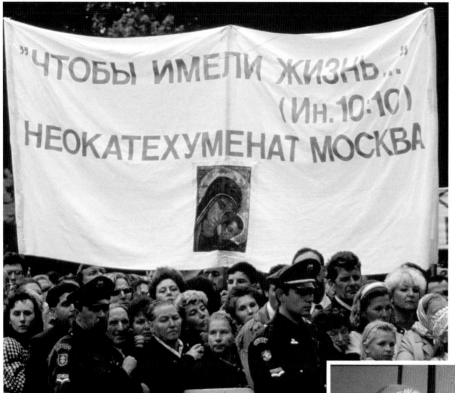

The visit that John Paul II made to Lithuania in 1993 was a pilgrimage to a nation of martyrs. More than 270,000 Catholics were arrested and put into prison between 1945 and 1955.

WHO IS THIS MAN?

A few weeks after Mikhail Gorbachev became the leader of the Communist Party, he sent Soviet foreign minister Andrei Gromyko to the Vatican to explore the possibility of establishing diplomatic relations between Moscow and the Holy See. He also suggested the possibility that Soviet authorities and Vatican personnel might conjointly take a look at the situation of Catholics in the USSR.

Gorbachev was not well known in March 1985, even within the Soviet bloc. (Some years later John Paul II said, "God in his Providence has given us this man.") The leaders of the Communist countries got to know him better at a meeting of the Political Committee of the Warsaw Pact that was held in Warsaw that April. Here Gorbachev talked for a

In 1988, when Cardinal Casaroli was delivering a letter to Mikhail Gorbachev, general secretary of the Communist Party of the Soviet Union, Gorbachev mentioned that a sacred icon was hidden behind a portrait of Lenin in his official residence.

visit to Poland from the pope in 1987, Jaruzelski realized that he had no choice but to include Solidarity leaders in a round table of negotiations for the future of Poland. Elections were held in 1989 with Solidarity candidates winning 261 of 262 seats in the new parliament.

CHANGES IN THE USSR

In November 1982 Leonid Brezhnev, general secretary of the Communist Party and president of the Union of Soviet Socialist Republics, died, and Yuri Andropov was elected to take his place. Andropov, former first head of the Committee of State Security (KGB), was a bitter enemy of the church in Poland. He died in 1984, and his elderly replacement died within the next year. In 1985 Mikhail Gorbachev was elected general secretary of the Communist Party of the Soviet Union.

Gorbachev, concerned about the economic inertia and spiritual stagnation in the Soviet Union, embarked upon a new policy of openness to ideas *(glasnost)* and of economic, political, and social restructuring *(perestroika)*. These initiatives were intended to strengthen the failing Soviet economic system, but they ended up undoing the terms of the Yalta Conference in Central Europe.

few hours with the Polish premier general Wojciech Jaruzelski, who explained the history of Christianity in Poland and the importance of church and the pope—whom Jaruzelski had known when he was a bishop back in Kraków—in keeping the country together. After their conversation Jaruzelski, in whom the Kremlin did not have much confidence, became Gorbachev's ally. He joined with Gorbachev to carry out his *perestroika* reforms. They hoped to transform the ailing Soviet Union into a modern country that respected people's social rights. Jaruzelski became an emissary between the Holy See and the Kremlin. Jaruzelski suggested to the pope that he should talk to Gorbachev, a new brand of Soviet leader.

WE'RE ALSO BAPTIZED

The Feast of the Millennium of the Baptism of the Rus People in Kiev became the first chance for a direct contact between the pope and the new Soviet leader. John Paul II, though, could not attend the festivities in Moscow in person, because the Russian Orthodox Church opposed his coming. A delegation from the Holy See, headed by secretary of state Cardinal Agostino Casaroli, arrived at the capital of the Soviet Union on June 13, 1988. He brought with him a letter from the Holy Father that was addressed to Mikhail Gorbachev. In it John Paul II outlined, from his point of view, the most important problems in the bilateral relationship between the Holy See and the Kremlin and suggested that it might be advisable for the two of them to go over the issues together in a private meeting. Casaroli delivered the letter on the last day of the Vatican delegation's stay in Moscow in the presence of the Soviet foreign minister Eduard Shevardnadze.

This was the first time since the Bolsheviks took over the Kremlin in 1917 that a cardinal from the Vatican had entered the Kremlin. Cardinal Casaroli, wearing his red cassock trimmed in purple, looked somewhat ill at ease despite the fact that he was a seasoned diplomat and world traveler. Gorbachev wanted to diffuse the tension, so he joked with Cardinal Casaroli. "There's no need for you to worry. Both Foreign Minister Shevardnadze and I were baptized when we were children!" he said. Then he read the entire letter from the pope but gave no reply.

Gorbachev answered the pope's letter 14 months later, when the Communist system in Central Europe was disintegrating. Poland had concluded roundtable negotiations and had just held partially free elections. In spite of its defeat, the Communist Party remained in power, as agreed upon by the opposition. In July the transitory power renewed diplomatic relations between Poland and the Holy See.

Other countries in the region were getting ready for the "autumn of the people," a time when former Soviet-bloc peoples could choose their own governments without the interference of Moscow.

"HE'S ONE OF US. HE'S A SLAV!"

On December 1, 1989, Mikhail Gorbachev went through the doors of the Papal Palace with his wife, Raisa. All cameras in the Vatican followed his every move and tried to capture his facial expressions. Raisa Gorbachev was invited to go visit the Sistine Chapel while her husband was directed to the papal apartments. The Holy Father received Gorbachev cordially but with a hint of reserve, since

he respected his guest but didn't share his point of view.

Their private conversation took place in the pope's library and went on for an hour and a half. When Mrs. Gorbachev met up with them, her husband turned to her and said, "I have the honor of presenting you to the highest moral authority on earth." Then he added, as if the thought just entered his mind, "He's one of us. He's a Slav!"

"The time has come for you to carry out what you already said you would do—that is, change your laws about religious freedom," the pope says to Gorbachev during his official visit to the Vatican in 1989.

In the official communiqué of the meeting, John Paul II mentioned the goal of his policy toward the East, which until a short time before had seemed to be a dream. He spoke about freedom of conscience and religion and being able to perform pastoral ministry in countries in which atheistic systems were in place. The general secretary's visit to the Vatican was the prelude to reform.

Gorbachev, for his part, said the meeting with Pope John Paul II was possible because of changes occurring in many countries. He considered diplomatic relations between Moscow and the Vatican as a *fait accompli* and promised he would see to it that religious freedom was a guaranteed right. At the end of the meeting, he unexpectedly invited the pope to visit the Soviet Union.

Diplomatic relations were formally reestablished in March 1990. The papal trip to the Soviet Union never took place, however, because scarcely a year after these two leaders met at the Vatican, the USSR collapsed.

On May 13, 1981, while Pope John Paul II was riding through St. Peter's Square, blessing a friendly, noisy crowd, two pistol shots were fired. Few people realized what had happened. At that single moment the fate of his pontificate hung in the balance.

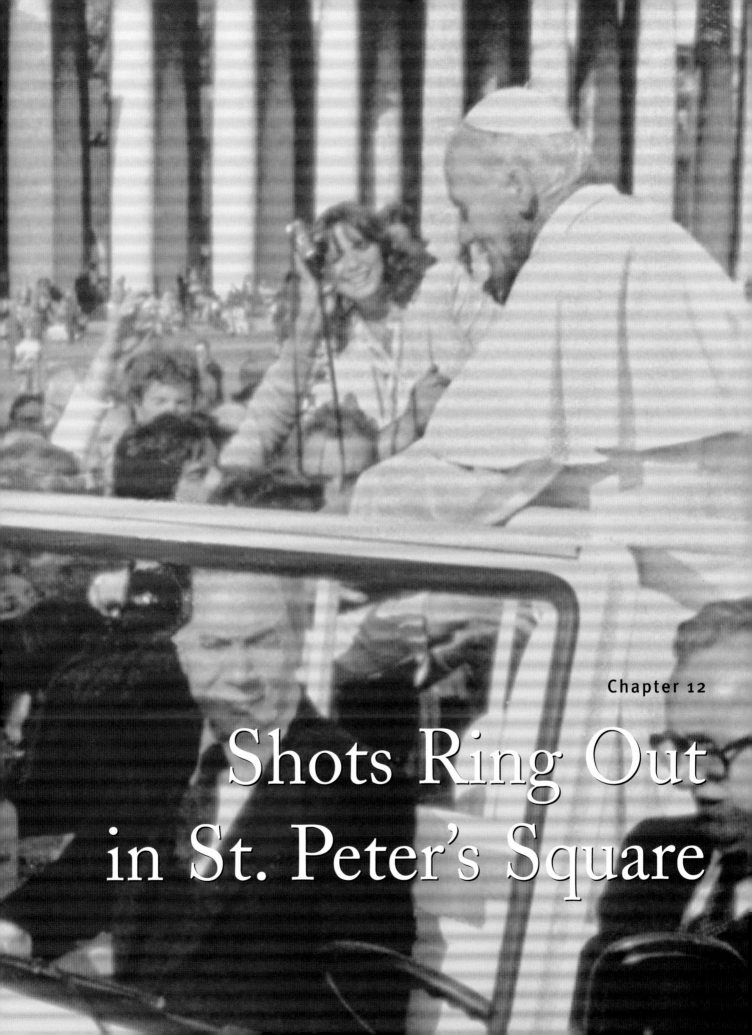

Chapter 12

Shots Ring Out
in St. Peter's Square

Tuesday, May 12, 1981, was drawing to a close. It had been a sad day for the pope. His private secretary, Bishop Dziwisz, had just returned from Warsaw with a letter from Cardinal Wyszynski. The seventy-nine-year-old primate of Poland was on his deathbed, and his days were numbered. There was nobody really ready to replace him. The only person who had enough authority to maintain and strengthen the church's role in Poland—keeping it stable

amid political turmoil—was the pope himself. The Holy Father was expecting difficult days ahead.

Wounded in the abdomen, John Paul II slumps into the arms of Bishop Dziwisz, who is standing beside him.

The next day started out sunny and warm. Outside, in St. Peter's Square, 25,000 people were waiting to see the pope. At his general audiences on Wednesday each week, the pope rode around the circular piazza in his popemobile, blessing the people and shaking their hands.

John Paul II got up very early, as usual. He had breakfast after morning Mass, worked in his study until eleven a.m., and then met people in a private audience in his library. Jerome Lejeune, a well-known genetics professor, and his wife joined the pope for his midday meal. After that, he spent some time in contemplative prayer.

Soon after five in the afternoon, the white popemobile came out of the Papal Palace through the Gate of the Bells into St. Peter's Square and began to slowly make its way through the smiling crowd. The pope usually circled the piazza once, sometimes twice, before stopping at a podium in front of the basilica, where he would speak to

the people. That Wednesday, May 13, 1981, the drive around the piazza lasted only 15 minutes. Just after the pope kissed a little girl named Sarah and handed her back to her parents, bullets were fired from somewhere in the crowd. A flock of doves scattered into the sky, but no one in the crowd realized what had happened—except for those standing near the man with the gun. The pope's bodyguard-driver sped away. The crowd didn't immediately connect the crackling noise with shots being fired. Seconds later people began to realize that the pope had been hit, and when this news spread around the piazza, the cheerful atmosphere turned into shock and horror. Standing beside the pope, as John Paul II slid back into his arms, Bishop Stanislaw Dziwisz could think of nothing but the outcome for the pope, his pontificate, and the whole world. This is how he tells what happened:

It was seventeen minutes after five. After driving around the piazza for a second time, shots rang out and hit the pope. Mehmet Ali Agca, a professional assassin, fired a pistol, and the bullets hit the Holy Father in the abdomen, right side, and his index finger. One of the bullets went through the pope's body and landed between us. I heard two shots. Two other persons were wounded. The bullets didn't get me, although they were so powerful they could have gone through several people. I asked the Holy Father, "Were you hit?"

"In the abdomen."

"Does it hurt?"

"Yes, a lot."

Then he began to slump down, and I managed to hold on to him because I was right beside him. Today, I have to say, an unseen power acted at that instant to save the life of the pope. Because he almost died, there was no time to think, no doctors nearby. If we made one bad decision, the result would have been disastrous.

The Holy Father's personal physician, Dr. Renato Bussonetti, arrived almost immediately. The pope was put in an ambulance, and as Bishop Dziwisz described, "We sped off for the emergency room at the Gemelli Clinic."

It took the ambulance eight minutes to get from St. Peter's Square to the clinic, a distance of six kilometers. The pope was conscious and praying in a soft voice. He lost consciousness as the ambulance reached the hospital.

When John Paul II became pope, he decided that if he ever became seriously ill, he wanted to be taken to a real hospital, not to the small infirmary in the papal apartments, as his predecessors had done. The Gemelli

En route to the emergency room, the Holy Father is half lying down, half sitting up, with his eyes closed. Signs of pain are clearly seen on his pale face.

medical staff was already on high alert and rushed the wounded pope to an intensive care unit and from there to the operating room.

Dr. Francesco Crucitti, a surgeon at the Gemelli Clinic, was caught in heavy city traffic when he heard about the attempt on the pope's life on the radio. He rushed to the hospital, determined to perform the surgery. At the clinic he brushed aside the guards—he had no time to talk to them—and burst into the operating room on the tenth floor.

The chair in front of St. Peter's Basilica, where the pope would have sat as he spoke about the faith, was now empty. Pilgrims from Poland put a picture of the Black Madonna of Czestochowa on it—a gift they had intended to give the Holy Father. A gust of wind knocked it down, and people who were close enough could read the inscription on it: "Mother of God, keep the Holy Father in your care. Protect him from evil."

The operating room was crammed with doctors and their attendants. The pope had lost a lot of blood, and the blood supply at the hospital did not have any plasma that matched his blood type. Members of the medical team did have the right match, however, and immediately donated as much as he needed to save his life.

"At one point, Dr. Bussonetti came up to me," Bishop Dziwisz remembered, "and asked me to anoint the pope with the holy oils of the sacrament of the sick, since he was in critical condition. His blood pressure was dangerously low, and his heartbeat was weak."

The blood transfusions made surgery possible, and when the pope's pulse rate began to return to normal, the

Mehmet Ali Agca is arrested right after he attempted to kill Pope John Paul II in St. Peter's Square on May 13, 1981.

hospital issued a bulletin to calm popular concern. "The pope has survived the attack on his life," it said, and the announcement was quickly relayed to the crowd in St. Peter's Square, who were saying the Rosary. Hope began to return.

Many dignitaries began to arrive at the clinic: cardinals, members of the Curia, and Italian politicians. Sandro Pertini, the president of Italy, was among them, and he stayed close to the Holy Father long into the night, refusing to leave until the pope was out of the operating room. The surgery took five hours and twenty minutes. At 12:45 a.m. a hospital spokesperson updated the pope's condition: The operation was a success; the pope was out of danger.

Agca had fired two bullets from a 9-mm Browning semiautomatic pistol. The doctors found that one bullet had struck the pope's abdomen and crossed his whole body. Fortunately, it had hit the pontiff's index finger first, thus diverting the projectile a fraction of an inch, enough to miss the aorta, which was in the direct line of fire.

Had the bullet punctured the blood vessel, he would have bled to death in a matter of minutes. The second bullet ricocheted off the pope's elbow, flew through the crowd, and hit two tourists. Theoretically, these two bullets could have killed someone, but they didn't.

PRAY FOR THE BROTHER WHO WOUNDED ME

After the surgery the pope was again taken to the intensive care unit to guard against complications. When he regained consciousness, he asked, "Have they said the Compline yet?" (The Compline is an official prayer of the church's liturgical hours, the prayer at the end of the day.)

Over the next two days the pope was in a great deal of

pain, but hope grew with each passing minute. After four days in the intensive care unit, he recorded a message that was to be broadcast over loudspeakers in St. Peter's Square. When his voice was heard once again, his words moved the whole world: "Pray for the brother who wounded me. I sincerely forgive him."

He would offer his suffering up for the church and the whole world, he continued, and then added, "Mary, I am all yours." The pope was totally convinced that the Holy Mother of God's intercession had saved his life. "One hand fired the bullet; another directed it," he would say later.

Mehmet Ali Agca was a Turkish terrorist who was captured and arrested minutes after he shot the pope. After firing the second time, he tried to escape into the crowd, but Sister Lucy, a Franciscan nun, lunged at him and managed to stop him. Others came to help, and together they knocked him down. The police arrived almost immediately, handcuffed Agca, and rushed him away.

It was always possible that efforts would be made to kill Agca in order to protect a possible mastermind behind the plot to kill the pope. But that never happened. The would-be assassin was taken to the high-security prison in Rebibbia, where he remained during his interrogation.

The police questioned Agca for a relatively short time, and on July 20 his trial began. He admitted to planning the assassination but refused to provide any details. His silence helped the jury arrive at a quick decision. He was found guilty on July 22, and Judge Sevrino Santiapichi sentenced him to life imprisonment.

Agca was a known terrorist in Turkey even before he shot the pope. Police had been keeping an eye on him since the late 1970s, when he was studying economics and was involved in student protests. He had even served time in jail. But his name blazed into the headlines for the role he played in one of the most publicized political assassinations in Turkey. His victim was Abdi Ipecki, a well-known journalist, newspaper editor, and liberal political analyst with leftist tendencies who wrote for the Istanbul newspaper *Milliyet*.

The police arrested Agca. He admitted killing Ipecki but would not reveal his political affiliation, if any. He was tried, convicted, and sent to prison, but he managed to escape, disguised as a soldier, even though he was incarcerated in a high-security facility. Later the police discovered that soldiers had helped Agca escape and furnished him with forged identity papers.

His arrest and escape coincided with final preparations

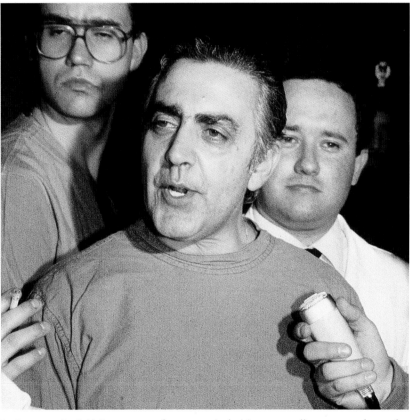

Dr. Francesco Crucitti informs waiting journalists that surgery on the pope was completed at 11:25 p.m., and he was in satisfactory condition.

for the pope's visit to Turkey. Soon after his election John Paul II had expressed an interest in meeting Patriarch Dimitrius, the ecumenical patriarch of Constantinople. (Before the Turks changed the city's name to Istanbul, Constantinople had been the capital of the Byzantine Empire and the fountainhead of Orthodox Christianity.) He wanted to continue the dialogue between Catholic and Orthodox Christians begun by Pope Paul VI and to demonstrate that he was ready to talk to Christians in the so-called "Second Rome" and the "Third Rome," which was Moscow.

A trip to Russia was out of the question at the time, and arranging the Turkish visit was not easy. The government agreed to his meeting the patriarch, but only if the pope would stop in Ankara on a state visit first. The pope saw the ecumenical visit as a small step toward one day meeting representatives of the Russian Orthodox Church in Moscow. He arrived in Turkey in November 1979.

Five days before the pope arrived, Ali Agca had escaped from prison, and before the day of the papal meeting with Patriarch Dimitrius, Agca sent a signed letter to *Milliyet*. He had escaped from prison, he said, in order to kill the pope. Meanwhile, he was hiding somewhere in Turkey. The rest of the letter was a mixture of political and fundamentalist rhetoric: "Western imperialists fear that Turkey and her sister Islamic nations are about to become political, economic, and military powers in the Middle East, so they sent the leader of their anti-Islamic

(CONTINUED ON PAGE 192)

189

The Suffering Pope

A new image of the Holy Father appeared in the photographs taken in St. Peter's Square the day he was shot. It was the picture of John Paul II falling into the arms of Bishop Dziwisz, with pain and suffering etched in his face. It was the first time the face of the pope in agony had been captured on film.

Until that day photographs had shown him only as a smiling, energetic, healthy, and sport-loving man. Over the years the photographic images changed to reflect signs of suffering and pain. But the change was not limited to his face. It emerged in his thinking as well.

In 1984, the Holy Year he had called to celebrate the 1,950th anniversary of the Redemption, he published an apostolic letter *Salvifici Doloris (On the Christian Meaning of Suffering)*, in which he explained the meaning of human suffering. The Hidden Mystery of the Redemption of the world, he wrote, is rooted in a special way in suffering, which he sees as man's encounter with God. A Christian who lives with suffering not caused by guilt for sin can always understand his suffering in light of the martyrdom of the Son of God.

"Suffering seems to be particularly *essential to the nature of man*. It is as deep as man himself, precisely because it manifests in its own way that depth which is proper to man and in its own way surpasses it. Suffering seems to belong to man's transcendence: It is one of those points in which man is in a certain sense 'destined' to go beyond himself, and he is called to this in a mysterious way," the pope wrote. "A certain idea of this problem comes to us from the distinction between physical suffering and moral suffering. This distinction is based upon the double dimension of the human being and indicates the bodily and spiritual element as the immediate or direct subject of suffering. Insofar as the words 'suffering' and 'pain' can, up to a certain degree, be used as synonyms, physical suffering is present when 'the body is hurting' in some way, whereas moral suffering is 'pain of the soul.' In fact, it is a question of pain of a spiritual nature, and not only of the 'psychological' dimension of pain which accompanies both moral and physical suffering."

In the years to come, the pope would bear personal witness to what he affirmed for all Christians.

JOHN PAUL II GETS READY TO MEET DEATH

Early in July 1992 John Paul II began to feel pain in his abdomen, which steadily got worse. Dr. Francesco Crucitti, the surgeon who had removed the bullet after the pope was shot, came to examine him. He ordered diagnostic tests, which showed that the pope had a tumor

John Paul II leaving the Gemelli Clinic on June 3, 1981. He blessed the young patients as he said good-bye.

in his large intestine. Surgery was essential. The Sunday after tests confirmed the diagnosis, John Paul II said the *Angelus* prayer with the crowd gathered in St. Peter's Square and then bade them good-bye, explaining he would be going to the hospital. The Holy Father was anointed with the sacrament of the sick to prepare himself for death.

The four-hour operation was performed on July 15 with the surgeons deciding that they should take out the gallbladder as well, since it had gallstones. A post-op biopsy confirmed that the tumor was benign. John Paul, at seventy-two, withstood the surgery well and was able to get out of bed and sit in a chair the next day. The pope left the Gemelli Clinic at the end of July and spent the rest of the summer at Castel Gandolfo. In October he was well enough to travel to Latin America.

WHAT NEXT?

In the wake of the surgery, media speculation about the pope's health mounted, fueled by the ambiguous medical bulletins the Vatican Press Office issued. Many doubted that the tumor was benign and interpreted the official silence as a Vatican attempt to cloud the truth.

The tumor, however, was not the real problem. The pope was suffering from rapidly progressing osteoporosis, meaning the pope's bones were becoming fragile. Also, he had Parkinson's disease, which caused his hands to tremble and his muscles to stiffen.

On November 11, 1993, John Paul II received in audience at the Hall of Blessings of the Papal Palace the Rome employees of the United Nations' Food and Agriculture Organization. Just as he was leaving the hall, the pope stumbled on a new floor mat, fell down a few stairs, and dislocated his right shoulder. The pain was sharp, but as he was taking his leave for the hospital, he waved his left hand to say good-bye and even joked in Italian, "*Sono saduto, ma non sono caduto.*" (I fell down, but I wasn't demoted.)

He was given anesthesia at the hospital before his shoulder was set. He had to keep his arm in a sling for a month, so he couldn't write. Instead, he dictated his thoughts to a priest from Kraków, Father Stanislaw Rylko, who worked in the Roman Curia. Father Rylko typed the pontiff's words on his laptop, printed them out, and gave them to the Holy Father for revisions and corrections. That would prove to be a very efficient way of working, especially after the pope began to have trouble with his handwriting.

Six months later, on the night of April 28, 1994, John Paul II slipped in his bath and broke his thighbone, another sign that his osteoporosis was getting worse. For the pope this latest bout of pain and suffering was a sign

On December 25, 1995, the pope gave his *Urbi et Orbi* (To the City and the World) message. He gave a blessing in French, took a deep breath, and tried to repeat it in English. He wasn't able to do so and moved away from his window in the Papal Palace. During the night a medical bulletin announced that the Holy Father just had a cold.

of God's Providence, even a gift from heaven. He spent the night in his apartment before calling for help. He was again rushed to the Gemelli Clinic, where he underwent bone-replacement surgery. The implant did not work as well as it should have, and the pope had trouble walking. He left the hospital after about a month, still limping a little bit. For about a year the pontiff couldn't walk without using a cane. As a result, he was forced to cancel a trip to the United States he had planned to make that October.

The first Sunday after his release from the hospital, he prayed the *Angelus* in St. Peter's Square and shared reflections about his hospital stay with the crowd. "I used to think that my vocation was to lead the Church of Jesus Christ into the third millennium and that I would do that by prayer and whatever good works I could do. I have just come to realize that is not enough. I must lead the church through suffering." He placed his suffering within the context of the Family Year then being celebrated and to ward off attacks on the family by those who promoted "population control."

Back in 1984, when so much of his pain and sufferings were still to come, he had written in *Salvifici Doloris* that suffering can bring about Christian conversion through man's discovery of the saving value of pain, and as a result of such suffering, man emerges anew. This discovery, moreover, is a reaffirmation of man's spirit, which is so much more important than his body. Sickness, even incapacitation to the edge of life itself, can bring forward inner maturity and greatness of spirit that can become a model for those who live in good health and without suffering.

Certainly these were qualities John Paul II displayed until the end of his days. His final illness was an example of how much this pope lived the life he preached, how deeply he felt the presence of a loving God, and how much he made suffering an integral part of his own life.

crusade to Turkey, where he will be masquerading as a religious leader. If the pope's visit is not canceled, I assure you I will kill him."

John Paul II was already on the plane to Ankara when he was told about the letter. "It's all in the hands of God," was all he would say.

That time Agca had no intentions of killing the pope. He would explain later that he wanted to create a situation that would force the police to focus on protecting the pope, thus making it easier for him to slip out of Turkey, which he did. He traveled to Germany and Bulgaria, then to northern Cyprus, which was under Turkish control, and then on to Lebanon. More trips

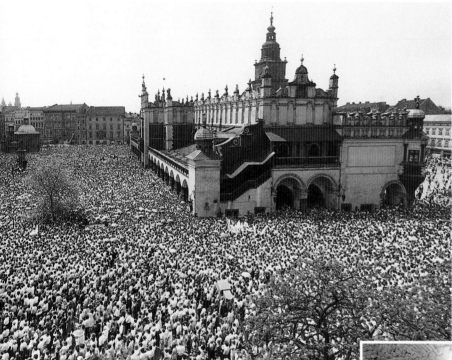

Above: The White March in Kraków: On May 17, 1981, a huge group of young people dressed in white parade through the city. Wearing white was their way of protesting evil in the world.

followed; he went to Iran and Switzerland. Although he had no job or any other visible source of income, he spent lavishly on false passports and lodgings during his travels.

Agca finally settled in Italy. He would admit later that he planned to kill Solidarity leader Lech Walesa in January 1981, when the Pole was in Rome for an audience with the pope. He hoped to put a bomb in Walesa's car, but the plot was foiled by the large contingent of police guarding the visitor. Weeks later Agca used another false passport, issued to a Faruk Ozgun, to register at the University of Perugia, even though he couldn't speak a word of Italian. He attended only one class, but as a student, he now had free access to all of Italy.

THE GRAY WOLF

Agca first told police that he was a member of the Bozkurtlar, or the Gray Wolves, a nationalist-minded terrorist organization in Turkey. The Gray Wolves believed that their great enemies were Imperialists in the West and Communists in the East—and that the pope was the worst of the lot. Agca's letter to Istanbul's *Milliyet* was a good summary of their ideology.

In Milan a Gray Wolf had given him the Browning automatic pistol he used in Rome on May 13. After he arrived at St. Peter's Square, he walked around watching people arrive and keeping a sharp eye out for police. At one point, he asked a Benedictine monk—in English—what gate the popemobile would use to enter the square. The monk, Martino Sciliani, inadvertently gave him the wrong answer: The car would drive through the Bronze Gate. The terrorist moved closer to a railing and waited. A religious sister came and stood next to him.

He carried his gun in a bag. When he assassinated the Turkish editor, he had walked up to the man's car as if he wanted to ask him a question. When Ipecki rolled down the window, Agca shot him straight in the face. This time the job looked a lot easier. The pope would be moving slowly past him in an open car, unaware of any danger as he waved and smiled, and he would be in Agca's full view. Shortly after five in the afternoon, the pope

Below: After hearing the news of the attack on the pope's life, people all over Poland attended Masses all night long.

entered St. Peter's Square but through another gate. Agca stayed calm and remained where he was standing in the crowd, following the man in white with his eyes. When Agca took out his gun, nobody realized what was happening.

During the trial Agca's attorney challenged the Italian court's jurisdiction. The case, the lawyer said, should be heard by a Vatican tribunal, since the shooting took place on Vatican territory. But the judge turned down the challenge, citing the Lateran Treaty, which specified that such cases were to be tried in Italian courts. Agca, who had argued before the challenge that he had acted alone and masterminded the plot by himself, abruptly refused to answer any more questions; nor did he appeal the sentence once it was handed down.

He was returned to the high-security Rebibbia prison, where no one could contact him, leaving many unanswered questions that puzzled judge, jury, and the public. Who ordered the shooting remained a mystery. Certainly the Gray Wolves never took credit for the attack. The investigation into the true facts behind the shooting would continue for years before Agca was willing to divulge the details.

THE CYTOMEGALOVIRUS, A SECOND KILLER

During the months that Mehmet Ali Agca was in jail awaiting trial, illness repeatedly threatened John Paul II's life. He was taken out of intensive care on his sixty-first birthday, May 18, five days after the shooting, and moved to a small apartment the clinic had reserved for him. It included bedrooms for himself and his private secretary, a bath, and a small conference room, where Cardinal Casaroli, the secretary of state, held daily meetings with doctors at Gemelli and other specialists from Western Europe, the United States, and Poland. Dr. Gabriel Turowski, an old kayaking friend and a surgeon at the Medical Academy of Kraków, was among those consulted.

After the pope was moved out of intensive care, the bulletins issued about his health were optimistic. He seemed to be recuperating rapidly. But a week later, on May 24, the pontiff developed a fever for which doctors could find no cause. Nevertheless, John Paul II wanted to

Mehmet Ali Agca

Ali Agca was born in 1958 into a poor family of coal miners in Yesiltepe in northern Turkey. His father died when he was six years old, leaving his family—his mother and three sisters—with only a very small income. He was described as lucid and intelligent, certainly enough so to seek higher education. At the University of Ankara, the Turkish capital, he first studied to be a schoolteacher, and then he switched to literature and geography.

His studies, however, were not his first love or interest. As a teenager he was a member of a street gang and engaged in petty crimes. Later he became a smuggler along the Turkish-Bulgarian border, where illegal trade in arms, drugs, and cigarettes was a lucrative business for him.

He left Ankara after a year to continue his studies at the University of Istanbul, where he changed majors again, deciding to study economics. That, in turn, got him interested in politics. He made contacts with both left-wing and nationalist student groups, even though they were opposed to each other. Thanks to his Bulgarian contacts he was sent to Syria for two months to study weaponry and terrorist tactics.

Back in Turkey, he joined the Gray Wolves, a right-wing terrorist group. The Bulgarians who financed Ali Agca were, of course, Communists, but they figured that the student group was a good vehicle for destabilizing Turkish society. Agca would later claim that he had no particular political ideology or affiliation and that he killed for money. His first "job" was the murder of a left-wing newspaper editor, Abdi Ipecki, whom he shot dead in 1978. He was jailed for his part in the plot but managed to escape with the help of right-wing soldiers.

He fled to Sofia where he would claim the Bulgarian secret service recruited him in a plot to kill the pope. It is a story the Bulgarians have steadily denied—as late as days before the pope died in 2005. He did receive enough money, however, to crisscross the Mediterranean region, change passports and identities, and thus destroy any evidence linking him to Sofia.

After he shot the pope, Agca was sentenced to life in prison, but he spent only 19 years in jail. In 2000, when the pope was celebrating his eightieth birthday, Agca asked John Paul II to help set him free, which he did. Ali Agca was released from the Rebibbia prison on June 13, 2000, and deported to Turkey. There he is serving a 10-year jail term to which he was sentenced in absentia.

Shortly before the pope's death, Agca sent a letter to prison authorities in Turkey claiming that members of the Curia had been in on the plot to kill the pontiff. But Agca had changed his story so often that few gave this latest version much credence.

telephone the cancer-stricken primate of Poland, Cardinal Stefan Wyszynski. The primate couldn't come to the phone, and the cord was too short to reach his bed. They did talk the next day, but it took all of Wyszynski's strength to overcome his pain. He asked for the pope's blessing. John Paul II blessed the aged cardinal's "mouth and hands," his way of paying homage to Wyszynski's words and deeds. Three days later the primate was dead.

The day after Wyszynski died, John Paul II began to have difficulty breathing. He suffered from pains in his chest. His fever rose alarmingly. His condition worsened, and the doctors could not determine its exact cause. On May 31 Pope John Paul II listened to a radio broadcast of

(CONTINUED ON PAGE 196)

In a World of Suffering

—Jacek Moskwa,
Polish correspondent

The day before John Paul II was to leave Cuba, he visited a hospital outside Havana called El Rincon (the Little Nook). An amateur orchestra was playing in a nearby home for the blind. A tiny church with white walls stood on a small square. No crowds had gathered to greet the pope, but inside the church blind children, some suffering from leprosy that had disfigured their faces, were waiting for him.

He walked up to the chair set up for him in front of the altar and sat down. His face looked tired. He had spent an exhausting four days in Cuba following a schedule crammed with one event after another. Then he began to speak. He spoke slowly, in a monotone voice: "The meaning of the parable of the Good Samaritan and of all the Gospel accounts is that man should feel obligated to show love and concern for those who suffer."

For the pope these were not empty words. When he finished speaking, he got up and approached the children, touching and blessing each one of them. His face was swollen, and his steps were very unsure. He looked like a leper himself. He noticed the tears that were streaming down the face of a little girl who was blind, and he kissed her on the forehead. A moment later everybody was crying.

This was the eighth time I had traveled with the pope, and during each journey the Holy Father talked about suffering, though one theme ran through his remarks—suffering strengthens the soul. And I noticed one other thing: He seemed to be suffering more on each trip we took. But only in Cuba did I begin to really understand the meaning of the pope's message, one that everyone, believers and nonbelievers, should try to understand.

The pope chose this meeting with leprous children to touch upon the problem of political prisoners in Cuba. This is how he spoke about them: "There is a suffering that is felt in the mind, a suffering people experience when they are cut off from the rest of society, when they are persecuted and condemned…for their ideas. Even when these ideas are peaceful, they are not accepted. The persons who are condemned to isolation and punishment, which they find hard to understand and accept…just want to be back in society, to live an active life, to find a place where they can express their thoughts and their opinions, and receive respect and tolerance."

SIGNS OF SUFFERING

Karol Wojtyla was barely eight years old when his mother died, and he was still very young when his brother, who was 12 years older and whom he loved very much, died. All he said about this sadness was, "It was God's will."

A few people close to Karol Wojtyla have shown "signs of suffering" in their lives. Cardinal Andrzej Deskur was a fellow student in the Kraków seminary but went to Rome soon after he was ordained. He remained a close friend not only because of his Polish origin or his successful climb through the Roman hierarchy but because on the night Wojtyla was elected pope, he suffered a devastating stroke.

When the pope learned of his friend's stroke, the pope hurried to the Gemelli Clinic to visit Deskur. When the pope left, he spoke to others lying ill in the hospital: "On the threshold of my pontificate, I hope always to rely on those who suffer and on those who unite their suffering, their martyrdom, and their pain with their prayer."

THE GIFT OF SUFFERING

Over the years the pope became very familiar with the Gemelli Clinic. He spent weeks there recovering from the the attempted assassination, and in 1992 he had a benign tumor removed from his large intestine. He returned once again in the autumn of 1996 for an appendectomy.

After that operation, on a day when he felt better and was able to sit in the patio of the clinic, he reflected on pain and the role it played in his life, a reflection prompted perhaps by a poem he had received on the day of his operation entitled "To a Friend Who Is Suffering."

He said, "During those days when I was very sick, I could better understand the value of the loving service to which God has called me. This service is also accomplished through the gift of suffering, thanks to which it is possible for me to complete with my suffering whatever was lacking in the suffering of Christ."

Those who were close to the pope wondered how he could put up with so much pain, so patiently. "The pope knows how to transform his pain into prayer," asserted André Frossard, author of *Don't Be Afraid! Conversations with John Paul II.*

Before leaving the clinic, John Paul II visited patients in the children's oncology ward, where most had no hope and some had only a few months to live.

How can children's suffering be compatible with God's mercy? That is one of the most difficult questions any theologian can try to answer. John Paul II went up to those young patients in the Gemelli ward who were undergoing their own suffering. Some still clung to hope. He went through all the rooms and stopped beside each bed.

"Look at me. I'm sick, too. I'm going home now, and you will also be going to your home in a little while," he kept saying to them.

Antonio Ramon, a Peruvian with short black hair, was one of the children the pope stopped to see. He was only nine years old and had already been operated on five times.

He was the one who had written the letter-poem to the Holy Father. Their roles were now reversed. This time a nine-year-old child wanted to help the grown man. Compassion is born in suffering.

THE MEANING OF SUFFERING

I questioned Professor Stanislaw Grygiel, a friend and fellow professor in the pope's Kraków days, about the meaning of suffering. Instead of answering my question, Grygiel just handed me a copy of his article, "The Meaning of Suffering in Today's World."

When I read it, I came across this idea: "Suffering and death carry man toward the future, and only from this perspective is it possible to understand suffering. We shouldn't worry about the fact that there are so many people who suffer, but about the fact that there are others who don't know how to suffer."

"Suffering is an issue better analyzed at a certain distance," the pope confessed to the Polish filmmaker Krzysztof Zanissi, when they were discussing his apostolic letter *Salvifici Doloris.* That letter was based on the pope's own life experience.

Recalling Job, the Suffering Servant, and the parable of the Good Samaritan, and even that of Christ himself, the pope said that "the meaning of suffering seems to belong to man's transcendence and is also truly human. It is transcendent because it is linked to the divine mystery of the Redemption. At the same time, it is profoundly human because it is in suffering that man encounters himself, his humanity, his dignity, and his mission."

These words from the apostolic letter come to my mind: "Christ taught man to bear witness through suffering while at the same time he helps others who suffer."

People who see John Paul II during huge open-air ceremonies and audiences under the blazing sun of Rome in St. Peter's Square and in places all over the world often ask, "Is it really necessary for him to suffer so much?"

The pope speaks slowly, his back is hunched, he limps, and still, he exerts himself for the whole world. Anyone could see that his hands are red and swollen from shaking hands with everyone who wants to touch him.

"There are many ways to communicate. One of them is to use words, and that is what the pope does in his sermons," the Austrian cardinal Christoph Schönborn has said. But there are also periods of silence when the Holy Father communicates using body language. He does this very well and can deliver a message more forcefully when he communicates in silence.

"We live in a society that tries to erase pain, suffering, infirmity, and death from our individual or collective memories," John Paul II said in June 1988, when he was with the patients and staff of the Rennweg Hospice, run by the Caritas Socialis organization in Vienna.

The pope did not deliver this message out loud; the text was distributed during a ceremony in the chapel. But then he went on to visit those who were dying, all of them bedridden and most of them in the last few days of their lives. No media was present. TV cameras were relegated some distance away, and no audio was permitted.

That day I saw a very weary and infirm elderly man, dressed in white robes, bending over the wasted figures of the patients, and I wondered what he might be saying to them. I came to realize he was saying absolutely nothing . The witness he gave them was himself.

Why the Gemelli Clinic?

Until John Paul II became pope, the health of pontiffs had always remained secret. Medical treatment was provided within the Papal Palace or at Castel Gandolfo, where there were private clinics. Karol Wojtyla immediately changed all that. Whenever he needed medical care, the new pope said, he wanted to go to the hospital—the reason why the ambulance drove him straight to the Gemelli Clinic moments after he was shot.

It's not an ordinary hospital; it's a huge medical complex equipped with the latest in medical technology. The Holy Father's choice of this clinic may have been influenced by a visit he paid to his friend Bishop Andrzej Maria Deskur, on October 13, 1978. Deskur had suffered a stroke, and he survived, thanks to being immediately taken to the Gemelli Clinic.

The clinic maintains an operating room on the tenth floor that is always kept ready to treat the pope, and he also has private accommodations on the eleventh floor, where he can spend the time he needs to recuperate. These medical preparations helped save his life on May 13, 1981.

the doctors didn't know why or what to do.

Finally a virologist came up with a diagnosis: One of the blood transfusions the pope had received during his operation was infected with the cytomegalovirus, a hard-to-detect infection that does not respond to antibiotics and can do major damage. The pope's physical strength needed building up to allow his body to fight off the virus. Doctors at once changed their treatment. They began to administer massive doses of vitamins, glucose, fever reducers, and analgesics. It worked. Within days the pope improved. But the pontiff was not well enough yet to leave the clinic, which, for the length of his stay, became the headquarters of the Catholic Church.

And it would prove to be a very busy one. With Wyszynski dead, John Paul II had to find a successor and quickly help defuse growing tension in his homeland. Internal conflicts between "reformers" and "hardliners" were tearing the Communists apart, and the party was clearly losing power. Solidarity, a dissident labor movement, was becoming more and more radical and taking on the trappings of an opposition party. The Communist Party congress was due to open on July 14, and Solidarity hoped to hold its first congress in September.

New church leadership had to be in place in Poland before the Communists met. On July 7 the pope named Joseph Glemp, once Wyszynski's secretary, now the bishop of Warmia and the late primate's personal choice for his successor, as the new head of the Polish church. Days later the party congress opened, and when it was over, party leader Edward Gierek had been expelled and tentative new leadership installed. For Glemp and the pope the next few months would pose new and serious challenges.

Wyszynski's funeral rites in Warsaw and prayed for the intention of the cardinal's eternal rest. He added, "I miss him. He was my friend. I need him."

Two days later the pope was much better, and the doctors agreed that he could convalesce at home in the Papal Palace. On June 7 he made a brief appearance at the balcony of St. Peter's Basilica, but on June 9 his condition worsened. His fever rose and fell, and his right lung became infected. By June 20 his health was so bad that he had to return to the Gemelli Clinic. However, neither the tomography scans nor the X-rays showed anything serious. The pope seemed to be visibly dying day by day, and

The pope must have known it because he now began to pressure his doctors to perform a necessary follow-up operation. The medical team was hesitant, wanting to wait for cooler weather. John Paul II insisted, however, and moved the date up to August 5, the Feast of the Virgin of the Snows. Dr. Crucitti, the doctor who had heard about the shooting on his car radio and rushed to

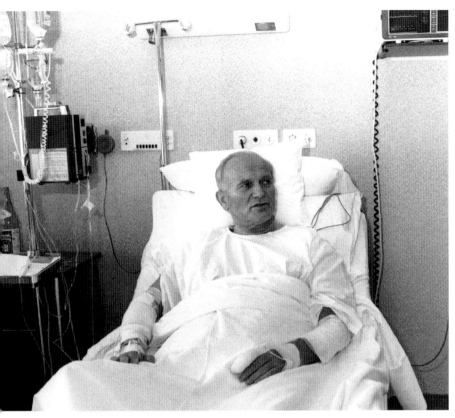

By May 18 the pope's condition has improved enough for him to be taken out of intensive care.

another conspirator, was on a truck that left the Bulgarian embassy, allegedly loaded with furniture, and headed for Yugoslavia.

More evidence was uncovered to confirm the "Bulgarian connection." But even as it was, new doubts arose. One of the Bulgarians Agca had named, Serguei Antonov, who worked for Bulgarian airlines, denied his involvement and charged that the Italian secret service had fed Agca the false information about him. He was set free. Many thought that even if Dyrzawna Sigurnost, the Bulgarian secret police, had masterminded the attempt on the pope's life, the KGB must have been involved.

Reader's Digest brought some new information to light when it published an article in 1982 written by Claire Sterling, an American journalist long based in Rome. She argued that the Kremlin was involved, information she received from Italy's attorney general. She also interviewed Agca in prison and showed him pictures of Bulgarian embassy employees. He picked out the three men he had cited without hesitation, but the plot behind the shooting—if indeed there was one—has never been clarified.

The pope himself took little interest in the investigation, but he dismissed the Bulgarian connection out of

the hospital, performed the surgery. The operation began at seven a.m., lasted for one hour, and was quickly pronounced a success.

On August 14 John Paul II went home to the Papal Palace, and on August 15 he celebrated the Feast of the Assumption of the Blessed Virgin in St. Peter's Square, where a crowd of 50,000 had gathered. Then the pontiff left for Castel Gandolfo, where he spent the rest of the summer.

AGCA STARTS TO TALK

Mehmet Ali Agca's conviction and sentencing did not halt the official investigation into the attempted assassination, but little progress was made until 1982. While the Holy Father was on a pilgrimage to Fatima, Agca began to talk about his accomplices. Clearly, he had given up hope that they would get him out of his Italian prison, as they had done in Turkey after he shot and killed the prominent newspaper editor. He gave the police seven names—four Turks and three Bulgarians. The Bulgarians held diplomatic passports, and the Turks were linked to terrorist groups.

One of his conspirators had planned to create an uproar after the shots were fired to give Agca cover to escape. He was to have been smuggled out of Italy the next day in a sealed shipping container and put on a truck with diplomatic license plates so that no one would examine the shipment at the border. Sister Lucy had foiled that plot, but plans had not been made in vain. Oral Celik,

Mehmet Ali Agca after receiving a sentence of life imprisonment. He spent only 19 years in an Italian jail and is now serving a 10-year term in a Turkish prison.

December 27, 1983, John Paul II visits Ali Agca in his Rebibbia prison cell.

hand. Vatican officials were not as certain, and they did believe that the idea of killing the pope had come out of Eastern Europe. Certainly secretary of state Agostino Casaroli and Achille Silverstrini, a top Vatican diplomat, thought so and said so publicly. Silverstrini said, "We can't forget the situation in Poland and Eastern Europe at that time. If the assassination attempt had been a success, it would have been a tragedy for Poland, for all those who were fighting against Soviet domination, and even for the Soviet system itself."

IT WAS THE WORK OF THE DEVIL

Soon after Christmas 1983 the pope went to the Rebibbia prison to visit the man who had tried to kill him. The world watched this astonishing event through the eyes of television cameras that accompanied the pontiff into the prison and to the door of Agca's cell. But they were not allowed inside.

"This is my home," Agca said when he motioned to the Holy Father to come into his cell. The two men met in one corner, under a barred window, where a chair for the pope and one for the prisoner were placed. They spoke face-to-face, but nobody really knows what they

A READER'S DIGEST EXCLUSIVE REPORT

Assassin aims his weapon (circle, above) over the heads of spectators seconds before shooting

BY CLAIRE STERLING

THE PLOT TO MURDER THE POPE

On Wednesday, May 13, 1981, a young man in St. Peter's Square shot and nearly killed Pope John Paul II. The gunman, captured at the scene, was soon identified as Mehmet Ali Agca (pronounced *Ahjah*), a 23-year-old Turk. Within hours the world learned that he had escaped from an Istanbul prison while awaiting a death sentence for the terrorist murder of a Turkish journalist. Front-page stories around the globe described him as a fascist thug working for Turkey's neo-

Reader's Digest publishes a special report on the assassination attempt in September 1982.

actually said. All the cameras could capture was a scene of two men—the assassin and the victim—speaking to each other in a low voice. Agca had learned Italian while in prison, and they spoke in Italian. John Paul II stretched out his hand to hold the prisoner's. They spoke for about a half hour.

Experts in lipreading tried to reconstruct their conversation later but could only decipher fragments. "Who ordered you to do it?" it seems the Holy Father asked. Agca answered something, and the Holy Father's face registered surprise. At the end of their conversation, Agca knelt down and kissed the pope's hand.

"The pope knows everything," Agca said later. But did Agca himself really know everything? Did he really know who had masterminded the plot? His behavior and conflicting statements would indicate that he was nothing more than a hired gun and that he just pulled the trigger. But the mystery remains.

Days before the pope died, German sources made public a précis of East German secret police records about the assassination. According to news items in March 2005, the KGB was responsible for plotting the assassination attempt. But perhaps typically for the mystery around the shooting, both the German and Bulgarian governments denied the report.

The pope did not seem to care very much about the identity of the plotters. "It's well known that this was the work of the devil, so no matter who it was that served him doesn't make any difference," the

198

Who Protects the Pope?

Papal security moved front and center after the attempt to kill John Paul II on May 13, 1981. But it was not something the pope was comfortable with. He saw all the protective measures as a curtain that shielded him from the global flock he was determined to serve. Nevertheless, he acquiesced even if he grumbled about the bullet proof glass that sheathed the white popemobile. And he was personally fond of the people assigned to secure his safety.

Camillo Cibin, the long-time chief of the "Vigilanza," the Vatican gendarmes or police—an organization separate from the colorful Swiss Guards but with sometimes overlapping duties—was in charge of the pope's security. Cibin was always at the pontiff's side, at audiences, liturgical celebrations, and during his extensive travels inside and outside of Italy. He had entered Vatican service in 1947 and still served the popes when he was past 80 years old.

His duties were not limited to official occasions, however. Cibin spent time with the pope when he was on vacation. When John Paul II was more vigorous, he even arranged skiing trips for him in the Italian Dolomite mountains.

And on one of his feast days—July 14, the feast of St. Camillus of Lellis—the pope was a member of the dinner party that had gathered to toast the "knight commander," as the tall, robust man with a shock of white hair, was called. A Venetian, he is married and has three children. He was close to the pope and was devastated when John Paul II was shot.

While Cibin traveled with the pope, a Jesuit priest, Father Roberto Tucci, acted as pontifical "advance man," making all the arrangements a papal trip abroad required. Tucci was another octogenarian, and extraordinarily close to the Holy Father. The pontiff honored his friend at the consistory in 2001 when he named the Jesuit a Cardinal. Tucci, however, declined a bishop's miter.

He is one of the more interesting Vatican officials. Born in Naples in 1921 of an Italian father and an English mother, he grew up as an Anglican who only converted to Catholicism as a young man. Among the many posts he has held was editor of the Jesuit Review *Civilita Catolica* and director general of the Vatican radio. He retired in 2001 and was succeeded by Monsignor Renato Boccardo.

The advance work was long and thorough. Father Tucci first toured a chosen country six months before the pontiff was scheduled to visit it. All vehicles parked along routes the pope would take were inspected, as were houses with windows facing the street. People who lived along the route were forbidden to invite anyone to their home during the pope's visit.

Every road on which the pope traveled was examined and the time determined it would take for him to reach point A or B. Alternate routes and safe houses were found to quickly move the pope to safety in case of need. Security agents carried electronic devices to prevent remote control bombs from being detonated. And all the pope's food was tested before he was allowed to eat it.

The protected space immediately surrounding the pope was called the "Zero Zone"—in a church, an area 90 feet around the altar in the open air, the zone was extended to about 150 feet; at airports, it was 180 feet. Each guard was assigned a specific duty and they were all trained to handle every possible situation.

Vatican security agents cooperated closely with local police and other authorities in countries the pope visited. With global terrorism on the rise, by the late 1990s such cooperation grew even closer as individual countries stepped up protective measures of their own.

When the pope visited Lebanon in 1997, for example, authorities mobilized 20,000 soldiers and policemen to protect John Paul II—that's one quarter of that country's available security forces, and the other 60,000 were put on ready alert. On a visit to Bosnia several months before, police found bombs on the route the pope was to travel and defused them before they could detonate.

John Paul II had visited Poland, his homeland, so often as pope that security forces there had the routine of protecting him down pat. The number two man in the ministry of the interior spent months supervising preparations for the papal mission in 1999, making sure, for example, that local community activities were closely coordinated.

The pontiff traveled to the former Soviet republic of Kazakhstan only weeks after the 9/11 terrorist attack in New York, and tensions ran high. Government security measures were "unprecedented," the foreign ministry announced. Almost 2,500 soldiers and police were on the streets when he visited its capital, Astana.

Just a year before John Paul II died, authorities in Rome took unprecedented security measures to guard him during Easter ceremonies. Easter in 2004 fell just weeks after terrorists had bombed a Madrid railroad station killing several hundred people. Italian police worked closely with Vatican officials to make sure that Easter ceremonies would be held safely. Parking was banned on the Via della Conciliazione. Manhole covers were sealed. Vatican visitors were screened much more carefully than they had been in the past. The measures paid off. Nothing happened, even though intelligence agencies had warned that terrorists were planning an attack.

Many people believe God's hidden plan was at work behind the scenes when Karol Wojtyla was elected pope.

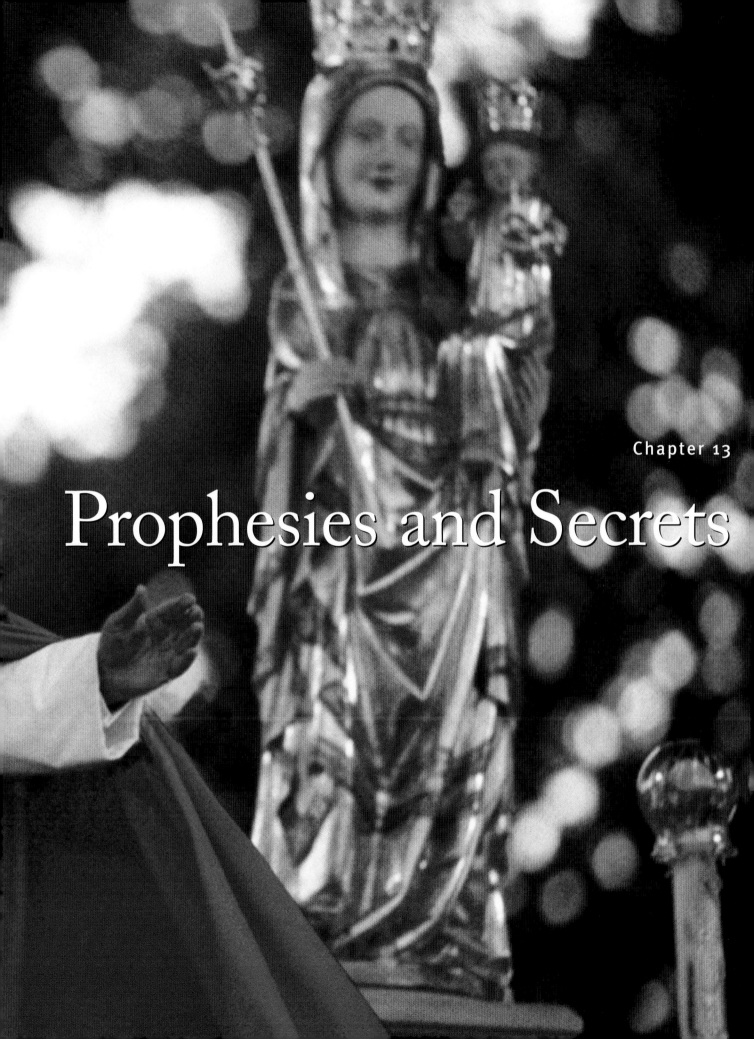

Chapter 13

Prophesies and Secrets

The advent of a Polish pope may have caught the world unaware—he was, after all, the first non-Italian pontiff in half a millennium—but there was no lack of prophesies and secrets unearthed after his election to show that some at least had predicted his accession.

One winter afternoon in Kraków during the German occupation, for example, Juliusz Kydrynski, with whose family Karol Wojtyla was then living, brought home a copy of a prophetic poem about Poland. The poem had been written in 1893 and was stored in the famed Ossolinski foundation library in Lvov until it surfaced in 1939, just before the war. Kydrynski had found a copy in an archive in Tegoborz. The poem reflected Poland's hopes in the nineteenth century when the country no longer existed as a separate state. Sometime in the future, the prophesy said, Poland would be free of foreign domination.

THE PROPHESY OF TEGOBORZ

The Polish nation would arise again during a "worldwide catastrophe" when "the two eagles will fall apart," the poem said. This prediction was widely interpreted as referring to World War I, when the three nations that had partitioned Poland—Germany, Austria-Hungary, and Russia—were defeated, and all three had eagles in their national emblems.

During and after World War II the prophesy was applied to the fall of the Third Reich, since it had predicted Germany's defeat and the return of Mazuria and Gdansk to Poland. Another excerpt from the poem, "To the East of the sun, the hammer will be smashed," was later reinterpreted as predicting the accession of a Pole to the Throne of Saint Peter and the fall of the Soviet Union.

When Karol Wojtyla first heard the Tegoborz prophesy, on that winter day long ago, he wasn't even thinking about becoming a priest. Years later Kydrynski wrote in his memoirs: "I remember that afternoon very well. Karol and I were in my room, and I was reading the poem out loud. One of the verses said, 'Three rivers of the world are conferring three crowns on the anointed one from Kraków.' As a joke, I tapped Karol and said, 'Well now, Karol. Let's see. I'm going to be the anointed one from Kraków. What will you be?'"

As things turned out, in October 1978, "the anointed one from Kraków" upon whom three crowns (in the papal tiara) were conferred was Karol Wojtyla, the cardinal archbishop from Kraków, when he was elevated to the Throne of Saint Peter. In fact, John Paul II did not have the papal tiara placed on his head—John XXIII was the last pope to wear the triple crown—but the tiara has been part of the papal emblem since Pope Clement V's time in the fourteenth century. It symbolizes the pope's ecclesiastical authority.

KAROL WOJTYLA GOES TO SEE PADRE PÍO

Millions of people around the world are convinced that God's will propelled Karol Wojtyla into Saint Peter's chair. Certainly enough enigmatic written and oral prophesies hinted at his election, prophesies given a more concrete focus after his election in 1978.

One of the most popular accounts—but one the Vatican has never confirmed—goes back to Wojtyla's student days in Rome, in 1947, when he traveled to the town of San Giovanni Rotondo to see Padre Pío, the Franciscan Capuchin friar who was a famous stigmatic and clairvoyant.

In 1918 Padre Pío was celebrating Mass in the Church of Santa Maria delle Grazie (Our Lady of Grace) in San Giovanni Rotondo. When he stopped to pray for a moment, he had a vision of Jesus Christ. He saw Christ standing at the back of the choir area with blood flowing from his wounds. Padre Pío, just thirty-one years old at the time, had experienced mystical phenomena before, but none were as vivid as what he saw at that Mass.

Soon after, he had another vision, and this time brown marks appeared on his hands, feet, and on the left side of his chest. It left him faint and trembling, so he started to walk unsteadily back to his room, where he noticed blood seeping from all three marks on his body. Padre Pío lived with this stigmata until his death, and only then did the open wounds close up.

Since Father Pío was also a famous clairvoyant who predicted events in the near future, his prophesies could be easily verified. He predicted that Italy would be defeated in World War II, for example, and would then be occupied.

Father Karol Wojtyla could see how much this great stigmatic suffered when blood gushed out of his wounds at the consecration of the Holy Eucharist. This happened every time Padre Pío celebrated Mass; the moment bread and wine were transformed into the body and blood of Jesus Christ, he would bleed. During his canonization procedure the general postulator of his cause, Father Bernard

Niedźwiedź upadnie po drugiej wyprawie,
Dunaj w przepychu znów tonie,
A kiedy pokój nastąpi w Warszawie,
Trzech królów pada w nim konie.

Trzy rzeki świata dadzą trzy korony
Pomazańcowi z Krakowa,
Cztery na krańcach sojusznicze strony
Przysięgi złożą mu słowa.

Węgier z Polakiem, gdy połączą dłonie,
Trzy kraje razem z Rumunią
Przy majestatu polskiego tronie
Wieczną połączą się unią.

A krymski Tatar, gdy dojdzie do rzeki
Choć wiary swojej nie zmieni –
Polski potężnej uprosi opieki
I wierny będzie tej ziemi.

Powstanie Polska od morza do morza.
Czekajcie na to pół wieku.
Chronić nas będzie zawsze łaska Boża,
Cierp i módl się człowieku.

The prophesy of Tegoborz was forgotten for many years but became well known after the Polish newspaper *Ilustrowany Kurier Codzienny* published it in March 1939, before the outbreak of World War II.

John Paul II after having placed
a crown on the image of Mary,
Merciful Mother of God, in
Kielce Cathedral in 1991.

Romagnoli, compared Padre Pío's sufferings to those of Jesus on the cross.

Legend has it that when young Father Karol Wojtyla was in San Giovanni Rotondo, Padre Pío predicted that he would become pope and also told him, "I see blood during your pontificate." This anecdote became widespread after Wojtyla became pope and was believed even more widely after the attack on his life. The pope has never confirmed Padre Pío's prophesy.

THE MYSTERIOUS FIGURE IN SLOWACKI'S POETRY

In 1848 Pope Pius IX left the Papal Palace and fled Rome when the revolutionary Italian army was advancing toward the city. The insurgents demanded that the pope, as temporal head of the Papal States, declare war on Austria, which then occupied much of northern Italy. The pope refused and took refuge in Gaete, near Naples, then under the rule of the king of the Two Sicilys, who was on good terms with Austria. After two years of exile, Pius IX returned to Rome with the help of the French army.

Juliusz Slowacki, the famous Polish poet, was living in exile in Paris at the time. He had tuberculosis and was in an extremely poor state of health. On his deathbed he heard the news that Pius IX had fled Rome, news that deeply disturbed him and inspired him to write this poem:

Since April 30, 2000, a photograph of Sister Faustina Kowalska hangs in the façade of St. Peter's Basilica. Sister Faustina was the first saint John Paul II canonized during the Jubilee. Two hundred thousand people, including Jerzy Buzek, the prime minister of Poland, attended the ceremony.

Among the jarring sounds of discord
God strikes a massive bell.
The throne lies open, waiting
For the Slavic pope.
Unlike the Italian,
He will not flee the sword
But full of courage, like his God,
Will run to face it.
To him, the world is dust!

One hundred and thirty years would pass before Slowacki's prophetic vision came true. Was it mere happenstance, or did these words of Karol Wojtyla's favorite poet really foretell the election of a Polish pope? Looking back from today's vantage point, it would certainly seem so, especially given the following verse in his poem:

He will spread his love all around
Like today's potentates pass out armaments.
He will tell of the powers of sacrament and symbol
And lead the world by his hand.

It is easy to interpret this stanza as a reference to the pope's call for a "civilization of love" and to his global pilgrimages. The next verse, finally, conjures up an image that closely resembles this pope at the beginning of his pontificate:

His face resplendent with the light of the Sun
Will be a lamp to lead the servants;
With him nations will travel
As they walk toward the light where is their God.

THE PROPHESY OF THE LIST OF POPES

Another prophesy that fits this papal mold goes back to the Middle Ages. Saint Malachy, bishop of Armagh in Ireland, compiled a list of 112 future popes. He didn't list popes by name but assigned brief allegorical symbols, in Latin, for each one. He also predicted that the world would come to an end during the reign of the last pope. Malachy gave his list to Pope Innocent II, who took no interest in it and buried it in the Vatican archives.

Malachy's prophesy reappeared in 1595, during the pontificate of Clement VIII, but as a copy of the original manuscript, so it could have been a forgery. When it was rediscovered, however, the document was taken at face value and connections were made between the names on the list and popes throughout history.

If the prophesies in this document can be believed, the symbolic name connected with John Paul II would be *De labore solis,* meaning either that in the year of his election the sun was extremely active or that he would be an intensely hardworking pontiff. As *De labore solis,* he would also be one of the last popes on the list.

The symbolic names immediately preceding *De labore solis* are:

The Crown Waits

—Adam Bujak, Polish photographer

After the attack on the pope's life in St. Peter's Square, the Holy Father went on a pilgrimage to Fatima to thank God for his miraculous escape from death. He prayed for a long time in front of the image of the Blessed Virgin, and before he departed, he left a votive offering behind. It was the bullet that almost took his life.

Father Luciano Guerra, director of the shrine, and others on his staff didn't know where to keep the pope's gift. Should they hang it around the neck of the statue of the Madonna or place it in the small space between her feet? Father Guerra worried that the small bullet might be lost when the statue was carried through the streets past large crowds.

Suddenly he decided to take the crown off the statue's head. When he turned it upside down, he noticed that the goldsmith had left a small round hole at the top of the crown. Perhaps the bullet would fit, Father Guerra thought. And it did, perfectly, to the amazement of everyone around him. The crown had waited 35 years for its final adornment.

De medietate lunae (Moon Divided in Two), a possible reference to Pope John Paul I, since his name, Albino Luciani, means "White Light" and to his birth in the diocese of Belluno—"*luna*" in Latin, means "moon."

Flos florum (Flower of the Flowers) could refer to Paul VI, since his papal emblem has a fleur-de-lis on it, which is thought to be the "flower of flowers."

Pastor et nauta (Pastor and Sailor) could fit John XXIII. As patriarch of Venice, he had roots in the city of sailors and navigators, and as pastor he led the church to the Vatican II Council.

Pastor angelicus (Angelic Pastor) is a generic symbol that could refer to Pius XII or any pope of the twentieth century.

Two more names come after *De Labore Solis*:

De gloria olivae (Of the Glory of the Olive), perhaps a reference to a coming era of peace.

Petrus romanus (Peter of Rome) could mean the coming of a second Peter to Rome, suggesting that the first Peter was there at the beginning of the church's history and that a second Peter would come to mark the end of the church's history and that of the world.

Malachy did not specify, however, that the names on his list would follow one another or whether other popes might come between the last two names on the document.

WHAT FATHER MARKIEWICZ HEARD

Another prophesy that alludes specifically to a pope from Poland is attributed to Father Bronislaw Markiewicz, a priest in the Przemysl diocese. He was in a local church on May 3, 1863, when he had a vision and heard a voice predicting the future of the Polish people:

> *Not only will they help each other, they will also extend themselves to help people of other nations, even nations that are their former enemies. They will inspire people to form a brotherhood of nations. God will pour out many graces and great gifts on the Polish people. Out of them will arise wise holy saints and masterful leaders who will fill outstanding positions in the world…. People of Poland, God will raise you up and you will give a great pope to the world. Have faith in the Lord.*

Father Markiewicz's vision and prophesy came at a time when Poland did not exist. Przemysl was in Galicia under relatively benign Austrian rule, but Poles in the Russian sector were engaged in a bloody insurrection, and in German-occupied Poland, Catholics were being persecuted. The idea that their oppressors would one day become their allies seemed as preposterous to Poles as the idea of a Polish pope.

Collevalenza

In the heart of Italy, between Rome and Perugia, lies the town of Collevalenza. It is a very old town, not very big, and is nestled in the Umbrian mountains. Karol Wojtyla came here twice, and although these two occasions are interesting episodes in his life, this is the first time they have been mentioned in a papal biography.

Collevalenza is the site of the Shrine of Merciful Love of God, and Karol Wojtyla paid it his first visit at the end of October 1964, when he was archbishop of Kraków and was in Rome to attend the Vatican II Council. He stepped off an Italian air force helicopter 17 years later, in November 1981, on his second visit, this time as head of the Catholic Church. It was his first pilgrimage since the attempted assassination on May 13.

Back in 1964 he had gone to Collevalenza by chance. The invitation to lead the Christ the King celebration had been issued to Cardinal Wyszynski, but since the cardinal was too ill to attend, he sent the archbishop of Kraków in his place.

Two religious orders called Collevalenza home at the time: an order of nuns, the Servants of the Love of God; and the Brothers of the Merciful Love of God. Mother Esperanza de Jesus had founded both in Spain. Father Alfredo Di Penta, the superior of the brothers' order, had invited the Polish bishops.

Mother Esperanza had arrived in Italy in 1936 and founded the Shrine of Merciful Love of God in Collevalenza in 1951. She was a visionary, and in time this shrine became a famous center of worship.

Mother Esperanza was born in 1893 as Maria Guiseppa Alhama y Valera in the province of Murcia in Spain. Fascinated by the personality and spirituality of Saint Teresa of Avila, the Spanish mystic she wanted to imitate, Mother Esperanza entered the Order of the Sisters of Calvary in 1915. Later it would be incorporated into the larger order of the Claretian Missionaries.

In 1929 Mother Esperanza told her superiors about her

Mother Esperanza (Maria Guiseppa Alhama y Valera). Born in 1893 into a poor rural family in Murcia, Spain, she entered the convent when she was twenty-two.

Cross of Merciful Love, in the Chapel of Christ Crucified.

mystical experiences, and as a consequence, she came under the scrutiny of the Holy Office of the Inquisition—a scrutiny, however, that would not prevent her from being in the process of canonization in the year 2005.

While praying in the chapel in 1929, she saw the figure of Christ on the cross. She wrote in her spiritual journal, that the good Jesus was letting her know how the image of his Merciful Love, and symbols connected with it, should be depicted.

Based on her specifications, Lorenzo Cullot, a Spanish

sculptor, created a moving image of Christ crucified. Jesus, dying, directs his gaze toward heaven, and in his side is a red heart with a banner that reads, *"Caritas"* (Latin for love). At his feet is a royal crown with the inscription MERCIFUL LOVE.

Two years later a Polish nun, Sister Faustina Kowalska (John Paul II canonized her in the year 2000), had a similar vision, in which Jesus instructed her to have a picture painted as she saw him, with his right hand raised in blessing, and his left hand slightly touching his chest, and

red and pale-colored rays of light streaming from his heart.

The Shrine of Merciful Love of God, with the bell tower of the basilica.

In 1934 Sister Faustina found a painter, Eugeniusz Kazimirowski, in Vilnius, Lithuania, who agreed to paint an image of the Merciful Jesus according to her specifications. A banner on it reads, "Jesus, I place my trust in you." The connection between the visions of the two nuns had clearly prompted the 1964 invitation that Archbishop Wojtyla accepted in place of Cardinal Wyszynski.

A few traces remain of Archbishop Wojtyla's first visit to Collevalenza. The brief homily he gave appeared in *L'Amore Misericordoso (Merciful Love),* the review published by the shrine, and he appears in two old and faded photographs from the archives. In one of them he is shown during the Christ the King ceremony distributing Holy Communion. In the other he appears in a very characteristic pose: He is listening to someone with his head leaning on his hand.

Father Ennio Fierro of the Merciful Love Order is firmly convinced that John Paul II's encyclical *Dives in*

Misericordia (On the Mercy of God) was inspired by his first visit to Collevalenza, when he spent a long time talking to Mother Esperenza. (The Slovak cardinal Józef Tomko, secretary of the Synod of Bishops, has confirmed that view.)

A year after Archbishop Wojtyla's visit, on September 8, 1965, Mother Esperanza wrote in her journal, "It has been revealed to me that the vicar of Christ will visit this shrine sometime. Perhaps this will happen very soon." Her words are now considered prophetic, even though a papal visit did not take place for some time.

Pope Pius XII did receive Mother Esperanza in a private audience, as did Pope John XXIII. Paul VI blessed her in the Papal Palace. In 1975 the patriarch and archbishop of Venice, Cardinal Albino Luciani, went to the shrine, but he was not yet pope John Paul I. Until 1981 no pope had ever come the shrine at Collevalenza.

In May of that year, Mother Esperanza's life hung by a thread. She had lived a long time—she would turn eighty-eight, though her health was not good. In the middle of the night of May 12, 1981, she thought she was dying. The next day, a few hours before the attack on the pope's life in Rome, she began to vomit blood and grow very weak quickly.

Her doctors did not know what to do. Late that afternoon, news came that the pope had been shot. Then, as doctors were discussing whether to give her a blood

In 1964 Archbishop Karol Wojtyla celebrates the Feast of Christ the King at the Shrine of Merciful Love of God.

transfusion to boost her rapidly falling red blood cell level, Mother Esperanza told them that she felt much better. A day later her red blood cell level was normal.

On the Feast of Christ the King in November 1981, the papal visit Mother Esperanza had foreseen in her journal came to pass. John Paul II entered the church and prayed in front of the cross she had brought from Spain showing the Merciful Jesus. After praying the *Angelus,* he explained why he had come again, citing both his encyclical *Dives in Misericordia,* which was published the year before, and the events of May 13, when he experienced God's mercy and care. Five months after that visit, John Paul II bestowed the title of Minor Basilica on the church in Collevalenza.

Mother Esperanza died in February 1983 and was buried in the crypt of the basilica; she was almost ninety years old. Rome is in the process of declaring her a saint.

Chapter 14

Guardian of the Moral Life

Any gift can be used for good or evil. Human intelligence and freedom are two great gifts from God.

It is easier for a camel to go through the eye of a needle than for someone who is rich to enter the kingdom of God (Mark 10:25). This well-worn quote from the Bible shows that right from the beginning, Christianity taught ethical norms to the faithful. Nevertheless, the Bible is not a manual of economics, politics, theology, or history. It is a guide for saving souls—it teaches truth and leads souls to God.

Church ministers serve the faithful who live within economic and political systems. Every Christian has the duty to act morally, to avoid evil, and try to do whatever is good. He or she can make the world a better place in which to live.

The church's teaching on faith and morality is clear and unambiguous. Social teachings are not, since different viable solutions to social problems exist. John Paul II has not promoted any particular economic or political theory, because he does not believe that one solution is the only acceptable one. Instead, he describes social conditions, offers advice, and denounces whatever he thinks is unjust or immoral.

POPE LEO XIII'S VISIONARY ASSESSMENT OF SOCIAL PROBLEMS

At the end of the nineteenth century, Pope Leo XIII promulgated *Rerum Novarum (On the Condition of the Working Classes)*, an encyclical that had great influence on the social concerns of his times. In it he foresaw many of the problems that would plague the dawning twentieth century. He predicted that the raw and often heartless capitalism of the late nineteenth century, with its blind faith in the ability of marketplace economics to resolve all social problems, would lead to injustice.

Capitalist exploitation of labor and the onerous working conditions imposed on workers, he held, would provoke a massive reaction likely to strengthen socialism in its more unsavory forms. In 1917 the Russian Revolution would prove him right. Communism was not based on the ideals of human dignity, equality, fraternity, and solidarity. Economies withered. Production became inefficient. Misery and degradation spread. In the end Communism would become one of the most murderous systems in history.

Leo XIII's proposals were visionary and realistic. John Paul II reiterated them in *Centesimus Annus (The Hundredth Year)*, the encyclical he promulgated

Pope Leo XIII promulgated his encyclical *Rerum Novarum (On the Condition of the Working Classes)* as a warning for the world as the twentieth century drew near. John Paul II's *Centesimus Annus,* written to commemorate *Rerum Novarum* on May 1, 1991, is a challenge to all societies as they enter the twenty-first century.

in 1991 to commemorate the 100th anniversary of Leo XIII's *Rerum Novarum*. But he added insights of his own about the dangers he saw coming at the dawn of the twenty-first century, especially after the fall of Communism in Central and Eastern Europe. He did this by asking questions: How do political and economic systems view their role in society? What good advice can be given to countries recently freed from Communist oppression? What types of systems, based on sound political and economic principles, would allow strong and healthy societies to flourish in these countries?

THE SYSTEM THAT DOES NOT UNDERSTAND HUMAN NATURE

John Paul II's predecessors analyzed the inner workings of social systems and judged them by that criteria. But this pontiff had lived under two oppressive totalitarian regimes, allowing him to evaluate other economic and political systems from a humanist perspective: Did they benefit humanity and safeguard the inherent dignity and rights of man, something socialism clearly had not done?

He continued to reflect on socialism through the 1990s, having observed as early as 1989 that it was in decline and moving toward the margins of history. Socialism, he argued, was based on an anthropological error: It did not fully understand human nature and therefore did not take its complexity into account in setting up social structures. In totalitarian systems individuals were absorbed into a collective body, into society as a whole. Men and women were not valued as separate, autonomous, and creative individuals but were turned into anonymous parts of the social organism. This mistaken concept of human nature created a false social ideal, and since the system was based on a fallacy, governments had to maintain it by the use of force.

THE DANGERS OF CAPITALISM

In his encyclical the pope also discussed the role of capitalism in the post-Communist world. In *Centesimus Annus* he wrote, "Can it perhaps be said that, after the failure of Communism, capitalism is the victorious social system and that capitalism should be the goal of the countries now making efforts to rebuild their economy and society? Is this the model which ought to be proposed to the countries of the third world that are searching for the path to true economic and civil progress?

"The answer is obviously complex. If by 'capitalism' is meant an economic system which recognizes the fundamental and positive role of business, the market, private property, and the resulting responsibility for the means of production, as well as free human creativity in the economic sector, then the answer is certainly in the affirmative, even though it would perhaps be more appropriate to speak of a 'business economy,' 'market economy,' or simply 'free economy.' But if by 'capitalism' is meant a system in which freedom in the economic sector is not circumscribed within a strong juridical framework that places it at the service of human freedom in its totality and that sees it as a particular aspect of that freedom, the core of which is ethical and religious, then the reply is certainly negative.

"The Marxist solution has failed, but the realities of marginalization and exploitation remain in the world, especially the third world, as does the reality of human alienation, especially in the more advanced countries. Against these phenomena the church strongly raises her voice. Vast multitudes are still living in conditions of great material and moral poverty. The collapse of the Communist system in so many countries certainly removes an obstacle to facing these problems in an appropriate and realistic way, but it is not enough to bring about their solution. Indeed, there is a risk that a radical capitalistic ideology could spread that refuses even to consider these problems, in the *a priori* belief that any attempt to solve them is doomed to failure, and blindly entrusts their solution to the free development of market forces.

"The church has no models to present; models that are real and truly effective can only arise within the framework of different historical situations, through the efforts of all those who responsibly confront concrete problems in all their social, economic, political and cultural aspects, as these interact with one another. For such a task the church offers her social teaching as an *indispensable and ideal orientation*, a teaching that recognizes the positive value of the market and of enterprise, but which at the same time points out that these need to be oriented toward the common good.

"The integral development of the human person through work does not impede but rather promotes the greater productivity and efficiency of work itself, even though it may weaken consolidated power structures. A business cannot be considered only as a 'society of capital

Karol Wojtyla's Pastoral Style
—Archbishop Ignacy Tokarczuk

What is a priest? A priest is someone who helps other people find Christ by proclaiming the Gospel to them and administering sacraments.

Karol Wojtyla has always been a priest. The only thing that changed is the breadth of his ministerial reach and pastoral responsibility.

As a new priest, he helped the pastor of a rural parish. Later he taught theology, wrote articles and poems, performed his duties as bishop of Kraków, and finally took over the enormous burden as head of the church.

What was his pastoral style like? When he became bishop, he chose the motto *Totus tuus* (I am all yours). He dedicated his priesthood to the Blessed Virgin Mary and all his strength, talent, and energy to the well-being of humanity.

Karol Wojtyla was guided by love of other people. This love was not just pretense or lip service, but a total gift of self in the service of others. Sacrifice of his time or his personal concerns did not matter.

As a priest, Karol Wojtyla was very demanding with people close to him but even more demanding of himself. Yet he was a realist who knew just how far he could go with people willing to follow his advice.

He did not fear difficulties, stood up to foes, did not wilt in confrontations, and always stated his position on issues forcefully and clearly. He believed in what he taught. More than a teacher, he was a witness to truth through his deep and authentic spirituality.

I worked with the Holy Father for several years. At that time, he was bishop of Kraków, and I was bishop of Przemysl. I invited him to my diocese for retreats, conferences, lectures, and meetings with the faithful, including young people. He consecrated several new churches at my request, including one in Stalowa Wola. We fought for years with Communist authorities over construction of this church. He came to birthday and anniversary celebrations, including one for the 600th anniversary of Przemysl.

Despite his many obligations, he always accepted my invitations gladly and was a frequent guest in my diocese. He was a man always on the go, busy with a host of different issues. He had energy to spare and never left a job unfinished. He taught me how to stand up for my convictions with courage and without concern for possible consequences.

He may have been Pope John Paul II, the successor to Saint Peter, but he was still a priest, even if he performed his priestly mission on a global scale. Indeed, he was the parish priest for the whole world. In that role, he reached out with loving concern not only to Catholics and other Christians but to all mankind.

goods'; it is also a 'society of persons' in which people participate in different ways and with specific responsibilities."

THE SYSTEM THAT RESPECTS FREEDOM

In short, the capitalist economic system, he explained in *Centesimus Annus*, can be morally sound when it responds to real needs without causing human misery or curtailing freedom, when wealth derives from labor and productivity.

Such capitalism teaches the values of courage, wisdom, cooperation, and mutual trust. Trust is key because it

John Paul II—Parish Priest for the Whole World

—Father Jaroslaw Bucholz

I can't exactly say why I became a priest, because it's still a mystery to me. A few years after I was ordained, while I was working in Belgium, I heard that I belonged to the "John Paul II Generation" of priests, since I had entered the seminary and was ordained during his pontificate. I imagined the term "generation" referred to the lifestyle these priests led, since they lived through the events of 1968 and people in Western Europe thought they were social activists or even revolutionaries. Unfortunately, most of these priests hardly ever left their parishes because they could not compete with all the modern forms of entertainment available to their potential parishioners.

Priests in the "John Paul II Generation" read their breviary, took the monstrance out of the old closet in the sacristy to venerate the Blessed Sacrament during Benediction, taught parishioners to say the old litanies in the tradition, and, at the same time, were not afraid to use modern electronic equipment to teach children the catechism. The social-service dimension of their ministry gave way to the spiritual dimension. That may be an oversimplification, but it points to a beautiful reality: Young people were finding inspiration in an old man, a man who reminded everyone that pastoral service was the most beautiful aspect of the priesthood.

For me, John Paul II was the parish priest for everyone on earth. Wherever he went, he celebrated Mass, gave homilies, baptized children, blessed marriages, prayed vespers, conducted Rosary novenas and ceremonies such as crowning the Blessed Virgin in May, the month dedicated to Mary. He did all this with deep personal commitment, as if he was hoping everyone on earth would become a saint.

He was never been afraid to face people who live in extreme poverty or are deeply distressed or sad. He treated adversaries with dignity and respect. In the way he lived his priesthood, both his very active ministry and his prayerful contemplation were evident to anyone who observed him. He showed many priests, myself included, how to perform priestly service and guide people of goodwill along the path to holiness. He encouraged people to be strong as they face challenges to their faith.

That's how we priests in the "John Paul II Generation" viewed the pope. For us he will always be a great fountain of inspiration.

make his point. Life for peasants in what is now Germany and France did not change very much from the second century on to the nineteenth. With the advent of the industrial revolution and capitalism's ability to produce wealth, however, enormous progress was made between 1800 and 2000. More wealth was created in those 200 years, and more beneficial social change achieved, than in the preceding 2,000 years.

The Bible, the pope noted, does not condemn wealth as such, and the meaning of "riches and the eye of the needle" must be anchored in the times. During Christ's stay on earth, wealth was accumulated through war, plunder, and financial speculation, not through economic development. Being rich meant "having stolen someone else's property," unless, of course, the money was inherited. Inheritance was morally all right; other ways of accumulating wealth were not, which is the point of the "eye of the needle" parable.

Jesus himself spoke about another aspect of wealth, warning that those who grew rich too often saw their wealth as a sign of divine Providence, meaning that God had meant them to be rich or had helped them to become so. Wealth, he preached, does not make a man a better person.

For John Paul II wealth imposes moral conditions on Christians who are rich. They can only make money legally, without breaking any laws. They must resist the temptation to cut corners on their way to wealth. He cited an old Polish saying, "You have to steal your first million," and countered the sentiment with the remark that nowhere is it written that you have to make your million all at once.

Many wealthy people have not stolen their first million, the pontiff pointed out. They paid their taxes, avoided corruption, and did not violate their ethical beliefs. The road to ethical accumulation of wealth may be difficult, but it does exist, and it is a wide road. Following such a path to wealth is the real challenge for Christians.

The rich should share their wealth with others, the pope insisted, especially with those who live in the "fourth world," people on the margins of society who cannot work to obtain their share of worldly goods—the handicapped, the old, the sick. Sharing the wealth, he argued, is a moral

makes the system more cost-effective and therefore more efficient. When managers believe that their workers are doing a good job, they see no need to control them by force—as good a way as any of instilling moral values.

In such an improved version of capitalism the concept of a joint labor-management effort is crucial because more is at stake than just efficient production values. People coming together in the workplace are linked by friendship and the sense of achievement that comes from successful cooperation. Moreover, companies that are respectful of their employees' dignity promote many other moral values.

The pope does not oppose ownership of material goods. Indeed, he believes that owning them and using them well are moral incentives. And he cites history to obligation for the rich. They have a duty to help the poor in their own society and indeed to help needy people everywhere.

THE POOR NEED HELP

Help from the rich for the poor and the defenseless was always a cause dear to the pope's heart. He backed monetary support for third-world countries, including at least some cancellation of their foreign debt. But before taking that step, donor nations should insist that the aid actually reach the poor and not be used to buttress oppressive regimes. Attaching conditions to debt relief is one way of making sure that monies are spent on concrete programs to alleviate poverty. Realism in helping poor countries is as indispensable as the grounding of such aid in faith, hope, and charity.

He warned, however, that economic sanctions against dictatorial countries are often ineffective. They hit the poorest the hardest and barely impact the lifestyles of the wealthy.

Whenever possible, therefore, governments should not become directly involved, but should support the charitable activities of private organizations and those of the church. Such an approach is both more humane and more cost effective. Societies that take care of their own help human potential and improve the overall social structure.

Finally, in his encyclical John Paul II supports fair and honest taxation as essential for the well-being of societies, but he holds governments responsible for setting reasonable and fair tax rates. Excessive or unjust taxes take money from those least able to pay and condemn them to a life of poverty and misery.

THE FAMILY IS ALSO AN ENVIRONMENT

Pope John Paul II is an environmentalist in the broadest sense of the word, ranging from the physical world around us to the family within us. The rapid growth of civilization has imperiled the fragile ecology that binds the globe together and, in a sense, has violated the Bible's admonition to *have dominion over the earth* (Gen. 1:26).

Below: The Caritas Association uses profits from the sale of candles to help the poor.

The earth exists to serve mankind, but men and women need to take care of their environment and not pollute and destroy it. They must learn to understand nature rather than force the earth to produce whatever man thinks he needs and wants from it. Launched in the 1960s, the ecological movement is only beginning to make up for the destruction and ecological tragedies wreaked over the centuries—with most of the damage done in the twentieth century.

CRITIQUE OF THE WELFARE STATE

The welfare state, the pope noted in *Centesimum Annus,* is an inadequate solution to the problems of global poverty. For one thing, social service bureaucracies tend to squander

Above: John Paul II's teachings inspired the members of the San José Club in the Catholic Association of Economic Clubs.

money and dehumanize interpersonal relations. The needy individual is transformed into a client for whom other members of society feel little responsibility, since the state has volunteered to take care of them.

Of course, state-run social organizations have to help when no one else will, but such aid should be goal oriented, limited in time, and disbursed wisely. If it is not, the "clients" become dependent on the bureaucracy and fail to develop their own initiative that might be able to break their dependence on state aid.

But for the pope, the environment is not limited to nature where trees grow tall, birds sing, and rivers run clear. The family in the culture is equally an environment to be cherished and cultivated. Families provide meaning to the lives of their members. They influence development of knowledge and of the subconscious. Children exposed to grotesque and vulgar language will grow up with an imperfect command of all language, while those surrounded by a cruel family environment will become harsh and cruel themselves. And cruelty leaves deep wounds on the human spirit. True ecology, therefore, begins within the family, the natural habitat of men and women.

Capitalism can threaten the family, especially when members are tempted to pursue their careers at the

expense of home and hearth. Work should not consume anyone's life to the exclusion of everything else. Children of divorce, for example, are themselves divorced more frequently than those who emerge from stable family life. They are more accident-prone because they have trouble concentrating, and they are more likely to wind up in psychiatric institutions and prisons or to become alcoholics or drug addicts. Without support from close family ties, they often feel helpless, abandoned, insecure, and unable to function normally in society.

John Paul II baptized several children each year on the Feast of Saint John the Baptist.

GOD CALLS EACH OF US BY NAME

The great drama of modern times is the disintegration of societies, a process in which individuals become faceless, blurred cogs in a machine. Totalitarian systems destroy the unique quality of individuals. They incorporate them into a mass collective where they are treated like worker ants. People sent to concentration camps were assigned numbers and for good reason—numbers stripped victims of their own distinctive personal identity.

Even after totalitarian regimes fell in many parts of the world, the danger of turning people into cogs of profit-making machines still exists. And as cogs, they remain isolated without ever coming to know one another as individuals. The state is not interested in them either except as sources of government funds through taxation. Social ties disintegrate in a sea of anonymity, and interpersonal relationships are destroyed. Therein lies the root cause of so much unhappiness. Each individual, however, is not anonymous; each individual is unique and irreplaceable and deserves a name of his or her own.

WEALTH MUST NOT LEAD TO IDOLATRY

Ownership of private property belongs on the positive side of capitalism's ledger because such ownership fosters human dignity and contributes to social peace. Those who have nothing tend to become restless, to engage in protest, and sometimes to take part in violent action.

Property owners are likely to take care of what they own. People who don't own property, and are therefore forced to live in other people's houses, tend not to bother. Why turn off lights in empty rooms when they don't have to pay the electric bill? Why bother keeping such houses neat and tidy?

The Ideal Priest

—Marcin Przeciszewski, Editor-in-Chief of the Polish Catholic Information Agency

John Paul II is an outstanding example of what it means to be a priest. The Holy Father believed that the example priests give when they live their lives according to radical Gospel values is the way to evangelize people in the secular world.

People were moved by the extraordinary personal testimony he gave during the celebration to honor him on the fiftieth anniversary of his ordination to the priesthood. He told them, "I am overcome with emotion when I visualize myself as I was then. I lay prostrate on the floor of Cardinal Sapieha's small private chapel. As I waited for him to confer the sacrament of orders on me, I listened to the strains of the hymn, *Come, Holy Spirit,* and heard the words of the Litany of the Saints. Then I received the call to proclaim the Good News, to lead the people to God, and to perform the holy ministries."

According to John Paul II, the core of priestly service is the priest's personal relationship with Jesus—and this is the theme of his extraordinary volume *Gift and Mystery.* Priests, he believes, do not fulfill their duties if they think only of their own perfection. But in his "Letter to Priests for Holy Thursday," April 9, 1979, he wrote, "If we want to help others to transform their lives, we have to progress in holiness in our own lives."

Addressing a group of Polish bishops in Rome, John Paul II told them: "People in today's world are calling for holy priests! The modern world is becoming more and more secularized, and truly holy priests need to witness Christ and the Gospel's message…. To be a leader and teacher, the priest must first be an authentic witness."

The Holy Father is a witness to what he proclaims, which is the secret of his global success. The modern world resists abstract ideological discourse and responds only to real-life examples of holiness. "The priest's very life is the indispensable testimony that makes Christ present in the world, that brings the Gospel message to the people of our time. People are more inclined to listen to witnesses rather than to teachers, to those who inspire by examples and not just by talk."

Priests lose credibility in society, John Paul II said on many occasions, when they are not faithful to the virtue of poverty. "Poverty is the source of the priest's readiness and freedom to go wherever his labor will be most useful, even at the cost of personal sacrifice. This form of evangelical poverty gives meaning to the lives of priests who submit their will to the workings of the Holy Spirit. It prepares them to 'go,' leaving all personal ties behind in order to fulfill only the will of the Master."

Priests often forget the virtue of poverty. In 1987 in Szczecin, Poland, the pope reminded them that "priests have to be in solidarity with the nation. The priest has to live a lifestyle similar to that of the average family or perhaps even that of a needy family. God will settle up accounts for those who live this simple lifestyle." He also stressed, "It would be a tragedy if the way priests lived their lives—since they are free of the many sacrifices that laypeople make in their daily lives—caused a deep chasm to open between priests and the faithful."

The pope once more reminded priests that they have a duty to serve the poor and weak. "Evangelical poverty frees priests from worldly concerns and allows them to align themselves in solidarity with the poor. Priests can then lend their strength to build a more just society; they are sensitive to the needs of the poor. The more priests understand economic and social realities, the more they will be able to push for getting help to the poor, a task everybody must face. No Christian is excluded from proclaiming the good news of the Gospels and helping others in need. But priests, more than others, must gravitate toward their brothers and sisters, who are marginalized and defenseless, to sinners, indeed to everyone who is unimportant in the eyes of society—the people, in short, to whom Christ ministered during his ministry as priest and prophet."

John Paul II urged priests "to read the signs of the times" and "to notice where society is heading in today's world" in order to respond to human hopes and expectations. Priests must plumb the deep material and spiritual needs of their flock and then define the pastoral means and methods that can help them. Immersing priestly lives and missions in prayer is one of them.

John Paul II, certainly, was an example of a man whose work was inspired and strengthened by prayer. Even though he was one of the busiest people in the world, he spent a few hours each day in prayer. Even when he traveled and was weary, he rose an hour before others did so he would have time to meditate.

But the division between haves and have-nots is not that clear, the pope believes. He warns property owners to beware of treating their possessions with idolatry. Liberal ideologies often talk about a "sacred" right to property. But God gave the earth to all mankind and instructed them to make good use of it. Ownership is one way of obeying God's command; so is using wealth to help others. Both are reasons why the pope defended the right to own property but admonished those with possessions to make good use of them.

(CONTINUED ON PAGE 218)

The Truth Will Make Us Free

In his very first encyclical, *Redemptor Hominis (On the Redemption of Man)*, John Paul II cited Jesus Christ's famous remark to his followers about truth: *You will know the truth, and the truth will make you free* (John 8:32). Analysts first interpreted this quotation as a papal challenge to those countries whose citizens were not free or enjoyed only limited freedom, more specifically to Communist leaders in Eastern Europe. But it soon became clear that John Paul II was the herald of human freedom the whole world over.

A LOOK AT GERMANY

The pope spoke about freedom in every country he visited on his pilgrimages, but the words he spoke on June 23, 1996, were particularly dramatic. He delivered a homily in front of the Brandenburg Gate in Berlin in which he said, "This place symbolizes better that any other on earth how a nation can yearn for unity after aggressors have divided it." The Brandenburg Gate, he noted, had been a prop for two dictatorships. The Nazis used it as a backdrop for their torches and parades. Communist ideologues feared freedom, and "so they closed this gateway and made it into a wall."

Helmut Kohl, then chancellor of the Federal Republic of Germany, said on that memorable day: "Holy Father, we derive our strength from you. You lend us your moral support and you have inspired the liberating movement in Poland and other Central and Eastern Europe countries. Even though the Communist system seemed indestructible, you knew that it could not withstand the test of time, because it was not based on human nature."

On November 2, 1993, John Paul II told Jas Gawronski of the Italian newspaper *La Stampa* that Christianity played a decisive role in restoring freedom to the Communist-bloc countries through proclamation of its religious and moral message and through its unshakable defense of human rights. "All I did was call Christian principles to mind, keep repeating them, and stressing that we all must obey and respect them," the pope told Gawronski.

He had said much the same thing in Prague on April 21, 1990. "Those who falsely claim they can build a social system without God will find that their effort is just an illusion. It cannot be otherwise! The only thing that remains to be seen is how and when they themselves will realize this."

CHRISTIAN PRINCIPLES OF FREEDOM

For John Paul II only biblical truths as embodied in the social teachings of the church can clarify the concept of human freedom. Any notion of freedom, he had stressed repeatedly, not based on the truth about man is not real freedom.

He explained what he meant in Czestochowa on June 13, 1987, when he said that "the difficulty of the gift of human freedom…is that it causes us to constantly mull over good and evil, to debate whether we will accept salvation or reject it. Freedom and liberty can be transformed into licentiousness, and licentiousness—as we know very well from our own Polish history—can fool men and women with the illusion of a 'golden liberty.' We have often seen how liberty lets individuals and whole societies slip into many forms of bondage. We become enslaved by pride, greed, sensuality, envy, laziness, hatred, and pride."

The main theme of John Paul II's *Redemptor Hominis* encyclical derives from St. Paul's Epistle to the Galatians 5:1: *For freedom Christ has set us free.* The freedom Christ gave mankind is freedom from sin, the source of all human bondage. Human freedom is both a gift and a fundamental duty for each Christian: *For you did not receive a spirit of slavery* (Rom. 8:15).

FREEDOM IS DIFFICULT

Today many governments offer their citizens total and unconditional liberty, a concept without morality and far from objective truth, which can lead to sin and to slavery. "Freedom is difficult," the pope said on June 7, 1991, in Plock, Poland. "We have to learn what freedom is and how to be truly free, so that our freedom does not enslave ourselves or others."

Christians can find freedom through the sacraments and prayer, the pope said, and thus experience the presence of the living God, who is liberty and the source of human freedom. For Christians holiness means living within the greatest possible freedom.

Freedom of religion is a fundamental human right, something John Paul II maintained since the beginning of his pontificate. This

In the Shadow of Auschwitz and Kolyma
—Father Józef Tischner

John Paul II is a child of the "most disgraceful age in history," the age of Auschwitz and Kolyma. Karol Wojtyla lived part of his life in the shadow of both. Auschwitz is the symbol of Nazi butchery, just as Kolyma in Siberia is that of Communist oppression. The pontiff learned to understand the inner workings of both systems—how they sustained themselves by presenting lies as truth and truth as lies.

He has experienced firsthand the impact truth and solidarity can have on society. He turned the slogans of "solidarity in truth" and "truth in solidarity" into the "strength of the weak" that in the end overthrew violence.

Still, the question remains, now that we have built democracies, can today's world, which is so far removed from the reality of Auschwitz and Kolyma, forget what happened there?

John Paul II understood the weakness of democracy and knew the roads people could take to run away from freedom. Democracy, it would seem, is the only system that can destroy itself. Totalitarian regimes, on the other hand, thrive even when people do not want them. Germans grieved over their lost freedoms, but only after they helped Hitler come to power. Communism held Eastern Europe in an iron grip for more than 40 years before its people overthrew the system. How could that have happened? Perhaps because human nature was undervalued and human solidarity was forgotten.

The pope had an answer: "History teaches us that democracy without values easily becomes open or hidden totalitarianism." (From *In the Country of the Closed Imagination*, Znak, Poland, 1977.)

right, however, is not based on indifference or relativity, which would suggest that absolute truth does not exist and that choice of one religion has the same merit as any other. Instead, it is founded on the dignity of every human being who seeks the truth, something only those who are truly free can search for.

No one, the pope contended, can ignore the innate religious dimension of every human being or, even worse, reject religion because they believe it is a source of discrimination and intolerance. Such rejection undermines the right to religious freedom, which, he says, is a fundamental human right.

RENDER TO CAESAR WHAT BELONGS TO CAESAR

Jesus Christ defined the relationship between politics and religion when he said: *Render unto Caesar the things that are Caesar's, and unto God the things that are God's* (Matt. 22:21). His meaning is clear: Church and state must remain separate. Temporal and spiritual power should never be held in the hands of any one person.

History has not always held to that biblical principle. Temporal rulers have wielded spiritual authority, and at times, the reverse has also been true. Over time, however, the concept of separation has taken hold in Christian nations. It has not been so clear-cut in other religions, however, with problematic results—for example, in Israel and the Islamic countries.

Separation of church and state does not mean an absence of religious values in society, John Paul II insisted, although contemporary Caesars seem to interpret the biblical stricture in that way, saying in effect, "We'll take care of everything in the temporal sphere. Religion really doesn't have anything to say about what we do."

But the church does, the pope believed. He saw democracy to be a public value, for example, and of great benefit to society. He cited Christianity's role in the creation and development of democracy, going back eight centuries to the democratic order Saint Dominic proclaimed for his band of brothers in 1220 in Bologna. He had not convened the assembly, he told members of his congregation, to give orders or spiritual direction. As the order's founder, Saint Benedict said, he was not the highest authority. That authority belonged to the group of assembled preacher brothers. Today the church spreads the message that all people—no matter what their religion—are equal because each one is created in the image of God.

Democracy and the church have been at odds in the past, especially when democratic policies turned hostile and the church replied in kind. But ever since Pope Pius XII saw democracy as a bulwark against the advance of Communism, the church has been a proponent of democratic values. John Paul II cherished the rights democracy grants its citizens in shaping the political process. The right to vote, which still does not exist in many countries, is a positive value because it allows for a way to change governments and overthrow the ruling classes without bloodshed.

In order to function properly, however, democracy needs an educated electorate that understands how democratic systems work. Voters must know what the politicians they elect stand for and where they come from—their education, their upbringing, their cultural background, their understanding of economic and social issues, and, finally, their concept of God.

The pope did have caveats about democracy, however. It cannot solve all social problems, he believed, and sometimes takes voting results too far. Valid decisions about

John Paul II traveled to Paris in 1980 to lend his support to Catholics, where Catholicism was in crisis, and where he addressed the United Nations Economic and Social Council on the importance of culture in human development.

theological and ethical issues cannot be based on election outcomes. Truth does not depend on votes. The earth revolves around the sun without benefit of electoral approval. Moral values are not subject to a majority vote, and moral principles cannot be determined in a democratic fashion.

Without ethical values democracy is not a viable political system, because it can too easily be turned into an openly totalitarian state or into one where oppression is disguised. Democracy without ethics, moreover, allows those with money or access to money to rise to the top. The uneducated, the frustrated, and the aggressive are equally dangerous to democracy. The pope cited Hitler's rise to power on the back of democratic votes as one example of democracy undone and noted that the last person burned at the stake was murdered in Geneva—in the showcase democracy of Switzerland.

LIBERTY IS A RESPONSIBILITY

Some American theologians have called John Paul II the "Pope of Liberty" for his devotion to individual freedom and his conviction that free men and women make good decisions about their lives. God created man in his image, which means he created him to be free, and the pope believed that human beings know how to make good use of their freedom. But that doesn't mean they always do so.

Reason is one of the many gifts God gave to men and women when he created them. Like any such gift, it can be used for good or evil. Take the automobile. It can be turned into an ambulance to save lives or the exhaust pipe can be reversed to make the same car into a gas chamber. Freedom, the pope urged, should be used wisely.

Nor should the gift of freedom be used indiscriminately. It has limits imposed by ethical norms. Individuals are really not "free" to harm others. Too often the nature of freedom is misunderstood by those who think they can do anything they want. The pope was always clear on that point: True freedom means consideration for others, and that is best learned through an understanding of the culture in which individuals live. Culture teaches us how to make the right choices—and how to avoid bad choices.

No matter where in the world the culture is rooted, it is an ethical guidepost pointing the way to ethical behavior in freedom. In some cultures children imitate one another and learn from each other, and such behavior is considered natural. In other cultures, however, imitation is considered offensive and is therefore discouraged. Cultural norms may differ, but they should always be respected.

LIVING IN THE GLOBAL VILLAGE

For the pope, globalization was both a challenge and an opportunity with no preset answers to the questions this new phenomenon raises.

True, globalization has the tendency of flattening differences that give the cultures of the world such color and vitality. Those with money and power seek to homogenize much that is offered on the global stage as they look for greater profits at lower cost, and they often do so at the expense of cultural sensitivities.

The opportunity globalization offers lies in the possibility for uniting mankind into one human family in which every individual can feel responsible for other members of that family. Modern communications have brought such a community much closer to reality.

As late as the first half of the twentieth century, most people were only interested in their hometowns and knew little of what went on beyond their local borders. Today the world is on everybody's doorstep with global economic, political, and cultural issues within easy reach through the global news media that transmit information visually and in print.

More than ever, people are becoming involved in the lives of other people. They are ready to help when tragedy strikes, whether it was the genocide in Kosovo when foreigners helped evacuate refugees or the tsunami in South Asia that sparked a counter-wave of global assistance. Europeans and Americans have gone to staff hospitals in remote African villages. A very Catholic spirit of fraternal love has begun to sprout in the wake of globalization.

The Internet has opened up the world even more, bringing diverse cultures into the living rooms of large cities or to remote villages. Even in the age of terror, restrictions on travel are far less than they once were. But all this activity still does not answer the question, How will individuals give meaning to their lives? The pope's reply was simple: "Look for the answer in the human heart."

During the beatification ceremony of Cardinal Aloizije Stepinac in Croatia in 1998, the pope emphasized the values Cardinal Stepinac lived by and those worth imitating: faith in God, unconditional love and forgiveness, and staying united with the church.

John Paul II traveled all over Europe, the Americas, and as far away as Asia. His main goals were to evangelize Catholics and work toward interfaith dialogue and unity among Christians, Muslims, and Jews.

Chapter 15

Pastor of All Peoples

In June 1992 John Paul II kneels and prays in front of a black figure of Christ in Angola, a country devastated by a bloody civil war. In his homily he declared that in its struggle for freedom, Angola has walked along its own way of the cross.

No pope in history traveled as much as John Paul II. Over the years, he developed a ritual that characterized his papacy and made him a familiar globe-trotter to millions everywhere.

Huge crowds were always on hand as his Alitalia jet landed at the international airport of whatever country he was visiting. The doors were flung open, and out stepped a man dressed in white robes, with a skullcap on his head. He greeted the waiting crowd with a warm smile and then knelt down to kiss the ground. During his later years, John Paul II's failing health did not allow him to kneel, but he still kissed—or at least blessed—some of the country's soil, which children held out before him on a big plate. The meaning of the gesture he started so long ago, however, had not really changed: It signified respect and love for the nation he was visiting.

Early in his pontificate John Paul II was asked why he traveled so much. His reply was typical for his wry sense of humor: Visiting other countries is easier than having the multitudes come to Rome to see me. Besides, he noted, Catholics have a right, even a duty, to meet their bishop at least once in their lifetime, and it is equally the duty of bishops to know their flocks. As bishop of Rome and head of the church, John Paul II was every Catholic's bishop, and therefore, he had the same duty as every other prelate.

Soon after his election he told reporters that he did not plan to travel outside the Vatican too much, but that he would follow Paul VI's example and embark on "pilgrimages." He was on the road almost constantly after that, and the "pilgrimage" became an integral part of his pontifical style. For the most part, he responded to the constant flow of invitations that came from the episcopate around the world, from foreign leaders, and from people who attended his general audiences.

Speaking to an Italian journalist, he said, "I realize my trips are a form of missionary outreach and pastoral ministry and, perhaps even more, that they show the collegial mission of the bishop of Rome. Since Vatican II they have become the church's method of self-realization."

In another interview the Holy Father said that his travels highlight the universality of the church and revitalize the value of local churches and the religious consciousness of those who attend them. A renascent spiritual life, moreover, can help bring about profound political change even in countries where authoritarian regimes rule.

In his early years he dismissed critics who faulted him for meeting heads of state and other political leaders in the countries he visited. He told the Vatican newspaper *L'Osservatore Romano* that such criticism is "an erroneous view of the supernatural nature of the church, as if dialogue with heads of states were simply a matter of my doing something sinful. Politics can at times be sinful, most likely when sinners are in power, but on the other hand, the political dimension of nations cannot be overlooked."

His travels, he stressed, were a response to the needs of the faithful in the modern world and, at the same time, reflected the missionary activities of the apostles who traveled the known world spreading the Word of God and establishing Christianity as a global religion.

During his pilgrimages the pope could not possibly meet the pastors and the faithful in every church of the 100-odd countries he visited. But more than any of his predecessors, he acquired firsthand knowledge of the problems and challenges various local Catholic churches were facing around the world.

JOHN PAUL II'S POLITICS OF TRAVEL

He was out of the starting gate early. On October 20, 1978, less than two weeks after his election, John Paul II left Rome for the first time on a visit to the Marian shrine at Mentor Ella, and on November 5 he visited the birthplace of Saint Francis of Assisi. Early in 1979 he went to Latin America—his first journey outside Italy.

Folk dancers swaying to the rhythm of tambourines welcome John Paul II to Papua, New Guinea, in 1995.

THE POPE TRAVELS TO LATIN AMERICA

Population alone explains the large role Latin America played in the pope's travels—almost half the world's Roman Catholics live in the region, and demographics indicate that their numbers will increase even more rapidly in coming decades.

Map of John Paul II's
Pilgrimages (up until December 2000)

1979
1. Dominican Republic, Mexico, Bahamas. 2. Poland. 3. Ireland, United States. 4. Turkey.

1980
5. Democratic Republic of the Congo (Zaire), Kenya, Burkina Faso (Upper Volta), Ivory Coast. 6. France. 7. Brazil. 8. Federal Republic of Germany.

1981
9. Pakistan, Philippines, United States (Guam and Alaska), Japan.

1982
10. Nigeria, Benin, Gabon, Equatorial Guinea. 2. Portugal. 12. Great Britain. 13. Brazil, Argentina. 14. Switzerland. 15. Republic of San Marino. 16. Spain.

1983
17. Portugal, Costa Rica, Nicaragua, Panama, El Salvador, Guatemala, Honduras, Belize, Haiti. 18. Poland. 19. France. 20 Austria.

1984
21. United States, South Korea, Papua New Guinea, Solomon Islands, Thailand. 22. Switzerland. 23. Canada. 24. Spain, Dominican Republic, Puerto Rico.

1985
25. Venezuela, Ecuador, Peru, Trinidad, Tobago. 26. Netherlands, Luxemburg, Belgium. 27. Togo,

Ivory Coast, Cameroon, Central African Republic, Democratic Republic of Congo (Zaire), Kenya, Morocco. 28. Switzerland, Liechtenstein.

1986
29. India, 30. Colombia, Saint Lucia. 31. France. 32. Bangladesh, Singapore, Fiji, New Zealand, Australia, Seychelles.

1987
33. Uruguay, Chile, Argentina. 34. Federal Republic of Germany. 35. Poland. 36. United States, Canada.

1988
37. Uruguay, Bolivia, Peru, Paraguay. 38. Austria 39. Zimbabwe, Botswana, Lesotho, Swaziland, Mozambique. 40. France.

1989
41. Madagascar, Réunion, Zambia, Malawi. 42 Norway, Iceland, Finland, Denmark, Sweden. 43. Spain. 44. South Korea, Indonesia, Mauritius.

1990
45. Cape Verde, Guinea-Bissau, Mali, Burkina Faso, Chad. 46. Czechoslovakia. 47. Mexico, Curaçao, 48. Malta. 49. Malta, Tanzania, Burundi, Rwanda, Ivory Coast.

1991
50. Portugal. 51. Poland. 52. Poland, Hungary. 53. Brazil.

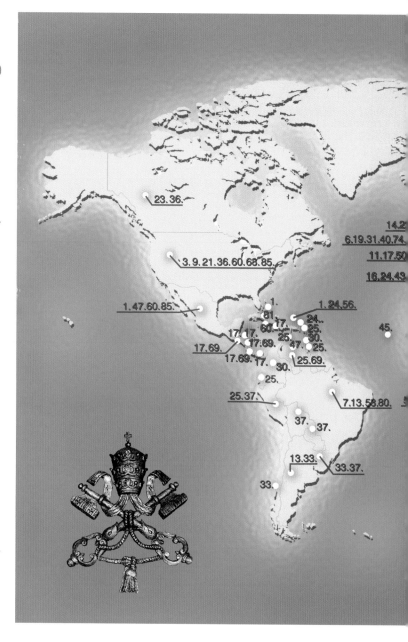

What adds to Latin America's importance in the future of the church are ominous signs pointing to a crisis of faith in Europe and North America, where churches are forced to deal with a massive decline of religious fervor and the consequent rise of secularization. New religious movements have also begun to undermine traditional church structures and sap church attendance.

The church in Latin America, in contrast, has displayed amazing strength despite facing a host of indigenous problems. The region has far too few priests to meet the manifold challenges, especially the rise of evangelizing

Protestant churches in many Latin American countries. Equally troubling for the pontiff was the spread of so-called "liberation theology" in a region many thoughtful Catholics believe represents the future of Catholicism and, for some, the future of Christianity itself.

The pope, therefore, intentionally chose Mexico, the Dominican Republic, and the Bahamas as his first overseas destination. Targeting the region first was a signal of the importance the pontiff attached to the status of the church there. And he would continue to focus on the hemisphere, making a total of 17 journeys to Caribbean,

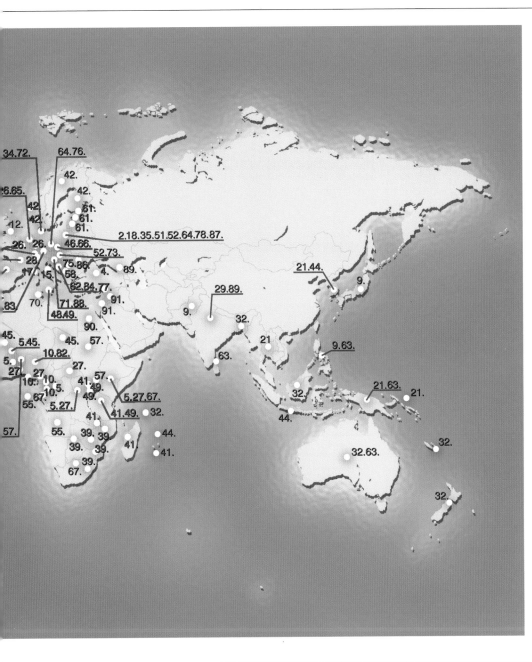

1992
54. Senegal, Gambia, Guinea,
55. Angola, São Tomé-Principe.
56. Dominican Republic.

1993
57. Benin, Uganda, Sudan.
58. Albania. 59. Spain. 60.
Jamaica, Mexico, United States.
61. Lithuania, Latvia, Estonia.

1994
62. Croatia.

1995
63. Philippines, Papua New
Guinea, Australia, Sri Lanka.
64. Czech Republic, Poland.
65. Belgium. 66. Slovakia. 67.
Cameroon, South Africa, Kenya.
68. United States.

1996
69. Guatemala, Nicaragua,
El Salvador, Venezuela.
70. Tunisia. 71. Slovenia.
72. Germany. 73. Hungary.
74. France.

1997
75. Bosnia-Herzegovina.
76. Czech Republic. 77. Lebanon.
78. Poland. 79. France. 80. Brazil.

1998
81. Cuba. 82. Nigeria. 83. Austria.
84. Croatia.

1999
85. Mexico, United States.
86. Romania. 87. Poland.
88. Slovenia. 89. India, Georgia.

2000
90. Egypt. 91. Jordan, Israel,
Palestine. 92 Portugal.

Central American, and South American countries. He made five trips to Mexico, four to Brazil, and three to the Dominican Republic. He also visited Argentina, Uruguay, Cuba, Peru, Venezuela, Guatemala, Nicaragua, and El Salvador.

JOHN PAUL II CONFRONTS LIBERATION THEOLOGY

The challenge of liberation theology was on the top of the pope's agenda as he flew across the Atlantic for the first time as pontiff. It was a challenge he would meet head-on by unequivocally condemning the doctrine. He chastised bishops, priests, theologians, and political activists for supporting armed struggle and other Marxist dogma in efforts to overcome injustice and poverty.

Introduction of elements foreign to the church's teaching, he noted, was inadmissible, and of all foreign elements, Marxism was clearly the worst. Struggle and hatred are not part of a priest's mandate, which should focus on the spread of love, forgiveness, and reconciliation, even with adversaries. Liberation theology, as the basis of church teaching, would turn priests into politi-

cians, soldiers, or government leaders, forcing them to neglect and perhaps abandon their fundamental pastoral duties. Besides, even as the name indicates, liberation theology should concentrate on man's relationship with God and not exclusively on human needs, as is so often the case in practice.

On the newly elected pope's first pilgrimage to Mexico in 1979, the faithful line the roadway and greet him with the popular song "Amigo."

His harsh tone shocked some and angered others while confirming a widely held opinion that the new pope adhered to conservative, even reactionary, political and ideological convictions. What critics overlooked, however, was John Paul II's equally unequivocal condemnation of all forms of social injustice and political oppression. The church, he preached, must commit to the service of the poor and the oppressed, and do so unconditionally.

IN THE NAME OF THE POOR AND DISCRIMINATED

While social problems exist on all continents, both in poor regions like Africa and wealthy ones like Europe, they are particularly acute in Latin America, and there the church has become deeply involved in efforts to solve them. The pope, therefore, could not overlook these issues; nor could he avoid taking a stand on what the church was doing—one reason he opposed liberation theology so strongly.

Instead, he favored other ecclesiastical methods of fighting poverty and social injustice. When he traveled to Brazil—the first time was in 1980—he encountered the phenomenon of the Base Church Communities

(Communidades Eclesiasticas de Base), a movement in which Catholic laymen play a larger role in keeping parishes without regular priests more closely connected. Communities meet regularly, study the Bible, and try to alleviate poverty as best they can.

John Paul II defends the rights of the poor in Mexico. Here he is welcomed with an outpouring of love in the small town of Cuilpan in Oaxaca in 1979.

The pope did warn Brazilian bishops against the base communities slipping into liberation theology and the dangers it posed to priests taking part in social justice actions and neglecting their pastoral duties. He stressed that only ordained priests can exercise these duties, leaving sociopolitical affairs to the lay community.

Nevertheless, he supported the fundamental thrust of Base Church Communities. They were deeply rooted in the church, he said, and performed a valuable function in educating the faithful and deepening their religious beliefs, especially given the lack of priests in Latin America. These laypeople were responding effectively to the needs of the church. But at the same time, the pope empowered Brazil's bishops to take firm action against any abuse that might arise in these communities through infiltration of left-wing doctrines.

In a lengthy interview published in *Tygodnik Powszechny* on July 16, 1980, the Holy Father put his position this way: "I think that my trip to Brazil…has allowed me and everyone else in the church to place the Brazilian church…within the context of the Universal Church—its way of life, experience, hopes, and problems. My trip fostered greater unity in prayer because it helped unite the global church in prayers for Brazil's Catholics. It encouraged the unity within the church and with the people of Brazil."

His voyage to Brazil, however, did more than that—it placed the papacy squarely on the side of the poor and disenfranchised. In São Paulo's soccer stadium, before 150,000 workers shouting, *"Libertade, libertade,"* the pope heralded "the right of the workers to unite in free associations, with the goal of making their voice heard, of defending their interests, and of contributing responsibility to the building of the common good." Many of those who cheered him that day had been on strike against Brazil's military regime for 42 days. The pope's support would strengthen the church across that vast land.

A CONTROVERSIAL MEETING IN SANTIAGO

The pontiff's trip to Chile in 1987 posed different problems and different issues. General Augusto Pinochet had ruled the country with an iron

Theology of Liberation
—Father Stanislaw Skobel

What exactly is liberation theology and why did the pope oppose it so harshly? Its roots lie in Latin American poverty and the extreme efforts to combat it. Theologians, the doctrine argues, should not be limited to theoretical discussions but should become participants in the ongoing struggle to liberate the oppressed.

Sin is not "individual, private, or merely interior reality," Gustavo Guitierrez, a major liberation theology theoretician maintains, but should be seen from "a social, historical fact, the absence of brotherhood and love in relationships among men." Capitalist nations, therefore, are sinful because they oppress and exploit poor countries.

But so, the theory holds, are the poor themselves because they allow themselves to be exploited and oppressed rather than resisting and overthrowing the oppressors, by violent means if necessary. Carried to an extreme, liberation theologists say murder can be justified if it is committed to free the oppressed. And the pope could not accept this extreme view, just as he refused incorporation of Marxist dogma.

But he could not argue with the root evil that sparked liberation theology—the combination of extreme poverty and political oppression. Rulers of underdeveloped countries in the hemisphere championed the interests of the rich and defended them with violence. They had, of course, done so over the centuries, but beginning in the 1960s theologians began to challenge the status quo. They argued that the church must help to battle poverty and to proclaim the good news of redemption to the impoverished.

The major proponents of liberation theology in Latin America were men like Ruben Alves, Joseph Comblin, Gustavo Gutierrez, Juan Segundo, the future cardinal Eduardo Pironio, José Miguez Bobino, and one of the most radical theologians in the group, Leonardo Boff.

The ideas these theologians professed were for the most part adopted and confirmed by the Latin American Bishops' Conference held in Medellin, Colombia, in 1968. In the conference document the bishops stressed that the struggle for a just society is a major factor in the history of salvation and that the church must take part in liberating men and women from all oppression.

Problems arose over the next decade as liberation theology moved closer to a Marxist analysis of society. José Carlos Mariategui was a leading exponent with his inclusion of "class struggle" and "revolution" as last resorts for establishing justice. Because he could not accept these points of view, John Paul II became a harsh critic of the movement.

His criticism was summed up in two Vatican documents the Congregation for the Doctrine of the Faith published: the *Instruction on Certain Aspects of the "Theology of Liberation"* in 1984 and the *Instruction on Christian Freedom and Liberation* in 1986. Both sharpened papal opposition and clarified the Vatican position.

The fall of Communism has helped modify the tenets of liberation theology. Increasingly, Latin American clerics have abandoned Marxist positions for having failed to alleviate hemisphere poverty, and they have found virtue in the capitalist approach of creating wealth that is able to help the poor.

Though it is no longer the radical movement it was in the '70s and '80s, liberation theology made major contributions to Catholic thought. Specifically, it insisted that theology should not indulge in abstract, speculative reflections about the world, but that theology should set out to transform it.

fist since staging a bloody military coup in 1973, and as a result, many other countries maintained some distance from the dictator, effectively isolating him and his country from the international community. However, since Pinochet was head of state, the pope had no choice but to meet with him, a meeting that embittered Communist countries and angered progressive church circles in the West.

Still, the pope did what he could to help victims of the dictatorship. In talks with Pinochet himself and during liturgical ceremonies, John Paul II asked about the *"desaparecidos,"* those who had disappeared because they had opposed the junta or had aroused its ire in some other way. He also met with representatives of 19 Chilean political groups, including some enemies of the junta.

But no matter where in the world he met political leaders, the pope always insisted that the religious and spiritual aspects of his journey come first, far ahead of any political consideration that might arise. The political fallout of his travels, however, was often significant. Certainly dictatorial regimes fell in Haiti, the Philippines, and in Chile not long after papal visits in the '80s—and his role in the Polish upheavals, of course, is well known.

The pope's travels had deeper significance than mere visits to countries that had extended invitations to him as Saint Peter's successor. As with all aspects of his pastoral ministry, they were part of his overall pastoral vision. In his "politics of pilgrimage" John Paul II visited other countries—or more accurately, local churches in them—to attend to whatever issue or problem was uppermost in his mind and theirs. It could be a matter of Catholic communities in crisis, for example, as they face holding on to Christ-like values in a secular world. Wealthy Christians in the

The pope visits poor neighborhoods— the *favelas*—on the outskirts of Vitória, Brazil, in 1991.

rich West are buffeted by consumerism, secularism, and other social trends hostile to church principles, the pope noted.

Young churches in the third world often display great dynamism, and their members are outstanding examples of living faith. Yet their beliefs are challenged by the social and political difficulties inherent in poor, underdeveloped countries, difficulties that have been overcome with, at best, uneven success. The pontiff took great care not to limit his travels to Catholic countries. Indeed, visiting the faithful in countries where Catholics are a minority was always one of his top priorities—Muslim nations, for example, where Catholics face problems inherent to living among people who profess a different religion.

EVANGELICALS IN LATIN AMERICA: A CONFRONTATION

Over the last few decades the church has begun to face a new challenge in Latin America: the rise of various evangelically oriented Protestant religions that have made great strides in many nations. Their doctrines often are opposed to some basic tenets of the Catholic faith, and they have made a habit of attacking the church.

Their motivation usually lies in different interpretations of the Bible. Jehovah's Witnesses, for example, devote themselves to careful study of the scriptures.

Above: Guatemalan women design a traditional sawdust walkway before John Paul II's arrival.

228

But their reading of them is so literal that they arrive at radical, unconventional, and fundamentalist ways of interpreting the text. The Mormons place the Bible behind the Book of Mormon, a dubious document in regard to scriptural importance.

Pentecostal churches are growing rapidly across the hemisphere as they push an unabashed evangelization. Their aggressive approach has led to frequent conflicts with the Catholic Church. Christian fundamentalists have also pushed their own interpretation of the Bible—every word in it is the literal truth—and made great headway in Latin America.

Other Protestant groups champion new doctrines and new commandments that forbid their followers to exercise normal, everyday activities. Many are openly hostile toward any traditional Christian denominations and not only the Catholic Church. Taken together, these different approaches to Christianity have "converted" almost half the population in some areas of Mexico and Central America.

Even worse, from the Vatican's point of view, are far-out "cults" that force members to break off ties with families and friends. Sect leaders insist on total control of their membership, often with tragic results—the Jonestown massacre in 1978 is perhaps the most dramatic and tragic example of such an unbridled cult.

Most of the new religious movements have roots in the United States and, therefore, look upon Latin America as a natural area of expansion. In the nineteenth century and early in the twentieth century, the United States viewed the region as its backyard, where it could intervene at will. The new religious groupings often seem to follow that expansionist view, using their money to "buy" poor farmers and factory workers in areas—mostly in Central America—where poverty is the daily norm.

"NORTH AMERICA" MEANS "HEAVEN ON EARTH"

North America has accumulated so much wealth that many people regard it as heaven on earth; yet many of those who live there face problems of their own, and they are not minor, even though they are not as severe as those in Latin America.

The Holy Father's many visits to the United States and Canada—he came seven times—were important events during which he addressed the United Nations in New York and the Organization of American States (OAS) in Washington, D.C. He spoke at a rally in New York's Shea Stadium, while on another papal visit 150,000 people turned Central Park into an open-air cathedral. In Denver some 200,000 gathered at a youth festival to see and applaud the pope.

Enthusiastic young people welcome John Paul II to Denver, Colorado, in 1993. He spoke about the crisis in the church and the serious problems of abortion and euthanasia in the United States.

Wherever he went in the United States, John Paul II was cheered and clearly loved. He had indeed conquered the hearts of most Americans, including the once powerful WASPS (White Anglo-Saxon Protestants), who have a tradition of hostility toward the Catholic Church. His wisdom, his personal magnetism, his firm grasp of theological issues, and his spirited defense of Catholic doctrines of faith and morals won him the respect even of those who regarded him and his church with some hostility.

He dealt with controversial issues with skill, detachment, and empathy. One such encounter took place on October 7, 1979, the last day of his first U.S. visit as pope. He arrived at the National Shrine of the Immaculate Conception in Washington, D.C., that Sunday morning and was welcomed by Sister Theresa Kane, president of the Leadership Conference of Women Religious. It was not the kind of welcome the pope had expected.

"As women," she said, "we have heard the powerful messages of our church professing dignity and reverence for all persons. As women, we have pondered upon these words. Our contemplation leads us to state that the church in its struggle to be faithful to its call for reverence and dignity for all persons must respond by providing the possibility of women as persons being included in all ministries of our church."

John Paul II heard her out calmly and then went on to deliver the homily he had prepared beforehand. He made no reference to Sister Kane's remarks but reaffirmed the traditional Vatican stance on women's role in the church. He stressed the importance of their religious mission but also pointed to the different parts men and women play in

CRUMBS FROM THE TABLE

In August 1993 the pope again traveled to the United States, this time in response to an invitation from America's bishops to attend World Youth Day in Denver. Reporters who covered the event wondered if, with so many young people in attendance, the festival might become a fiasco.

Instead, it turned into a triumph that resounded across the world despite the fact that the pope did not mince words. Christians must be faithful to God, he said. The church's moral teachings must be upheld, and they included premarital chastity. He criticized materialism without, however, demanding that Americans, who lived in a wealthy society, renounce their material possessions. The rich, he said, must share their wealth with the poor and help those in need. For the pope this had been a constant refrain going back to his first papal visit to the United States in 1979 when he said, "Don't just give poor people the crumbs from your table!"

On his visits to the United States, the pope always stressed the importance of freedom—freedom of speech, of religion, of the press, and all the other freedoms Americans enjoy. He urged that "export" of these freedoms be made a U.S. priority. But at the same time, he warned against misuse of the "gift of freedom," stressing that "freedom is based on truth."

For the pope, freedom of worship obviously had priority, and given the variety of religious denominations in the United States, ecumenical unity and interfaith dialogue were especially important for him. In every American visit, John Paul II engaged members of other religions—meeting regularly, for instance, with Jewish leaders—both separately and at larger ecumenical gatherings.

WE ALL BELIEVE IN THE ONE GOD

The pope traveled to Africa for the third time in August 1985—he had gone there first in 1980—visiting Togo, the

The Holy Father after addressing a session of the United Nations Organization in New York City during his "Pilgrimage to the World" in 1979.

Ivory Coast, Cameroon, the Central African Republic, the Democratic Republic of the Congo (former Zaire), Kenya, and Morocco.

The journey was yet another sign of how important that continent loomed in John Paul II's vision for the future of the Catholic Church. He saw Africa as a last frontier, a bastion against the spread of secularism. The African church is one of the oldest in Christendom, but over the centuries missionaries have had a hard time proclaiming the Word of God to a basically tribal culture.

In recent decades a process of acculturation has begun to take hold—that is, an effort to adapt Christianity to local conditions so it can take root in indigenous social customs. That required integration of tribal rituals into the Catholic religion, something John Paul II found difficult to accept until a synod of African bishops persuaded him to change his mind.

The church in Africa has also faced other challenges. It has been struggling to survive among competing faiths: tribal animist religions, a muscular Islam, and well-financed Protestant denominations from the United States. All of them have complicated the already difficult task of proclaiming the Word of God to people who know nothing about it. Nevertheless, Catholic missionaries continue to strive for new ways of evangelizing the African peoples and to forge bonds of understanding with other religions. Thus, John Paul II made a point of meeting leaders of Islam and animist denominations during his African travels.

A MAJOR STEP IN CASABLANCA

One of the most effective meetings of the mind between Catholicism and Islam took place on the pope's third voyage to Africa. In Casablanca the pope spoke to 90,000 Muslim youths from across the continent, and what he said had an enormous impact. Islam and Christianity have a great deal in common, he told his youthful audience, and the two religions need to engage in more dialogue as a way of increasing mutual understanding and respect.

"Abraham is, for all of us, the example of having faith in God and surrendering to God's will while trusting in God's goodness. We all believe in the same true God, the Living God, who created this world and who leads the human beings he created to perfection," he said. He urged the youths to give witness to God and to work to make the world a better place to live.

In Casablanca John Paul II also addressed social conditions in this modern age. All people should be treated equally, he said, and in turn, all of them should be open and tolerant of one another. They should work to improve living conditions, and they should make every effort to grow spiritually. At the end of his remarks, he prayed, "God, Creator of justice and peace, grant us true joy and true love, as well as permanent bonds of fellow-

In 1980, the faithful gather in front of the People's Palace in Kinshasa, in the Democratic Republic of the Congo. After Mass the crowd constructed a tiny chapel of tall reed stalks to house the chair where John Paul II sat.

ship among nations. May you always shower us with your gifts! Amen."

THE MISSION TO ASIA

In Asia the church faces problems similar to those in Africa. Here, too, it must adapt Catholic beliefs to indigenous cultures. Here, too, interfaith dialogue is an important missionary tool, and one the pope used well during his seven journeys to Asia, Australia, and Oceania that spanned 17 countries including the Philippines, India, and South Korea. In Asia, Catholics make up only three percent of the population, and the Philippines is the only country where they represent a majority. This low representation has sometimes led to confrontation.

Perhaps the most dramatic encounter took place during the pope's three-day visit to New Delhi in November 1999, his second trip to India. His visit, church officials said, had no special agenda. But it came at a time of growing concern about Hindu attacks against Christian clerics and the opposition of some Hindu groups to Christian

The pope arrives in a helicopter to attend the World Youth Day celebrations in the stadium in Manila in 1995.

missionary work. Months before the pope's arrival, an Australian Baptist missionary, his two sons, and an Indian priest were murdered in the countryside.

Fundamentalist Hindu groups demanded that the pope apologize for atrocities Portuguese missionaries committed in Goa in the sixteenth century against Hindus who resisted conversion. They also charged that the church was backing an aggressive program of converting Hindus to Catholicism and using foreign money to do so.

But John Paul II was not an easy man to intimidate despite heightened Indian security during his trip. He released an Apostolic Exhortation entitled *Ecclesia in Asia* the day after he arrived. In it the pope wrote that "we can pray that in the Third Christian Millennium *a great harvest of faith* will be reaped in this vast and vital continent…. The people of Asia need Jesus Christ and his Gospel. Asia is thirsting for the living water that Jesus alone can give." The document was the result of a Synod for Asia that was held at the Vatican in the spring of 1998. John Paul II regularly visited regions

At the Vigyan Bhawan Convention Center in New Delhi in 1999, the Holy Father meets with representatives of the many religious faiths in India: Hinduism, Islam, Buddhism, Jainism, Judaism, Zoroastrianism,and Brahmanism.

after special synods had discussed problems and issues that affected them.

During ceremonies held at the Sacred Heart Cathedral in New Delhi, attended by 100 bishops (60 from outside India), the pope followed up his exhortation:

Kali, Goddess of Death, is the patroness of Calcutta, India. In 1986, the Holy Father meets with Mother Teresa and tours her Asram Nirmal Hriday (House of the Pure Heart), in Calcutta, where many people live in poverty.

"You, the bishops, are being asked to make ever greater efforts to spread the Gospel of salvation throughout the length and breadth of the human geography of Asia." And, he continued, "if this most basic of rights is denied, then the whole edifice of human dignity and freedom is shaken…. In parts of Asia explicit proclamation is forbidden, and religious freedom is denied or systematically restricted."

Reaction to the pope's remarks was mixed. A prominent Hindu nationalist accused John Paul II of abusing "the hospitality that India has extended to him" and of starting a drive to evangelize the subcontinent. "He should not have said it," Rajender Chadha, spokesman for RSS, a prominent Hindu nationalist group, told the Press Trust of India. The pope, he continued, had confirmed Indian fears that the church had "grand plans to convert India into a Christian country."

Archbishop Alan Basil de Lastic, president of the Catholic Bishops' Conference of India, faced a barrage of media questions about the pope's real meaning in his exhortation to evangelize Asia. De Lastic insisted that John Paul II had not championed any "stepping up" of conversions. "We will carry on proclaiming the Word of

Christ, and it is for others to accept. There is no question of using force or allurements." He dismissed Hindu demands for a ban on conversion as "a perversion that denies the fundamental freedom of individuals to choose one's religion according to one's conscience."

What's more, even the pope admitted that "the effort to share the gift of faith in Jesus as the only savior is fraught with philosophical, cultural, and theological difficulties," difficulties compounded, he said, by the fact that "Jesus is often perceived as foreign to Asia. It is paradoxical that most Asians tend to regard Jesus—born on Asian soil—as a Western rather than an Asian figure."

VOYAGES TO THE SOURCE OF CHRISTIANITY

On two pilgrimages during the Year 2000 Jubilee, the pope traveled back in time to places where the church had its roots in the Old Testament and the New Testament.

He went first to Mount Sinai in Egypt in February and then spent two days in Cairo, where he met with Christians of various rites and with several Muslim leaders, including the rector (president) of Al Azhar University, the oldest and the most prestigious institute of higher learning in the Islamic world.

A month later the pope fulfilled a long-held dream to visit the Holy Land, something he had not been able to do because of diplomatic and political difficulties, even though Paul VI had furtively visited Israel for 11 hours in 1964. Diplomatic relations were not established until 1994, and in the Jubilee Year many feared John Paul II's arrival could exacerbate Jewish-Arab tensions and might trigger a terrorist attack.

It did not happen. He visited sites holy to three religions and all the places where Jesus had lived and worked. He also went to Yad Vashem, the Holocaust museum in Jerusalem, where he said, "As bishop of Rome and successor of the Apostle Peter, I assure the Jewish people that the Catholic Church, motivated by the Gospel law of truth and love, and by no political considerations, is deeply saddened by the hatred, acts of persecution and

John Paul II at Mount Nebo, in Jordan, in 2000, where God showed Moses the Promised Land.

displays of anti-Semitism directed against the Jews by Christians at any time and in any place."

He put a letter in the western wall in Jerusalem; met with Ezer Weizman, then Israel's president, and spoke with Holocaust survivors, some from Wadowice, and with Palestinians. These contacts gave political relevance to the religious dimensions of his journey.

EUROPE, CRADLE OF CHRISTIANITY AND OF ATHEISM

Despite the global reach of his pilgrimages, the pope did not neglect his backyard—Europe, a place that was the cradle of the church and remained a key player in political, economic, cultural, and religious life despite the emergence of other global power centers. More than half of his travels took place within the confines of the Old World.

The continent's problems were massive and engaged the pope's intensive scrutiny. Populations were aging. Consumerism was running rampant and in lockstep with

secularization as more and more people fell away from religion and the church. As he traveled the continent, he encountered increased opposition. Various groups protested his visits, attacked him personally, and challenged his authority as head of the church. Of course, he was also received with love and respect.

That Poland would be one of the first countries he visited outside Italy was only natural, and he would return to his homeland over and over. But he maintained close contact with all the other European nations, including states that emerged from the breakup of the Soviet Union, Yugoslavia, and Czechoslovakia. Christianity, after all, had shaped Europe, and nowhere else has faith in God impregnated the culture and the civilization as much as it has in the Old World.

Next to Poland, Pope John Paul II visited France more often than he did any other country—a total of six times between 1980 and 1997—and whenever he went, he tried to address the problems of the moment, to encourage the French in their faith, and to oppose the threats they faced.

His first trip to France took place from May 30 to June 2, 1980, and his schedule would have broken the back of a lesser man. Barely off the plane, he met with the mayor of Paris at the Hôtel de Ville (city hall) and never looked back. Next he celebrated Mass at Notre Dame and spoke to the priests from the Ile-de-France gathered in the cathedral. He ended that day with a broadcast message to the French people. The next day he celebrated Mass for French workers at St. Denis Basilica and met with Poles, Muslims, Jews, and representatives of other Christian denominations.

On June 1 he traveled to Le Bourget Airport outside

Paris for an open-air Mass on the airfield where *Lucky Lindy* had landed in 1927 and where people from all over France had gathered to hear him preach. At the end of his homily, the pope asked the congregation this question: "France, you who are the elder daughter of the church, are you faithful to the oaths you pledged at your baptism?... France, daughter of the church and teacher of other peoples, are you in keeping with eternal wisdom for the well-being of mankind?"

France is often called the elder daughter of the church because at the beginning of the sixth century, the Frankish kingdom, occupying what is today France, became the first political entity in Europe to be "baptized" as a state. France was also the first country in Europe to separate church and state—that is, to remove church influence from civil government, which it did in the wake of the French Revolution of 1789.

More than 50,000 French youth jammed the Parc des Princes stadium on the night of June 1 to hear the pope answer 20 questions they had pre-submitted in writing. To all of them, he gave detailed answers in which he exhorted the young to remain true to the spirit of the church and to God. His reception was tumultuous. The spirituality the young people displayed surprised many.

On the day he left France, he addressed a meeting of UNESCO—the United Nations Organization for Education, Science, and Culture—the first pontiff ever to do so. In his remarks he stressed the role of education and culture in the lives of men, that it was essential to the existence and well-being of mankind. "Culture is always placed in an essential and necessary relationship to what man is and what man can be." And he pointed to the role culture had played in his native Poland in keeping alive national identity during the time Poland did not exist as a state.

In September 1996 the pope again traveled to France to celebrate two important Christian anniversaries—the sixteenth centenary of Saint Martin's death and that of the baptism of Clovis, king of the Franks, at the end of the fifth century. In his general audience on September 25, 1996, the pope said: "Martin's missionary work and Clovis's baptism gave rise to a deep faith life, which was expressed in abundant fruits of holiness down the centuries. I witnessed this, for example, in Brittany, where Saint Anne, Mother of the Virgin Mary, is especially venerated. Here faith in Christ and fidelity to the church have been preserved, even at the cost of martyrdom."

John Paul II in Lourdes in 1983, praying in the grotto where the Holy Virgin Mary, dressed in white, is believed to have appeared to Saint Bernadette Soubiroux.

This time, opposition to the pope's pilgrimage was fierce. Opponents argued that using public funds to finance the trip violated the French constitution, and they questioned whether Clovis had actually been baptized, throwing the purpose of the pope's journey into doubt.

John Paul II was not deterred, and the results bore him out. He not only met young people again, but he also visited those "wounded by life"—the poor, the abandoned, alcoholics, drug addicts, AIDS victims, and prostitutes—noting in a liturgical celebration in Tours that nothing can erase the image of God reflected in all human beings.

235

THE FEDERAL REPUBLIC, EDITH STEIN, GERMANY REUNIFIED

The German people were another major target of papal travels and pilgrimages. He first went there as pope in 1980, and his trip had a distinct ecumenical focus—joint religious services and meetings with Protestant leaders and with representatives of foreign "guest workers," many of them having lived in Germany for decades.

The pope told them that they had a right to dignified

In 1997, nearly one million young people from all over the world attend the twelfth World Youth Day in Paris.

treatment, adequate compensation, and access to health care and to other benefits given German natives. But he also urged them to preserve their national heritage and religious identity, to care for families they left behind, and to pass on their traditions and culture to the next generation.

His 1987 pilgrimage was much more controversial. He traveled to Cologne for the beatification of two martyrs who were murdered by the Nazis: Father Rupert Mayer and Edith Stein, the Jewish intellectual who converted to Catholicism and took the name Sister Teresa Benedicta of the Cross when she entered the Carmelite Order.

Beatifying Edith Stein (a preliminary step before she was canonized as a saint) provoked violent protests from Jews in Germany and many other countries. Jews who convert to another religion, and especially to Christianity, lose Jewish identity, many Jews believe. Edith Stein converted and entered a convent, changing her name and diving deep into her new religion.

Names played an important role in Judaism. Change

it, and you change your identity. So when Edith Stein became Sister Teresa Benedicta of the Cross, she denied her own self and did this against the greatest tragedy ever inflicted on the Jewish people—the Holocaust. No wonder so many Jews opposed her beatification.

The pope, however, would not be deterred. Her beatification took place on May 1, 1987, in Cologne, where she had entered the Carmelite Order in 1933. In the ceremonnies John Paul II called her "a gift, a call, and a promise for our times. She abandoned herself to God as an 'offering for true peace,' for the sake of her threatened Jewish people."

John Paul II's third visit, in 1996, was to a reunited Germany, and it, too, had special meaning. Together Chancellor Helmut Kohl and the pontiff walked through the newly opened Brandenburg Gate that had once divided Berlin and had symbolized the division of Europe between Communism and democracy. In walking through the gate, it was as if the pope were sanctioning both German reunification and the prospects of European unity.

During this visit Pope John Paul II beatified two other German clerics who had been murdered by the Nazis—Bernhard Lichtenberg and Karol Leisner. Both had openly opposed the Nazi dictatorship. He also met for the third time with the Central Council of German Jews, this time at the Bernhard Lichtenberg House, named for the martyred priest, in Berlin.

In his remarks the pope proclaimed a "message of life" so that Jews and Christians could live together in peace and mutual understanding. "We ask God to bless our common path. May Germany and Europe succeed in resisting the forces of death, open up to the message of life, and to stride into the third millennium under the sign of a new hope. Shalom!"

In his reply Ignatz Bubis, president of the Central Council, called for renewed cooperation between Jews and Christians to combat all forms of anti-Semitism. He thanked the pope for his efforts to build new bridges between the two faiths but also warned against the outbreak of a new anti-Semitism in Europe. He recalled a pogrom in Poland immediately after the war and called upon all religions to cooperate in combating anti-Semitism wherever it occurred.

AUSTRIA: MEMORY OF THE TURKS AND OF EUROPE

John Paul II visited Austria three times during his pontificate. It was a region he knew well from his sojourns as archbishop of Kraków when he had often stayed there. On his first pilgrimage in 1983, he recalled the 300th anniversary of the second Turkish siege of Vienna in 1683 that was lifted by allied armies under the command of Polish king Jan III Sobieski. That victory, he noted, stopped Islamic expansion into Europe and began the decline of the Turkish Empire. Seen from today's perspective, however, that conflict could be seen as a new opportunity for interethnic and interfaith coexistence in Austria and Europe.

And as the pope did in most countries he visited, he used the occasion for ecumenical meetings with leaders of other religions. In Vienna he saw representatives of the Eastern Orthodox churches of Serbia, Romania, Russia, Bulgaria, leaders of the Armenian, Coptic, and Syrian churches, and Anglicans, Evangelical Christians, and Baptists.

In a homily at St. Stephen's Cathedral in Vienna, the Holy Father pointed out the basic unity of Europe's cultures and stressed their common roots in Christianity. These bonds, he predicted, would prove stronger than the physical wall in Berlin and the Iron Curtain, which then divided the European continent and seemed to have become a permanent institution. John Paul II's vision foresaw European unity based on common Christian traditions.

When he visited Austria for a third time, in 1998, he noted that the political divisions in Europe may have ended but that new invisible forces continued to divide and separate people—economic disparities, materialism, moral permissiveness, and the loss of faith in so many places.

SPAIN: AN APPEAL TO FAITH AND YOUTH

The Holy Father traveled to Spain five times during his pontificate, with his last visit in 2003. He came first in November 1982 and spent 10 days crisscrossing the country and visiting 17 holy sites before ending his journey in Santiago de Compostela, the city of Saint James the Apostle, an ancient pilgrimage site.

The pope recalled the role of the city over the centuries when pilgrims from across Spain and all over Europe flocked to the cathedral to pray and renew their faith in God. "The road to Santiago sparked a vigorous spiritual and cultural exchange among the peoples of Europe," the pope said, urging Europe to find itself again. "Europe, know thyself! Rediscover your roots. Make them send up vigorous shoots again. Bring back to life the authentic values that shaped your glorious history and made your presence and your contributions to other countries so beneficial."

The pontiff returned to Santiago de Compostela in August 1989 for the Second World Youth Day, and it seemed as if pilgrims heeded the advice he had given seven years before. Some 600,000 flocked to the burial

During his 1996 visit to the Federal Republic of Germany, John Paul II and Chancellor Helmut Kohl walk through the Brandenburg Gate, which had once been the border between East Berlin and West Berlin.

place of Saint James, and they came from everywhere. They used trains, buses, planes, boats, and bicycles, and many of them walked, as pilgrims of old had done and as John Paul II did, along the footpath to the shrine.

He wore a penitent's cloak and carried a pilgrim's staff. Seven hundred young people, also robed as penitents, accompanied him. They sang the Litany of the Saints as they marched, and in his homily the pope likened the road they had traveled to an "expression of a profound spirituality of conversion." He urged his young audience to live their lives in love and concern for others. "The road that leads to Christ is not an easy one, since it may lead to the cross. But no other road leads to truth and life."

The pope would return to Spain twice more—in 1993 to attend the celebrations of the 46th International Eucharistic Congress held in Seville, and again in 2003,

(CONTINUED ON PAGE 240)

Trip Logistics

The white Alitalia jet is poised and waiting on the Fiumicino airport runway near Rome. A flurry of last-minute preparations for the pope's flight are under way, and the scene resembles an action-packed adventure film. Armored police vans patrol the area with sharpshooters inside, ready to move against any threat. Another van pulls up beside the plane and will stay there until takeoff.

John Paul II usually arrived in a helicopter minutes before his flight was scheduled to leave. He would greet all those gathered to see him off—some of his Vatican staff, several members of the Italian government, and a few Rome City officials. The black cassocks of waiting priests flap in the wind. Swiss Guards would line up behind the armed security guards, discreetly keeping watch. As the Holy Father made his way toward the aircraft, the Swiss Guard would raise their swords in a farewell salute. The jet with the Holy Father aboard would take off for a foreign land.

John Paul II always left Rome on an Alitalia jet and returned in an aircraft of the country he had visited. The pope was a modest person with simple needs. He eschewed the impressive conference rooms that are standard on corporate jets and made do with a table and four chairs placed near the front of the aircraft. Usually he sat next to the window, which had a cross hanging over it.

Cardinal Angelo Sodano, the Vatican secretary of state, and about 30 top papal aides would occupy a larger space behind the pope's enclave. Among those who usually traveled with the pontiff were Bishop Piero Marini, master of ceremonies; Archbishop Giovanni Baptists Re, undersecretary of state; Joaquín Navarro-Valls, director of the Vatican Press Office; Dr. Renato Buzzonetti, the pope's personal physician and director of health services at the Vatican; Angelo Gudel, a member of the pope's household staff; and Camillo Cibin, Vatican chief of security.

Another section of the plane was reserved for minor Vatican officials and support staff, and finally, the rear of the plane was set aside for journalists from all over the world, television and camcorder technicians, photographers, and others. Since the same group of people usually traveled with the pope, they knew one another quite well.

Even though the clergy wore religious garb, the atmosphere was relaxed. Vik Van Brantegem, Navarro-Valls's assistant, managed the press corps, whose flight program was carefully laid out so that each one would get his or her allotted time with Vatican officials.

As the pope flew over various countries, telegrams were sent to heads of state (with copies going to journalists). Each message said the following:

Your Excellency,
I am undertaking my next pilgrimage to (country name is mentioned). As I fly over the airspace of your country, I would like to express warm wishes to you and your entire nation.

John Paul II, Pope

Arturo Mari, the official photographer, would snap hundreds of pictures of the pope wherever he went, and people shown with him in the photographs usually wanted to buy them. Profits from their sale helped defray expenses.

Father Roberto Tucci, S.J., commander of the Swiss Guard, was in charge of the pope's schedule. The slim white-haired priest in his early sixties always had a microphone attached to the collar of his jacket so he could give orders to guards and other personnel.

WHEN THE POPE FROM POLAND IS INVOLVED, SOMETHING UNEXPECTED ALWAYS HAPPENS

Once a decision was reached on which country to visit next, Father Tucci took over as the advance man. Six months before the pope's scheduled arrival, he would scout the new terrain. He previewed scheduled events. He checked the route the pope would travel to highlight potential danger spots. He recorded the time it would take to get from one place to another, and he jotted down, in meticulous detail, information about places where the pope would meet with other people and where he would officiate at religious ceremonies.

The popemobile waits inside a container truck, ready for the next papal voyage.

A detailed itinerary was then developed from his notes. The final draft, usually about 100 pages long, contained all the details of the pope's proposed schedule: where he would go and what time he would arrive at each place; venues of meetings and how long they would last; where the pope would sit or stand at events; who would take photos and when and where cameras would be placed. Copies of the schedule were distributed to everyone on the plane, including journalists.

Such careful planning helped assure smooth sailing except when John Paul II decided to do something not on the schedule, which happened often. In Kraków in 1992, the Holy Father announced he wanted to return to the Main Square. Police and papal guards had to scramble in order to secure the surrounding area. The "papal whim" in Kraków lasted just a few minutes, but it threw the whole day off schedule. Meals were another problem. Nobody seemed to know just when the pope would eat and with whom—especially when he went home to Poland.

John Paul II's tight schedule often made it difficult for him to arrive on time. But he tended to joke about his habitual tardiness. "The two-hour delay proves the pilgrimage was a complete success," he said in Ireland. When his schedule in Canada was impossible to keep, he just smiled and said, "It's not my fault. Blame the people who organized my trip."

WHY ALL THOSE TRIPS?

The pope was on the road the better part of every year.

"Why do you keep going all over the world all the time?" Alessandro Monno, an eleven-year-old boy, asked the Holy Father when he visited St. Benedict parish in Rome.

"Because the whole world is not here," the pope replied.

"Do you travel around like a tourist?" the boy asked.

"That would be wonderful, if I could, but I have to stick to protocol. Why are you asking me all these questions?"

The boy didn't answer, so John Paul II then finished his own thoughts. "Have you ever read what Jesus said about going and proclaiming the Gospel to the whole world? That's why I travel all around the world."

THE PALLIUM AND THE SHOES

The pope's household staff packed his luggage for every trip with great care and attention to detail. John Paul II always brought the crucifix Pope Paul VI carried when he traveled. He wore the ring with the papal insignia on it. Texts of his homilies and speeches were placed in a special briefcase.

Angelo Gudel selected the pope's clothing, making sure that all the vestments he would need for various events were packed and that they would be suitable for the climate of the places he visited. Sister Matilde, one of the five sisters of the Servants of the Sacred Heart of Jesus from Kraków who lived at the Vatican, double checked to ascertain that the pope's cassocks, skullcaps, liturgical robes, and miters were in his suitcases. Often he didn't need them, however, because they were generally given to him as gifts.

The pallium, a white woolen band about five centimeters wide and embroidered with black crosses that symbolize the pope's supreme ecclesiastical power, was packed in a special box. His shoes, white socks, and white woolen slippers were not to be overlooked. The pope ordinarily wore comfortable cordovan-colored, soft leather shoes, size nine. He also liked heavy-duty shoes specially made for him by the British shoemaker Airwair.

John Paul II prepared carefully for each pilgrimage. He wrote most of his greetings, addresses, and homilies, and whenever the pope could, he spoke the native language of each country he visited—especially his replies to those who welcomed him upon his arrival. He practiced the greetings before departing. In preparation for his journey to Brazil, he celebrated daily Mass in Portuguese in his private Vatican chapel and asked two religious sisters from Brazil and Portugal to correct him. In the end, as always, he surprised the crowds of the faithful with his fluent Portuguese.

John Paul II with Vaclav Havel, president of the Czech Republic, in 1995.

when 700,000 young people gathered to hear him at an airfield outside Madrid. He repeated then what he had told another young audience in Santiago de Compostela 20 years before: "I continue to believe in you. You are the hope of the church, no less than of society."

THE NETHERLANDS, SO DIFFICULT

Not all the pope's pilgrimages proved as easy and as fruitful as those he made to Spain. In 1985 he traveled to the Benelux countries and ran into virulent opposition, especially in the Netherlands. Anticlerical groups distributed pamphlets and brochures attacking the pontiff's stand on sexual education, abortion, euthanasia, and the ordination of women. Some were downright offensive.

Protesters took to the streets carrying banners that said, "Pope Go Rome" and "Jesus Christ, Yes. The Church, No." Television programs poked fun at the pope's kissing the earth and blessing people on his arrival.

John Paul II made no conciliatory overtures to his less-than-gracious hosts. He talked to Dutch crowds the same way he spoke to people in other countries. He stressed the traditional teachings of the church. He reminded his audiences that the church in Holland could look back on 1,500 years of glorious history. He praised the social activism the Dutch church had displayed through more than 5,000 missionaries who worked across the globe.

But he also addressed the identity crisis the Dutch church had experienced during Vatican II, when it had challenged aspects of traditional church teachings about morality. Religious vocations were in dramatic decline. Laymen were taking over ministerial functions the church reserved for priests. Some even officiated at religious services of other denominations and without ecclesiastical approval.

In a meeting with priests in Utrecht, the pope praised the consecrated life of priests as a "sign of contradiction" to the secular world, and he urged them to bear witness to their vocation and to their mission in today's rapidly changing world. Leading a consecrated life, he told them, brings important values to the fore, such as life in priestly communities, the practice of obedience as a virtue, and spirituality imbued with prayer.

In Belgium the pope spoke to the faithful in the nation's two languages—French and Flemish—and paid

The pope greets young people at the World Youth Day in Santiago de Compostela in Spain in 1989.

special attention to the problems different nationalities face when they live together in one country and both have to strive for the common good. He also addressed a host of other issues of concern: the mission of laypeople in the church, the religious dimension of fine arts, the role of the Catholic University in Louvain, and the lifestyle of Christians who live and work in any large and modern metropolis such as Brussels.

Given his tight schedule, the pope could not hold a press conference or meet with individual members of the media. So he left them a written message that stressed the dignity of every man, woman, and child on earth. "No one can be completely defeated; every person can always discover his or her true strength and radiance."

THAT THEY MAY ALL BE ONE

The pope's journey to the Scandinavian countries in 1989 must have seemed a pilgrimage into a hostile land, given that most Scandinavians are Lutheran. But for this pope, the voyage was an ecumenical opportunity. His reception was often frosty, especially in Denmark, where the bishops of Roskild barred him from speaking to general audiences, and he was restricted to Catholic churches for holding ecumenical services. And while far fewer people came out to see him than in other, more Catholic countries, he still met with thousands of well-wishers. His reception in Finland and Sweden, moreover, was much friendlier, since those countries had more Catholics.

Wherever he spoke, John Paul II stressed the need for greater openness among the various Christian communities. He praised the progress that had already been achieved and pledged that Rome would continue to foster ecumenical dialogue and develop friendly ties with other Christian churches.

Back home, the pope told a general audience at the Vatican on June 14, 1989, that his inspiration for this pilgrimage lay in the Gospel where Jesus had said: *That they may all be one. As you, Father, are in me and I am in you* (John 17:21). His journey, he said, had been "a pilgrimage to the beginnings of Christianity in Nordic Europe," which dated back to the ninth century.

"The sincere and cordial reception we received often seemed more like a joyful reunion of brothers who were reunited after many years. We renewed our promise of love and expressed it by praying together. This was an affirmation of the hope that inspires the ecumenical movement. A mutual love was born of the strong promise that we would do everything we could to overcome existing difficulties."

AFTER THE FALL: EASTERN EUROPE BECKONS

For more than 10 years, Poland was the only Communist country willing to have John Paul II visit. The regime had no choice, given that the new pope was Polish.

In the 1980s Yugoslavia also seemed ready to welcome the pontiff. And for a while in 1984, it seemed as if the trip would come off. Cardinal Franjo Kuharic, the archbishop of Zagreb, even announced that preparations for a papal journey had begun. But negotiations dragged on, and the visit kept being postponed. And the rest of Eastern Europe, of course, continued to be off-limits.

All that changed in 1989 as Communism began to disintegrate. The pope wanted to visit Hungary first, and in August of that year, the Communist government and the nation's bishops extended a joint invitation for 1991, but events dictated a different schedule.

During his 1985 visit to the Netherlands, some people go all out to show the pope he is not welcome.

On December 29, 1989, Vaclav Havel was elected president of Czechoslovakia and made one of his first trips abroad to the Vatican. A date was set quickly—John Paul II would visit that country on April 20–21, 1990. What a change! Only months before, this had been a virulently anti-Catholic state, especially hostile to the Polish pope.

One purpose of his trip was to pay homage to Cardinal Frantisek Tomasek, the ninety-year-old archbishop of Prague, who had spent decades in heroic opposition to the Communist regime. Another was to pay tribute to the missionary activities of saints Cyril and Methodias, the apostles to the Slavs, by visiting Welehrad, a small town in Moravia, linked to their activities.

In Prague the pope delivered a homily to priests and other religious people gathered in St. Vitus Cathedral, part of Hradcin Castle overlooking the city. He praised them for keeping the faith despite harsh persecution and called on them to confront the challenges of their newly won freedom. At a meeting with theologians, he said the case of Jan Hus, a dissident theologian who was burned at the stake for heresy during the Council of Constance in 1415, should be reviewed and reevaluated.

The pope went again in 1995, and this trip was far more controversial. His purpose was to canonize Jan Sarkander, a priest murdered by Czech Protestants in 1619 and whom the church had long considered a martyr. Czech Protestants were outraged and demanded the pontiff scrap the ceremony. They charged that Father Sarkander had been engaged in forcible conversions of Protestants. Not so, the pope said, citing scholarly research that showed the priest had never engaged in violence against Czech Protestants, and he went ahead with the canonization.

Protestants boycotted an ecumenical ceremony to show their displeasure. The pope sent a handwritten letter offering to explain his decision. It was refused. So at the end of the canonization Mass in the town of Olomuniec, the pope asked his opponents to forgive Catholics for the harm they had done them in the past and offered to pardon all those who had ever done violence to the Catholic Church. His offer touched everyone present at the ceremony, but it did not bridge the gap and Czech Protestants were still angry.

It took longer to arrange the journey to Hungary, but in August 1991 Hungarian president Arpad Goench was on hand to welcome the pontiff and to recall the deep bonds of friendship between Hungarians and Poles. John Paul II traveled across the country and, as was his habit, met with Protestant and Jewish leaders.

The pope visited Hungary for a second time in 1996 to celebrate the thousand-year anniversary of the Benedictine Abbey in Pannonhalma. The abbot suggested that this ancient cloister, founded before the split between the Catholic and the Orthodox churches in 1054, might be a good place for a meeting between the pope and the Orthodox patriarch of Moscow and all Russia, Aleksij II.

The Holy Father was delighted. He had long sought to visit Russia and meet with the Orthodox hierarchy. But Patriarch Aleksij delayed the meeting on one pretext after another, and it never happened.

ALBANIA: A CHURCH REBORN

On April 25, 1993, the pope visited Albania, a country that for a quarter of a century had proclaimed that it was the world's first atheist state. John Paul II consecrated four Albanian bishops in the recently restored cathedral in Shkodra. In his homily he spoke of a church reborn with the newly consecrated bishops restoring a hierarchy devastated during the Communist regime. He recalled the tragic past Albanian Catholics had endured and said, "We must not forget what happened! It's good to look ahead to the future, to build it in freedom so that men and women will benefit from it, but we must also remember the lessons of the past in order to avoid repeating their errors in the future." He went on, "What happened in Albania is unprecedented in the history of the world.... Albania sank into an abyss and only through a miracle found its way out without bloodshed. When everything seemed lost, freedom arrived."

THE BALTICS: A CHURCH RESTORED

In September of that year, the Holy Father traveled to the three Baltic states—Lithuania, Latvia, and Estonia—that had been under Soviet rule for almost 50 years and where the church had also been repressed.

He had hoped to visit Lithuania before the collapse of the Soviet Union when Mikhail Gorbachev's *perestroika* had seemed to offer a chance and everyone thought that the road to the Baltic countries ran through Moscow. Instead, when he landed in Vilnius, the president, the prime minister, and the nation's bishops were lined up at the tarmac to greet him.

As he had done across Eastern Europe, the pope recalled the recent past, paid homage to those who had suffered under the Communist regime, and proclaimed the new challenges the church faced in all three countries. He cited Lithuania for special attention because the nation has the largest Catholic population in the region. Ethnic Polish communities, for example, had suffered from religious discrimination, and it was high time to improve relations among national groupings.

One highlight of his pilgrimage was a visit to the Mountain of Crosses, near the town of Szawly. Over the decades Lithuanian pilgrims had placed thousands of crosses in the woods near town. No matter how hard the Communists tried to stop the planting of new crosses, they could not do so. As soon as crosses were destroyed, new ones sprouted, often the next day.

This place, the pope said, was testimony to the mystery of the power of the cross. Planting them "became a

When he arrives in Albania to consecrate four bishops in 1993, John Paul II proclaims that the church in Albania was reborn out of the blood of martyrs.

providential fountain of blessings for the church and a sign for reconciliation within this nation and with other peoples."

In Lithuania, where 10 percent of the population is of Polish descent, the pope spoke in Lithuanian and Italian, not in Polish, in order to avoid offending Lithuanians. In Latvia, however, he often spoke Polish even though far fewer Poles lived there. While in Latvia he placed the peoples of the Baltic nations under the care of the Blessed Mother of God.

His visit to Estonia was brief, only 10 hours, because that small country has only a few Catholics. Still, he managed to visit a small Catholic community of about 100 people. He assisted at an ecumenical service in the Lutheran church of St. Nicholas and celebrated Mass in the main square of Tallinn, the Estonian capital.

ON THE PATHS OF A BLOODY WAR

The Balkans would prove another matter. As Yugoslavia fell apart, bloody war erupted and papal pilgrimages became impossible. Over and over, the pope pleaded with combatants to stop fighting and return to peace and justice, but to no avail. He did, however, recognize the

right of every nation in Yugoslavia to go its own way and form independent states. And the Vatican was the first government to recognize Slovenia, Croatia, and, later, Bosnia-Herzegovina. (The Holy See also recognized an independent Slovakia when that country peacefully broke up the Czechoslovak union.)

Not until September 1994 did the pope travel to the region, and at that he had to postpone a planned visit to Bosnia-Herzegovina. The day before he was to start out, on September 8, United Nations peacekeepers told the Vatican they could not guarantee the pope's safety. Two days later, however, John Paul II arrived in Croatia, the scene of bloody fighting with Serbia only the year before.

He received a warm reception from the government, church leaders, and the people. In his first address he called for reconciliation and the rebuilding of trust and mutual respect. On his second Croatian pilgrimage in 1998, he paid the highest church tribute to perhaps the most tragic figure in Catholic Croatia, Cardinal Alojzie Stepinac, who had suffered imprisonment under the Nazis and the Communists. An unshakable defender of human dignity, he had spent years in harsh confinement, first in jails and later under house arrest. During a Mass he celebrated in Zagreb, John Paul II beatified this heroic figure of the Catholic faith.

In April 1997 the pope finally made it to Sarajevo, spending a day in the war-ravaged capital of Bosnia-Herzegovina. The visit turned into a spectacular success

The pope holds a press conference during one of his many flights abroad.

as the pontiff called for establishing a lasting peace and met with representatives of all religious groups in the country—Muslims, Jews, and members of the Orthodox Church.

Although the pope has not managed a trip to Moscow, he did have a chance to visit a country where the majority of the population was Orthodox—Romania. For a long time this dream, too, seemed out of reach because of tensions between Greek Catholics, who acknowledge the sovereignty of Rome, and the Orthodox Christians who do not.

Finally tensions between the two religious groups began to relax, and in May 1999 the pope set foot on Romanian soil. He was warmly received by both Catholics of various rites and by Orthodox Christians. His message was the same one he had given elsewhere in the region—a call to unity, a call echoed by thousands of the faithful at the end of an open-air Mass he celebrated in Bucharest's main square. Again he praised those who had kept their faith during all the years of Communist persecution.

A legacy of that persecution remained. Back in 1948 the Communists had dissolved the Greek Catholic Church and handed its property to the Orthodox clergy. Deep hatred between the two religions resulted, and if they had not begun to mend their differences, the pope could not have traveled to Romania.

The Holy See is a political entity with the pope as its chief of state, a role that makes the pope a player on the global stage.

Chapter 16

Keeping the Peace

Politics and international relations are not the primary focus of the Catholic Church, especially in the post–Vatican II Council era. The council fathers had emphasized the spiritual nature of the church and urged the clergy to stay out of politics. This principle may be correct, but it is frequently compromised. Unlike other Christian denominations, the Catholic Church is a political state subject to international law. It occupies a very small territory (112 acres), in which the Holy See is located. Its official name is the Vatican City State, and it maintains diplomatic relations with other nations, belongs to a number of international organizations, and takes an active part in the political life of the world.

Consequently, the pope is not only the head of the Catholic Church but also a political leader, just like any other head of state. John Paul II's involvement in the political arena started at the beginning of his papacy when he sent an envoy to mediate a Chile-Argentina dispute, attended a meeting of Latin American bishops to caution them against the Marxist ideas in liberation theology, and began his campaign to bring freedom to the Soviet-bloc states of Eastern Europe, starting with his beloved Poland.

THE OLDEST DIPLOMATIC TRADITION IN THE WORLD

His efforts were part of a long-standing tradition. For 2,000 years the Catholic Church has been active in international affairs. The Holy See has one of the oldest and most effective diplomatic corps in the world. Vatican diplomats and employees in nunciatures are ordained priests, bishops, and consecrated religious sisters, and they combine professional diplomatic practices with active ministry in the church.

The papal ambassador, or apostolic nuncio, to a country is always an archbishop who takes an active role in the religious life of the country in which he exercises his diplomatic duties. As an apostolic minister, he takes part in conferences of the country's bishops, participates in liturgical ceremonies, and ordains priests and bishops if necessary. At the same time, he is a member of the diplomatic corps; in countries that are predominately Catholic, he is usually a senior member. Lesser members of the church's diplomatic corps take part in the life of the local church.

All Vatican diplomats are graduates of the Pontifical Ecclesiastic Academy. Founded in 1706, this academy trains clerics who will serve in the Vatican diplomatic corps with a two-year course

This building houses the Vatican Secretariat of State.

of study that includes Canon Law, world history, church history, principles of diplomacy, and languages, among other subjects. About 20 students graduate each year. After graduation, church diplomats-in-training work for two years in various offices of the Roman Curia, especially in the Secretariat of State, where they gain practical experience. The training is arduous and thorough; five graduates of the pontifical diplomatic academy have gone on to become pope. To gain additional experience, the diplomats-in-training are next assigned to advisory positions in different countries for an average stay of three or four years. Only after many years of living and working abroad are they assigned as papal nuncio to a particular country. At that time, the pope nominates the new papal nuncio as a titular archbishop. The papal nuncio will usually be assigned to a country for four or five years before he is transferred. Some nuncios, however, have stayed 10 years or more in one country.

The history of the papacy has many examples of popes and their diplomats who worked toward peace among nations. While kings in the Middle Ages waged constant wars, the church proposed the *Treuga Dei*, or God's Truce, as a way to suspend (and limit) warfare on certain feast days and during the liturgical seasons of Lent and Advent. Popes took similar initiatives in mediations between European sovereigns both during and after the Renaissance. The Holy See was the chief arbiter between Catholic rulers.

ON EVERYONE'S BEHALF

John Paul II has revitalized Vatican diplomacy and raised its prestige. October 20, 1978—four days after he was elected pope but before he officially began his pontificate—he held a special audience with the diplomatic corps of the Holy See. In this address John Paul II presented the Catholic Church's principles of diplomacy and his own expectations of diplomacy in general and Vatican diplomacy in particular.

"The church has always desired to take part in the life of all nations and to contribute to the development of all people. The church has always recognized the plurality of cultures and the contribution that the history and language of each culture make to the rich diversity of cultures. In many cases, the church has made its own particular contribution to the formation of these cultures, and it continues to believe that international relations should be based on the respect for the rights of every nation."

Reflecting on the role of diplomatic relations, the pope went on to say that this does not mean that church

John Paul II meets with then recently elected president of the United States, George W. Bush, at Castel Gandolfo on July 23, 2001.

diplomats should confuse the realms of church and state; nor should they pass judgment on any given regime. Their role is just to recognize positive worldly values in national states and be willing to carry on a dialogue with legitimate political leaders who are in charge of the welfare of their society. The church diplomats must be aware that their role will always be difficult as they try to understand human aspirations and help to promote them. They accomplish this sometimes by intervening directly but, most of all, by helping to make people aware of justice and peace issues.

Mindful of the example of Jesus Christ, the pope continued, the Holy See must not abandon its pastoral task. Every pontifical diplomat must carry out Christ's directives, show interest in the welfare and development of nations, and teach people salvation. "Is this not the main responsibility and task of the church?" he asked.

Pope John Paul II waits to deliver his address to the United Nations General Assembly on October 2, 1979.

At the same time, John Paul II stressed how important it was for nations to take people's religious needs into account and to guarantee religious freedom so that people can profess their beliefs without penalty. They should be allowed to take part in the life of their society as full-fledged citizens. The Holy See acts in everybody's interest without exception. Respect for people's life, freedom, and dignity is the foundation of harmonious relations in societies. A person is never just an instrument or a means to an end. Progress for each citizen and for the cultural life of any society as a whole is based on treating all people as fundamentally equal, performing work with professional competence, and everybody working together for the common good with a mind-set of reconciliation and openness to spiritual values.

THE VATICAN RECONCILES ENEMIES

John Paul II's active interventions in the international scene were made by discourses, letters, sermons, and meetings with political leaders both on their home territory and in Rome. His concern was for the dignity and innate rights of the common man and, above all, the right to life from the moment of conception to the point of natural death. He opposed abortion and the use of contraceptives, and he opposed the death penalty. The pope's stance was not limited to a narrow religious interpretation, since on many occasions he interceded on behalf of the rights of all human beings, no matter what philosophical or faith belief they professed.

John Paul II's many trips (see Chapter 15) demonstrated the Holy See's presence and the pope's personal interest in the public and political life of the world. He always presented himself to the world as the head of the Catholic Church and Vatican chief of state and was welcomed by officials at the highest levels of government, as well as local church bishops. John Paul II has also met with government leaders and foreign diplomats in his offices at the Vatican or in Castel Gandolfo. Government leaders frequently asked John Paul II to intervene to help resolve conflicts in their countries.

MEDIATION BY THE HOLY SEE

One such intervention was the Vatican's mediation—including John Paul II's personal involvement—in a territorial conflict between Argentina and Chile that had been threatening to break into war for some time. The problem concerned a dispute about territorial rights to three islands in Beagle Channel in the Strait of Magellan and the waters that surround them. In 1972 Pope Paul VI and Cardinal Antonio Samore had begun an attempt to mediate the dispute. At first, their deliberations were fruitless, but in the end, the foreign affairs ministers of both countries signed documents in Montevideo on January 6, 1979, making a mutual promise not to resort to the use of armed forces and to again ask for the official intervention of the Holy See. John Paul II, who had just become pope, sent a Vatican representative to both countries. This time negotiations were no swifter, but they eventually came to a favorable conclusion. On January 23, 1984, the chancellors of both countries signed a joint declaration of peace and friendship that went into effect after an exchange of ratifying documents on May 2, 1985, at the Vatican.

Peace was an integral part of John Paul II's message as he traveled the world. During his visit to Ireland in 1979, he said, "Don't place your trust in military might; don't rely on violence. This is not the Christian way. This is not the way of the Catholic Church. Believe in peace, forgiveness, and love, because they are of Christ."

During the 1980s, in the first part of John Paul II's pontificate, world peace was threatened by the cold war between the West and the Soviet bloc in the East. The arms race between the United States and the Soviet Union, the only countries with major nuclear arsenals, kept nuclear war at bay—at least until the collapse of the Soviet Union, when the equation changed. The emergence of other, smaller countries with nuclear arms capabilities, like India and Pakistan, then Iran and North Korea, offered new threats.

THE ACT OF PENANCE

After a trip to India in 1986, when John Paul II addressed an audience of Hindus, Muslims, Sikhs, Buddhists, Jainists, Parsees, and Christians, he got the idea for organizing an interfaith World Day of Prayer for Peace. He envisioned a great prayer to God—invoked in many names and many languages—to save the world from nuclear annihilation, end the cold war, and bring universal peace. He picked Assisi, the home of Saint Francis, the most peace-loving of Christian saints, for the ecumenical assemblage.

On October 27, 1986, representatives of 27 Christian denominations, 37 delegations from 13 non-Christian religions, and a group of more than 150 bishops of the Catholic Church, whom the pope personally invited, gathered together in the churches and cathedrals of Assisi to pray. They

A supplicant's hands asking the pope's blessing in Damascus on May 7, 2001.

met John Paul II on an open plain. Together the religious participants represented 4 billion believers from 65 faiths and denominations.

"For the first time in history, we have met with people from all over the world—Christians of other denominations and those who believe in other religions—in this holy sanctuary dedicated to Saint Francis," the pope said. "Each of us, according to our own faith beliefs, give testimony before the whole world that peace has a transcendent character. At the same time, I must recognize in all humility that Catholics have not always been faithful to the convictions of our faith. We have not always 'kept the peace.'"

John Paul II stressed that for him, the valid path to take included dialogue, respect for freedom, freedom of religion, and solidarity with the poor. Truth is the force that sustains peace that is born in the heart of any person who has the courage to not recognize divisions. The wellspring of peace is reconciliation with God, the Creator, and all of God's creation.

PRAYERS THAT STOPPED WARFARE

A few weeks before the World Day of Prayer for Peace, the pope launched an appeal for a universal truce on that day; it would be a symbolic halt to all the armed conflicts around the world. He and his bishops and nuncios contacted all the warring parties. Armies and guerilla groups in Ireland, Lebanon, the Philippines, Nicaragua, El Salvador, Chile, India, Sri Lanka, Sudan, and Angola suspended warfare for all or part of the day. Governments not involved in wars, at the church's request, organized a moment of silent meditation.

To John Paul II the day was a success. He saw the event as a living illustration of the type of ecumenism and interreligious dialogue that had been urged in the Vatican II Council. He also believed that the World Day of Prayer for Peace marked a turning point in the cold war and the nuclear arms race.

FREE US FROM PESTILENCE, HUNGER, AND WAR

John Paul II followed the disintegration of the former Yugoslavia attentively and used every means within his power to terminate war in the Balkans during 1992 and 1993. He warned, "We cannot look on this tragedy with indifference!" He proclaimed Sunday, January 24, 1994, as a Day of Prayer for the Gift of Peace in the Balkans and called for a two-day period of fasting to accompany the day of prayer. In September of the same year, after the cancellation of his pilgrimage to the Balkans, the pope celebrated Mass in Castel Gandolfo for the intention of peace in this region. He prayed: "Our Father…I, the bishop of Rome, the first Slavic pope, am on my knees before you and to you do I place my petition. Free us from pestilence, hunger, and war! I know that many join me in this request. Not only here but also in Sarajevo, in Bosnia-Herzegovina, in all of Europe, and beyond its borders."

The pope's pilgrimage to Sarajevo finally took place in April 1997. Here the pope said: "No more war! No more hatred and intolerance!... That is what this century and the millennium that is just about to end have taught us…. We have to substitute the inhuman logic of oppression by the constructive logic of peace. The wiping out of vengeance has to make way for the liberating strength of forgiveness, which is opposed to the nationalist fanaticism that leads to ethnic conflicts."

John Paul II returned to defend peace in the Balkans in the spring of 1999 as hundreds of thousands of Albanian refugees were driven out of Kosovo by the Federal Republic of Yugoslavia's and Serbian troops. NATO bombed Serbia to stop the "ethnic cleansing" of the Albanians and sent in a peacekeeping force. The Holy Father took advantage of any opportunity to publicly express his firm conviction that "the sequence of hatred and violence can only be broken by the force of brotherhood, rights, and justice."

A similar sequence of hatred and violence generated mass genocide of the civilian population in Rwanda. Hutus killed some 800,000 Tutsis and moderate Hutus and sent two million refugees across the country's borders in 1994, while the United Nations and the world looked on without interfering. Many priests and three bishops (among them the archbishop of Kigali) were killed. John Paul II called for a Synod of African Bishops to protest "the violations, the tragedies, and the fighting among brothers." He cried: "Let go of hatred, put down the weapons that have shed so much blood in this beaten-down region. In the name of God, put down your weapons immediately! Rwanda and all of Africa are in need of peace."

The pope also interceded on behalf of victims of civil wars in East Timor, Sudan, Chad, and Peru. He expressed his solidarity with persons deprived of essential human rights when he visited the Palestinian refugee camp in Dehiesheh during his trip to the Holy Land in 2000. In March 2003, before the imminent invasion of Iraq by the United States and Great Britain to depose the dictator Saddam Hussein, the pope challenged those two nations to first exhaust all diplomatic means to force Iraq to comply with United Nations Security Council regulations regarding weapons of mass destruction.

WE ARE ALL RESPONSIBLE

During his pilgrimages the pope did not overlook the wars that had caused genocide. He visited the Nazi concentration camps in Auschwitz, Majdanek, and Mauthausen, and he visited the sites of atomic bombings in Hiroshima and Nagasaki, Japan. On June 7, 1979, at Auschwitz, the pope said: "Auschwitz is a place that I cannot visit as if it were just a museum. As we visit this place, we have to fearfully reflect about the broad extent of hatred. Auschwitz is a witness to war and war brings with it the limitless increase of hatred, destruction, and cruelty. We cannot deny that human courage, heroism, and patriotism were also demonstrated here, but the overall result is a negative one. And over time, war is becoming a struggle of the technology of destruction, which has increased negative effects. Those who directly cause war and those who do not do everything within their power to stop war are both equally responsible for it."

FOR THE NEW MILLENNIUM

In a millennium address on January 10, 2000, John Paul II said: "This person who is speaking to you was a companion on the road with several generations in the past century. He was a participant in the painful experiences of his own nation and he lived through the darkest moments in the history of Europe. Since that time, he has been Successor of St. Peter for more than twenty-one years and feels called to a universal fatherhood that reaches all people of our time without exception.

"Today…he wants to share with everyone the following thought. At this moment when the doors to the new millennium are opening, the pope is convinced that humanity can finally come to conclusions about the past. Therefore, in the name of God, I beg you to abhor the inhumanity of war, to respect human life and family life, to close the gap between the rich and the poor, and to realize that we are all responsible for each other. That is what God is asking of us, and God never asks us anything that is beyond our strength. God also gives us the strength to accomplish whatever God asks of us."

THE RIGHTS OF NATIONS ARE HUMAN RIGHTS

During his pontificate John Paul II spoke many times before international organizations such as the United Nations General Assembly, the United Nations Economic and Social Council, the International Labor Organization, and the United Nations Food and Agriculture Organization. On these occasions he presented the Catholic Church's position on world issues.

Concern for peace and international security, the need for human solidarity, and the inherent dignity of the human being are the themes he returned to over and over. The pope was not guided solely by ideological and religious issues. He cared for everybody—Catholics and Christians of other denominations, non-Christians, and atheists. He condemned the embargo the United Nations imposed on Iraq in August 1990 because he thought it mainly affected the Iraqi people, not their leaders. John Paul II admonished Iraq as an aggressor state that endangered peace in the world. The pope also did everything he

could to stop the invasion of Iraq by the United States and Great Britain in March 2003 because they had not first exhausted every diplomatic means of dealing with Iraq. The pope also suggested that the Security Council of the United Nations had not put enough political pressure on Iraq.

Representatives of many religions pray together for peace at the World Day of Prayer for Peace in Assisi, sponsored by John Paul II, on October 27, 1986.

The United Nations was always close to the pope's heart, going back to his first visit on October 2, 1979, when he told the secretary-general that "the message I want to leave with you is a message of assurance and of hope, assurance that peace is possible if it is based on the recognition of the fatherhood of God and the brotherhood of mankind; the hope that the sense of moral responsibility that every person should assume will make it possible to create a better world in liberty, in justice, and in love."

Speaking before the General Assembly the same day, he said: "Not only does the Holy See hold collaboration with the United Nations in high regard but from the birth of the organization has always expressed the high esteem and approval in which it holds this highest forum of international life and contemporary humanity." This high regard, the pope added, "is not the result of political reasons alone, but stems from the same moral and religious nature of the Roman Catholic Church's mission."

When he visited the United Nations for a second time 16 years later, many of the problems that had faced the world body back then had changed radically. In his speech before the General Assembly on October 5, 1995, he pointed to some of the changes—the fall of Communism, the tearing down of the Berlin Wall, and the end of the cold war.

"The moral dynamics of this universal quest for freedom clearly appeared in Central and Eastern Europe during the nonviolent revolutions of 1989," the pontiff said. "Unfolding in specific times and places, those historical events nonetheless taught a lesson which goes far beyond a specific geographical location. For the nonviolent revolutions of 1989 demonstrated that the quest for freedom cannot be suppressed. It arises from a recognition of the inestimable dignity and value of the human person, and it cannot fail to be accompanied by a commitment on behalf of the human person.

"Modern totalitarianism has been, first and foremost, an assault on the dignity of the person, an assault which has gone even to the point of denying the inalienable value of the individual's life. The revolutions of 1989 were made possible by the commitment of brave men and women inspired by a different, and ultimately more profound and powerful, vision: the vision of man as a creature of intelligence and free will, immersed in a mystery which transcends his own being and endowed with the ability to reflect and the ability to choose—and thus capable of wisdom and virtue. A decisive factor in the success of those nonviolent revolutions was the experience of social solidarity: In the face of regimes backed by the power of propaganda and terror, that solidarity was the moral core of the power of the powerless, a beacon of hope and an enduring reminder that it is possible for man's historical journey to follow a path which is true to the finest aspirations of the human spirit."

But the pope also spoke of the freedom of nations when he said: "The Universal Declaration of Human Rights, adopted in 1948, spoke eloquently of the rights of persons; but no similar international agreement has yet adequately addressed the rights of nations. This situation must be carefully pondered, for it raises urgent questions

251

about justice and freedom in the world today. In reality the problem of the full recognition of the rights of peoples and nations has presented itself repeatedly to the conscience of humanity, and has also given rise to considerable ethical and juridical reflection.

"I am reminded of the debate which took place at the Council of Constance in the fifteenth century, when the representatives of the Academy of Krakow, headed by Pawel Wlodkowic, courageously defended the right of certain European peoples to existence and independence. Still better known is the discussion which went on in that same period at the University of Salamanca with regard to the peoples of the New World. And in our own century, how can I fail to mention the prophetic words of my predecessor, Pope Benedict XV, who in the midst of the First World War reminded everyone that 'nations do not die,' and invited them 'to ponder with serene conscience the rights and the just aspirations of peoples.'

"Our respect for the culture of others is therefore rooted in our respect for each community's attempt to answer the question of human life. And here we can see how important it is to safeguard the fundamental right to freedom of religion and freedom of conscience, as the cornerstones of the structure of human rights and the foundation of every truly free society. No one is permitted to suppress those rights by using coercive power to impose an answer to the mystery of man." ("To the Peoples at War and Their Leaders, July 28, 1915.")

AGAINST THE STATUS QUO IN EUROPE

Much has already been said or written about John Paul II's influence on events in Central and Eastern Europe, but some are worth repeating because they put the contributions he has made to peace and freedom in better perspective.

When he became pope, Europe was still divided by the Iron Curtain and the organizations that had been built up on both sides to maintain the status quo. NATO protected Western Europe from military attack while the European Union built up economic integration. America's "nuclear umbrella" and the thousands of troops it had stationed on the continent guarded both American and European interests.

The Soviet Union had built up a comparable military alliance in the Warsaw Pact, and they had kept control of the Eastern economies through COMECON (the Council for Mutual

Economic Cooperation), which directed the thrust of economic development, mostly to the benefit of the USSR.

As unnatural as this division, which was agreed upon at the Yalta Conference in February 1945, appeared to most people, it seemed impervious to change. The church on both sides of the Iron Curtain learned to adapt to the then new realities. Both John XXIII and Paul VI accepted what they could not change and tried to normalize relations with the Communist states in order to make life easier for those trapped behind the front lines of the cold war.

This policy involved compromises with Communist regimes that were not always well received in the West and often did not work out. For example, in 1973 Pope Paul VI nominated three members of the Patriotic Pax Priests, a Communist organization in Czechoslovakia, as bishops, figuring that they would get a better deal for Czech Catholics from Czech authorities.

Prague bureaucrats did not see it that way. They interpreted his choice of bishops as confirming the party's hard-line policy toward the church. Paul VI felt humiliated, grieved over his failure, and never launched any new conciliation initiatives. As a result, the Czech church suffered from a severe shortage of bishops, which before the "velvet revolution" ended Communist rule in 1989, left the country with three bishops.

From the beginning of his pontificate, John Paul II adopted a very different attitude. Concessions, he knew, would not work, since the Communists were not willing to trade favors. He was, of course, willing to talk to Communist leaders at any time, but he always had his eye on an overall settlement, not piecemeal negotiations that would never lead very far.

He showed off the Vatican's new approach and novel style on his first visit back to Poland after his election. In June 1979 millions of Poles attended his rallies, and the

Pope John Paul II talks to elderly and underprivileged citizens of Czestochowa outside the Holy Family Cathedral on June 6, 1979.

government did not dare interfere. It was a muscular demonstration of church power and a trigger for the changes that began to pulsate through Eastern Europe.

HALF THE CATHOLICS IN THE WORLD

Latin America presented a totally different challenge for the new pope, but one that was just as critical for the future of the Catholic Church. Marxist and Communist ideologies played a key role in the hemisphere, especially in Cuba, but the number of Catholics who live in the Latin American countries is much greater. They account for almost half of the world's faithful, and their number is increasing along with the overall population.

Soon after his election the pope visited Mexico and the Dominican Republic, the first of many visits he would pay to Latin America, where he ended up traveling to nearly every country in the hemisphere at least once and to Brazil, the largest country in the region, four times.

Liberation theology was one of the first problems the Holy Father faced in Latin America (see Chapter 15). His opposition was based on the doctrine's focus on man, not God, which therefore did not merit the appellation of theology. He also objected to the religious immersion in daily politics that liberation theology seemed to require.

An early test came in July 1979. In Nicaragua a leftist guerilla group, the Sandinista National Liberation Front, overthrew the corrupt Somoza family dictatorship. When the guerillas seized power, they appointed four Catholic priests as government ministers. The Vatican demanded they quit. When they didn't, he expelled them from the priesthood.

His stand on both issues earned him vigorous criticism from the left, but the course of events would prove him right. With the demise of Communism in 1989, liberation theology lost much of its appeal with proponents opting for more effective and less ideological approaches to ending poverty, a goal the pope has espoused since long before his election.

But politics are not the only hurdle facing the church in Latin America. The region must overcome a severe shortage of priests and other religious personnel to minister to the spiritual needs of a rapidly growing population. Progress has been slow, but the number of vocations has rebounded in recent years, with attendance at some hemisphere seminaries up sharply.

The seminary in Guadalajara, Mexico, has more than a thousand young men preparing for the priesthood and is the largest training ground for priests in the world. The number of seminarians is also up in Brazil and Argentina. One result has been a sharp increase in the number of Latino cardinals. At the February 21, 2001, consistory, the pope named 44 new cardinals—11 of them Latino.

CHANGES IN VATICAN POLITICS

Over the course of John Paul II's pontificate, the number of states with which the Holy See maintained full diplo-matic relationships almost doubled, from 96 countries in 1978 to 174 in 2005. The Holy See also maintained diplomatic relations with the European Union, the Order of Malta, and "special" relations with the Russian Federation and the Palestine Authority. This increase reflected the emergence of more than 20 new countries during the 1990s, a by-product of the disintegration of the Union of Soviet Socialist Republics, Yugoslavia, and Czechoslovakia. At the same time, the so-called German Democratic Republic disappeared from the world map.

Traditionally the Vatican had maintained diplomatic relations with Europe and the Americas, but during John Paul II's pontificate, ties with African and Asian nations came to the fore, particularly where Islam is the dominant religion. The Holy See used these relationships to improve the condition of Catholics and other Christians living in Muslim countries, not always to the good, since religious tolerance is not tolerated. This was especially true in the former Soviet republics in central Asia, which are Muslim-dominated and often hostile to Christianity in general and to the Catholic Church in particular, with anti-Catholic propaganda quite commonplace.

"The land you just kissed is honored by your presence," President Fidel Castro said as he welcomed the Holy Father during his papal visit to Cuba on January 21, 1998. During the pope's visit President Castro replaced his usual military uniform with a business suit.

The Holy See had also been the target of other secular attacks in recent years. Thus the world news media reacted with spite and vitriol when the Vatican recognized Croatia and Slovenia as independent states in 1992. Cartoons published at the time depicted the Vatican as a "Satanic State." But overall, this pontificate enjoyed growing respect in the international community, where its role gained in importance that is largely attributed to John Paul II's active and forceful diplomacy.

The Prolific Writer

No pope in history wrote as much John Paul II and in as many different literary forms—poetry, drama, autobiography, philosophy, theology, anthropology, and politics. He published five books with commercial publishers—the first pope ever to do so—and they have sold millions of copies across the world, with royalties flowing to John Paul II's favorite charities. The stream of encyclicals and other apostolic documents written in Latin and in other languages has been unmatched.

All told, he published more than fifty works, the bulk with the Vatican and other Catholic presses. His first book as pope appeared in the United States and the United Kingdom in 1979. It was a collection of poems he had written in Polish in the 1950s and 1960s. Random House published an English version of this work in 1982 as *Easter Vigil and Other Poems*. His plays and other writings on theater were published by the University of California Press in 1987 under the title *The Collected Plays and Writings on Theater*.

His books intended for lay audiences worldwide are direct, easy-to-read, and readily understandable. That is why they have had such wide appeal, and none more so than the first, *Crossing the Threshold of Hope*, published in 1994. As Philip Zaleski, professor of religion at Smith College, wrote in the religious journal *First Things* in March 2000, the book is "a splendid distillation of Catholic thought, the Catechism in miniature, the essential teachings of the world's largest religious body distilled into 244 elegant pages.... The book crackles with a vitality that, twenty years into his papacy, one takes for granted with John Paul II. One finds this energy in the declaration that began his reign and begins this book: 'Be not afraid!' One finds it in the exhilaration that courses through the text, the sense that totalitarianism and atheism are on the run and that the future brims with hope for Christians, indeed for all men and women of goodwill."

Two years later the pope published a tautly written autobiography entitled *Gift and Mystery: On the Fiftieth Anniversary of My Priestly Ordination*. In it the pontiff covered his Polish roots and life under the Nazi occupation, and, later, under Communism. But typically for him, he says little about his own role in helping to bring about Communism's downfall. Instead, he focuses on the dangers of consumerism, which, he believed, poses a greater threat than Communism ever did.

His workload as pontiff was too great to allow him much time for drama or poetry. But in the spring of 2003, John Paul II broke the long silence of his poetic voice with the publication of *Roman Triptych—Meditations*. He wrote it in Polish, beginning his labor at the end of his 2002 visit to Poland that August and completed it in the Vatican at Christmas.

Delia Gallagher, writing in *Catholic Culture*, analyzes the three-part poem's structure and meaning this way:

The first, "The Stream," is a mystical contemplation of nature, highlighting its beauty and man's search for God.

The second, "On the Book of Genesis at the Threshold of the Sistine Chapel," is a reflection on man, the image of God, from Creation to the Last Judgment. (In this part, he recalls the conclave of August 1978 in which Pope John Paul I was chosen, and the one in October, when he himself was elected. Here also is where the pope refers to his own death and the conclave that will follow to elect his successor.)

The third, "A Hill in the Land of Moriah," evokes Ur of the Chaldeans, Abraham's homeland, and the conversation between the patriarch and his son Isaac, whom he was about to sacrifice on Mount Moriah as proof of his loyalty to God.

The pope ends the poem with these enigmatic words:

I carry your name in me,
this name is the sign of the
Covenant which the Primordial
Word made with you
even before the world was created.
Remember this place when you
go away from here,
This place will await its day.

In his writings John Paul II preached to all mankind—from heads of state to youngsters such as this Croatian boy.

His encyclicals and letters are no literary bonbons; they are hefty tomes that give rigorous exposition to his thoughts and feelings. Thus his volume entitled *Ecclesia in America (The Church in America)* runs to 140 pages in its English text. In it the pope calls on the church in the Americas to *preach the Gospel to all creation* (Mark 16:15). Genuine personal encounters will bring forth a renewal of the church, he writes, for "the encounter with the living Jesus Christ is the path to conversion, communion, and solidarity." The Holy Father concludes by inviting all Catholics of America to "take an active part in the evangelizing initiatives which the Holy Spirit is stirring in every part of this immense continent."

Major encyclicals run even longer. *Vita Consecrata (The Consecrated Life)* takes up 208 pages in his plea for a commitment to the consecrated life. Others demand conciseness and clarity. One example is the 14-page document on ecology, *The Ecological Crisis—Common Responsibility.*

Other works address family, the elderly, women, and education. The breadth of the pope's erudition is truly stunning.

As Michael Nowak wrote about the pope in the *National Review* in 2003 :

> *In his intensive studies in modern philosophy and distinguished teaching career, Wojtyla gained distinctive intellectual strengths and broader horizons than any of his recent predecessors. His skills in languages and knowledge of several cultures, not to mention his hard face-to-face dealings with Communist adversaries,*

> *toughened his mind and deepened his quest for sustained, systematic reflection. It will be a few decades before the church as a whole catches up with some of the initiatives he launched and some of the lines of thought he opened up.*
>
> *I once heard the great philosopher Alistair MacIntyre say of one of John Paul II's encyclicals on moral thought,* Veritatis Splendor, *that it was the deepest and most subtle philosophical meditation on truth since Kierkegaard.* Centesimus Annus *is the greatest work among all papal letters on the free society, cultural, economic, and political; add his companion encyclicals,* Laborem Exercens *and* Sollicitudo Rei Socialis, *and you have the most distinguished body of reflections on the social and economic order produced by any religious body in any time. His path-breaking discourses on the theology of the human body may be the so far least noted of the bombshells he has left for future generations to unpack.*
>
> *Those who are inclined to call this pope "John Paul the Great" do so because of the extent, range, and depth of his contributions in reshaping the horizons of the world in which we live, not only the political world (which perhaps more than anyone he contributed, with Margaret Thatcher and Ronald Reagan, to altering), but also the intellectual world. Although few would have thought it possible, John Paul II has surpassed Leo XIII not only in length of service but in the range and depth and importance of his literary endowment.*

Neither age nor illness slowed the pontiff's literary output. In 2004 he published *Arise, Let Us Be Going,* a book that covered the pope's years as a diocesan bishop, from 1958 to 1978, when he was particularly active with students and young married couples. And he described the long series of conflicts with the Communist government that culminated in his clash over construction of a church in the industrial town of Nowa Huta. He made the Communists back down by celebrating Mass at the site week after week in defiance of government orders.

Even as he was taken to the Gemelli Clinic in February 2005 with an illness that would take his life weeks later, Rizzoli, his Italian publisher, rushed a new work into print: *Memory and Identity: Conversations Between Millenniums.* In the book the Holy Father addresses some of the major issues of the twentieth century and his own feelings about the 1981 assassination attempt that almost killed him. It is based on long conversations the pontiff held in the summer of 1993 with two Polish philosophy professors, Krzysztof Michalski and Father Józef Tischner. It is something of a last will and testament, since it covers a host of issues close to his heart and his thinking—democracy, freedom, the concepts of nation, homeland and state, human rights, and church-state relationships. And John Paul II also reflected on the presence of evil in modern life and how it can often end up as an invitation to do good.

"Jesus Christ is the center of the universe and of history," John Paul II said. At another time he added, "God has made way for a great Christian spring to come in the third millennium."

Chapter 17

A New Christian Spring

Pope John Paul II geared his whole pontificate toward steering the church safely, with moral values intact, into the third millennium. In doing so, he embarked on a dangerous journey between the demands of the modern age and the traditions of Christianity. It is a measure of his success that he was both one of history's most beloved and most controversial pontiffs.

More than any other contemporary pope, he understood the revolution in communications that shook the second half of the twentieth century. He was able to take radio, television, film, the Internet, and other new technologies that could reproduce high-quality sound and pictures, along with helicopters and ever faster jet aircraft, and harness them in the best interests of the church.

Through his voice, language became a tool of faith that he was able to project around the globe, and because he spoke so many languages, he was able to lend a personal touch to his message so millions could feel his words in their hearts as well as understand them in their minds.

REACHING OUT

John Paul II was never a distant communicator. He logged 600,000 miles in journeys to 120 countries, and in each one of them, he gave people a sense of the church as drama reminiscent of ecclesiastical plays of the Middle Ages. He brought with him to his pontificate the tools of theater, honed in his youth as an amateur actor, director, and playwright, and used them to teach the faithful.

Over the decades he began to take on the patina of a rock star, something he proved in Colorado in 1993 when he attended World Youth Day. Half a million young people witnessed the pope sharing the podium with genuine rock stars, and pictures of the pontiff with the musicians were projected on giant TV screens for all to watch.

His world travels gave literally billions of people, Christians and non-Christians alike, a new vision of the Catholic Church—robust, muscular, confrontational, in your face, loose, even "cool"—all things the church had never been before. But John Paul II was no McLuhanite: The media he used with such great effect were not his message.

That was manifold. His compassion for the poor and disadvantaged around the globe was genuine, no matter how much he may have differed with those in the Latin American clergy who espoused liberation theology to combat poverty and oppression. His rhetoric on

The Catacombs of St. Sebastian date back more than 1,700 years to the first millennium of Christian times. Emperor Constantine the Great constructed a basilica over them in the fourth century.

poverty was fierce. He saw the alleviation of misery as the duty of both rich nations and wealthy individuals.

He took a strong stand on social issues and on the role work plays in modern society. His second encyclical, *Laborem Exercens*, promulgated in 1981, outlined his position on the dignity of labor and showed off his modern way of thinking about the problems afflicting the world today. A few excerpts will illustrate the point:

Work...is always relevant and constantly demands renewed attention and decisive witness. Because fresh questions and problems are always arising, there are always fresh hopes, but also fresh fears and threats connected with this basic dimension of human existence: Man's life is built up every day from work, from work it derives its specific dignity, but at the same time, work contains the unceasing measure of human toil and suffering, and also of the harm and injustice, which penetrate deeply into social life within individual nations and on the international level.

WORK IN AN AGE OF TECHNOLOGY

Work provides man with the food he needs to keep his body intact, but it also is the engine that produces science and progress, civilization and culture. Work is not easy, the pope wrote, and the truism that man will earn his bread by the sweat of his brow remains valid. Work is often accompanied by "many tensions, conflicts, and crises," which can disrupt daily life.

New technologies will impact the workaday world, he wrote, much as the industrial revolution did in the nineteenth century. Automation is one example. The rising cost of energy and other raw materials is changing the workplace, as is the spread of "save the environment" ecology and the emergence of third-world people demanding their place in the sun. *These new conditions and demands will require a reordering and adjustment of the structures of the modern economy and of the distribution of work. Unfortunately, for millions of skilled workers these changes may perhaps mean unemployment, at least for a time, or the need for retraining. They will very probably involve a reduction or a less rapid increase in material well-being for the more developed countries. But they can also bring relief and hope to the millions who today live in conditions of shameful and unworthy poverty.*

The church, the pope went on, is not in a position to analyze these changes, but it should always stand up for

A detail of a Byzantine mosaic of Christ in the Basilica of Hagia Sophia (Holy Wisdom) in Istanbul. Emperor Justinian constructed the basilica from AD 532 to 537 during the first millennium of the Christian era.

A New Advent

From the day he became pope, John Paul II looked to the horizon of the third millennium as the lodestar of his papacy. In his first encyclical, *Redemptor Hominis (On the Redemption of Man)*, he urged the faithful to live in a "New Advent"—a period of hope that was upon them. Certainly the pope himself did, so much so that his pontificate has been called a "Season of Advent."

The culmination of that season came in the Year 2000 Jubilee when John Paul II called upon his flock to use the celebration for their own personal conversion and for the renewal of Christian life, a renewal he saw largely in terms of ecumenism. The year offered an opportunity to work for unity among Christians with honesty, humility, and courage. "If we don't do this," he said, "we are not faithful to the words of Christ."

His ecumenism has not gone unchallenged. Some are fearful it will undermine the bedrock of faith and morals and lead to greater divisions among Christians rather than less. Others worry that the obstacles in the way of achieving unity are too great to remove safely. The pope stood fast against both sets of critics, swimming resolutely upstream.

The church is not out to convert everyone to Catholicism or to make them renounce their own faith; nor does it mean to obliterate "the frontiers of truth taught by the church." But ecumenism does mean reaching out to members of other faiths, something the pope did through all his seemingly endless travel. "We arrived at churches on all continents and paid special attention to ecumenical relationships," he explained.

His goal was to be a witness to the faith and to inspire others to be witnesses also, to persuade them to examine their conscience and to reflect on their faith. And he succeeded in as much as his pilgrimages always left a distinctive mark among the nations and peoples he visited.

Brother Roger, shown here in 1966, founded the ecumenical Taizé movement in France in 1940. With the pope's approval he organized ecumenical meetings in many parts of the world.

temporal state, Vatican City, but also because the moral authority of the church must be exercised on the temporal stage of world politics. John Paul II honed his political skills in decades of negotiating with Communists in Poland. His role in bringing Poland and Eastern Europe safely out of the Soviet grip is well known, but it is not the only role he played on the world stage. He was an articulate opponent of war and an equally articulate champion of human rights. And he did not care who started the wars or oppressed the people.

He spoke out forcefully against both American invasions of Iraq and opposed economic sanctions against that country and indeed against others as well. He believed that sanctions hurt the poor and did little damage to their intended targets—the despots in power. He took an active part in efforts to mediate the collapse of Yugoslavia and the bloody wars that followed that country's disintegration. Indeed, it is hard to find any international conflict in which John Paul II did not play an important role or raise a warning and often chiding voice.

CHRISTIAN UNITY

Like no other pope before him, John Paul II championed ecumenism and moved forcefully toward Christian unity from the moment he was elected. He worked hardest to heal the breach with the Orthodox Church that has now lasted more than a thousand years and laid out his position in an apostolic letter written in 1995 entitled *Orientale Lumen*:

> We believe that the venerable and ancient tradition of the Eastern churches is an integral part of the heritage of Christ's church, the first need for Catholics is to be familiar with that tradition, so as to be nourished by it and to encourage the process of unity in the best way possible for each.

Members of the Orthodox and Eastern Catholic rites know that they are the "living bearers" of this tradition, and, the pope wrote, Latin Catholics should be as aware of the rich spiritual treasures of the East and share the pope's passion for Catholic unity, a unity he did not see in a single tradition or in the opposition of the various communities but in the "undivided heritage of the Universal Church."

the dignity and rights of those who work when these changes threaten or violate them in order to "ensure authentic progress by man and society."

In that context he always showed himself to be open to the natural sciences, welcoming advances that promote human well-being and values and opposing those he deemed not to do so. As a polymorph, the pope was eager to discuss the sciences with their practitioners, a practice that went back to his early days as a bishop in Kraków when he invited scientists for seminar-like discussions of their work and its implications.

THE POPE AS DIPLOMAT

He proved himself an adept and adroit politician, a role all popes must play not only because they are the head of a

Opus Dei

One of the most powerful organizations within today's Catholic Church is Opus Dei, which enjoyed a close relationship with, and support from, John Paul II because it is devoted to boosting spirituality and the spiritual life among Catholic laymen. The organization is also one of the most controversial within the church.

It was founded in Madrid in 1928 by a young Spanish priest named Josemaria Escriva de Balaguer. Ever since he was a teenager, Escriva had pondered God's mission for him. Then, on October 2 of that year, he heard church bells pealing and saw the revelation of the thoughts of God. It became clear to him that God wanted him to found Opus Dei, the Work of God.

The new organization, he wrote, would "tell men and women of every country and of every condition, race, language, milieu, and state of life...that they can love and serve God without giving up their ordinary work, their family life, and their normal social relations."

The message had resonance. His book, *The Way*, has sold 3 million copies worldwide. Membership in Opus Dei tops 80,000 worldwide, with 3,000 in the United States, where the organization has a 17-story headquarters in Manhattan worth $43 million. Opus Dei has enormous financial and political clout. Its role at the Vatican to this day is reminiscent of the role that the Jesuit order played during the Counter-Reformation.

John Paul II favored the organization, giving it special status that makes members independent of local bishops and subject only to the authority of the Opus Dei bishop in Rome, Javier Echevarria, and the pope. More important, the pope moved swiftly to canonize Monsignor Escriva, beginning the process only six years after the Spaniard died in Rome in 1975. He was made a saint within record time in 2002, with 250,000 gathered at the Vatican for the ceremonies.

What appealed most to the pontiff was the emphasis Opus Dei put on "sanctifying the workplace," as papal biographer George Weigel put it, "through apostolically committed professional men and women." Most members live in the lay world, although 2,000 priests belong to the organization. Some lay members have opted for a celibate, communal life, but most have not. Among the most prominent members is Joaquín Navarro-Valls, the Spanish doctor who served as John Paul II's principal press spokesman.

Only a few members are rich and powerful—their number includes at least two cardinals, while 40 other princes of the church attended the founder's canonization. However, most of the Opus Dei members come from all walks of life: They are farm workers, doctors, housewives, and students.

The organization is controversial on several grounds. Forged in the Spanish civil war of the 1930s, it was widely perceived as a supporter of General Francisco Franco's dictatorship, although toward the end of his rule, the organization began to oppose his ruthless methods. Members have meddled in politics—two were ministers in Spain's right-wing government in the 1990s—and have been active in international finance.

And before the Year 2000 Jubilee he urged Catholics to take advantage of the celebration "to work for unity among Christians with honesty, humility, and courage. If we don't do this," he said, "we are not faithful to the words of Christ." Clearly he hoped that Christianity would enter the third millennium once again united. But he also knew that unity would be difficult to achieve.

Wherever he traveled, the pope met with leaders of other Christian denominations. Ecumenism was a constant on his travel agenda. Few encyclicals or apostolic letters or other documents lacked some reference to a restored Christian unity and expressed his willingness—and eagerness—to work for it. Yet he was often misunderstood and criticized, even within his own church.

His forceful reply to doubters was made early in his papacy in his first encyclical letter, *Redemptor Hominis*, where he wrote:

There are people who in the face of the difficulties or because they consider that the first ecumenical endeavors have brought negative results would have liked to turn back. Some even express the opinion that these efforts are harmful to the cause of the Gospel, are leading to a further rupture in the church, are causing confusion of ideas in questions of faith and morals and are ending up with a specific indifferentism. It is perhaps a good thing that the spokesmen for these opinions should express their fears. However, in this respect also, correct limits must be maintained. It is obvious that this new stage in the Church's life demands of us a faith that is particularly aware, profound, and responsible.

Ecumenism, the pope went on, requires openness on all sides, a willingness to engage in dialogue and in shared exploration of evangelical truth. But it does not mean abandoning divine truth as the church has taught it. As for those who oppose ecumenism, John Paul II put this question: "Have we the right not to do it? Can we fail to have trust—in spite of all human weakness and all the faults of past centuries—in our Lord's grace as revealed recently through what the Holy Spirit said and we heard during the council?"

Here is the intersection between the pope's bold confrontation of present and future and his insistence on traditional Christianity. That intersection, too, was the source of much of the criticism John Paul II faced during his pontificate.

In *Redemptor Hominis* he laid out both positions. He committed his pontificate to Vatican II, promised to continue the reforms of his predecessors John XXIII and Paul VI, and pledged to work for Christian unity. But he also anchored his pontificate in his now famous exhortation "Open the doors to Christ," a thought he developed in that first encyclical.

"Our spirit is set in one direction, the only direction for our intellect, will, and heart—toward Christ our Redeemer, toward Christ, the Redeemer of man. We wish to look toward him—because there is salvation in no one else but him, the Son of God—repeating what Peter said: 'Lord, to whom shall we go? You have the words of eternal life.'"

A celebration of Poland's 1,000 years of Christianity was held at Gniezno, Poland, in 1977. Evoking similarities to a celebration held in the millennium year 1000, it became a symbol of hope for unity in Europe.

For the church Christ's words are eternal. They are repeated over and over, as is the story of the life Christ led on earth. "The church never ceases to relive his death on the cross and his Resurrection, which constitute the content of the church's daily life. Indeed, it is by the command of Christ himself, her Master, that the church unceasingly celebrates the Eucharist, finding in it the 'fountain of life and holiness.' "

Jesus Christ, the pope said, is at the heart of Christian doctrine, and the Christian way of life consists of imitating Jesus Christ. Christianity is a constant invitation to encounter Christ. This form of Christocentric theology lay at the core of John Paul II's beliefs. For him Jesus was both alive forever and an eternal presence in human history. The nature of God and man can be understood only through Jesus, and without him the dual nature of God, both human and divine, could not be revealed.

His faith, therefore, was firmly rooted in the values that sustained the early Christians, who, this pope believed, have inspired Catholic reformers across the ages. And this belief in tradition formed John Paul II's thinking about major church issues. It is behind his refusal to bend ecclesiastic and evangelic rules, and the root of his opposition to changing fundamental church dogma.

No matter how great the pressure, for example, this pope would not relax church rules that forbid the use of birth control. He remained as staunchly opposed to abortion as he was against the death penalty—another issue that often put him at odds with countries like the United States, where the state continues to put people to death. More than once John Paul II pleaded with U.S. authorities for the life of a condemned man and failed.

He refused Holy Communion to divorced Catholics who remarry or priests who leave the clergy to marry. He regarded homosexuality as a sin—though he prayed for the sinners—and considered gay marriages an abomination, something that could seriously disrupt and distort the sacrament of marriage in the eyes of the church. He always put the future and the survival of the Catholic Church first, which may explain his mild condemnation of priestly pedophilia and the cover-ups that followed in the United States and Europe. John Paul II feared for the viability of his church under the onslaught of those who sought revenge for past wrongs.

JOHN PAUL II ON THE ROLE OF WOMEN

He never gave way on the issue of ordaining women, breaking sharply with the practice of many Protestant denominations, where women have long been ministers of the church. But the pope spent much time and thought on the role of women in the modern church and in the modern world.

In a letter written to the 1995 Beijing conference on women—to which he sent a woman to represent the church—the pontiff wrote: "We are heirs to a history which has *conditioned* us to a remarkable extent. In every time and place, this conditioning has been an obstacle to the progress of women. Women's dignity has often been unacknowledged and their prerogatives misrepresented; they have often been relegated to the margins of society and even reduced to servitude. This has prevented women from truly being themselves, and it

John Paul II: Saint Maker

The Polish pope will always be remembered for the extraordinary number of saints and blesseds that he sanctioned. In fact, in 26 years he created more saints and blesseds by himself than all his predecessors put together, going back to the 1620s when Pope Urban VIII began the formal practice of declaring the worthiness of such Christians. (Before that time, martyrs and saintly people—some real and some mythical—were elevated by popular acclaim.)

John Paul II beatified more than 700 men and women and declared more than 300 saints. Blesseds are usually on the last step to sainthood—Mother Teresa, the Albanian nun who cared for Calcutta's poorest of the poor, for example, died in 1997, was made a blessed in 2003, and will probably receive sainthood in another 10 years or so. The pontiff clearly saw blesseds and saints as role models and heroes for Christians all over the world. They are exemplars of the holy life and show others how to enter heaven. John Paul II chose many men and women who showed Christian courage in the modern world; for example, a nun who was killed by a soldier in Zaire rather than submit to rape, and members of religious orders killed by Fascist regimes for not denying their faith. The Holy Father believed in the communion of saints as a dimension of the church on earth and spoke of those whom he beatified or canonized as "saints for the third millennium."

In the Catholic Church the attainment of sainthood means that a person has been declared to be reliably in heaven by the pope and is thus worthy of universal devotion. A blessed is also declared to be in heaven but worthy of only local devotion. Even the relics of saints and blesseds—their bones or objects with which they were associated—are thought to have special power. Catholics are encouraged to pray to these sanctified individuals for help in coping with life problems.

The process of creating a blessed or a saint traditionally has taken many, many years—sometimes even centuries. Long after the candidate's death, a local bishop might propose that person for beatification. The candidate's exemplary life would be thoroughly researched and carefully documented. Then a church lawyer, the devil's advocate, would challenge each of the claims of holiness for the candidate before church officials.

In addition, miracles of healing or helping must be associated with the candidate as a sign from heaven that the individual is truly blessed or saintly. These miracles must be declared by doctors or scientists "inexplicable" by the laws of nature. In a scientific age these miracles are more difficult to quantify.

In January 1983 John Paul II published an Apostolic Constitution called *Divinus Perfectionis Magister (The Devine Master of Perfection)*. This new law for creating blesseds and saints reduced the process to a matter of years. He abolished the devil's advocate role, which has made it harder for people to criticize or object to a candidate. In the beatification of Opus Dei founder Josemaria Escriva de Balaguer, for example, only one person of eleven who had asked to speak against his candidacy actually was invited to express doubts. John Paul also reduced the number of miracles required as testimony to blessedness or saintliness.

John Paul II beatified and canonized Christians from many eras and from all over the world. Among them are Pope John XXIII, the popular outgoing instigator of Vatican II, and Pope Pius IX, a prisoner of the Vatican who was responsible for the doctrine of papal infallibility in 1870. He beatified native Madagascan Victoria Rasoamanarivo in 1989, and the first Gypsy so honored was Cererini Jimenez Mallo, in 1997. Pope John Paul II celebrated his eightieth birthday in 2000 by canonizing 27 saints in St. Peter's Square.

---

has resulted in a spiritual impoverishment of humanity."

Yet Jesus always treated women with respect, openness, and tenderness, and he did so against the norms of his times. The church goes back to the Gospel in its efforts to free women from exploitation, John Paul II wrote, and he expressed his conviction that women are pivotal to solving current social issues—dealing with leisure time, quality of life, migration, social services, euthanasia, drugs, health care, and the ecology. Their presence will soften the contradictions of a society geared to efficiency and productivity, and further the process of humanizing that marks the "civilization of love."

This was central to the pope's thought and action, for if there is one word that sums up John Paul II's pontificate, it is "love"—love of God in general and Jesus and Mary in particular; love of his church, whose traditions he defended with all his might and which he took into the modern world, fusing both tradition and change into a single new whole; love of mankind everywhere and in every place; love and compassion for human frailty; love of religious freedom as a God-given right. This was truly a pope who offered the strength of his love to the whole world as he has returned the Office of Peter to its evangelical roots.

"We can be sure that our beloved pope is standing today at the window of the Father's house, that he sees us and blesses us."
—Cardinal Joseph Ratzinger

Chapter 18

The World Pays Homage to the Pilgrim of Hope

Pope John Paul II died at 9:37 p.m. Rome time on Saturday, April 2, 2005, just 46 days shy of his eighty-fifth birthday. As tradition demands, close associates called out his given name three times, "Karol, Karol, Karol." When he didn't respond, he was pronounced dead. Again according to tradition, his papal ring was removed and smashed.

He died as he had lived: on his own terms. He had returned from his second stay within six weeks at Rome's Gemelli Clinic just before Easter, and he declined to go back when his health took a precipitous turn for the worse. He knew he was dying, and he was prepared to go.

Minutes after John Paul II died, Archbishop Leonardo Sandri, a senior Vatican official, stepped outside to announce the pope's death to the tens of thousands who had gathered in St. Peter's Square. An hour later the bells of the Vatican heralded the sad news to *Urbi et Orbi* (the City and the World). Sunday morning another huge crowd assembled for an outdoor Mass that would begin the formal period of mourning. Later in the day the pope's body was laid out in the Clementine Hall—which John Paul II had used for general audiences—for the first private viewing by cardinals, bishops, and other members of the clerical hierarchy, as well as Italy's top dignitaries, led by Prime Minister Silvio Berlusconi and President Carlo Ciampi. The body was dressed in red and white papal

To Keep Rome Safe and Moving

With multitudes converging on Rome for John Paul II's funeral, the municipal government pulled out all the stops to keep the city not only secure but moving. Rome has a population of 3.7 million. An estimated 3 to 4 million mourners doubled the city's population when they came to pay their respects to their beloved pope over the four days of his lying in state and the day of the funeral.

It took 15,000 police and military personnel to patrol the streets and monitor the lines leading into St. Peter's Basilica to view John Paul II's body. The patient pilgrims who waited as long as 10 hours to say their brief good-byes in St. Peter's Basilica during the first part of the week were screened by metal detectors and X-ray machines. Municipal officials then provided them with bottled water and, if they had to spent the night on the cobblestones to save their places in line for

An aerial view of the Vatican, where mourners would gather to pay final tribute to John Paul II.

the next day, a blanket. Since hotel rooms were sold out immediately, Rome set up tent cities to accommodate the overflow, and citizens were urged to offer beds to the travelers. Hundreds of thousands of Poles, for example, jumped onto buses and trains and headed for Rome to honor their beloved countryman.

To protect the 80 heads of state that came to Rome for the funeral, police helicopters and air force combat jets patrolled the skies. During the Mass a five-mile radius of sky over Rome was closed to all traffic except television and patrol helicopters and an AWACS surveillance jet deployed by NATO. Italian naval vessels stood offshore and kept watch on the Tiber River.

Elite carabinieri, Italy's national police force, were stationed at all of Rome's major intersections. Sharpshooters were placed on rooftops overlooking St. Peter's Square. Even distinguished guests had to go through metal detectors and submit their bags to X-ray machines before taking their seats to the right of the casket at the funeral.

Businesses and schools were closed the day of the ceremony, and all traffic was banned from the area around St. Peter's Square; limos with dignitaries had to zip in and out quickly. Because the square could not possibly hold the crowds for the funeral, 27 billboard-size television screens were set up around the city to provide the crowds with live coverage of the events as they unfolded.

Rome can be proud of its efforts to manage the masses of pilgrims. Despite the extra millions who poured into its borders in a matter of days, there was no major violence. The only mishap, which turned out to be benign, was a miscommunication after the funeral that prompted Italian F-16s to force a small plane that had inadvertently strayed into the forbidden zone to land at a nearby airport.

vestments with a white miter trimmed in gold on his head, which rested on three shimmering gold pillows. His silver staff, the crosier, was cradled under his left arm.

Italian television cameras were switched on at this viewing, beginning what was to be almost nonstop global coverage of the pope's funeral. Papal spokesman Joaquín Navarro-Valls later announced that the Vatican had issued press credentials to 3,500 journalists.

The pope lay in state in St. Peter's Basilica from the afternoon of Monday, April 4, until the funeral on Friday, April 8. A river of humanity poured into St. Peter's Square for a brief glimpse of the pontiff in the basilica, which was all they were allowed. Half-a-million people walked past his bier on Tuesday and an incredible one million the next day, with many of the world's notables among them. President George W. Bush; his wife, Laura; his father, former President George H. W. Bush; and former President Bill Clinton knelt in prayer soon after arriving in Rome on Wednesday evening.

As the days went on, pilgrims arrived by plane, train, bus, car, and even motorcycle. The length of time spent standing in line grew longer and longer for those hoping to catch a glimpse of the pope. A 5-hour wait was the norm on Monday; by Wednesday it had stretched to 10 hours. The crush grew so bad that on Thursday the Rome daily *Il Messagero* headlined its story PILGRIMS, STOP. The appeal was in vain. Some 4 million visitors were believed to have come into the city.

A BEWILDERING INFLUX

For the Romans the influx was sometimes bewildering: Americans in shorts, Africans in native dress, Filipinos in flowered shirts, monks in homespun habits and sandals—all with cell phones in their hands. However, after a week, even Polish motorcyclists, dressed in leather from head to toe, did not cause a stir.

That so many Europeans had journeyed to Rome was not a surprise, but that so many others came from much farther away was amazing. One young woman from the Congo had a simple explanation for a reporter from the French newspaper *Le Monde:* "The pope never stopped coming to see people all over the world. In learning of his death, people left their villages to give back to him what he had given to them."

On the day of the funeral, people crawled out of their sidewalk sleeping bags by five a.m. and began to trudge toward St. Peter's Square. Authorities had all but shut down central Rome. Traffic was banned except for the motorcades bearing the dignitaries—an astonishing procession that included 4 kings, 5 queens, 44 heads of state, and 25 prime ministers.

Some 1,400 people were seated in the space just outside the basilica, facing 600 prelates seated behind the casket in the middle and grouped according to their clerical rank. President Bush, flanked by his wife, Laura, on one side and his father and Bill Clinton on the other, sat in the second row, close to French president Jacques Chirac, who, at one point, bent over to kiss the hand of U.S. Secretary of State Condoleezza Rice.

THE GATHERED DIGNITARIES

John Paul's status in global politics was reflected in the number of heads of state who attended. President Horst Koehler, Chancellor Gerhard Schroeder, and Foreign Minister Joschka Fischer represented Germany. Prime Minister Tony Blair and Prince Charles, who postponed his wedding by a day to attend, represented Great Britain. King Juan Carlos of Spain came with his wife, Queen Sophia, and so did the President of Brazil, Luiz Inacio da Silva. U.N. Secretary-General Kofi Annan represented the world community. Lech Walesa, the founder of Solidarity and the first president of Poland after the fall of Communism, joined Poland's current president.

Some 300,000 people jammed into the Bernini colonnade that surrounds St. Peter's Square, while another 250,000 crowded into the streets around the basilica. Half-a-million mourners gathered outside to watch a broadcast of the Mass on the 27 giant television screens placed in major sites across the city. In one location a Polish interpreter took over the microphone for Polish pilgrims; in another the commentary was in German.

Before the casket was brought into the square from the basilica, Archbishop Stanislaw Dziwisz, following ancient ritual, covered the pope's face with a white silk cloth. Cardinal Piero Marini, master of liturgical ceremonies, placed two items in the casket: a small bag of gold and silver Vatican coins minted during John Paul II's pontificate and a metal cylinder holding his life story written in Latin. Cardinal Eduardo Martinez Somala splashed holy water over the body, and then the cypress wood casket was nailed shut.

At precisely 10:06 a.m. the 12 papal Swiss Guards, in formal attire with white gloves, carried the casket out of the church and placed it on an Oriental carpet covering the stone floor in front of an outdoor altar. A timid sun poked through the clouds. A brisk wind blew across the square, billowing the scarlet cloaks of the cardinals. On the casket Cardinal Marini placed a red leather-bound copy of the scriptures, whose pages fluttered in the wind.

Bells pealed in mourning as the pope's body was put down gently. The choir of the pontifical chapel sang the *Requiem in Aeternam (Lord Grant Him Eternal Rest)* to open the Mass celebrated by the dean of the College of Cardinals, Joseph Ratzinger, a Bavarian who had known the pope for 30 years and who serves as prefect of the Congregation for the Doctrine of

Joaquín Navarro-Valls, the pope's longtime representative.

the Faith. The Mass was concelebrated by dozens of his fellow cardinals.

The music was muted, according to the precepts laid down by the Vatican II Council. An organ just inside the basilica accompanied two choirs singing Gregorian chants. The Mass was read in Italian and Latin and included the Nicene Creed. Readings from the Acts of the Apostles followed, read in six different languages by six different people. An American seminarian read the only English segment, a letter of Saint Paul to the Philippians. The readings all focused on Saint Peter's calling.

During the Mass the square was awash with flags that whipped in the wind, many of them the red-and-white banner of Poland. Some flags sported the Polish eagle, the symbol of nationhood and freedom. Others recalled the names of Polish cities so close to the pope's heart. The crowd hoisted banners proclaiming *"Santo Subito,"* meaning that John Paul II should be made a saint at once. They also shouted the slogan out loud, at one time holding up the Mass for five minutes while doing so.

Cardinal Ratzinger read his 20-minute homily in Italian. It was, for this generally cool and unflappable churchman, an extremely emotional experience:

"Follow me." The Risen Lord says these words to Peter. They are His last words to this disciple, chosen to shepherd his flock. Follow me—this lapidary saying of Christ can be taken as the key to understanding the message that comes to us from the life of our late beloved Pope John Paul II. Today we bury his remains in the earth as a seed of immortality—our hearts are full of sadness, yet at the same time of joyful hope and profound gratitude.

…The Holy Father was a priest to the last, for he offered his life to God for his flock and for the entire human family, in a daily self-oblation for the service of the church, especially amid the sufferings of his final months. And this way he became one with Christ, the Good Shepherd who loves his sheep. Finally, abide in my love: The Pope who tried to meet everyone, who had an ability to forgive and to open his heart to all, tells us once again today, with these words of the Lord, that by abiding in the love of Christ we learn, at the school of Christ, the art of true love.

…In the first years of his pontificate, still young and full of energy, the Holy Father went to the very ends of the earth, guided by Christ. But afterward, he increasingly entered into the communion of Christ's sufferings…. And in the very communion with the suffering Lord, tirelessly and with renewed intensity, he proclaimed the Gospel, the mystery of that love that goes to the end…. None of us can ever forget how in that last Easter Sunday of his life, the Holy Father, marked by suffering, came once more to the window of the Apostolic Palace and one last time gave his blessing Urbi et Orbi. *We can be sure that our beloved pope is standing today at the window of the Father's house, that he sees us and blesses us.*

The Pope's Will

Never one to accumulate material goods, Pope John Paul II was concerned mostly with other matters in his will, which he wrote during Lenten retreats over a period of 21 years, starting in 1979.

Early in his papacy, he seemed to envision his burial in Poland and suggested that the clergy there could make the arrangements. Later entries, however, gave the final say to the College of Cardinals. He did make note that he wanted to be buried "in the bare earth" with a "simple tombstone."

The will was written by hand in Polish, then translated into Italian by the Vatican before its release. In the early 1980s he wrote of his frustrations with the Communists in Poland: "The path of the church has become difficult and tense—as much for the faithful as for the pastors," he commented. In the 1990s he thanked God that the Communist regimes had fallen in Eastern Europe without a nuclear war.

After the assassination attempt in 1981, the pope wrote that his life belonged to God. "I hope that He will help me to recognize how long I must continue in this service. I ask him to recall me when He himself wants to."

In the will John Paul II asked his personal secretary, Archbishop Stanislaw Dziwisz, to burn his notes and to distribute his effects. The royalties from his books had already been designated for charity. He ended his will with these words:

As the end of my earthly life approaches, I return to the memory of the beginning, to my parents, my brother and sister (whom I did not know because she died before my birth), the parish of Wadowice, where I was baptized, that beloved city of mine, my peers, friends from elementary school, high school, university, up until the time of the occupation when I was a worker, and then the parish of Niegowice, and that of St. Florian in Kraków, the pastoral ministry of academics, the milieu …all milieux… Kraków and Rome…the people who in a special way have been entrusted to me by the Lord. To all I want to say one thing: "May God reward you."

A Nation Grieves: Poland Mourns the Loss of Its Own

Nowhere did the pope's death have as great an impact as it did in Poland, his homeland. President Aleksander Kwasniewski ordered flags flown at half-mast, and special Masses drew thousands even before the funeral.

A day earlier, Thursday, April 7, nearly a million people gathered on Blonie Meadow in Kraków, where John Paul II had often celebrated Mass on his return to the city he had led as bishop, archbishop, and cardinal for almost 20 years. Another 800,000 stayed to watch the funeral on giant television screens. The crowd sang along with the familiar hymns being broadcast. Many who attended were the young people the pope had worked so hard to attract, and many of them wore white clothing or white ribbons to honor his papacy.

Several hundred thousand other Poles gathered in Warsaw's Pilsudski Square to watch while public life in the capital and elsewhere in Poland ground to a halt. Factories, stores, and schools were closed. Outside St. Anna's Church in the old city of Warsaw, an endless ocean of flowers and candles covered the streets. After the funeral Mass, Polish artillery fired a 26-gun salute—one salvo for each year of his papacy. Catholics and Jews met in Warsaw's only synagogue to mourn the man who had done so much to bring the two religions closer together. In Wadowice, the small town where Karol Wojtyla was born in 1920, some 15,000 people gathered outside the church where he had been baptized.

Polish mourners were not limited to Poland. Thousands traveled to Rome to take part in the ceremony. Special trains left Warsaw on Wednesday night for the 30-hour trip to the Ostia Station on the outskirts of the Eternal City, where they arrived around midnight on Thursday.

Eight people were jammed into each compartment. The train did not have a single empty seat. When it passed Czestochowa, site of the Black Madonna icon that John Paul II held so dear, the young people chanted the Lord's Prayer and the Hail Mary. Efforts for a moment of silence on the train at the exact hour of the pope's death failed, since the train's public-address system had broken down.

One student summed up the feelings of many when he told Christophe Chatelot of *Le Monde* that the group felt both joy and sadness. The pope may not have been present in the heart of every Pole, he said, "but we're all sad to have lost somebody like him."

As he spoke, Ratzinger pointed to the papal palace window where John Paul II had stood so often—and was clearly overcome by emotion.

Ratzinger's homily was interrupted 13 times by heavy applause, unusual in American churches but common in Europe. As the Mass proceeded, clouds grew thicker and the sun disappeared from time to time. The wind picked up and blew the cardinal's thick silver hair into some disarray. As the service continued, the congregation gave the peace sign to their neighbors, a part of the ceremony introduced by the Vatican II Council. The crowd began to chant *"Magnus, Magnus,"* signifying their desire that John Paul II be given the rare honor of being called "the Great." Then as the time approached for Holy Communion, 320 priests spread among the crowd to distribute the host to the hundreds of thousands ready to receive it.

The Litany of Saints was sung near the end of the Mass, and then the patriarchs of the Eastern rite churches gathered around the casket to sing their own hymns. With holy water and incense, Ratzinger blessed the casket before leading the 140 cardinals back into St. Peter's Basilica. Silence fell on the square when the papal pallbearers again lifted the casket to their shoulders. At the top of the steps of the basilica, they turned the casket toward the people one last time; then they slowly turned the casket again and disappeared inside the basilica.

The casket was taken into the grotto beneath the nave, where John Paul II was placed alongside many other popes. An honor guard of cardinals stood outside the crypt—their red skullcaps removed in a last sign of respect—as the cypress casket was lowered into a zinc coffin and, finally, into a walnut coffin, which was lowered into the ground. The same gravesite was formerly occupied by the body of John XXIII until his beatification, after which time his coffin was moved into the basilica above the nave.

"It was total silence," Cardinal Roger Mahoney of Los Angeles told the *Washington Post*. "After the Holy Father had passed by and everybody left and was out of sight, we turned to go back and take off our vestments. No one said a word, not a word."

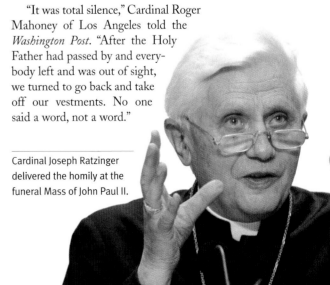

Cardinal Joseph Ratzinger delivered the homily at the funeral Mass of John Paul II.

Polish Pronunciation Guide

Polish is a difficult language for Americans to learn to speak. This brief guide is designed to help readers of this book pronounce the names of Polish people and places that appear frequently in this biography. It does not include Polish alphabet marks, like accents over consonants or the special character through the *l*. In Polish the accent is usually—but not always—on the penultimate, or next-to-last, syllable, indicated by bold-faced caps.

LETTERS	POLISH SOUND	ENGLISH SOUND
c	"ts"	as in "cats"
ch	"ch"	as in Scottish "loch"
dz followed by i or e	"j"	as in "jelly"
dz not followed by i or e	"dz"	as in "adze"
h	"ch"	as in Scottish "loch"
i	"ee"	as in "teeth"
j	"y"	as in "yes"
l	"w"	as in "way"
o	"oo"	as in "boot"
oh	"o"	as in "go"
rz	"rz"	similar to the "s" in "pleasure"
s	"sh"	as in "shout"
v	"w"	as in "winter"
w	"v"	as in "vine"
y	"y"	similar to the short "i" in "hit"
z	"z"	similar to the "s" in "pleasure"

Pronounce the following words as shown:

Baziak	**BA**-zhak	Pilsudski	pew-**SUD**-ski
Boleslaw	bow-**LESS**-waf	Sapieha	sa-**PYEH**-ha
Czestochowa	chens-toe-**HOE**-vah	Srodowisko	sheh-ro-do-**VEE**-sko (short "o" as in "go")
Dziwisz	**JEE**-vish		
Jadwiga	yah-**DVEE**-gah	Stanislaw	**STAH**-nee-swaf
Jagiello	ya-**GYEH**-wa	Tadeusz Kurowski	ta-**DAY**-oosh koo-**ROF**-ski
Kalvaria Zebrzydowska	kal-**VAR**-ya ze-bzheh-**DOF**-ska	Turowicz	too-**RO**-vich
Kononiczna	**KA**-no-nee-chna	*Tygodnik Powszechny*	tee-**GO**-dneek pof-**SHEF**-nay
Kraków	**KRA**-koof	Tyranowski	tee-ra-**NO**-fski
Lwów (Lvov)	li-**VOOF**	Wadowice	vah-do-**VEET**-sa
Mieczyslaw Kotlarczik	**MYEH**-cheh-swaf kot-**LAR**-chick	Wawel	**VAH**-vel
		Wojtyla	voy-**TI**-wah
Niegowic	nyeh-**GO**-vitz	Wyszynski	vi-**SHIN**-skee (short "i" in "vi")

For Further Reading

About John Paul II

Allergi, Renzo and Marsha Diagle-Williamson. *John Paul II, a Life of Grace.* Saint Anthony Messenger Press and Franciscan Communications, 2005.

Beigel, Gerard. *Faith and Social Justice in the Teaching of Pope John Paul II.* Peter Lang, New York, 1997.

Bernstein, Carl and Marco Politi. *His Holiness: John Paul II and the Hidden History of Our Time.* Doubleday, New York, 1996.

Blazynski, George. *Pope John Paul II: A Man from Krakow.* Sphere, London, 1979.

Buttiglione, Rocco. Karol Wojtyla: *The Thoughts of the Man Who Became Pope John Paul II.* Eerdmans, Grand Rapids, Michigan, 1997.

Chicago Tribune. *John Paul II, the Pope Who Changed History.* Triumph Books, Chicago, 2005.

Cornwell, John. *The Pontiff in Winter.* Doubleday, New York, 2004.

Coyne, George V., ed. *John Paul II on Science and Religion.* University of Notre Dame Press, Notre Dame, Indiana, 1990.

Craig, Mary. *Man from a Far Country: A Portrait of Pope John Paul II.* Hodder and Stoughton, London, 1979.

Dionne, Robert J. *The Papacy and the Church.* Philosophical Library, New York, 1987.

Dulles, Avery, SJ. *The Splendor of Faith: The Theological Vision of Pope John Paul II.* Crossroad, New York, 1999.

Frossard, André and Pope John Paul II. *Be Not Afraid!* St. Martin's Press, New York, 1984.

Hanson, Eric O. *The Catholic Church in World Politics.* Princeton University Press, Princeton, New Jersey, 1987.

Hebblethwaite, Peter. *Paul VI: The First Modern Pope.* Paulist Press, New York/Mahwah, New Jersey, 1993.

Hebblethwaite, Peter and Ludwig Kauffman. *John Paul II: A Pictorial Biography.* McGraw Hill, New York, 1979.

Henze, Paul. *The Plot to Kill the Pope.* Charles Scribner's Sons, New York, 1983.

Hofman, Paul. O Vatican: *A Slightly Wicked View of the Holy See.* Congdon and Weed, New York, 1984.

Kelly, George A. *Keeping the Church Catholic with John Paul II.* Ignatius Press, San Francisco, 1993.

Koralak, Tadeusz. *John Paul II: The Pope from Poland.* Interpress Publishers, Warsaw, 1979.

Kwitny, Jonathan. *Man of the Century: The Life and Times of Pope John Paul II.* Henry Holt, New York, 1997.

Malinsky, Mieczyslaw. *Pope John Paul II: The Life of Karol Wojtyla.* Seabury, New York, 1979.

McDermott, John M. SJ, ed. *The Thought of Pope John Paul II.* Editrice Pontificia Universita Gregoriana, Rome, 1993.

Moody, John. *Pope John Paul II.* Park Lane Press, New York, 1997.

O'Carroll, Michael. *Poland and John Paul II.* Veritas Publications, Dublin, 1979.

Oram, James. *The People's Pope: The Story of Karol Wojtyla of Poland.* Chronicle Books, San Francisco, 1979.

Parker, Michael. *Priest of the World's Destiny: John Paul II.* Faith Publishing Company, Milford, Ohio, 1995.

Sterling, Claire. *The Time of the Assassins: Anatomy of an Investigation.* Holt, Rinehart and Winston, New York, 1983.

Szulc, Tad. Pope *John Paul II: The Biography.* Scribner, New York, 1995.

Weigel, George. *Witness to Hope: The Biography of Pope John Paul II.* Cliff Street Books, New York, 2001.

Willey, David. *God's Politician: Pope John Paul II, the Catholic Church and the New World Order.* St. Martin's Press, New York, 1993.

Williams, George Huntston. *The Mind of John Paul II: Origins of His Thought and Action.* Seabury Press, New York, 1981.

Winn, Wilton. *Keeper of the Keys: John XXIII, Paul VI, and John Paul II: Three Who Changed the Church.* Random House, New York, 1988.

By John Paul II

John Paul II. *The Loving Heart: Private Prayers of Pope John Paul II.* Atria, 2005.

_____. *Memory and Identity: Conversations at the Dawn of a Millennium.* Rizzoli International, 2005.

_____. *Crossing the Threshold of Hope.* Alfred A. Knopf, New York, 1994.

Wojtyla, Karol. *The Place Within: The Poetry of Pope John Paul II.* Random House, New York, 1994.

_____. *The Collected Plays and Writings on Theater with introductions by Boleslaw Taborski.* University of California Press, Berkley, 1987.

_____. *Blessed Are the Pure of Heart.* St. Paul Books and Media, Boston, 1983.

_____. *The Acting Person.* D. Riedel, Dordrecht, Netherlands/Boston, 1979.

Index

Page numbers in *italic* refer to photographs.

Photo Credits